The Economics of Justice

THE ECONOMICS OF JUSTICE

Richard A. Posner

Harvard University Press
Cambridge, Massachusetts
and London, England

For Kenneth and Eric

Library of Congress Cataloging in Publication Data

Posner, Richard A
    The economics of justice.

    Includes index.
    1. Justice—Addresses, essays, lectures.   2. Social justice—
Addresses, essays, lectures.   3. Economics—Addresses, essays,
lectures.
I. Title.
JC578.P67   320'.01'1   80-25075
ISBN 0-674-23525-8 (cloth)
ISBN 0-674-23526-6 (paper)

Preface, 1983

In rereading this book after two years of almost total immersion in an activity very different from academic teaching and research—being a judge in a federal court of appeals—I have almost the sense of reading something written by a different person, and yet I am not inclined to think it ought to be reworked in some fundamental way. The purpose of the book is to demonstrate the power and promise of economics in illuminating areas of social behavior not ordinarily thought of as economic, and although many of the specific applications and judgments in the book are and will long remain controversial, its purpose will have been served if the reader is persuaded of the power, not necessarily the omnipotence, of the economic approach to the subjects considered.

The book uses economics in two quite different ways, the positive and the normative—and I recognize that the latter is much more controversial. In this time of anarchy in ethics, the ethic that is implicit in price or value theory—the ethic that I have called "wealth maximization"—deserves to be put out on the counter along with other ethical wares being sold in a disorderly market; but I hope I have not "oversold" this approach by insufficient attention to the rather bizarre results that its unflinching application could produce. Imagine a case where human growth hormone is exceedingly scarce, is allocated strictly on a market, or willingness-to-pay, basis, and is purchased by a wealthy man who wants to put a couple of inches on his normal height and can outbid a poor dwarf who could use the hormone to attain a normal height. No doubt one can argue that allowing human growth hormone to be allocated by the market will increase the supply for everyone by increasing the incentives to produce the hormone, and yet one recoils from the implications of allowing the market to control its allocation completely. Ethical theories seem to invite and receive shocking applications, yet I hope the ethical theory propounded in Part I of this book will be taken in the spirit in which it was intended: as a subject of speculation rather than a blueprint for social action. With this reservation, which is perhaps insufficiently emphasized in the book, I reoffer this book as a contribution to an exciting field—the use of modern economics to elucidate problems of law and justice.

Preface to the First Edition

The essays in this book deal with four subjects: the efficiency or "wealth maximization" theory of justice; the social, including legal, institutions of primitive and archaic societies; the law and economics of privacy and related interests; and the constitutional regulation of racial discrimination and "affirmative action." As explained in Chapter 1, these seemingly disparate subjects turn out to be interrelated from the standpoint of economics.

I use "justice" in approximately the sense of John Rawls. "For us the primary subject of justice is the basic structure of society, or more exactly, the way in which the major social institutions distribute fundamental rights and duties and determine the division of advantages from social cooperation. By major institutions I understand the political constitution and the principal economic and social arrangements" (*A Theory of Justice,* 1971, p. 7). This book is not a comprehensive analysis of "the political constitution and the principal economic and social arrangements," but it does examine a number of important political, economic, social, and legal arrangements, and it tries to show how economic analysis can advance our understanding of them. The book is nontechnical and is addressed to philosophers, political scientists, historians, anthropologists, sociologists, and classicists as much as to lawyers and economists. If the book seems overly ambitious in its sweep, I can defend only by emphasizing that the book is exploratory rather than definitive.

More friends and colleagues than I can hope to mention commented helpfully on prepublication drafts of the essays included in this book. I particularly want to thank Gary Becker, Lea Brilmayer, Ronald Coase, Jules Coleman, Frank Easterbrook, Richard Epstein, Charles Fried, Paul Friedrich, Victor Fuchs, Jack Hirshleifer, Gareth Jones, Stanley Katz, Anthony Kronman, John Langbein, William Landes, Bernard Meltzer, Frederic Pryor, James Redfield, Steven Shavell, George Stigler, Geoffrey Stone, and James White. Each of them made an important contribution to one or more of the chapters. I also want to thank the sponsors, participants, and audiences at various lectures and workshops at the University of Chicago, New York University, the University of Pennsylvania, the Centre for Socio-Legal Studies at Oxford University, the State University of New York at Buffalo, the University of Georgia, and the Public Choice Society, where drafts of some of these essays were first presented.

Robert Bourgeois was a devoted and effective assistant in my research for several of the chapters in this volume; other valuable research assistance was provided by Carole Cooke, Gordon Crovitz, Donna Patterson, Helene Serota, Susan Stukenberg, and Pamela Trow. I am grateful to the Center for the Study of the Economy and the State at the University of Chicago and to the Law and Economics Program of the University of Chicago Law School, for financial assistance. Above all I want to acknowledge my intellectual debts to the economists who have shaped my approach: Gary Becker, Ronald Coase, Aaron Director, and George Stigler. Without their guidance and inspiration, the papers gathered here would not have been written.

All of the chapters except the first have been published before in some form, but the revisions made for this book have been extensive. Chapter 2 is based on an article published in volume 19 of the *Journal of Law and Economics* (1976). Chapter 3 is based on an article in volume 8 of the *Journal of Legal Studies* (1979) and on pages 189–191 of my book *Economic Analysis of Law* (2d ed. 1977). Chapter 4 is based on an article in volume 8 of the *Hofstra Law Review* (1980) and also on an article in volume 9 of the *Journal of Legal Studies* (1980). Chapter 5 is based on an article in volume 90 of *Ethics,* published by the University of Chicago (1979). Chapter 6 is based on Part I of an article in volume 23 of the *Journal of Law and Economics* (1980), and Chapter 7 on Part II of that article. Chapter 8 is based on an article published in volume 9 of the *Journal of Legal Studies* (1980). Chapters 9 and 10 are based on two articles: one published in volume 12 of the *Georgia Law Review* (1978) and one in volume 28 of the *Buffalo Law Review* (copyright © 1979 by *Buffalo Law Review*). Chapter 11 is based on an article in the 1979 volume of the *Supreme Court Review,* edited by Philip B. Kurland and Gerhard Casper, published by the University of Chicago. Chapter 12 is based on Chapter 27 of *Economic Analysis of Law.* Chapter 13 is based on an article in the 1974 volume of the *Supreme Court Review,* edited by Philip B. Kurland, published by the University of Chicago; and Chapter 14 on an article in volume 67 of the *California Law Review* (copyright © 1979, California Law Review, Inc.). I thank the copyright holders for permission to use this material.

I regret not having seen the articles, apart from Jules Coleman's and my own, that appeared in the "Symposium on Efficiency as a Legal Concern," in volume 8 of the *Hofstra Law Review* (1980), after this book was in page proof. Many of the papers in the symposium deal with issues examined in Part I of this book; although they do not change my conclusions, I would have liked the opportunity to refer to some of them. I console myself with the reflection that the last word has not been said on any of the topics discussed here.

Richard A. Posner

September 1980

CONTENTS

The Economics of Justice

1

An Introduction to the Economics of Nonmarket Behavior

This book takes an economic approach to issues—including the meaning of justice, the origin of the state, primitive law, retribution, the right of privacy, defamation, racial discrimination, and affirmative action—that are not generally considered economic. Is not economics the study of the economic system, the study of markets? None of the concepts or activities in my list are market concepts or activities.

Although the traditional subject of economics is indeed the behavior of individuals and organizations in markets, a moment's reflection on the economist's basic analytical tool for studying markets will suggest the possibility of using economics more broadly. That tool is the assumption that people are rational maximizers of their satisfactions. The principles of economics are deductions from this assumption—for example, the principle that a change in price will affect the quantity of a good by affecting the attractiveness of substitute goods, or that resources will gravitate to their most remunerative uses, or that the individual will allocate his budget among available goods and services so that the marginal (last) dollar spent on each good and service yields the same satisfaction to him; if it did not, he could increase his aggregate utility or welfare by a reallocation.

Is it plausible to suppose that people are rational only or mainly when they are transacting in markets, and not when they are engaged in other activities of life, such as marriage and litigation and crime and discrimination and concealment of personal information? Or that only the inhabitants of modern

Western (or Westernized) societies are rational? If rationality is not confined to explicit market transactions but is a general and dominant characteristic of social behavior, then the conceptual apparatus constructed by generations of economists to explain market behavior can be used to explain nonmarket behavior as well.

The question of how fruitful this extension of economics is cannot be answered on logical grounds and should not be answered on intuition. I happen to find implausible and counterintuitive the view that the individual's decisional processes are so rigidly compartmentalized that he will act rationally in making some trivial purchase but irrationally when deciding whether to go to law school or get married or evade income taxes or have three children rather than two or prosecute a lawsuit. But many readers will, I am sure, intuitively regard these choices, important as they are—or perhaps because they are so important—as lying within the area where decisions are emotional rather than rational. The only way to assess the fruitfulness of extending economics into the nonmarket sphere is to make economic studies of nonmarket behavior and evaluate the results.

At the outset of the modern development of economics stands one man who believed that people were rational maximizers of their satisfactions in all areas of human life. This was Jeremy Bentham, who plays a prominent, if somewhat sinister, role in Part I of this book. Bentham's application of economics to crime and punishment was neglected by economists for almost two hundred years, although it had an enduring influence on penology. Bentham did not try to marshal evidence for his view that people were always and everywhere in rational pursuit of their self-interest. He merely asserted it, and subsequent generations of economists apparently found the assertion too implausible to want to test it.

The modern revival of interest in applying economics to nonmarket behavior begins with Gary Becker of the University of Chicago, although, as always in the history of thought, one can find predecessors.[1] Beginning with the publication of his doctoral thesis on the economics of racial discrimination in 1957,[2] Becker and his students and disciples pushed economics into such diverse areas as education, fertility, the utilization of time in the household, the behavior of criminals and of prosecutors, charity, prehistoric hunting, slavery, suicide, adultery, and even the behavior of rats and pigeons.[3] This is not the place to attempt an evaluation of a large, diverse, and frequently technical literature—much of it controversial even within the economics profession[4]—that attempts nothing less than a redefinition of economics as the study of rational choice, not limited to the market. It is enough to say that because of this literature it is no longer absurd to suggest that justice, privacy, primitive law, and the constitutional regulation of racial discrimination might be illuminated by the economic approach.

My interest in the economics of nonmarket behavior began with, and remains centered on, the field known as economic analysis of law or, somewhat confusingly, "law and economics." This book represents a broadening of my interests to include aspects of social experience beyond the strictly legal. But everything in the book grew out of the economic analysis of law. It may therefore be helpful if I describe the field briefly and relate it to the specific problems addressed in this book.[5] The eco-

1. E.g., Sidgwick's discussion of externalities in 1883 and Mitchell's of household production in 1912. See Henry Sidgwick, *The Principles of Political Economy* 406–408 (3d ed. 1901); Wesley C. Mitchell, "The Backward Art of Spending Money," 2 *Am. Econ. Rev.* 269 (1912), reprinted in his book *The Backward Art of Spending Money, and Other Essays* 3 (1950).

2. See Gary S. Becker, *The Economics of Discrimination* (2d ed. 1971).

3. The best introduction to the economics of nonmarket behavior is Becker's book of essays, *The Economic Approach to Human Behavior* (1976). See especially his introductory chapter. Other such analyses include *Essays in the Economics of the Family* (Theodore W. Shultz ed. 1975); John H. Kagel et al., "Experimental Studies of Consumer Demand Behavior Using Laboratory Animals," 13 *Econ. Inquiry* 22 (1975).

4. See, e.g., Ronald H. Coase, "Economics and Contiguous Disciplines," 7 *J. Legal Stud.* 201 (1978).

5. For a general survey of the field, see Richard A. Posner, *Economic Analysis of Law* (2d ed. 1977), and for a recent review article, Richard A. Posner, "Some Uses and Abuses of Economics in Law," 46 *U. Chi. L. Rev.* 281 (1979).

nomic analysis of law has two branches. The older—the analysis of laws regulating explicit economic activity—dates back at least to Adam Smith's discussion of the economic effects of mercantilist legislation. Such studies remain an important part of the economic analysis of law today—indeed, quantitatively the most important part. They include studies of antitrust, tax, and corporation law; public utility and common carrier regulation; and the regulation of international trade and other market activities.

The other branch, the analysis of laws regulating nonmarket activities, is for the most part very recent. It is this branch that provides the background of the present book. The pioneers here are Ronald Coase and Guido Calabresi. In his famous article on social cost, published in 1961, Coase analyzed the relationship between rules of liability and the allocation of resources.[6] This was also the subject of Calabresi's first article on accident law, written independently of Coase's work and published the same year as Coase's article.[7] Coase observed—almost in passing, for this was not the focus of his paper—that the English courts, in interpreting the common law doctrine of nuisance (the doctrine governing pollution and related types of interference with the enjoyment of property), had decided cases in a way that seemed to accord with the economics of the problem. In fact they had exhibited a surer, if wholly instinctive, grasp of those economics than the economists had! Coase's insight into the economizing character of common law doctrines remained for a time undeveloped. Since 1971, however, in a series of studies that is now quite extensive, I and others have examined the hypothesis that the common law is best explained as if the judges were trying to maximize economic welfare.[8] The hypothesis is not that the judges can or do duplicate the results

6. See R. H. Coase, "The Problem of Social Cost," 3 *J. Law & Econ.* 1 (1960). (This issue was actually published in 1961.)

7. See Guido Calabresi, "Some Thoughts on Risk Distribution and the Law of Torts," 70 *Yale L. J.* 499 (1961).

8. For discussion and references see Posner, "Some Uses and Abuses of Economics in Law," 46 *U. Chi. L. Rev.* 281, 288–291 (1979).

of competitive markets, but that within the limits set by the costs of administering the legal system (costs that must be taken into account in any effort to promote efficiency through legal rules), common law adjudication brings the economic system closer to the results that would be produced by effective competition—a free market operating without significant externality, monopoly, or information problems.

Evidence for the implicit economic structure of the common law has been found in many studies of legal rules, institutions, procedures, and outcomes. These studies are not limited to the occasional instances where the courts have adopted a virtually explicit economic formulation of the law, as in Judge Learned Hand's formula for negligence.[9] He said that negligence is a failure to take care where the cost of care (he called it the "burden of precautions") is less than the probability of the accident multiplied by the loss if the accident occurs. An economist would call the product of this multiplication the expected costs of the accident. The Hand formula is a tolerable, although not perfect, approximation of an economically efficient concept of care and negligence.[10] But the economic logic of the common law is more subtle than this. In analyzing a wide variety of legal doctrines—a few scattered example are assumption of risk in tort law, the degrees of homicide, the principles of tort and contract damages, proximate cause, mistake and fraud in contract law, the principles of restitution, the doctrine of "moral consideration," the structure of property rights in water, the law of joint tortfeasors, and the rules of salvage in admiralty law[11]—economists and economically minded lawyers have found that the law uncannily follows economics.

9. See United States v. Carroll Towing Co., 159 F.2d 169 (2d Cir. 1947); Conway v. O'Brien, 111 F.2d 611 (2d Cir. 1940).

10. See John Prather Brown, "Toward an Economic Theory of Liability," 2 *J. Legal Stud.* 323 (1973); Richard A. Posner, *Economic Analysis of Law* 122–123 (2d ed. 1977).

11. See references in Posner, supra note 8, at 290; William M. Landes & Richard A. Posner, "Joint and Multiple Tortfeasors: An Economic Analysis," 9 *J. Legal Stud.* 517 (1980).

The Plan of the Book

Part I deals with the relationship between the concept of efficiency as wealth maximization, which has guided the positive economic analysis of the common law, and an acceptable concept of justice. The relationship of efficiency to justice is an interesting subject in its own right, but my interest derives mainly from the occasional suggestion that the efficiency theory is implausible because no judge could be guided by so crude a concept of justice as wealth maximization.[12] One possible reply is that the judge's preferences do not enter into his decisions. Efforts have been made to show that the common law would evolve in the direction of efficiency even if the judges' decisions were random,[13] but the argument is persuasive only under strong assumptions.[14] My reply is different. It is that efficiency as I define the term is an adequate concept of justice that can plausibly be imputed to judges, at least in common law adjudication. The reasons for this conclusion, it turns out, also point the way toward a reconciliation of the efficiency theory of the common law with the interest-group or redistributive theories that dominate current economic analyses of legislation. Part I also attempts to explicate the differences between economics and classical utilitarianism as guides to legal and political action.

Part II of the book deals with the social and legal order of primitive, including ancient, societies. Many common law doctrines have ancient roots, and most law in primitive societies, like the common law itself, is customary rather than legislated or codified.[15] It seems worth inquiring, therefore, whether the economic theory of the common law might be able to explain the law of primitive societies as well. Furthermore, a study of primitive law may illuminate questions in the positive economic

12. See, e.g., Frank I. Michelman, "A Comment on *Some Uses and Abuses of Economics in Law*," 46 *U. Chi. L. Rev.* 307 (1979).

13. See references in Posner, supra note 8, at 289 n.31.

14. See William M. Landes & Richard A. Posner, "Adjudication as a Private Good," 8 *J. Legal Stud.* 235, 259–284 (1979).

15. Customary law is defined more precisely in Chapter 6.

analysis of the common law. One such question is why in the nineteenth century strict liability declined in importance relative to negligence as the standard of liability. It is pertinent to note that strict liability is the general standard of liability (sometimes for crimes as well as torts) in primitive law and to ask what features of primitive society might explain this difference between primitive and modern law. Indeed, I began my research on primitive law and society by asking why strict liability looms so much larger in the liability systems of primitive than of modern societies.

Part III first develops an economic theory of privacy and related interests and then asks whether the relevant common law doctrines (including unfair competition, assault and battery, defamation, and the privacy tort itself) are consistent with the theory. If the argument of these chapters is accepted, it provides a further illustration of the power of economics to explain legal doctrines far removed from a concern with "economic" activities in the narrow sense.

Part IV explicates a nonefficiency, in fact antiefficiency, concept of justice: justice as individualized assessment beyond the point where a dollar in additional search would yield a dollar's worth of additional information. The argument is that much racial and related discrimination probably is efficient because it economizes on the costs of information, but that the equal protection clause of the Fourteenth Amendment to the U.S. Constitution embodies a theory of justice that rejects efficient discrimination. The role of economics in the analysis is thus not to explain the legal position but to distinguish economic from noneconomic concepts of justice. Part IV focuses on affirmative action because that is the cutting edge of legal policy toward discrimination.

Part IV provides evidence that although efficiency can explain common law doctrines, it seems not to explain some important constitutional rules. There is further evidence relating to this point in Part III, dealing with privacy. Not only are state and federal privacy statutes seemingly antiefficient, but the Supreme Court has evolved a constitutional doctrine of privacy that has no systematic relationship to the economics of the problem.

The various parts of the book are connected with each other not only through a common origin in the positive economic analysis of law but also through a convergence on the economics of uncertainty. Uncertainty is a source of risk, which most people dislike, and so also a source of demands for the reduction of risk through various forms of insurance. Uncertainty also creates a demand for information. An important branch of nonmarket economics, the economics of information, pioneered by George Stigler,[16] studies how rational maximizers allocate their time and other resources to searching out profitable opportunities to buy and sell. The field has focused on information in markets, but it can properly be regarded as an area of nonmarket behavior because the information itself is rarely bought or sold. Economists of information have extended their inquiry to investments in fraud and in reputation.

The analysis of uncertainty both as risk and as ignorance is fundamental to each of the topics discussed in this book. Because many injuries, including many breaches of contract, arise out of uncertain events, out of accidents, it is superficial to criticize the legal system as unjust because it does not always require compensation for injury; as I show in Part I, there may often be compensation ex ante even if there is no compensation ex post. In Part II, uncertainty both as risk and as misinformation is shown to be fundamental to the structure of primitive social and legal institutions. The primitive emphasis on informal insurance arrangements is related to the lack of alternative insurance mechanisms, and the primitive emphasis on strict liability is related to the high costs of information about care and inten-

16. See George J. Stigler, "The Economics of Information," in his book *The Organization of Industry* 171 (1968); for a good review article, see J. Hirshleifer, "Where Are We in the Theory of Information?" 63 *Am. Econ. Rev. Papers & Proceedings* 31 (1973). On risk and uncertainty see Kenneth J. Arrow, *Essays in the Theory of Risk-Bearing* (1971). And on the entire area of information and uncertainty see J. Hirshleifer & John G. Riley, "The Analytics of Uncertainty and Information—An Expository Survey," 17 *J. Econ. Lit.* 1375 (1979). This last is comprehensive and up to date, but also technical.

tion. Privacy, the subject of Part III, is, in its most interesting sense, the concealment of personal information. The most attractive case, although ultimately unconvincing, for protecting privacy in this sense is that people will misinterpret personal information—will attach excessive weight to the discovery that someone is a homosexual or an ex-convict or that he has a history of mental illness. The objection to "efficient" (statistical) discrimination is the same—that people will attach excessive weight to knowing that someone is black or female. But since these facts cannot be concealed, the focus of policy shifts from protecting secrecy to forbidding use of the information as a basis for deciding to employ or otherwise transact with the individual, the type of prohibition analyzed in Part IV.

The economics of uncertainty establishes more connections among the parts of the book than are suggested by this discussion; for example, the concept of reputation (a form of information capital) is used in Chapter 8 to explain retribution and in Chapter 10 to explain why libel and slander are torts. However, the purpose of this introduction is not to recapitulate the book, but to introduce the reader to the economics of nonmarket behavior in general and of law in particular, to relate the subsequent chapters to the efficiency theory of the common law, and to alert the reader to the importance of uncertainty, risk, and information as economic concepts central to the aspects of justice explored in the book.

I
JUSTICE AND EFFICIENCY

2

Blackstone and Bentham

The purpose of this chapter is mainly negative—to arouse the reader's mistrust of utilitarianism by examining the thought of its most thorough practitioner, Jeremy Bentham. Utilitarianism has not wanted for critics, and many of my criticisms are old ones. What is perhaps new is that not only do I agree with Bentham that people are rational maximizers of their satisfactions in all areas of life, but I believe that economic efficiency is an ethical as well as scientific concept—and is not economics simply applied utilitarianism? It is not, as I hope to show. My angle of attack on utilitarianism is also novel in that I search for a clue to the basic character of Bentham's thought in his passionate dislike of William Blackstone.

Blackstone's *Commentaries*

William Blackstone was elected to the first chair in English law at Oxford in 1758. Between 1765 and 1769 he published the four volumes of his *Commentaries on the Laws of England,* based on his Oxford lectures. In 1776 Jeremy Bentham, who had attended Blackstone's lectures as a sixteen-year-old student, published his *Fragment on Government*—a fierce attack on the *Commentaries.* The *Fragment* consisted of a preface roundly denouncing the *Commentaries,* but with few particulars, followed by a microscopic critique of seven pages in the introduction to the *Commentaries* in which Blackstone discussed the nature of law. Bentham gave the impression that a scrutiny of the other 2,000-odd pages of the *Commentaries* would reveal a similar incapacity for reasoned analysis.

The *Fragment* made two fundamental criticisms: first that Blackstone was a shameless apologist for the status quo,[1] and second that his analysis of the nature and sources of legal obligation was shallow, amateurish, and contradictory—that, as Samuel Johnson is reported to have said, Blackstone "thought clearly, but he thought faintly."[2]

There is indeed much to criticize in the *Commentaries*,[3] but there is also much to praise, apart from the clarity and concision which are its most obvious virtues. Blackstone joined two strands of legal writing. One, typified by Montesquieu's *L'Esprit des lois,* analyzed the social functions of law considered in the abstract, with no more than passing references to any actual legal

1. This theme has been developed recently, at great length and from a Marxist perspective, in Duncan Kennedy, "The Structure of Blackstone's Commentaries," 28 *Buff. L. Rev.* 205 (1979).

2. Quoted without citation to source in C. H. S. Fifoot, *Lord Mansfield* 26 (1936).

3. In particular:

(1) Blackstone was complacent about the English legal system of the time. He closed his eyes to a number of notorious abuses in the practical administration of the law (such as delay in the Chancery court), and accepted uncritically many serious deformities in legal doctrine, such as the rule forbidding a party to a lawsuit to appear as a witness in the suit. He was also excessively tolerant of the many anachronisms of the law of his time. It was mayhem (a kind of aggravated battery) to knock out someone's "foretooth," but not to knock out a "jaw-tooth," because to commit mayhem you must impair the victim's capacity to defend himself against violent attacks. Blackstone records this distinction without comment, 3 William Blackstone, *Commentaries on the Laws of England: A Facsimile of the First Edition of 1765–1769* 121 (1979), hereinafter cited as *Comm.* All page references are to the facsimile of the first edition, published by the University of Chicago Press with introductions by Stanley N. Katz (vol. 1), A. W. Brian Simpson (vol. 2), John H. Langbein (vol. 3), and Thomas A. Green (vol. 4). In quoting from Blackstone, I have omitted footnote references without indication.

(2) Blackstone was also guilty at times of circular reasoning, as when he "explained" the various legal disabilities of married women by the principle that husband and wife are one in contemplation of law, without offering any explanation of the principle itself. See 1 *Comm.* 430.

(3) There are a number of apparent inconsistencies in the *Commentaries* on major issues. For example, laws that contravene natural law are invalid—but no human agency can invalidate a law duly enacted by Parliament. Compare 1 *Comm.* 54 with 1 *Comm.* 91. The judges are "the living oracles" of the law—but they are also judicial statesmen (not Blackstone's term, but his meaning) who use legal fictions to nullify laws they don't like. Compare 1 *Comm.* 69 with 2 *Comm.* 116–117. The right of property is described as an aspect of the law of nature in Book I and as an artifact of populous societies in Book II. Compare 1 *Comm.* 138 with 2 *Comm.* 7.

system. The other, illustrated by Bracton's treatise on English law or Pothier's on civil law,[4] described the actual laws of a society. Blackstone demonstrated how the laws of England operated to achieve the economic, political, and other goals of the society. His functionalism may be seen as a distant ancestor of the positive economic analysis of the common law sketched in Chapter 1 of this book.

Blackstone's aspiration in the *Commentaries* was to present the law as a "rational science."[5] To what extent did he achieve this? To answer that question we must examine Blackstone's analysis of the scope and nature of English law.

To Blackstone the ultimate objective of law was to secure fundamental rights. By this he seems to have meant nothing more pretentious than the conditions for maximizing social welfare in approximately the sense in which I discuss social wealth maximization in the next chapter. The fundamental rights—sometimes referred to as "the liberties of Englishmen"—"consist, primarily, in the free enjoyment of personal security, of personal liberty, and of private property."[6] Blackstone's conception of a free society was close to that of Adam Smith and other "liberals" in the original and nearly forgotten sense of that term: people should be free to behave as they please so long as they do not invade other people's freedom.

Blackstone's conception of economic liberty was not so spacious as Adam Smith's, but for its time it was impressive.[7] His conception of civil liberties, while less spacious than that of John Stuart Mill, say, was also impressive for its time. On religious liberty, Blackstone stated: "All persecution for diversity of opinions, however ridiculous or absurd they may be, is contrary to

4. See Henry de Bracton, *On the Laws and Customs of England* (Samuel E. Thorne trans. 1968); Robert Joseph Pothier, *A Treatise on the Law of Obligations, or Contracts* (William David Evans trans. 1853).

5. 2 *Comm.* 2.

6. 1 *Comm.* 140.

7. Especially good, I think, is his discussion of why lending money at interest should be permitted, contrary to medieval Christian opinion on the subject. See 2 *Comm.* 456–458.

every principle of sound policy and civil freedom."[8] His discussion of liberty of the press is justly famous:

> The liberty of the press is indeed essential to the nature of a free state: but this consists in laying no *previous* restraints upon publications, and not in freedom from censure for criminal matter when published. Every freeman has an undoubted right to lay what sentiments he pleases before the public: to forbid this, is to destroy the freedom of the press: but if he publishes what is improper, mischievous, or illegal, he must take the consequence of his own temerity. To subject the press to the restrictive power of a licenser, as was formerly done, both before and since the Revolution, is to subject all freedom of sentiment to the prejudices of one man, and make him the arbitrary and infallible judge of all controverted points in learning, religion, and government. But to punish (as the law does at present) any dangerous or offensive writings, which, when published, shall on a fair and impartial trial be adjudged of a pernicious tendency, is necessary for the preservation of peace and good order, of government and religion, the only solid foundations of civil liberty. Thus the will of individuals is still left free; the abuse only of that free-will is the object of legal punishment. Neither is any restraint hereby laid upon freedom of thought or inquiry: liberty of private sentiment is still left: the disseminating, or making public, of bad sentiments, destructive of the ends of society, is the crime which society corrects.[9]

In this passage the modern reader is struck by the dichotomy between advance censorship and post-publication criminal punishment; only the former offends Blackstone's conception of liberty of the press. The explanation for this dichotomy may lie in the political role that Blackstone assigned to the English jury. As we shall see, he considered the jury an important bulwark

8. 4 *Comm.* 53.
9. 4 *Comm.* 151–152.

against oppression by royal officials. Presumably it could be trusted not to convict a journalist prosecuted because of writings not truly seditious or libelous but merely offensive to the King or his ministers. The real danger to liberty of the press was the censor, a royal official acting outside of the jury system.

Despite Blackstone's vigorous defense of freedom of religious belief and of the press as he understood the concepts, there is no mention of these freedoms in his discussion of personal liberty in Book I of the *Commentaries.* Nor is there any mention of freedom of speech as such—yet Blackstone deemed fundamental and inalienable the right to petition king and Parliament for redress of grievances. Blackstone understood the importance of civil liberties, but his analysis was not systematic.

Although the exercise of fundamental rights was in Blackstone's view subject to "necessary restraints—Restraints in themselves so gentle and moderate, as will appear upon farther inquiry, that no man of sense or probity would wish to see them slackened," they were indefeasible: "no human legislature has power to abridge or destroy them, unless the owner shall himself commit some act that amounts to a forfeiture."[10] The force of this statement is weakened by Blackstone's later denial that a court can invalidate a duly enacted Parliamentary statute. He saved himself from fundamental inconsistency by adopting Locke's view, reflected a few years later in the American Declaration of Independence, that abridgments of fundamental rights legitimize revolution. But given the costs of revolution, it can hardly be considered a satisfactory remedy for deprivations of fundamental right; also, this view is inconsistent with Blackstone's contention, considered below, that every legal right implies a legal (that is, judicially cognizable) remedy and that a right without a remedy is a contradiction in terms. Blackstone no doubt believed that the main protection of fundamental rights lay not in legal remedies or violent revolution but in the balance of power among the political forces in the society, which had been achieved by the British constitution of his day.

10. 1 *Comm.* 140, 54.

Blackstone assumed that the fundamental rights were rights not only against the government but also against private coercion, so that an Englishman had an indefeasible right to the enactment and enforcement of an effective system of criminal laws. The American view of the matter is different. Rights under the U.S. Constitution are basically rights against public officials. Protection against private coercion is a matter of legislative discretion. This implies that there are no federal common law crimes, which has indeed long been the American view. The contrasting English acceptance of common law crimes flows naturally from the idea, implicit in Blackstone, that the basic liberties of Englishmen are protected against private as well as public invasion—an intriguing and by no means foolish idea that incidentally reinforces my earlier point that Blackstone viewed rights broadly as the conditions for social welfare. The social welfare obviously requires protection against private as well as public coercion.

Yet Blackstone also emphasized, very much in the spirit of 1776, the danger of official infringements upon the liberties of Englishmen. For example, he stated:

> To preserve these [liberties] from violation, it is necessary that the constitution of parliament be supported in its full vigour; and limits, certainly known, be set to the royal prerogative. And, lastly, to vindicate these rights, when actually violated or attacked, the subjects of England are entitled, in the first place, to the regular administration and free course of justice in the courts of law; next, to the right of petitioning the king and parliament for redress of grievances; and, lastly, to the right of having and using arms for self-preservation and defence.[11]

Correlative to the notion of liberty in the *Commentaries* is the idea that law is concerned with social or public, rather than with private, behavior:

11. 1 *Comm.* 140.

Let a man . . . be ever so abandoned in his principles, or vicious in his practice, provided he keeps his wickedness to himself, and does not offend against the rules of public decency, he is out of the reach of human laws . . .

Thus the statute of king Edward IV., which forbad the fine gentlemen of those times (under the degree of a lord) to wear pikes upon their shoes or boots of more than two inches in length, was a law that savoured of oppression; because, however ridiculous the fashion then in use might appear, the restraining it by pecuniary penalties could serve no purpose of common utility. But the statute of king Charles II., which prescribes a thing seemingly as indifferent (a dress for the dead, who are all ordered to be buried in woollen,) is a law consistent with public liberty; for it encourages the staple trade, on which in great measure depends the universal good of the nation . . . [T]hat constitution or frame of government, that system of laws, is alone calculated to maintain civil liberty, which leaves the subject entire master of his own conduct, except in those points wherein the public good requires some direction or restraint.[12]

Adam Smith would have regarded Blackstone's example of a utilitarian law as ludicrously inapt, but the general principle is well stated: the "common utility," or public welfare, requires that law leave everyone "entire master of his conduct" save as his conduct may infringe the rights of others or otherwise reduce the social welfare.

A related point is Blackstone's attempt to divorce law from conscience. Anticipating Holmes's "bad man" theory of law by more than a hundred years, Blackstone wrote that "the main strength and force of a law consists in the penalty annexed to it."[13] Thus, there was no legal right without a legal remedy, and the absence of a remedy implied the nonexistence of the right.

12. 1 *Comm.* 120, 122.
13. 1 *Comm.* 57.

A further implication that Blackstone, like Holmes, drew was that

> in relation to those laws which enjoin only *positive duties,* and forbid only such things as are not *mala in se,* but *mala prohibita* merely, without any intermixture of moral guilt, annexing a penalty to non-compliance, here I apprehend conscience is no further concerned, than by directing a submission to the penalty in case of our breach of those laws: for otherwise the multitude of penal laws in a state would not only be looked upon as an impolitic, but would also be a very wicked thing; if every such law were a snare for the conscience of the subject. But in these cases the alternative is offered to every man; "either abstain from this, or submit to such a penalty," and his conscience will be clear, which ever side of the alternative he thinks proper to embrace.[14]

Blackstone's view of the role of law in society was a secular and liberal one. Its role was not to improve people's chances of getting into heaven but to discourage, by penalizing, conduct that reduces social welfare. Implicitly in Blackstone's account, legal sanctions act as prices that influence the demand for and hence incidence of proscribed activities.

As I have thus far described it, Blackstone's conception of the nature and purpose of law was somewhat abstract, but what is notable about the *Commentaries* is the thoroughness and precision with which he traced the articulation of the concept in specific rules and institutions of the legal system of his time. Blackstone was emphatic that to be protected effectively, the fundamental rights to life, liberty, and property needed to be buttressed by a host of ancillary procedural and substantive rights—and what he described in the *Commentaries* as the rights of Englishmen are most of the rights later codified in the Amer-

14. 1 *Comm.* 57–58.

ican Bill of Rights. Blackstone was especially eloquent about the rights of habeas corpus and of trial by jury in both civil and criminal matters:

> To assert an absolute exemption from imprisonment in all cases, is inconsistent with every idea of law and political society, and in the end would destroy all civil liberty, by rendering its protection impossible; but the glory of the English law consists in clearly defining the times, the causes, and the extent, when, wherefore, and to what degree the imprisonment of the subject may be lawful. This it is, which induces the absolute necessity of expressing upon every commitment the reason for which it is made; that the court upon an *habeas corpus* may examine into its validity; and according to the circumstances of the case may discharge, admit to bail, or remand the prisoner.[15]

As a political thinker Blackstone is usually considered a minor disciple of Montesquieu, who developed, although he did not invent, the idea of separation of powers (that is, the allocation of executive, legislative, and judicial authority to separate branches of government). But Blackstone viewed the formal tripartite separation of powers as only one element in a broader system of political power diffusion, in which authority was to be split up among a number of governmental organs in a system of checks and balances[16] and in which the underlying political power (as distinct from formal legal authority), based on wealth or other factors, was also widely diffused. In the evaluation of alternative rules governing inheritance, he assigned wealth-distribution effects an important place,[17] and he defended property qualifications for voters on the ground that those who had

15. 3 *Comm.* 133.
16. See 1 *Comm.* 50–51, 149–151.
17. 2 *Comm.* 373–374.

no property would sell their votes and thereby magnify the political influence of the wealthy.[18]

Blackstone has been criticized for giving an excessively idealized picture of how the eighteenth-century British constitution operated, and there is merit to the criticism. Many votes for members of the House of Commons were indirectly controlled by the king and a few powerful aristocrats. English government of the period was more oligarchic than Blackstone let on.[19] Yet the *Commentaries* contain hints of a more realistic awareness of the nature of the constitution. Blackstone criticized the narrowness of the suffrage,[20] and he realized that the decline in royal prerogative did not tell the full story of the king's political power. He alluded to the system of influence by which the king and his aristocratic allies kept their hands firmly on the levers of power:

> Whatever may have become of the *nominal*, the *real* power of the crown has not been too far weakened by any transactions in the last century. Much is indeed given up; but much is also acquired. The stern commands of prerogative have yielded to the milder voice of influence: the slavish and exploded doctrine of non-resistance has given way to a military establishment by law: and to the disuse of parlia-

18. 1 *Comm.* 165. This defense of property qualifications is not so self-evident as Blackstone thought. Giving the propertyless the vote would increase their political power either directly or, by giving them a marketable asset and thus increasing their wealth, indirectly. Blackstone's apparent concern was that the availability of votes for sale, presumably at low prices, would magnify the political power of the wealthy aristocrats vis-à-vis the rest of the propertied class. The concern is not groundless, but Blackstone failed to articulate its ground. While in principle coalitions of the lesser (but more numerous) property owners might increase their political power by the cheap purchase of votes from people without property, organizing the necessary coalitions might encounter serious free-rider problems. A single very wealthy aristocrat or a small group of wealthy aristocrats might find it simpler to purchase votes. Thus the elimination of property qualifications in the eighteenth century might have aggravated the oligarchic tendencies of the period.

19. See, e.g., J. A. W. Gunn, "Influence, Parties and the Constitution: Changing Attitudes, 1783–1832," 17 *Hist. J.* 301 (1974); J. H. Plumb, *The Origins of Political Stability: England 1675–1725* (1967).

20. 1 *Comm.* 165–166.

ment has succceded a parliamentary trust of an immense perpetual revenue.[21]

Blackstone emphasized the importance of an independent judiciary[22] and of the jury as a counterpoise to the Crown-appointed judges:

[If the administration of justice] be entirely intrusted to the magistracy, a select body of men, and those generally selected by the prince or such as enjoy the highest offices in the state, their decisions, in spite of their own natural integrity, will have frequently an involuntary bias towards those of their own rank and dignity: it is not to be expected from human nature, that *the few* should be always attentive to the interests and good of *the many*. On the other hand, if the power of judicature were placed at random in the hands of the multitude, their decisions would be wild and capricious, and a new rule of action would be every day established in our courts. It is wisely therefore ordered, that the principles and axioms of law, which are general propositions, flowing from abstracted reason, and not accommodated to times or to men, should be deposited in the breasts of the judges, to be occasionally applied to such facts as come properly ascertained before them. For here partiality can have little scope: the law is well known, and is the same for all ranks and degrees; it follows as a regular conclusion from the premises of fact pre-established. But in settling and adjusting a question of fact, when intrusted to any single magistrate, partiality and injustice have an ample field to range in: either by boldly asserting that to be proved which is not so, or by more artfully suppressing some circumstances, stretching and warping others, and distinguishing away the remainder. Here therefore a competent number of sensible and upright jurymen, chosen by lot from among those of the middle rank, will be found the

21. 1 *Comm.* 325–326.
22. See 1 *Comm.* 259–260.

best investigators of truth, and the surest guardians of public justice. For the most powerful individual in the state will be cautious of committing any flagrant invasion of another's right, when he knows that the fact of his oppression must be examined and decided by twelve indifferent men, not appointed till the hour of trial.[23]

Blackstone was aware that if the definition of legal rights were left to the whim of the judges, the judges would be no better than despots.[24] But at the time he was writing, most of the laws of England were not statute laws; they were common law, that is, law previously declared by the judges. Thus it would seem that English judges *were* despots, albeit petty despots since they were subject to legislative check if they abused their despotic power too much. But Blackstone rejected this view:

The judges in the several courts of justice . . . are the depositaries of the laws, the living oracles, who must decide in all cases of doubt, and who are bound by an oath to decide according to the law of the land. Their knowledge of that law is derived from experience and study . . . and from being long personally accustomed to the judicial decisions of their predecessors. And indeed these judicial decisions are the principal and most authoritative evidence that can be given of the existence of such a custom as shall form a part of the common law . . . For it is an established rule to abide by former precedents, where the same points come again in litigation: as well to keep the scale of justice even and steady, and not liable to waver with every new judge's opinion; as also because the law in that case being solemnly declared and determined, what before was uncertain, and perhaps indifferent, is now become a permanent rule, which it is not in the breast of any subsequent judge to alter or vary from, according to his private sentiments.[25]

23. 3 *Comm.* 379–380.
24. See 3 *Comm.* 327–328; see also 3 *Comm.* 422–423.
25. 1 *Comm.* 69.

In Greek mythology an oracle is not an interpreter, but merely a passive transmitter, of divine utterances. To compare any judge, let alone a common law judge, to an oracle thus seems absurd. But once it is understood what Blackstone was about, the oracle metaphor becomes apt. He viewed the common law as a set of customs of immemorial antiquity. The Norman conquerers had submerged the old customs under the oppressive institutions of feudalism, and the task of the modern English judge was to scrape away the Norman incrustations with which the common law, that is, immemorial custom, had been overlaid, and restore it to its pristine Saxon form. This view of the judicial function may seem to give the judge an active role in law reform, but actually, once he has succeeded in reconstructing the Saxon custom, he is a passive spokesman for legal concepts of immemorial antiquity.

Taken literally, Blackstone's conception of the judicial function raises many questions. Had the Saxons really developed a set of legal institutions appropriate to the eighteenth century? Did Blackstone have any but the haziest idea of Saxon laws and legal institutions? Did the judges of his time really adopt so archaeological a view of their function? But these questions miss the real point of Blackstone's theory of common law adjudication: he was trying to rationalize judicial creativity in adapting the common law to contemporary social needs. Before Gibbon's *Decline and Fall of the Roman Empire* (published after the *Commentaries*), social progress or improvement was usually conceived in terms not of evolution toward new and higher levels of social welfare but of restoration of some long-ago state of bliss.[26] Legal institutions, in Blackstone's view, changed and evolved, but the evolution was toward a set of ideal concepts that, in keeping with the spirit of his time, he located in a remote and largely imaginary past state of grace. Out of elements by no means original with him,[27] Blackstone thus constructed a concept of common law adjudication that gave the judges latitude for sub-

---

26. See, e.g., H. R. Trevor-Roper, "Gibbon and *The Decline and Fall of the Roman Empire*," 19 *J. Law & Econ.* 489 (1976).

27. See J. G. A. Pocock, *The Ancient Constitution and the Feudal Law* (1957).

stantive law reform, as they endeavored to bring the law into
harmony with the contemporary ideals of liberty that he
ascribed to Saxon times, while at the same time disclaiming an
outright judicial activism that would have smacked of the despotic.

Although Blackstone's is not the modern answer to the question of judicial legitimacy, it resembles the modern answer. The
justices of the U.S. Supreme Court do not acknowledge that
they fashion law out of their personal predilections. They claim
rather to be operating within a system of precedent designed to
reconstruct the intentions—broadly conceived, to be sure—of
the framers of the Constitution. But as we shall see in Chapter
11, in discussing the Supreme Court's privacy decisions, in the
hands of the modern judge the Constitution of 1787 is an essentially fictive construct, like the customs of an idealized pre-Nor-
man society in Blackstone's time. Two hundred years after Gibbon, we still prefer to think in terms of the restoration of
ancient, rather than the acquisition of new, liberties.

The exercise of judicial creativity in the conceptual framework described by Blackstone inevitably results in a heavy reliance on legal fictions as the agency of legal reform. Although
Blackstone was not a slavish adherent of the principle of *stare
decisis* (decision according to precedent)—a prior decision could
be overruled if "contrary to reason"[28]—his preferred method of
judicial creativity was the legal fiction, especially as this was the
only method available for getting around unreasonable legislation; judges had, in Blackstone's view, no power to invalidate
legislation. The law of real property illustrates the method.
That law had been shaped by the feudal system introduced by
the Normans, and many provisions of the medieval law, which
had been functional in the context of a feudal society, had become dysfunctional—indeed, if followed, they would have
paralyzed the market in real estate. Yet the medieval law was
firmly established, not only in precedents but in statutes. The
English judges got around it by an ingenious use of legal fic-

28. 1 *Comm.* 69.

tions, such as the method of obtaining a clear title known as "common recovery." They were

> fictitious proceedings, introduced by a kind of *pia fraus,* to elude the statute *de donis,* which was found so intolerably mischievous, and which yet one branch of the legislature would not then consent to repeal . . . [T]hese recoveries, however clandestinely introduced, are now become by long use and acquiescence a most common assurance of lands; and are looked upon as the legal mode of conveyance, by which tenant in tail may dispose of his lands and tenements: so that no court will suffer them to be shaken or reflected on, and even acts of parliament have by a sidewind countenanced and established them.[29]

The Warren Court could have used this passage as historical precedent for its (implicit) view that it is proper for the courts to assume the mantle of legislative reform if the legislature is for some reason unable to act effectively.

The political uses of the legal fiction are nicely illustrated by Blackstone's discussion of the maxim, "The king can do no wrong."[30] At first blush it might seem that the purpose of this maxim was to place the king above the law. But Blackstone's discussion suggests that the real purpose was to make it easier to subject the king to the restraints of law. The fiction that the king could do no wrong, and its corollary that any wrong done by the king was to be attributed to "evil counselors,"[31] made it possible to check royal abuses through actions against the king's agents rather than against the king himself; direct confrontations between the courts or the legislature and the king were avoided. The fiction had essentially a face-saving function.

Blackstone emphasized the role of courts in making law because when he wrote, most law in England was judge-made. He did not ignore the role of legislation, but he assigned it a limited

29. 2 *Comm.* 117.
30. 1 *Comm.* 238–239.
31. 1 *Comm.* 237.

role—its proper office was to resolve conflicts between common law precedents, and otherwise to supplement and patch common law doctrine.[32] The modern view is that legislatures are free to make sweeping changes in existing law within the broad bounds set by constitutional limitations on legislative action. Blackstone, a thoroughgoing incrementalist, deprecated sweeping social change by any governmental organ.

Book IV of the *Commentaries,* which deals with criminal law and procedure, has been much praised. The eloquent attack on excessive reliance on capital punishment as a sanction for criminal acts[33] is the passage usually singled out for commendation, but with the qualification that Blackstone got his views on capital punishment from Beccaria. What is overlooked is not only Blackstone's wide-ranging discussion of many other questions of criminal jurisprudence but also the difference between his purposes and those of Beccaria and other jurists from whom he borrowed ideas about criminal jurisprudence. Beccaria's *Essay on Crimes and Punishments* was an elegant theoretical analysis of the principles of punishment.[34] Blackstone took Beccaria's theoretical propositions and applied them to the actual system of criminal justice in England.[35] In at least one respect—the rele-

32. See 3 *Comm.* 327–328; 1 *Comm.* 353.

33. 4 *Comm.* 18–19: "It is a melancholy truth, that among the variety of actions which men are daily liable to commit, no less than an hundred and sixty have been declared by act of parliament to be felonies without benefit of clergy; or, in other words, to be worthy of instant death. So dreadful a list, instead of diminishing, increases the number of offenders. The injured, through compassion, will often forebear to prosecute: juries, through compassion, will sometimes forget their oaths, and either acquit the guilty or mitigate the nature of the offence: and judges, through compassion, will respite one half of the convicts, and recommend them to the royal mercy."

34. See Caesar Beccaria, *An Essay on Crimes and Punishments* (Edward D. Ingraham ed. 2d Am. ed. 1819).

35. Among the notable features of Blackstone's discussion of the criminal law is his adoption of a deterrent rather than a retributive rationale for punishment: "As to the *end* or final cause of human punishments. This is not by way of atonement or expiation for the crime committed . . . but as a precaution against future offences of the same kind. This is effected three ways: either by the amendment of the offender himself; for which purpose all corporal punishments, fines, and temporary exile or imprisonment are inflicted: or, by deterring others by the dread of his example from offending in the like way, . . . which gives rise to all ignominious punishments, and to such executions

vance of concealability to the optimal severity of punishment—
Blackstone was clearer than Beccaria (though it remained to
Bentham to define expected punishment cost rigorously as the
product of the probability and severity of punishment). According to Blackstone:

> As punishments are chiefly intended for the prevention of
> future crimes, it is but reasonable that . . . among crimes
> of an equal malignity, those [should be most severely pun-
> ished] which a man has the most frequent and easy oppor-
> tunities of committing, which cannot be so easily guarded
> against as others, and which therefore the offender has the
> strongest inducement to commit.[36]

Blackstone's discussion of marginal deterrence, while derivative
from Beccaria, indicates the way in which he related Beccaria's
theoretical analysis to the actual laws of England (and other
countries):

> It has been . . . ingeniously proposed [by Beccaria], that
> in every state a scale of crimes should be formed, with a
> corresponding scale of punishments, descending from the
> greatest to the least: but, if that be too romantic an idea, yet
> at least a wise legislature will mark the principal divisions,
> and not assign penalties of the first degree to offences of an
> inferior rank. Where men see no distinction made in the
> nature and gradations of punishment, the generality will
> be led to conclude there is no distinction in the guilt. Thus

---

of justice as are open and public: or, lastly, by depriving the party injuring of the power
to do future mischief; which is effected by either putting him to death, or condemning
him to perpetual confinement, slavery, or exile. The same one end, of preventing future crimes, is endeavoured to be answered by each one of these three species of punishment." 4 *Comm.* 11–12. The retributive theory is discussed in Chapter 8.

36. 4 *Comm.* 16. Beccaria's entire discussion of this question is as follows: "That a
punishment may produce the effect required, it is sufficient that the *evil* it occasions
should exceed the *good* expected from the crime, including in the calculation the certainty of the punishment, and the privation of the expected advantage." Beccaria,
supra note 34, at 94.

in France the punishment of robbery, either with or without murder, is the same: hence it is, that though perhaps they are therefore subject to fewer robberies, yet they never rob but they also murder. In China, murderers are cut to pieces, and robbers not: hence in that country they never murder on the highway, though they often rob. And in England, besides the additional terrors of a speedy execution, and a subsequent exposure or dissection, robbers have a hope of transportation, which seldom is extended to murderers. This has the same effect here as in China; in preventing frequent assassination and slaughter.[37]

Blackstone was an early supporter of the right to counsel in criminal cases:

But it is a settled rule at common law, that no counsel shall be allowed a prisoner upon his trial, upon the general issue, in any capital crime, unless some point of law shall arise proper to be debated. A rule, which (however it may be palliated under cover of that noble declaration of the law, when rightly understood, that the judge shall be counsel for the prisoner; that is, shall see that the proceedings against him are legal and strictly regular) seems to be not at all of a piece with the rest of the humane treatment of prisoners by the English law. For upon what face of reason can that assistance be denied to save the life of a man, which yet is allowed him in prosecutions for every petty trespass?[38]

Blackstone was also well aware of the danger of political abuse of the criminal process. I quoted earlier his discussion of the political importance of the jury in criminal matters; in the same vein is his discussion of the evidentiary requirements in trials for treason:

37 4 *Comm* 18
38 4 *Comm.* 349.

In cases of treason also there is the accused's oath of allegiance, to counterpoise the information of a single witness: and that may perhaps be one reason why the law requires a double testimony to convict him; though the principal reason, undoubtedly, is to secure the subject from being sacrificed to fictitious conspiracies, which have been the engines of profligate and crafty politicians in all ages.[39]

Finally, Blackstone was concerned with the problem of selective enforcement created by archaic laws: "It is true, that these outrageous penalties [for being seen in the company of Gypsies], being seldom or never inflicted, are hardly known to be law by the public: but that rather aggravates the mischief, by laying a snare for the unwary."[40]

Bentham's Antipathy to Blackstone

I have quoted so extensively from Blackstone's views on criminal justice in part to show that he was not the enemy of reform caricatured in Bentham's *Fragment on Government;* indeed, Blackstone anticipated (influenced?) some of Bentham's own views on criminal justice. Not only was Blackstone a trenchant critic of the excessive use of capital punishment and of other features of both civil and criminal law, but he sought to justify—obliquely, to be sure—judicial innovation and creativity. Liberty and utility were his criteria for evaluating laws. By identifying, describing, and explaining the basic features of his (and our) society's legal system—the evolutionary nature of common law rulemaking, jury trial, statutory interpretation, legal fictions, the political context of judicial action, the interrelation among the branches of government, and the relationship between law and morals—Blackstone made an important contribution to the scientific study of law. Merely to have summarized the laws of England in four highly readable volumes was an important

39. 4 *Comm.* 351.
40. 4 *Comm.* 4.

step in demystifying law and making it accessible to lay understanding, criticism, and reform.[41]

How then are we to explain Bentham's ferocious antipathy to
the *Commentaries*?[42] The answer requires an understanding of
his goals and methods. Although he made important contribu-

41. Professor Langbein's recent assessment of Blackstone is worth quoting here:
"Whatever his shortcomings, Blackstone was an intellectual. He tried throughout the
Commentaries to do more than describe; he sought to understand, to rationalize, to explain. His reasoning was, we think, sometimes mistaken. But the subsequent treatise
tradition owes a good deal to his conception of the legal writer's job. More than anyone
before him, Blackstone took it upon himself to try to identify the deeper purposes of
the rules and practices of the common law." Langbein, Introduction to 3 *Comm.* at iv.

42. The ferocity cannot be doubted. Along with the *Fragment* there is Bentham's no
less vitriolic *A Comment on the Commentaries* (Charles Warren Everett ed. 1928), a much
longer work than the *Fragment* and one that Bentham worked on throughout his life
and left incomplete at his death (the *Fragment* was in fact a "fragment" of the *Comment*).
Elsewhere in Bentham's writings we find these examples of his fury against Blackstone:

His hand was formed to embellish and to corrupt everything it touches. He
makes men think they see, in order to prevent their seeing.

His is the treasury of vulgar errors where all the vulgar errors that are, are
collected and improved.

He is infected with the foul stench of intolerance, the rankest degree of intolerance that at this day the most depraved organ can endure.

In him every prejudice has an advocate, and every professional chicanery an
accomplice.

His are crocodile lamentations.

He carries the disingenuousness of the hireling Advocate into the chair of the
Professor. He is the dupe of every prejudice, and the abettor of every abuse. No
sound principles can be expected from that writer whose first object is to defend
a system.

Extracts from Bentham's *Commonplace Book,* in 10 *Works of Jeremy Bentham* 141 (John
Bowring ed. 1843), hereinafter cited as Bentham *Works*.

I should mention here the extreme difficulty of ascertaining Bentham's views, which
requires that the reader treat my analysis of Bentham's thought as tentative. Bentham
wrote some seven and a half million words during his lifetime, only a small fraction of
which he published. Much of his other writing has been edited for publication, but the
accuracy of the edited writings is frequently questionable, in part because of the extreme disarray in which his papers were left. And much of his writing has never been
published or even deciphered. Until the completion of the authoritative edition of
Bentham's work, being prepared under the direction of H. L. A. Hart and expected to
run to forty volumes, Bentham's readers can have only an approximate idea of his
views on many questions, including some of those discussed here. Another difficulty is
that he changed many of his views during his very long lifetime; still another problem,
which is acute in the case of one who wrote so much and failed to indicate what he
thought publishable and what not, is distinguishing between his considered views and
his casual ruminations.

tions to law, economics, and philosophy, Bentham regarded himself not as a theoretical or academic thinker but as a legislative reformer. He got his ideas for legislative reform by deduction from the "greatest happiness," or utility, principle. Already stated clearly in the writings of Priestley, Beccaria, and others, this principle was that the test of sound social policy was whether it promoted the greatest happiness of the greatest number of people.[43] Bentham translated the greatest-happiness principle into a host of specific public policies that he worked out in great detail. His best-known proposals were in the area of criminal justice, although, except for prison reform, he, like Blackstone, got most of his basic ideas in that area from Beccaria.

The utility principle carried Bentham in two different directions. One was toward freedom from governmental interference, especially in economics and religion. Among other things, he criticized as paternalistic Adam Smith's support of laws forbidding usurious loans. The other direction was toward intrusive, moralistic, and frequently paternalistic governmental interventions; laws against mistreating animals, laws for the forcible reeducation of criminals, laws requiring passers-by to rescue people in distress spilled from his pen. The schizoid character of Bentham's proposals was the result not of an inconsistency in the utility principle or in his application of it but of the spongy, nonoperational character of the principle itself. The happiness of millions of different people cannot be measured and aggregated for purposes of comparing the utility of alternative policies. He thought, for example, that the greatest-happiness principle required that "the legislator must prohibit all acts which tend to produce a spirit of inhumanity."[44] On this account, and also because animals experience suffering (unhappiness), he urged that the law prohibit cruelty to animals. He even wanted to prohibit sport fishing.[45] Benthamites play the

43. See, e.g., 22 *The Theological and Miscellaneous Works of Joseph Priestley* 13 (John Towill Rutt ed. 1832).

44. F. Boutros, *Principles of Legislation from Bentham and Dumont* 238 (1842).

45. See Jeremy Bentham, *Principles of Penal Law,* in 1 Bentham *Works* 367, 562.

game of deriving public policy from the greatest-happiness principle without rules, and the set of public policies he proposed resembles nothing so much as his personal preferences (he was notoriously fond of animals, especially cats).

Consider Bentham's proposal for dealing with beggars. He wanted to outlaw begging and put all the beggars into prisons; however, they could be released into a kind of indentured servitude that would continue until they had reimbursed the prison for its expenses in maintaining them and had thereby earned "full emancipation."[46] Bentham justified his solution—slavery —to the problem of begging on the ground that begging could have but two effects on the people begged from—to cause them either the "pain of sympathy" or, if they lacked sympathy, another kind of pain, disgust. The sum of these pains was greater than the difference to the beggars' welfare between begging and working.[47] Bentham did not explain how he made this calculation.

Thus far there is little to explain his antipathy to Blackstone, who also believed, if less emphatically than Bentham, that "common utility" should be the object of laws and who was also a follower of Beccaria, an early advocate of prison reform,[48] and a believer in private property and free exchange. (Blackstone was more emphatic about property,[49] and Bentham about free exchange. Like Adam Smith after him, Blackstone supported

46. Jeremy Bentham, *Tracts on Poor Law and Pauper Management*, in 8 Bentham *Works* 361, 402.

47. See 8 Bentham *Works* 401.

48. See, e.g., Blackstone's description of the recently established "penetentiary houses" for offenders previously punished by transportation (banishment) in 4 *Comm.* 371–372 (Edward Christian ed. 1830).

49. Bentham's support of private property rests on somewhat narrow foundations. He inferred, from a combination of the principle of diminishing marginal utility of (money) income and a hunch that people's utility functions were similar or identical, that the greatest happiness of the greatest number would require equalizing wealth were it not for the disincentive effects of thereby impairing the security of property. See, e.g., "The Philosophy of Economic Science," in 1 *Jeremy Bentham's Economic Writings* 81, 115–116 (W. Stark ed. 1952); and "The Psychology of Economic Man," in 3 *id.* at 421, 442. Bentham viewed economic freedom as an instrumental value in maximizing the wealth of the poor people of the society. I discuss this issue further in Chapter 3.

usury laws.[50]) In general, their differences in matters of substantive policy do not seem insurmountable, and in many areas where they did differ, Bentham was, as it were, carrying on where Blackstone had left off.[51]

Moreover, the sharp substantive differences that do exist between the two do not exhibit a fundamental or at least consistent ideological cleavage. Blackstone held conventional views on marriage and women's rights; Bentham, notably modern ones.[52] But Blackstone supported and Bentham opposed the privilege against self-incrimination; Bentham admired the Court of Star Chamber[53] and despised juries; Blackstone defended the jury and condemned the Star Chamber. Although Blackstone was more comfortable with rank and privilege than Bentham, he never denounced "levelling" so fiercely as did Bentham, who wrote that "the cry for equality is only a pretext to cover the robbery which idleness perpetrates upon industry."[54]

Bentham's antipathy to Blackstone derived, I believe, from another quarter of his intellectual activity than the formulation of substantive reforms, having to do with his efforts at "selling" his reform proposals. He was not content to think up brilliant ideas for policy change; he passionately desired to see his ideas translated into the public policy of England (and of Mexico and Russia and everywhere else). A large number of Bentham's ideas seem to have been devised for the express purpose of facilitating the adoption of his substantive reform proposals; his theory of the nature of law, his theory of fictions and other semantic theories, and his political theory are examples.

50. See reference in note 7 supra.

51. As noted earlier, Blackstone had proposed that defendants in capital cases be allowed counsel; Bentham proposed that the state pay for counsel if the defendant was indigent. Bentham urged the formal merger of law and equity; though not proposed by Blackstone (who minimized the conflict between the law and equity courts), this was certainly in the spirit of his views on the subject. See 3 *Comm.* 440–441.

52. See Jeremy Bentham, *Principles of the Civil Code*, in 1 Bentham *Works* 299, 352–358.

53. See Mary P. Mack, *Jeremy Bentham: An Odyssey of Ideas* 425 (1963).

54. Bentham, supra note 52, in 1 Bentham *Works* 312; see also 358–364. But this may not have been Bentham's mature view. See note 42 supra.

Bentham saw three things standing in the way of speedy adoption of his reforms: (1) the common law system of lawmaking, and the lawyers and judges who had a vested interest in the system; (2) intellectual confusion rooted in semantic ambiguity; and (3) England's elaborately balanced, imperfectly representative governmental system. On points (1) and (3) he was probably right. The English common law system of rulemaking *was* quintessentially incremental, indeed glacial. Using the methods of judicial reform described in the *Commentaries,* it would have taken hundreds of years to implement Bentham's reform program; it had taken hundreds of years to achieve less far-reaching reforms in the feudal land law. And the history of England in the nineteenth century suggests that a broadening of the franchise and a greater concentration of power in the House of Commons—the goals of Bentham's program of political reform—may indeed have been preconditions to the adoption of his specific substantive policies, which occurred mainly after the passage of the Reform Act of 1832.

Blackstone's appointment as the first university professor of English law and the publication of the *Commentaries* had enhanced the prestige of the common law, and this alone made the *Commentaries* a natural target for Bentham. Moreover, the *Commentaries* coupled enthusiasm for common law rulemaking with skepticism about the use of statutes to effect sweeping legal reform. Blackstone even attacked the principle of codification. To Bentham, who invented the word, codification meant the enactment of comprehensive statute law based on the greatest-happiness principle to replace whatever patchwork of statutes and common law or customary principles might occupy the field. But Blackstone had written that

> when laws are to be framed by popular assemblies, even of the representative kind, it is too Herculean a task to begin the work of legislation afresh, and extract a new system from the discordant opinions of more than five hundred counsellors. A single legislator or an enterprizing sovereign, a Solon or Lycurgus, a Justinian or a Frederick, may

at any time form a concise, and perhaps an uniform, plan of justice: and evil betide that presumptuous subject who questions its wisdom or utility. But who, that is acquainted with the difficulty of new-modelling any branch of our statute laws (though relating but to roads or to parish settlements), will conceive it ever feasible to alter any fundamental point of the common law, with all its appendages and consequents, and set up another rule in its stead?[55]

In the early period of his career from which the *Fragment* dates, Bentham thought that the major obstacle to reform was the ignorance or confusion of the people in power—if only their minds could be cleared, his suggested reforms would be promptly implemented.[56] And he thought intellectual confusion was rooted in linguistic imprecision. Figurative language in particular shielded people from recognizing the error of habitual belief. His hatred of Blackstone may have stemmed in part from Blackstone's masterful use of metaphor and other figurative devices.[57] Though himself a master of metaphor for polemical purposes (for example, "nonsense upon stilts"), Bentham thought that metaphor was to the Enemy of Reform what flattery had been to the Serpent. Bentham said of Blackstone, "His hand was formed to *embellish* and corrupt" (my emphasis). Blackstone not only urged common law incrementalism instead

55. 3 *Comm.* 267.

56. See 1 Leslie Stephen, *The English Utilitarians* 176, 196 (1900).

57. As in his explanation of how the common law judges were able to reform the feudal land law without the help of legislation: "Yet they wisely avoided soliciting any great legislative revolution in the old fashioned forms, which might have been productive of consequences more numerous and extensive than the most penetrating genius could foresee; but left them as they were, to languish in obscurity and oblivion, and endeavoured by a series of minute contrivances to accommodate such personal actions, as were then in use, to all the most useful purposes of remedial justice . . . The only difficulty that attends [these contrivances] arises from their fictions and circuities, but, when once we have discovered the proper clew, that labyrinth is easily pervaded. We inherit an old Gothic castle, erected in the days of chivalry, but fitted up for a modern inhabitant. The moated ramparts, the embattled towers, and the trophied halls, are magnificent and venerable, but useless. The inferior apartments, now converted into rooms of convenience, are chearful and commodious, though their approaches are winding and difficult." 3 *Comm.* 268.

of "legislative revolution," he did it so winningly, with such a generous and effective use of figurative expressions, as to deceive the people who could have effected such a revolution into believing that it was unnecessary and undesirable.

Another aspect of the *Commentaries* that made the work an effective defense of gradualism was Blackstone's portrayal of the body of laws as the outcome of an evolutionary process—extending over hundreds of years and embracing the efforts of thousands of lawyers, judges, and legislators—which had produced a complex, intricately reticulated system. Blackstone implicitly disparaged the claims of any single individual, a Bentham, to be able to excogitate an equally good or better system. Bentham's attack on Blackstone typifies the antagonism of radicalism in its familiar modern sense to meliorist or "liberal" approaches to social problems.

In his early years, as I have mentioned, Bentham had conceived of the reform process as proceeding from the top down. When this approach of "selling" the authorities on the desirability of enacting his codes failed to produce swift results, he decided that reform would not occur unless the structure of government was altered drastically. He began to urge universal suffrage so that political power would be allocated proportionately to all of the adults in society, which he argued would lead to the adoption of policies designed to maximize the greatest happiness of the greatest number. And he urged that all political power be vested in the House of Commons to expedite the translation of popular preferences, which he assumed would coincide with the greatest-happiness principle, into legislative reform. Bentham was aware that in such a system the majority could exploit the minority in a fashion that would violate the greatest-happiness principle,[58] but he thought this danger could be averted by educating the people to realize that benevolence produced the greatest happiness.

Bentham again found Blackstone standing in the way of reform. The British constitution approvingly described in the *Commentaries* was based on the sharing of political authority

58. Jeremy Bentham, "Greatest Happiness of the Greatest Number," in *Bentham's Political Thought* 309–310 (Bhikhu Parekh ed. 1973).

among a hereditary monarch, an appointed judiciary, an aristocratic House of Lords, and a House of Commons that, because of property qualifications and rotten boroughs, was unrepresentative. Although Blackstone favored broadening the franchise, he would not have supported universal suffrage in elections to the Commons, let alone removal of all political authority from the other branches of the government. His views on government resemble in a general way those of many of the framers of the U.S. Constitution—notably Madison—who borrowed heavily from the British constitution as described by Blackstone and Montesquieu and who, like Blackstone, feared the tyrannical potential not only of monarchy and aristocracy but of democracy as well. Bentham, writing *his* constitutional code years after the adoption of the U.S. Constitution, consciously rejected the American model.

Blackstone and Bentham Compared

Blackstone and Bentham typify polar approaches to the study of social phenomena. Blackstone studied the operations of an actual social system, the system of English law as it had evolved against the background of the nation's disordered political history. His study revealed a system of enormous intricacy, with impressive survival and growth characteristics and a significant capacity for reform—in short, a resilient, adaptable, viable social organism.[59]

59. In light of this theme, the oft-criticized organization of the *Commentaries* (Book I—rights of persons, Book II—rights of things, Book III—private wrongs, Book IV—public wrongs) is seen to be inevitable, indeed masterful. It is true that things don't have rights and that if Book IV had been placed directly after Book I the work would have been divided more logically into public and private law. But juxtaposing the powerful, albeit respectful, criticisms of criminal justice in Book IV with the eulogistic discussion of the British constitution and the role of judges in Book I would have undermined the view of the English legal system that Blackstone wanted to convey. Book I was an encomium to the adaptability, the resiliency, the progressiveness of the English legal system. Book II buttressed this encomium by showing in detail how the judges threw off the Norman Yoke in the field of land law, and Book III completed the picture of judge-created law. The area in which progress had been least satisfactory—the criminal law—was naturally left to the end. An additional reason for placing criminal law last was that it was less important than private law to most practitioners. But by this criterion Book I should have been placed after Books II and III.

Justice and Efficiency

Bentham never studied systematically any social or legal institution, English or foreign, contemporary or historical. He never tried to master the working principles of the institutions he sought to reform. Instead he deduced optimal institutions from the greatest-happiness principle and then tried to work out the details of their implementation. This is a mode of social research that breeds utopianism and its bitter cousin radicalism. Lacking an understanding of the real world to which his reforms must be fitted, the utopian reformer grows increasingly impatient at society's failure to implement his ideas and proposes increasingly radical measures to force a refractory world into his imagined mold. The lessons of history, English and Continental (for example, French), should have convinced Bentham of the virtues of incrementalist reform within a system of balanced government, though he might have quarreled with the pace of such reform and with the details of the constitutional structure. But they did not. Finding the English system an obstacle to his ideas, he proposed to sweep it away and substitute a system in which power might be dangerously concentrated in a single branch. Finding conventional modes of thought and language inimical to prompt implementation of his proposals, he urged that language be purified of metaphor and ambiguity. Seeing legislation as the swiftest route to implementation of his reform ideas, he proposed to abolish the common law, the natural rights of Englishmen, and the independent judiciary.

Many of Bentham's radical proposals, including codification and criminal rehabilitation, would probably not have worked or at least not well. Others would have worked only too well. Bentham's assault on traditional language and the habits of thought encapsulated in it prefigured the totalitarian assault on language by Newspeak, Hitler, and the Soviet press. In his suggestions for prison reform, Bentham was a pioneer in developing techniques of brainwashing.[60] He toyed with the idea of having everyone's name tattooed on his body to facilitate criminal law enforcement.[61] Compulsory self-incrimination, tor-

60. See Boutros, supra note 44, at 206.
61. Bentham, supra note 45, in 1 Bentham *Works* 557.

ture,[62] anonymous informers, abolition of the attorney-client privilege and of the jury, and depreciation of rights[63] are other parts of Bentham's legacy to totalitarian regimes.

Bentham might have gone further down the road toward the totalitarian state had he not believed that security of private property was necessary to create adequate incentives for hard work, a view seemingly inconsistent with his faith in the efficacy of education and reeducation. Otherwise he might have recommended a much more intrusive public sector, for he believed that the greatest-happiness principle would probably require the equalization of income and wealth were it not for the disincentive effects of depriving the more successful people of the fruits of their labor.[64]

However, to stress only the repressive tendencies in Bentham's thought is to do injustice to an individual of prodigious intellect, energies, and good will. One must not forget either his advocacy of religious freedom, civil divorce, a rational punishment system, procedural reform, the removal of unnecessary restrictions on economic freedom, and other social improvements, or his scientific contributions—to utility theory,[65] to the theory of evidence, and to the economic analysis of law and other nonmarket activities. By making explicit what had been only implicit in Beccaria and Blackstone—that punishment is a method of imposing costs on criminal activity and thereby altering the incentives to engage in it—Bentham laid the foundation for the modern economic analysis of crime and punishment.[66] Particularly important to the approach of this

62. W. L. Twining & P. E. Twining, "Bentham on Torture," in *Bentham and Legal Theory* 39 (M. H. James ed. 1973).

63. He described the Declaration of Independence as "a hodge-podge of confusion and absurdity." Bentham's "Account of Lind and Forster," in 10 Bentham *Works* 63.

64. See note 49 supra.

65. See George J. Stigler, "The Development of Utility Theory," in his *Essays in the History of Economics* 66–155 (1965).

66. The seminal modern work is Gary S. Becker, "Crime and Punishment: An Economic Approach," 76 *J. Pol. Econ.* 169 (1968). Bentham's analysis of criminal punishment appears at its best in his *Introduction to the Principles of Morals and Legislation*. See, e.g., Jeremy Bentham, *A Fragment on Government and an Introduction to the Principles of Morals and Legislation* 293–294 (W. Harrison ed. 1948).

book is Bentham's insistence that human beings act as rational maximizers of their satisfactions in all spheres of life, not just the narrowly economic:

> NATURE has placed mankind under the governance of two sovereign masters, pain and pleasure. . . They govern us in all we do, in all we say, in all we think.

> Men calculate, some with less exactness, indeed, some with more: but all men calculate. I would not say, that even a madman does not calculate.[67]

Bentham's major weaknesses as a thinker were the sponginess of the utility principle as a guide to policy, his lack of interest in positive or empirical analysis, and his excessive, if characteristically modern, belief in the plasticity of human nature and social institutions. He exaggerated the feasibility of making sweeping social reforms through statutory codification, the possibility of instilling public-spiritedness, the potential for rehabilitating criminals, the humanizing effects of education, and the perfectibility of public administration. His unexamined faith in his own altruistic motivation and in the power of individual intellect (his own), his restless do-goodism, his love of mechanical and intellectual gimmickry, his impatient prose, his neologisms —"codification," "minimize," "international," and the rest—but above all, his faith in *plans,* make him uncannily contemporary. "Bentham was clearly the victim of a common delusion. If a system will work, the minutest details can be exhibited. Therefore, it is inferred, an exhibition of minute detail proves that it will work."[68]

Bentham attacked Blackstone for complacent optimism, but in reality he was the greater optimist. In particular, he had no anxiety that England might once again slide into tyranny or civil war, the poles between which the country had oscillated with disturbing frequency before 1688. An implicit concern of the

67. *Id.* at 125, 298.
68 1 Leslie Stephen, supra note 56, at 283.

Commentaries is with the problem of maintaining social order, that is, of so distributing and organizing political power as to avoid the extremes of tyranny and civil war and thus minimize the role of violence and threats in the society. Bentham, concerned with the distinct problem of welfare or utility, had little interest in this problem.[69]

The difference between the political concept of social order and a narrowly economic concept of utility or welfare can be illustrated with reference to the problem of the control of crime. The economist is interested in how the machinery of criminal justice, constituting a system of governmental coercion, is used and how it could be used more effectively to prevent wasteful private activities, such as theft and murder. He generally takes for granted that the machinery is firmly in the control of the law-abiding majority.[70] But from the standpoint of the political scientist concerned with the social order, the interesting question is not how to deploy the criminal law machinery to deal most effectively with private coercion but how to prevent that machinery from coming into the control of a faction.

Or consider the question of the role of the state in altering the distribution of income or wealth. The economist is concerned with the efficiency consequences of redistribution, but only in a limited sense—he disregards the possibility that the social fabric will be torn apart by the redistribution or the failure to redistribute. But society is not "disordered" merely because its institutions permit some state-compelled wealth redistributions. The question to be asked about such a society from the standpoint of social order is whether the redistributions avoid (or in some cases encourage) recourse to more drastically coercive forms of reallocating social wealth in accordance with power. (As Chapter 5 shows, this point is fundamental to understanding the social organization of primitive societies.)

---

69. But see Bentham, supra note 45, in 1 Bentham *Works* 570–578.

70. For an exception, see Daniel Landau & Michael D. Bordo, "The Supply and Demand for Protection: A Positive Theory of Democratic Government with Some Suggestive Evidence" (U. Toronto, Faculty of Law, Law & Econ. Wkshp. Ser. no. WSII-20, Dec. 1979).

Consider Blackstone and Bentham's implicit disagreement with respect to the nature of language as a human institution. To Bentham, language is valuable in proportion as it conveys precisely and unambiguously the speaker's or writer's ideas. Consequently Bentham is very impatient with language and in his writings is constantly struggling with it—trying to remake it, to purify it of ambiguity, to increase its transparency. Blackstone's implicit attitude toward language was different. His frequent, sometimes extravagant, reliance on simile and metaphor, the loving care with which the sentences in the *Commentaries* are shaped and honed, the sensitivity to language and rhetorical skills evident throughout the *Commentaries,* show Blackstone's concern to cast his ideas in language that is graceful, polished, arresting, even colorful.[71]

At the time when Blackstone and Bentham were writing, there was an ancient tradition—one finds evidence of it, among other places, in the New Testament, in Cicero, and in early eighteenth-century writers such as Pope and Swift—in which linguistic forms were regarded as bound up with fundamental characteristics of civilization, including the preservation of social order. In Pope's *Dunciad,* for example, abuse of language is treated as an extended metaphor of social disintegration.[72] A distinguished contemporary manifestation of the tradition is George Orwell's novel *1984.* These writers believed that to control language is to control thought, communication, and ultimately action. In their view traditional language, as distinct from Newspeak or other invented languages, is a social institution with an enormous stabilizing influence because it embodies and perpetuates habits of thought, modes of reasoning, and traditional values that act as a bulwark against precipitate change and absolute government.[73] Language is like the free market.

71. Incidentally, Blackstone was a competent poet, whereas Bentham despised poetry as a willful means of obscuring communication.

72. See Aubrey L. Williams, *Pope's Dunciad: A Study of Its Meaning* (1955), especially pp. 156–158.

73. This idea is suggested in a striking passage from Wittgenstein that reminds one of Blackstone's Gothic-castle metaphor of the common law (See note 57 supra): "Our

No legislature or bureaucracy prescribes the forms of speech, the structure of language, or the vocabulary that individuals use. Like a free market, a language is an immensely complicated yet private and decentralized institution.[74]

Reading the rhetoric of totalitarian states, one senses that political absolutism both fosters and is buttressed by attempts to reshape language,[75] while conversely a traditional language is one of the barriers to absolutism. Thus, as I suggested earlier, Bentham's belief in the plasticity of language has an unintended political significance. Perhaps not so unintended: Bentham's attack on Blackstone in the *Fragment* is in no small part an attack on the conventional way of speaking about such things as sovereignty.

A related difference between Blackstone and Bentham is in their attitudes toward the limits of the individual's reasoning powers. Although "reason" is found more often in Blackstone's writings than in Bentham's, it is clear that Blackstone subscribed to the view, more articulately expressed by Edmund Burke, that the individual's reasoning power is limited and should be exercised with humility.[76] Bentham evinced no misgivings about the power of reason—in particular his own—to decide any question of policy *de novo,* without benefit of authority, consensus, or precedent.

The idea of the fallibility of human intellect has roots in Christian theology, which contrasts the impaired reasoning power of fallen man with the perfect reason of the angels. Blackstone echoes this notion in his discussion of immemorial custom. The Saxon period described in the *Commentaries* recalls the Garden of Eden, as described, for example, in *Paradise Lost,*

---

language can be seen as an ancient city: a maze of little streets and squares, of old and new houses, and of houses with additions from various periods; and this surrounded by a multitude of new boroughs with straight regular streets and uniform houses." Ludwig Wittgenstein, *Philosophical Investigations,* ¶18 (G. E. M. Anscombe trans., 2d ed. 1958).

74. The resemblance of language to customary law is discussed in Chapter 5.

75. See Leon Lipson, *How to Argue in Soviet* (forthcoming).

76. See, e.g., 1 *Comm.* 69–70; Edmund Burke, *Reflections on the Revolution in France* 99 (Thomas H. D. Mahoney ed. 1955).

where man exercised his mental faculties with a clarity and force never recaptured after his expulsion. In Blackstone's version of the Christian myth, the Saxon period in English history was the time when the principles of the law were completely understood by man, without the mediation of any authority, whereas after the Norman Conquest men had to struggle to recapture the Saxon clarity of vision, assisted by crutches such as precedent. The English courts corresponded to the Christian church as the intermediary between divine wisdom and (impaired) human rationality after the Fall.

Consider finally the disagreement between Blackstone and Bentham over the issue of "natural" versus "positive" law. Stated most baldly, the issue is whether, as Blackstone thought, the criterion of law is its consistency with divinely inspired and sanctioned natural law, and therefore a bad law is a contradiction in terms—a bad law is no law—or whether, as Bentham thought, the only law worthy of the name is positive law, that is, law promulgated or enacted by some state organ having the authority to make laws. The dispute may seem merely terminological, but it disguises a significant aspect of the fundamental cleavage between concern with social order and concern with welfare. Natural law appears to have meant something like constitutional law in the American sense, in a period when the idea of written constitutional safeguards was as yet unfamiliar; that is, natural law was a criterion of the validity of enacted (positive) law. In the American constitutional system we indeed confound the ideas of bad law and of no law; they come together in the statute that is invalidated as being unconstitutional.

The problem of limiting the executive and legislative branches is central to any responsible analysis of power and social order, and Blackstone, writing before the American Revolution and the U.S. Constitution, was more sensitive to the problem than Bentham, writing afterward. Imagine how Blackstone's views would have been strengthened by the quite different lessons that could be drawn from the outcomes of the American and the French Revolutions! Bentham did not draw either the positive lesson from the American Revolution—the possibilities for institutionalizing a pluralist balance of power within a state—or the negative lesson from the French Revolution—the dangers of Jacobinism.

As a normative social theorist, Bentham is rather frightening. But is he frightening because he was so thoroughgoing a utilitarian or because he lapsed from utilitarianism? If the former, may it be possible to find in economics a principle of social choice alternative to the utilitarian or greatest-happiness principle, a principle that supports Blackstonian rights and other stabilizing features of social structure? Or does Benthamism exhaust the normative content of economics? These questions are addressed in the next two chapters.

3

Utilitarianism, Economics, and Social Theory

My doubts that Benthamism, utilitarianism in its most un-compromising form, is an adequate ethical system may seem also to undermine the economic analysis of law in both its positive and normative versions—as a theory of what the common law is (for is it plausible to ascribe to the common law judges an indefensible legal norm?) and even more clearly as a theory of what the law should be. It is therefore not surprising that among the severest critics of the economic approach to law are those who attack it as a version of utilitarianism.[1] Their procedure is to equate economics with utilitarianism and then attack utilitarianism. Whether they follow this procedure because they are more comfortable with the terminology of philosophy than with that of the social sciences or because they want to exploit the current philosophical hostility to utilitarianism[2] is of no moment. The important question is whether utilitarianism and economics are distinguishable. I believe they are and that the economic norm I shall call "wealth maximization" provides a firmer basis for ethical theory than utilitarianism does.

Utilitarianism and normative economics are often and easily confused. Utilitarianism, as ordinarily understood and as I shall use the term here,[3] holds that the moral worth of an action,

1. For recent examples see Richard A. Epstein, book review, "The Next Generation of Legal Scholarship?" 30 *Stan. L. Rev.* 635, 645 n.35 (1978), and his "Nuisance Law: Corrective Justice and Its Utilitarian Constraints," 8 *J. Legal Stud.* 49, 74–75 (1979).

2. For examples of the tendency in modern philosophy to treat utilitarianism dismissively, see Robert Nozick, *Anarchy, State, and Utopia* 62, 201 (1974); and Bernard Williams, "A Critique of Utilitarianism," in J. J. C. Smart & Bernard Williams, *Utilitarianism For and Against* 77, 149–150 (1967).

3. The term is sometimes used more broadly to refer to any consequentialist ethical theory. So used, it would embrace the normative economic theory presented in this chapter. In the sense I use the term, it should perhaps be called "classical utilitarianism" to distinguish it from the constrained utilitarian theory that I advance.

practice, institution, or law is to be judged by its effect in promoting happiness— "the surplus of pleasure over pain"[4]—aggregated across all of the inhabitants (in some versions of utilitarianism, all of the sentient beings) of "society," which might be
a single nation or the whole world. Normative economics holds
that an action is to be judged by its effect in promoting the social
welfare, a term often defined so broadly as to be synonymous
with the utilitarian concept of happiness, except that ordinarily
the satisfactions of nonhuman beings are not included in the
concept of social welfare. The identification of economics with
utilitarianism has been reinforced by the tendency in economics
to use the term "utility" as a synonym for welfare,[5] as in the expression "utility maximizing," and by the fact that many prominent utilitarian theorists, such as Bentham, Edgeworth, and
John Stuart Mill, were also prominent economists. Furthermore, many practitioners of "welfare economics" (the most
common term for normative economics) describe their activity
as applied utilitarianism.[6]

Even viewed as applied utilitarianism, economics is a distinct
field of intellectual activity from philosophical utilitarianism; it
has a technical vocabulary, theorems, and methodology of
which a utilitarian philosopher might be—and many are in fact
—unaware. The history of utilitarianism and of economics in
legal theory makes this clear. Although the origins of utilitarianism, like those of economics, are earlier than *The Wealth of
Nations*—they are found in the writings of Priestley, Beccaria,
Hume, and others—utilitarianism did not reach a state of de-

---

4. Henry Sidgwick, *The Methods of Ethics* 413 (7th ed. 1907).
   5. A special use of the term utility in economics must be distinguished. Two outcomes are said to differ in utility but not in value when they have the same actuarial
value, that is, the same value to a risk-neutral person, but the person choosing between
the outcomes is not risk neutral. Thus a certainty of $1 and a 10 percent chance of
winning $10 are said to have the same value, but a risk-averse individual would prefer
—would derive greater utility from—the certain $1. This idea of utility is consistent
with a purely economic approach to questions of value in the broad sense; utility as
happiness, as we shall see, is not.
   6. On the utilitarian basis of welfare economics see, e.g., I. M. D. Little, *A Critique of
Welfare Economics* 42 (2d ed. 1957); A. C. Pigou, *The Economics of Welfare* 20 (4th ed.
1932).

velopment comparable to economics until Bentham's work in
the generation after Smith. But while legal theory began to feel
the impact of utilitarianism in Bentham's time, economics had
no real impact on legal theory (with the exception of a few
fields like antitrust law, where the legal norm was explicitly economic) until the 1960s.

By that time utilitarianism had achieved a strong hold over
the legal imagination.[7] The theory of criminal punishment was
explicitly utilitarian.[8] In constitutional adjudication, the rejection of the concept of "absolute" rights in favor of a balancing
test not only had a strongly utilitarian flavor[9] but reflected a
pervasive emphasis on utilitarian considerations as determi-
nants of legal rules and outcomes. Torts and contracts were also
approached in utilitarian terms.[10] Yet despite their belief in utilitarianism, legal scholars rarely used economic concepts explicitly. The occasional efforts at an "economic" approach to law
are better described, in the main, as pseudoeconomic,[11] although some of the scholarship of the period reveals an intui-

7. See, e.g., Henry M. Hart & Albert Sacks, *The Legal Process: Basic Problems in the Making and Application of Law* 113–114 (tent. ed. 1958).

8. See, e.g., Herbert L. Packer, *The Limits of the Criminal Sanction* (1968), especially ch. 13.

9. For a good example concerning free speech, see United States v. Dennis, 183 F.2d 201, 212 (2d Cir. 1950) (L. Hand, J.), aff'd, 341 U.S. 494 (1951).

10. See, e.g., Henry T. Terry, "Negligence," 29 *Harv. L. Rev.* 40 (1915); Lon L. Fuller, "Consideration and Form," 41 *Colum. L. Rev.* 799 (1941). Holmes's rejection of any moral obligation to fulfill a promise, expressed in his famous adage that the obliga-tion created by contract is to perform or pay damages, has a strongly utilitarian flavor. See Oliver Wendell Holmes, "The Path of the Law," in his *Collected Legal Papers* 167, 175 (1920). And Ames had stated: "The law is utilitarian. It exists for the realization of the reasonable needs of the community. If the interest of an individual runs counter to this chief object of the law, it must be sacrificed." James Barr Ames, "Law and Morals," 22 *Harv. L. Rev.* 97, 110 (1908). Much earlier references to utility can be found in legal writings. James Stephen, *A General View of the Criminal Law of England* 106 (1890), quotes a medieval English nuisance case: "Le utility del chose excusera le noisomeness del stink." And Blackstone's *Commentaries* contain, as we saw in the last chapter, signifi-cant references to utility.

11. An example is the "economic" theory of torts, effectively criticized in Roscoe Pound, "The Economic Interpretation and the Law of Torts," 53 *Harv. L. Rev.* 365 (1940). The theory was that tort decisions were motivated by the personal economic interests of the judges deciding them

tive grasp of economic theory,[12] as do, of course, many of the judicial decisions.[13]

Until recently, then, utilitarianism held sway in legal theory, but overt economic analysis was rare. The position is now reversed. Today most legal theorists who discuss utilitarianism reject it as a basis of normative legal theory,[14] a tendency that led H. L. A. Hart to state recently that utilitarianism is "currently on the defensive" so far as American legal theory is concerned.[15] At the same time, as noted in Chapter 1, a substantial literature has developed that applies the concepts of economics to law with an explicitness and sophistication unknown to legal theory in the period when utilitarianism was dominant. The question remains, however, whether economics and utilitarianism are different or the same.

Some Problems of Utilitarianism

Two features of utilitarian theory require clarification at the outset.[16] First, it is a theory of both personal morality and social

12. See, e.g., Fuller and Terry articles, supra note 10; and United States v. Carroll Towing Co., 159 F. 2d 169 (2d Cir. 1947) (the "Hand formula"), discussed in Chapter 1.

13. See *id.*; and Richard A. Posner, *Economic Analysis of Law*, pt.II (2d ed. 1977).

14. See, e.g., Ronald Dworkin, *Taking Rights Seriously* (1977); Richard A. Epstein, supra note 1, and his "A Theory of Strict Liability," 2 *J. Legal Stud.* 151 (1973); Charles Fried, *Right and Wrong* (1978); Duncan Kennedy, "Form and Substance in Private Law Adjudication," 89 *Harv. L. Rev.* 1685 (1976); Harry H. Wellington, "Common Law Rules and Constitutional Double Standards: Some Notes on Adjudication," 83 *Yale L. J.* 221 (1973). However, in his recent work Epstein, at least, has spoken more kindly of utilitarianism as a source of constraints on the single-minded pursuit of nonutilitarian norms. See Epstein, "Nuisance Law," supra note 1, at 75–102.

15. H. L. A. Hart, "American Jurisprudence through English Eyes: The Nightmare and the Noble Dream," 11 *Ga. L. Rev.* 969, 986 (1977).

16. For some recent expositions of utilitarianism see John Plamenatz, *The English Utilitarians* (1958); J. J. C. Smart, "An Outline of a System of Utilitarian Ethics," in Smart & Williams, supra note 2, at 3; Rolf E. Sartorius, *Individual Conduct and Social Norms: A Utilitarian Account of Social Union and the Rule of Law* (1975). Among the classical expositions see in particular Jeremy Bentham, *Introduction to the Principles of Morals and Legislation* (1789); Henry Sidgwick, supra note 4; Leslie Stephen, *The English Utilitarians* (1900). As noted earlier (see note 3 supra), I decline to empty the term utilitarianism of much of its distinctive meaning by defining it as the class of ethical doctrines in which the morality of a course of action is judged by its social consequences.

justice. A good man is one who strives to maximize the sum total of happiness (his own plus others'), and the good society is one that seeks to maximize that sum total. Second, the maximand, as most utilitarians view it, is not a particular psychological state—ecstasy or euphoria or whatever—but is the broadest possible concept of satisfaction. Happiness, or utility, is maximized when people (or creatures) are able to satisfy their preferences, whatever those preferences may be, to the greatest possible extent. But this formulation does not exclude the possibility that A may know B's true preferences better than B does—the possibility, that is, of paternalism.

One of the principal criticisms of utilitarianism is that its domain is uncertain. Whose happiness is to count in designing policies to maximize the greatest happiness? Does the happiness of animals count? This issue has been addressed by J. J. C. Smart:

> Perhaps strictly in itself and at a particular moment, a contented sheep is as good as a contented philosopher. However it is hard to agree to this. If we did we should have to agree that the human population ought ideally to be reduced by contraceptive methods and the sheep population more than correspondingly increased. Perhaps just so many humans should be left as could keep innumerable millions of placid sheep in contented idleness and immunity from depredations by ferocious animals. Indeed if a contented idiot is as good as a contented philosopher, and if a contented sheep is as good as a contented idiot, then a contented fish is as good as a contented sheep, and a contented beetle is as good as a contented fish. Where shall we stop?[17]

Smart does not answer his last question. Although he finds it "hard to agree" to equating the contented sheep with the contented philosopher, he can find no basis in utilitarian theory for distinguishing them and is left in the end to remark rather lamely that "the question of whether the general happiness

17. Smart, supra note 16, at 16.

would be increased by replacing most of the human population by a bigger population of contented sheep and pigs is not one which by any stretch of the imagination could become a live issue."[18]

Since utility in its broad sense is something possessed by many animals, the theory seems to require including sheep and pigs in the population whose happiness is to be maximized. Smart suggests as much. But there is something amiss in a philosophical system that cannot distinguish between people and sheep. In utilitarian morality, a driver who swerved to avoid two sheep and deliberately killed a child could not be considered a bad man, because his action may have increased the amount of happiness in the world.

We could say, with Frank Knight, that people don't *want* happiness or any other version of satisfaction that might embrace what animals want: "The chief thing which the common-sense individual actually wants is not satisfactions for the wants which he has, but more, and *better* wants."[19] But this is just a version of the old utilitarian game, which leads nowhere, of dividing preferences into "higher" and "lower" on inevitably shifting and subjective grounds.

Another boundary problem of utilitarianism concerns foreigners. Should American policy be to maximize the happiness of Americans, with foreigners' happiness given a zero weight? Or is a more ecumenical perspective required? And how about the unborn? To include them in the population whose happiness is to be maximized may yield policies on abortions, adoptions, homosexuality, savings, and other issues different from those indicated if only the currently living are counted in the happiness census. Whether to include foreigners or the unborn is not an issue that utilitarianism can resolve directly, yet again it seems that if maximizing utility is to be taken seriously, the broadest possible conception of the relevant population must be used.

18. *Id.* at 24–25.
19. Frank Hyneman Knight, *The Ethics of Competition, and Other Essays* 22 (1935); see also *id.* at 32.

The problem of foreigners and the unborn is related to the old dispute over whether the utilitarian goal should be to maximize average or total happiness. If the poorer half of the population of Bangladesh were killed, the standard of living—and, for all one knows, the subjective happiness as well—of the remaining half would rise because of the higher ratio of people to land and other natural resources. However, the *total* happiness might be less. Similarly, a high birth rate may cause a reduction in the standard of living of a crowded country and, along with it, in the average happiness of the country, but this loss may be more than offset by the satisfactions, even if somewhat meager, of the added population. There is no clear basis in utilitarian theory for choosing between average and total happiness, but the latter is more consistent with a simple insistence on utility as the maximand.

In summary, the logic of utilitarianism seems to favor setting as the ethical goal the maximization of the total amount of happiness in the universe. Since this goal seems attainable only by making lots of people miserable (those of us who would have to make room for all the foreigners, sheep, or whatever), utilitarians are constantly seeking ways to contract the boundary. But to do so they must go outside of utilitarianism.

Another problem is the lack of a method for calculating the effect of a decision or policy on the total happiness of the relevant population.[20] Even within just the human population, there is no reliable technique for measuring a change in the level of satisfaction of one individual relative to a change in the level of satisfaction of another.

The Pareto approach may seem to offer a solution to the problem of measuring satisfaction. A change is said to be Pareto superior if it makes at least one person better off and no one worse off. Such a change by definition increases the total amount of (human) happiness in the world. The advantage of the Pareto approach is that it requires information only about marginal and not about total utilities. And there seems ready at

20 As Hayek puts it, the practice of utilitarianism presupposes omniscience. 2 F. A. Hayek, *Law, Legislation, and Liberty* 17–23 (1976).

hand an operational device for achieving Pareto superiority, the voluntary transaction, which by definition makes both parties better off than they were before. However, the condition that no one else be affected by a "voluntary" transaction can only rarely be fulfilled. Moreover, the voluntary-transaction or free-market solution to the problem of measuring utility begs two critical questions: whether the goods exchanged were initially distributed so as to maximize happiness (were the people with money those who derive the most happiness from the things money can buy?) and whether a system of free markets creates more happiness than alternative systems of resource allocation would.

Difficulty in deriving specific policies from ethical premises is not, however, unique to utilitarianism; it seems characteristic of ethical discussion generally. Among contemporary Kantian legal rights theorists,[21] one has only to compare Charles Fried and Richard Epstein, who, starting from seemingly identical premises regarding human respect and autonomy, derive sharply different policy implications.[22]

However, the fact that utilitarianism is no more indefinite than competing theories of moral obligation may not reconcile one to utilitarianism, especially if one favors limited government. Suppose, for example, that Bentham was correct in his belief that, lacking any real knowledge of the responsiveness to income of different individuals' happiness, we should assume that every one is pretty much alike in that respect. Then we need make only one additional, and as it happens plausible, assumption—that of the diminishing marginal utility of money income—to obtain a utilitarian basis for a goal of equalizing incomes. For on these assumptions it is easily shown that an equal distribution of income and wealth will produce more happiness

21. I follow Bruce A. Ackerman, *Private Property and the Constitution* 71–72 (1977), in using the term "Kantian" to refer to a family of related ethical theories that subordinate social welfare to notions of human autonomy and self-respect as criteria of ethical conduct. Such theories need not, and usually do not, resemble closely the thought of Immanuel Kant, on which see Bruce Aune, *Kant's Theory of Morals* (1979).

22. Among many other differences, Fried rejects Epstein's position that, *prima facie*, tort liability should be strict liability. See Charles Fried, supra note 14, at 107; and his *An Anatomy of Values: Problems of Personal and Social Choice* 187–189 (1970).

than any other distribution[23] unless the costs of achieving and maintaining such a distribution equal or exceed the benefits. The qualification is critical, but it places the burden of proof on the opponent of income equalization in an area where proof is notoriously difficult to come by. This example illustrates a point made in the preceding chapter: if the impracticality of the felicific calculus is taken to justify the utilitarian's use of guesswork, the possibilities for plausible public intervention in private activities are unlimited.

The problem of indefiniteness blends into a related objection to utilitarian thought: what one might term the perils of instrumentalism. If happiness is maximized by allowing people to own property, marry as they choose, change jobs, and so on, then the utilitarian will grant them the rights to these things, but if happiness can be increased by treating people more like sheep, then rights are out the window. People do not seem to be happier in totalitarian than in democratic states, but if they were, the consistent utilitarian would have to support totalitarianism. Utilitarianism thus seems to base rights of great importance on no firmer ground than an empirical hunch that they promote "happiness." That hunch cannot be verified by any tools we have or are likely to acquire—though some people will find one bit of evidence or another (for example, the Berlin wall) persuasive. Even within the framework of the liberal state, utilitarians who are not shy about making bold empirical guesses concerning the distribution of happiness can produce rather monstrous policy recommendations.[24]

"Moral monstrousness" is indeed a major problem of utilitarianism. Two types of monstrousness should be distinguished. One stems from the utilitarian's refusal to make moral distinctions among types of pleasure. Suppose that A spends his lei-

23. See Jeremy Bentham, "The Philosophy of Economic Science," in 1 *Jeremy Bentham's Economic Writings* 81, 115–116 (W. Stark ed. 1952); Abba P. Lerner, *The Economics of Control: Principles of Welfare Economics* 35–36 (1944); Sartorius, supra note 16, at 131.

24. It should be mentioned, in fairness to the utilitarians, that Bentham is the principal, and inexhaustible, source of bizarre policy deductions from utilitarian premises. Nonetheless, utilitarians are frequently interventionist. See, e.g., 3 Stephen, supra note 16, at 228–229, on J. S. Mill's interventionist proposals.

sure time pulling wings off flies, while B spends his feeding pigeons, and because A has a greater capacity for pleasure than B, he derives more happiness from his leisure time. Putting aside the unhappiness of the fly, and the happiness of the pigeons, the consistent utilitarian would have to judge A a better man than B, because A's activity adds more to the sum of happiness than B's.

The other type of moral monstrousness arises from the utilitarian's readiness to sacrifice the innocent individual on the altar of social need. Alan Donagan gives the following example:

> It might well be the case that more good and less evil would result from your painlessly and undetectedly murdering your malicious, old and unhappy grandfather than from your forebearing to do so: he would be freed from his wretched existence; his children would be rejoiced by their inheritances and would no longer suffer from his mischief; and you might anticipate the reward promised to those who do good in secret. Nobody seriously doubts that a position with such a consequence is monstrous.[25]

Donagan seems correct in arguing that a consistent utilitarian would have to judge the murderer a good man. The utilitarian could, of course, point out that a *practice* of murdering obnoxious grandfathers would probably reduce happiness. Knowledge of the practice would make grandfathers very unhappy and in the long run would probably not benefit the heirs, because the practice would deter people from accumulating estates. But any utilitarian objections to creating an exception to the murder laws for killers of obnoxious grandfathers have no force at the level of personal morality once it is stipulated that the murder will go undetected. Yet to call the murderer in Donagan's example a "good man" does unacceptable violence to conventional moral notions.

Monstrousness is a less serious problem of utilitarianism at the level of social than of personal choice. It is one thing to pick

25. Alan Donagan, "Is There a Credible Form of Utilitarianism?" in *Contemporary Utilitarianism* 187, 188 (Michael D. Bayles ed. 1968).

an innocent person at random and kill him to achieve some social end and another to establish an institutional structure—
criminal punishment, for example—which makes it inevitable
that some innocent people will suffer. No punishment system
could be devised that reduced the probability of erroneous conviction to zero. Yet even at the level of social choice, utilitarianism can lead to monstrous results. Were there a group of
people at once so few relative to the rest of the society, so miserable, and so hated that their extermination would increase the
total happiness of the society, the consistent utilitarian would
find it hard to denounce their extermination, although he
would be entitled to note the anxiety costs that might be imposed on people who feared they might be exterminated next.

If monstrousness is a peril of utilitarianism, moral squeamish-
ness, or fanaticism, is a peril of Kantian theorists. Bernard Williams poses the case of Jim, the guest of an officer in a backward
country who is about to have a group of political prisoners
shot.[26] The officer tells Jim that if Jim will shoot one of the prisoners, he will release the others. Williams argues that Jim has no
obligation to shoot a prisoner because there is a difference between doing evil and failing to prevent evil. But the difference is
hard to see in the example. If Jim declines the officer's invitation, all the prisoners will die; if he accepts it, all but one will be
saved. There is no trade-off. No one will be better off if Jim declines the invitation; all but one will be worse off.

Most Kantians try to avoid fanaticism by carving exceptions to
the categorical duties they impose.[27] They will say that torture is
wrong even if it could be shown (as Bentham believed) to maximize happiness on balance, but will then admit that if torturing
one person were necessary to save the human race it would not
be wrong to torture him. Once this much is conceded, however,
there is no logical stopping point. What if two innocents must be
killed to save 200 million Americans—ten to save three million

26. See Bernard Williams, "A Critique of Utilitarianism," in Smart & Williams, **supra**
note 2, at 77, 98–99.
27. For an example of this approach see Fried, supra note 14, at 10.

Chicagoans—twenty to save 60,000 residents of one Chicago neighborhood?

The tendency of Kantianism to merge into utilitarianism is illustrated by the moral philosophy of John Rawls. Although his premises are Kantian and he rejects utilitarianism because it "does not take seriously the distinction between persons,"[28] he defines justice as the outcome of collective choice by individuals in the "original position," that is, stripped of all their individual characteristics. He assumes that these shades choose principles of justice that will maximize their own utility, and because they are also assumed to be highly risk averse, they choose a principle that trades away much individual economic liberty for social insurance. Rawls's principle of social justice resembles Bentham's principle of maximizing income equality subject to the constraint of preserving the individual's incentive to engage in productive activity. In both cases, the optimal degree of equality depends on empirical hunches regarding the size and shape of individuals' marginal-utility schedules and the disincentive effects of egalitarian policies. The necessity of making such hunches imparts to Rawls's theory the same indefiniteness that plagues Bentham's. Rawls's concept of the "veil of ignorance" resembles the method by which the economist Abba Lerner deduced a norm of income equality from the greatest-happiness principle.[29] Lerner said that given our ignorance of the height of people's marginal-utility functions, the best assumption was that they are uncorrelated with income.[30] It is not surprising that another welfare economist, John Harsanyi, anticipated the core of Rawls's principle of justice (rational choice by people in the original position) by many years.[31]

28. John Rawls, *A Theory of Justice* 27 (1971).
29. I am indebted to Gary Becker for this point.
30. See Lerner, supra note 23.
31. See John C. Harsanyi, "Cardinal Utility in Welfare Economics and in the Theory of Risk-Taking," 61 *J. Pol. Econ.* 434 (1953). Rawls acknowledges Harsanyi's contribution. See Rawls, supra note 28, at 137 n.11, 162 n.21. Harsanyi remains a sophisticated exponent of utilitarianism. See his "Morality and the Theory of Rational Behavior," 44 *Soc. Res.* 623 (1977). I discuss the "original position" of Rawls and Harsanyi further in Chapter 4.

To summarize, utilitarianism has serious shortcomings whether viewed as a system of personal morality or as a guide to social decision making; but Kantianism, the usual alternative, has its own serious defects; one of these is its resemblance to utilitarianism. Against this background let us consider economic analysis as an alternative moral system.

Wealth Maximization as an Ethical Concept

Wealth versus Utility

Since Adam Smith, the term "value" in economics has generally referred to value in exchange, value as measured or at least measurable in a market, whether explicit or implicit. From the concept of value derives the concept of the wealth of society as the sum of all goods and services in the society weighted by their values.[32]

Although the concept of value is inseparable from that of markets, value is not the same thing as price. The market price of a good is its value to the marginal purchaser, and intramarginal purchasers will value it more in the sense that they would pay more for it if the price were higher. The wealth of society includes not only the market value in the sense of price times quantity of all goods and services produced in it, but also the total consumer and producer surplus generated by those goods and services.[33]

The most important thing to bear in mind about the concept of value is that it is based on what people are willing to pay for something rather than on the happiness they would derive from having it. Value and happiness are of course related: a person would not buy something unless having it would give

---

32. For a useful taxonomy of welfare definitions, including wealth, see Frank I. Michelman, "Norms and Normativity in the Economic Theory of Law," 62 *Minn. L. Rev.* 1015, 1019–1021, 1032–1034 (1978).
33. Cf. Figure 1 and note 57 infra.

him more happiness, in the broad utilitarian sense, than the alternative goods or services (including leisure) that he must give up to have it. But while value necessarily implies utility, utility does not necessarily imply value. The individual who would like very much to have some good but is unwilling or unable to pay anything for it—perhaps because he is destitute—does not value the good in the sense in which I am using the term "value."

Equivalently, the wealth of society is the aggregate satisfaction of those preferences (the only ones that have ethical weight in a system of wealth maximization) that are backed up by money, that is, that are registered in a market. The market, however, need not be an explicit one. Much of economic life is still organized on barter principles. The "marriage market," child rearing, and a friendly game of bridge are examples. These services have value which could be monetized by reference to substitute services sold in explicit markets or in other ways. They illustrate the important point that wealth cannot be equated to the Gross National Product or any other actual pecuniary measure of welfare. A society is not necessarily wealthier because of an (involuntary) shift by women from household production to prostitution, or because a wealthy person who used to give money to charity (thereby increasing the consumption of others) now spends it on himself.

Another type of nonexplicit market, the hypothetical market, is also important in analyzing the wealth of society. Compare two situations. In one, I offer you $5 for a bag of oranges, you accept, and the exchange is consummated. The wealth of the society must now be greater. Before the transaction, you had a bag of oranges worth less than $5 to you and I had $5; after the transaction you have $5 and I have a bag of oranges worth more than $5 to me. However, suppose that instead of buying the oranges from you, I accidentally smash them. A court applying the Learned Hand formula of negligence liability[34] would ask

34. See Chapter 1.

whether the expected cost to you of the accident was greater or
less than the expected gain to me of whatever activity produced
the accident as a by-product. To answer, the court would have
to make a judgment as to how much those oranges were worth
to you, how much walking fast was worth to me, and so on. The
purist would insist that the relevant values are unknowable since
they have not been revealed in an actual market transaction, but
I believe that in many cases a court can make a reasonably accurate guess as to the allocation of resources that would maximize
wealth. Since, however, the determination of value made by a
court is less accurate than that made by a market, the hypothetical-market approach should be reserved for cases, such as the
typical accident case, where market-transaction costs preclude
use of an actual market to allocate resources efficiently.

Hypothetical-market analysis plays an important role in the
economic analysis of the common law. Much of that law seems
designed, consciously or not, to allocate resources as actual markets would, in circumstances where the costs of market transactions are so high that the market is not a feasible method of allocation. Hypothetical-market analysis also makes clear that
maximizing wealth and maximizing happiness are not the same
thing. Suppose a polluting factory lowers residential property
values in an area by $2 million, but that it would cost the factory
$3 million to relocate (the only way to eliminate the pollution),
and on this basis the factory prevails in the property owners'
nuisance action. The unhappiness of the property owners may
exceed the happiness of the owners of the factory (who might
consist of thousands of shareholders, each with only a small
stake in the enterprise) at avoiding a $2 million judgment. Now
reverse the numbers and assume that the property owners are
wealthy people and that if the factory has to close down, its
workers will suffer heavy relocation costs and many small local
merchants will be pushed into bankruptcy. A judgment that
forces the factory to close will be efficient but it will probably not
maximize happiness.

As another example of why wealth maximization is not just a
proxy for utility maximization in the sense of classical utilitari-

anism, consider a poor man who decides to steal a diamond necklace for his wife. The necklace has a market value of $10,000, which is also, let us assume, its subjective value to the owner. That is, the owner would be willing to sell it for any price above $10,000. The optimum fine for this theft (based on the value of the necklace, the probability of apprehending and convicting the thief, the costs of the criminal justice system, the costs of self-protection, and so on) is, let us say, $25,000; for the indigent thief, a term of imprisonment has been set that equals the disutility of a $25,000 fine to a thief who could pay it. In these circumstances, we can be reasonably confident that if our poor man goes ahead and commits the theft, the total happiness of society will rise, even though he cannot pay the fine. The thief must obtain greater utility than the disutility he imposes on society (in the cost to the victim, the costs of operating the criminal justice system, the insecurity generated by crime, and so on) since that disutility is brought to bear on him in the form of an expected disutility of imprisonment yet he commits the theft anyway. But the theft does not increase the wealth of society, because it is the outcome of neither a voluntary nor a hypothetical-market transaction. In actual-market terms the thief's unwillingness (based on inability) to pay for the necklace shows that the necklace is worth less to him than to the owner. Hypothetical-market analysis is unwarranted because there is no problem of high market transaction costs that would justify allowing the thief to circumvent the market. Even if the hypothetical-market approach were used in this example, it still would not result in awarding the necklace to the thief, for it is not worth more to him than the owner in a willingness-to-pay sense. The hypothetical-market approach would, however, be applicable if someone of monetary means broke into an unoccupied cabin and stole food in order to avert starvation. Transaction costs would be prohibitive and there would be reason to believe that the food was more valuable, in the economic sense of value, to the thief than to the owner.

The uncertainty of the relationship between wealth and happiness is further suggested by the fact that the inhabitants of wealthy countries appear to be no happier than those of poor countries, although within countries the wealthy seem to be happier than the poor.[35] Adam Smith, who was not a utilitarian or a "welfare economist," thought people were deluded in believing that they would be happier if they were richer, though he had no doubt that this belief was prevalent and was an essential stimulant to human progress.[36]

Not only can wealth not be equated to happiness, but, to state the same point in the language of economics, people are not just wealth maximizers. Wealth is an important element in most people's preferences, and wealth maximization thus resembles utilitarianism in assigning substantial weight to preferences, but it is not the sum total of those preferences. That is why positive economic theory assumes that people are utility maximizers in a broad, utilitarian sense, and is another reason for the frequent confusion of economics and utilitarianism as ethical systems.

Before concluding my exposition of the meaning of wealth maximization, I want to clarify an ambiguity in the critical concept of "willingness to pay." Suppose I own a home that has a market value of $100,000. It is possible that I would not sell the house for less than, say, $125,000 (the market value is the value to the marginal purchaser in the market, and I may not have the same preferences as he). But it is also possible that if I did

35. See two papers by Richard A. Easterlin: "Does Money Buy Happiness?" *Public Interest,* No. 30, Winter 1973, at 3; "Does Economic Growth Improve the Human Lot? Some Empirical Evidence," in *Nations and Households in Economic Growth: Essays in Honor of Moses Abramovitz* 89 (Paul A. David & Melvin W. Reder eds. 1974).

36. It is therefore surprising that *The Wealth of Nations* is sometimes regarded as a utilitarian tract, as by Plamenatz, supra note 16, at 111. Rawls, supra note 28, at 22–23 n.9 and 184–188, describes the Smith of *The Theory of Moral Sentiments* as utilitarian because the "impartial spectator" of Smithian ethics resembles, in Rawls's view, the "aggregate man" of the utilitarians. If anything, the impartial spectator resembles man in the Rawlsian original position: the stress in both conceptions is on disinterest as fundamental to the concept of justice. Little, supra note 6, at 79 n.2, notes (without developing the point) that Adam Smith wrote of "wealth," not "welfare" or "happiness." On Adam Smith's ethical views see R. H. Coase, "Adam Smith's View of Man," 19 *J. Law & Econ.* 529 (1976); James M. Buchanan, "The Justice of Natural Liberty," 5 *J. Legal Stud.* 1 (1976); Donald J. Devine, "Adam Smith and the Problem of Justice in Capitalist Society," 6 *J. Legal Stud.* 399 (1977).

not own the house—it is my principal asset—I would not be willing to pay more than $75,000 for it, because that is all I could "afford" to pay. Is the house, then, worth $75,000 or $125,000? The answer depends on whether or not I own the house. But this does not conclude the analysis because, assuming I own the house, we must consider whether my ownership is consistent with ethically proper principles by which rights are assigned (the principles of distributive justice). As a dramatic example of this point, consider a totalitarian society in which a small group of government officials possesses immense amounts of that valuable commodity, power. If the price they would demand to surrender their power is considered an element in determining the wealth of the society, then it would be unclear whether introducing democratic institutions would increase that wealth. But except in the unlikely event that the bosses had obtained power through market or hypothetical-market transactions, the "value" of their power to them would be no more relevant in measuring social wealth than the "value" that the thief derives from the goods he steals.

Wealth Maximization, Morality, and Justice

If wealth is not just another name for happiness, and it surely is not, why should the pursuit of wealth be considered morally superior to the pursuit of happiness? That is the central question of this chapter and the next.

What makes so many moral philosophers queasy about utilitarianism is that it seems to invite gross invasions of individual liberty—whether in the name of animal happiness, or the happiness of Nozick's "utility monster,"[37] or Bentham's speculations on what really makes people happy. But uncompromising insistence on individual liberty or autonomy regardless of the consequences for the happiness or utility of the people of the society seems equally misplaced and unacceptable. Hence there is increasing interest in trying to combine utilitarianism and the Kantian tradition in some fashion, as in the recent work of

37. Nozick, supra note 2, at 41.

Richard Epstein.[38] The ethics of wealth maximization can be viewed as a blend of these rival philosophical traditions. Wealth is positively correlated, although imperfectly so, with utility, but the pursuit of wealth, based as it is on the model of the voluntary market transaction, involves greater respect for individual choice than in classical utilitarianism.

Compare once again the man who is willing to pay $10,000 for a necklace with the man who has no money but is willing to incur a nonpecuniary disutility equivalent to that of giving up such a sum. The position of the first man is morally superior because he seeks to increase his welfare by conferring a benefit on another, namely the owner. Moreover, the buyer's $10,000 was in all likelihood accumulated through productive activity—that is, activity beneficial to other people besides himself, whether to his employer, customers, or his father's customers. If we assume that a person's income is less than the total value of his production,[39] it follows that the productive individual puts into society more than he takes out of it. Hence, not only does the buyer in our example confer a net benefit on the owner of the necklace (who would not accept $10,000 otherwise), but at every stage in the accumulation of that money through productive activity, net benefits were conferred on other people besides the producer. The thief, in contrast, provides no benefit to the owner of the necklace or to anyone else. His "claim" to the necklace, which the utilitarian would honor, is based on a faculty—the capacity to experience pleasure—that may be worth nothing to other people. The term "thief" is used pejoratively even in societies where theft, being punished very severely, is unlikely to occur unless the utility to the thief exceeds the victim's disutility; this fact is a datum about our ethical beliefs that utilitarianism cannot account for, and wealth maximization can.

This discussion is relevant to the question whether the utility that a thief obtains from theft should be taken into account in

38. See nuisance-law article cited in note 1 supra, where Epstein advocates legal principles based on notions of personal autonomy constrained by utilitarianism.
39. See note 57 infra.

the design of an efficient system of penalties.[40] If all thefts were pure coercive transfer payments extracted in a setting of low transaction costs, the utility of the thief would be entitled to no consideration, because such thefts do not create wealth. But not all thefts are of this type. Consider my earlier example of the person lost in the woods who breaks into an empty cabin and steals food that he must have to live. The cost of transacting with the owner would be prohibitive, and the theft is wealth maximizing because the food is worth more in a strict economic sense to the thief than to the owner. It follows not that the thief should go unpunished in this case—we may want to punish him to ensure that no one will commit a theft unless it really is wealth maximizing (that is, yields a gain to the thief greater than the loss to the victim)—but only that the punishment should be set at a level that deters stealing *unless* it is wealth maximizing. In contrast, if theft never had social value, the size of the penalty would be limited only by the costs of imposing it.

Economic liberty is another value that can be grounded more firmly in wealth maximization than in utilitarianism. It is the almost universal opinion of economists (including Marxist economists) that free markets, whatever objections can be made to them on grounds of equity, maximize a society's wealth. This is, to be sure, an empirical judgment, but it rests on firmer ground than the claim that free markets maximize happiness.

Most of the conventional pieties—keeping promises, telling the truth, and the like—can also be derived from the wealth-maximization principle. Adherence to these virtues facilititates transactions and so promotes trade and hence wealth by reducing the costs of policing markets through self-protection, detailed contracts, litigation, and so on.[41] Even altruism (benevolence) is an economizing principle, because it can be a substi-

40. Compare Gary S. Becker, "Crime and Punishment: An Economic Approach," 76 *J. Pol. Econ.* 169 (1968), with George J. Stigler, "The Optimum Enforcement of Laws," 78 *J. Pol. Econ.* 526 (1970).

41. See *Altruism, Morality, and Economic Theory* (Edmund S. Phelps ed. 1975); Posner, supra note 13, at 185–186.

tute for costly market and legal processes.[42] And yet even the
altruist might decide to sell his services to the highest bidder
rather than donate them to the neediest supplicant. Because of
the costs of determining need other than through willingness to
pay, allocation by price may confer greater net benefits on the
rest of society than allocation by "need" or "desert."[43] Allocation by price will also result in a greater accumulation of wealth.
This wealth can be given away in whole or in part—though
again the altruist will not want to spend so much time screening
applicants for charity that he greatly reduces his productive
work and the benefits it confers on other people.

To summarize, the wealth-maximization principle encourages and rewards the traditional "Calvinist" or "Protestant" virtues and capacities associated with economic progress.[44] It may

42. For a concrete example see William M. Landes & Richard A. Posner, "Salvors,
Finders, Good Samaritans, and Other Rescuers: An Economic Study of Law and Altruism," 7 *J. Legal Stud.* 83, 95 (1978).

43. Hayek has put this well: "We still esteem doing good only if it is done to benefit
specific known needs of known people, and regard it as really better to help one starv-
ing man we know than to relieve the acute need of a hundred men we do not know; but
in fact we generally are doing most good by pursuing gain . . . The aim for which the
successful entrepreneur wants to use his profits may well be to provide a hospital or an
art gallery for his home town. But quite apart from the question of what he wants to do
with his profits after he has earned them, he is led to benefit more people by aiming for
the largest gain than he could if he concentrated on the satisfaction of the needs of
known persons. He is led by the invisible hand of the market to bring the succour of
modern conveniences to the poorest homes he does not even know." 2 Hayek, supra
note 20, at 145.

44. Not everyone, of course, agrees that the market brings out the best in man. John
Ruskin stated: "In a community regulated only by laws of demand and supply, but protected from open violence, the persons who become rich are, generally speaking, indus-
trious, resolute, proud, covetous, prompt, methodical, sensible, unimaginative, insensi-
tive, and ignorant. The persons who remain poor are the entirely foolish, the entirely
wise, the idle, the reckless, the humble, the thoughtful, the dull, the imaginative, the
sensitive, the well-informed, the improvident, the irregularly and impulsively wicked,
the clumsy knave, the open thief, and the entirely merciful, just, and godly person."
Ruskin, *Unto This Last* 74–75 (Lloyd J. Hubenka ed. 1967), quoted in Knight, supra
note 19, at 66.

Many of these assertions are implausible. It is a business asset to be imaginative (for
example, in devising new products, production processes, and methods of distribution), sensitive (in handling partners, employees, customers, and suppliers, and in anticipating shifts in consumer demand), and knowledgeable, at least within a narrow

be doubted whether the happiness principle also implies the same constellation of virtues and capacities, especially given the degree of self-denial implicit in adherence to them. Utilitarians would have to give capacity for enjoyment, self-indulgence, and other hedonistic and epicurean values at least equal emphasis with diligence and honesty, which the utilitarian values only because they tend to increase wealth and hence *might* increase happiness.

Wealth maximization is a more defensible moral principle also in that it provides a firmer foundation for a theory of distributive and corrective justice. It has been argued that the source of rights exchanged in a market economy is itself necessarily external to the wealth-maximization principle.[45] In fact the principle ordains the creation of a system of personal and property rights that ideally would extend to *all* valued things that are scarce—not only real and personal property but the human body and even ideas. Sometimes, to be sure, these rights have to be qualified because of the costs of protecting them—that is why the patient, copyright, and related laws protect only a subset of valuable ideas—or because of transaction costs or because of the problems of conflicting use (should I have the right to burn trash on my property or should my neighbor have the right to be free from smoke?). Nonetheless, the commitment of the economic approach to the principle of rights is stronger than that of most utilitarians—or, for the matter, of those Kantians who allow redistributive concerns to override property rights.

To many students of moral philosophy rights and economics

---

sphere. Why then should a well-informed, thoughtful, and entirely wise person fail to become wealthy in a market economy *because* he has these qualities? Perhaps Ruskin thinks that such a person would not desire wealth. But if so, it would presumably be so however the economy were organized. Nor need a merciful, just, or godly man be at a competitive disadvantage in a market economy—unless these qualities (especially the last) are taken to imply an aversion to producing for the market. For a broad-ranging and inconclusive debate on the morality of the market system, see papers collected in *Markets and Morals* (Gerald Dworkin, Gordon Bermant & Peter G. Brown eds. 1977).

45. See Dworkin, supra note 14, at 97–98; Kennedy, supra note 14, at 1763–1764.

seem incompatible concepts, but they are not. The theory of
property rights is an important branch of modern microecono-
mic theory.[46] A property right, in both law and economics, is a
right to exclude everyone else from the use of some scarce resource.[47] Such a right is absolute within its domain (an important qualification, which I will take up shortly) in the sense that
someone who wants a resource in which another has a property
right cannot take the right from him by appealing to the general welfare. For example, if A parks his car in B's garage and B
seeks an injunction against him, A cannot defend by arguing to
the court that the garage is really worth more to him than to B
(perhaps because A's car is more expensive than B's). Nor can A
take the garage and remit B to a lawsuit for its market value. He
must negotiate with B for the garage. The fact that the right
cannot be extinguished or transferred without the owner's consent makes it absolute.

Absolute rights play an important role in the economic theory
of the law. The economist recommends the creation of such
rights—to ideas, land, or labor, for example—when the costs of
voluntary transactions are low, as in my garage example. But
when transaction costs are prohibitive, the recognition of absolute rights is inefficient. Hence I do not have an absolute property right against sound waves that penetrate my house or air
pollution that deposits dirt on its window sills. The difference
between these examples and the garage case is that in the latter,
voluntary transactions provide a sure way of moving resources
to their most valuable uses. In the former, transaction costs preclude the use of voluntary transactions to thus move resources,
and alternative allocative mechanisms to property rights must
be found—such as liability rules, eminent domain, or zoning.

To make property rights, although absolute, contingent on
transaction costs and subservient or instrumental to the goal of

46. See, e.g., Eric Furubotn & Svetozar Pejovich, "Property Rights and Economic
Theory: A Survey of Recent Literature," 10 *J. Econ. Lit.* 1137 (1972).

47. See Guido Calabresi & A. Douglas Melamed, "Property Rules, Liability Rules,
and Inalienability: One View of the Cathedral," 85 *Harv. L. Rev.* 1089 (1972); Posner,
supra note 13, at 49–51.

wealth maximization is to give rights less status than many "rights theorists" claim for them. Although the property rights of economic analysis are absolute and embrace the person as well as nonhuman goods (I have within broad limits the absolute right to decide whom to work for, or to marry), these rights are not transcendental or ends in themselves, and they operate, in general, only in settings of low transaction costs. Nevertheless, they are rights in a perfectly good sense of the term—unless the idea of a right is held to exclude rights, however absolute, that are justified as instruments to some end outside of the protection of rights as such.

The economist does not merely decree that absolute rights be created and then fall silent as to where they should be vested. To be sure, if market transactions were costless, the economist would not care where a right was initially vested. The process of voluntary exchange would costlessly reallocate it to whoever valued it the most. But once the unrealistic assumption of zero transaction costs is abandoned, the assignment of rights becomes determinate. If transaction costs are positive (though presumably low, for otherwise it would be inefficient to create an absolute right), the wealth-maximization principle requires the initial vesting of rights in those who are likely to value them most, so as to minimize transaction costs.[48] This is the economic reason for giving a worker the right to sell his labor and a woman the right to determine her sexual partners. If assigned randomly to strangers, these rights would generally (not invariably) be repurchased by the worker and the woman; the costs of the rectifying transaction can be avoided if the right is assigned at the outset to the user who values it the most. Similarly there is no mechanism for initially identifying, and vesting the right in, someone who in fact values it so highly that he might not resell it to the "natural" owner. The inherent difficulties of borrowing

48. The analysis of a technical difficulty in applying the wealth-maximization criterion—the possibility that the initial assignment of rights may affect prices and thereby make values derivative from the assignment of rights rather than determinative of it—is discussed in Chapter 4

against human capital[49] would no doubt defeat some efforts by the natural owner to buy back the right to his labor or body even from someone who did not really value it more highly than he did, but that is simply a further reason for initially vesting the right in the natural owner.

Charles Fried objects that it is improper to think about rights in this way, because a decision that the individual values his life, body, or mind more than anyone else presupposes that the individual is an entity already possessing life, body, or mind.[50] But possession is not ownership. Although Fried thinks it especially ridiculous that a person's teeth should be up for grabs, as it were, consider the following hypothetical case. Because the teeth in my head are brilliantly lustrous and pearly, the Colgate company hires a photographer to follow me about and photograph me whenever I smile, and the best of the pictures is then published without my consent in an advertisement for Colgate toothpaste. The New York Court of Appeals once thought there was no invasion of one's legal rights in such a case.[51] The court in effect assigned the right to a brilliant smile away from its "natural" owner. Although this view was economically incorrect and has been generally rejected, it did not involve any contradiction or absurdity.

A further consideration relevant to the initial distribution of rights is the inefficiency of monopolies. This consideration argues for parceling out rights in small units to many different people in order to raise the costs of assembling the rights into a single bloc large enough to confer monopoly power. Thus it would be inefficient to assign to one person the right to the labor of all electrical or foundry or restaurant workers, because that assignment would result in monopolization of a part of the labor supply and therefore in a reduction in the wealth of the society.

49. I abstract from avoidable difficulties such as the bankruptcy laws and the legal prohibitions against voluntary indentured servitude.
50. See Fried, supra note 14, at 103–104.
51. See Roberson v. Rochester Folding Box Co., 171 N.Y. 538, 64 N.E. 442 (1902); and Chapter 9.

All the same, an initial distribution of rights that was consistent with a goal of wealth maximization might be extremely unequal. But inequality of results is not what concerns those who argue that the economic theory of law is a theory of rights masquerading as a species of utilitarianism. They allege that wealth or happiness maximization is not consistent with the protection of rights, yet a theory of rights is in fact an important corollary of the wealth-maximization principle.

I want to turn now to the place of corrective justice in a theory of wealth maximization.[52] The classic analysis of corrective justice is in Book V, Chapter 4 of Aristotle's *Nicomachean Ethics*. Aristotle explains that if one person injures another by an act of injustice, the injury is wrongful, and rectification in some form required, even if the injurer is a better man than the victim according to the principle of distributive justice (distributive justice as distribution according to merit) described in the previous chapter of Book V. The idea that the wrongfulness of an injury can be determined apart from the relative merit of the injurer and his victim, and the closely related idea of distributive neutrality in legal disputes, seem to be the heart of the Aristotelian concept of corrective justice. But the precise mode of rectification assumed by Aristotle, that is, a private damages action brought by the victim against the injurer, reflects the privatized character of the legal system in Athens at the time[53]; it does not appear from Aristotle's discussion that he thought the private damage action the only possible mode of rectification that was compatible with his concept.

The Aristotelian concept of corrective justice is consistent with, and indeed required by, the wealth-maximization approach. If a wrongful act results in injury, rectification in some form is necessary if the efficiency of resource use is not to be undermined. To be sure, this conclusion requires equating wrongful with inefficient, an equation Aristotle did not make. But the concept of corrective justice in Aristotle is a procedural

52. For a fuller discussion of corrective justice see my article "The Concept of Corrective Justice in Recent Theories of Tort Law," 10 *J. Legal Stud.* (Jan. 1981).

53. I discuss that system in Chapter 8.

rather than a substantive idea. It prescribes rectification for wrongful acts that cause injury, regardless of the relative merit of injurer and victim considered apart from the act, but it does not define what acts are wrongful; this definition is not itself part of the concept of corrective justice. So it is compatible with that concept to define an act of injustice as an act that reduces the wealth of society; and once that step is taken, it is easy to show that a failure to rectify such acts would reduce the wealth of society by making such acts more common. It is also easy to show that a failure to observe distributive neutrality in adjudicating claims arising from such acts would reduce the wealth of society. For example, if two people having different earnings are disabled in the same accident resulting from a wrongful act of the injurer, it would be inefficient to give them each the same damages, on the ground that they are in some sense, perhaps a Kantian sense, entitled to an equal distribution of the world's goods. Nor, if the injurer were a wealthier or a better man than his victims, would it be efficient on that account to give the victims less than their lost earnings and other items of damage; this would lead to too many accidents, or to the wrong (suboptimal) precautions.

Wealth maximization provides a foundation not only for a theory of rights and of remedies but for the concept of law itself. "Law" is often defined simply as a command backed up by the coercive power of the state. By this definition, any order emanating from the sovereign power is law. But that strains the ordinary meaning of the term, and it has been suggested that the definition, to be descriptive of the term as it is actually used, must include the following additional elements: (1) to count as law, a command must be one that can be complied with by those to whom it is addressed; (2) it must treat equally those who are similarly situated in all respects relevant to the command: (3) it must be public; (4) there must be a procedure for ascertaining the truth of any facts necessary to the application of the command according to its terms.[54] These elements are part of the economic theory of law.

---

54. See Rawls, supra note 28, at 237–239, and references cited there.

The basic function of law in an economic or wealth-maximization perspective is to alter incentives. This implies that law does not command the impossible; a command that is impossible to fulfill will not alter behavior. The impossible command must be distinguished from the legal sanction that is unavoidable only because the cost of avoidance is greater than the cost of the sanction. There is no incongruity in making the party who breaches a contract liable in damages in a case where he had no real choice because the cost of performing the contract would have greatly exceeded the damages from nonperformance (or even because performance would have been literally impossible). The law has simply placed the risk of nonperformance on the party who fails to perform. The proper criticism of the various pockets of strict liability in the criminal law (for example, reasonable mistake is no defense in a prosecution for bigamy or statutory rape) is not that they are inconsistent with the idea of law but that the risk imposed is greater than the circumstances warrant.

The requirement that law must treat equals equally is another way of saying that the law must have a rational structure, for to treat differently things that are the same is irrational. Economic theory is a system of deductive logic: when correctly applied, it yields results that are consistent with one another. Insofar as the law has an implicit economic structure, it must be rational; it must treat like cases alike.

Law as a system for altering incentives and thus regulating behavior must also be public. If the content of a law becomes known only after the occurence of the events it applies to, the existence of the law can have no effect on the conduct of the parties subject to it.

Finally, the economic theory of law presupposes machinery for ascertaining the facts necessary to correct application of a law. The deterrent effect of a law is weakened (and in the limit would disappear) if enforced without regard to whether the circumstances are those to which the law was intended to apply. Suppose there is a law against price fixers, but no effort is made to ascertain who is fixing prices; instead, one in 10,000 people is selected at random and punished as a price fixer. Then there will be no incentive to avoid price fixing. The only difference between the price fixer and others is that the former has profits from price fixing; the expected liability is the same for all.[55]

The Criticisms of Utilitarianism Revisited

How far do the criticisms of utilitarianism apply also to economic analysis? The boundary problem is the least serious. Animals count, but only insofar as they enhance wealth. The optimal population of sheep is determined not by speculation on their capacity for contentment relative to people, but by the intersection of the marginal product and marginal cost of keeping sheep.

Another implication of the wealth-maximization approach, however, is that people who lack sufficient earning power to support even a minimum decent standard of living are entitled to no say in the allocation of resources unless they are part of the utility function of someone who has wealth. This conclusion may seem to weight too heavily the individual's particular endowment of capacities. If he happens to be born feeble-minded and his net social product is negative, he would have no right to the means of support even though there was nothing blameworthy in his inability to support himself. This result grates on modern sensibilities, yet I see no escape from it that is consistent with any of the major ethical systems. Rawls and others have promoted the view that the individual's genetic endowment is a kind of accident devoid of moral significance, but that is inconsistent with the Kantian notions of individuality from which the view purports to derive. To treat the inventor and the idiot equally concerning their moral claim to command over valuable resources does not take seriously the differences between persons.[56] And any policy of redistribution impairs the autonomy of those from whom the redistribution is made.

With regard to the status of the unborn, the critical question from the standpoint of wealth maximization is how far one is

55. See Posner, supra note 13, at 430–433.
56. See text at note 28 supra.

willing to push the notion of hypothetical markets. It is possible in principle to calculate whether additional population would be economically self-supporting. Additional population might reduce the wealth of a very crowded society but increase that of a sparsely settled country with abundant natural resources. In suggesting that the proper inquiry is whether the social product of the additional population exceeds its social cost, rather than whether the rest of the population will be made wealthier, I may seem implicitly to be resolving the boundary question in favor of including the additional population in the population whose wealth we are interested in maximizing. But these formulations are actually equivalent. As shown in Figure 1, productive people put more into society than they take out of it.[57] Hence, so long as the additional population is productive, the existing population will benefit.

57. In Figure 1, D, the demand for (some type of) labor, represents the schedule of prices that workers or other producers could command for various quantities of their labor. If there is competition among the workers, the output of their labor will be carried to the point, q, where the marginal product of their labor—what demanders will pay at the competitive margin—is just equal to the supply price (S), representing the opportunity costs of workers' time and other inputs (education, etc.). Thus the rectangle PBqO represents the total income of the labor force, while the larger area ABqO represents the total social product of their work. The difference is a form of "consumer surplus," on which see John R. Hicks, "The Rehabilitation of Consumers' Surplus," in *Readings in Welfare Economics* 325 (Kenneth J. Arrow & Tibor Scitovsky eds. 1969); Robert D. Willig, "Consumer's Surplus without Apology," 66 *Am. Econ. Rev.* 589 (1976).

The diagram exaggerates the size of the surplus, because some of it might represent a return to suppliers of inputs that were responsible for the worker's productivity. It is generally assumed, however, that producers in a competitive economy are unable to appropriate all of the value of their output. Even a patent owner can appropriate only the first seventeen years of the value produced by his invention. And even during that period, he could not appropriate all the consumer surplus of the invention unless he were able to price discriminate *perfectly*—and that is never possible.

A further qualification is that the *marginal* producer by definition creates no consumer surplus—he takes out exactly what he puts in—so if each producer is marginal, none would reduce the wealth of other people by withdrawing from the market. However, not every producer is marginal; we may be reasonably confident that the American people would be poorer if Henry Ford had decided to become a Trappist monk rather than an automobile manufacturer. More important, even in an industry where each producer is marginal and his withdrawal from the industry would not reduce consumer surplus, the withdrawal of a group of producers would. Each producer's contribution to consumer surplus is negligible, but the sum of their contributions is not.

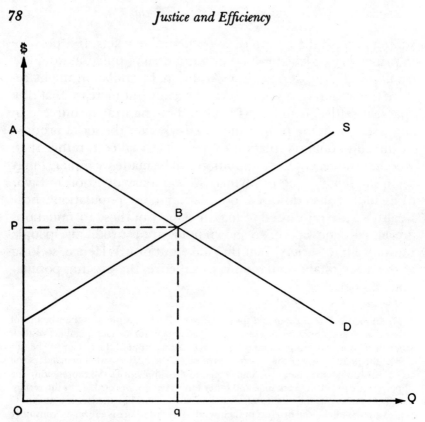

Figure 1. Consumer surplus: production for others. Q = workers' output; S = supply price; D = demand for labor; area $PBqO$ = total income of labor force; area $ABqO$ = total social product of their work.

As for foreigners, a policy coupling free immigration with no public support of the immigrant will ensure that only wealth-maximizing immigration occurs. No one will immigrate who anticipates an income lower than the costs of maintaining himself. Since (putting aside mistake) his income will be smaller than his total social product and larger than his maintenance cost, he will contribute to the rest of the population more than he takes from them in goods and services. There is no conflict between average and total in a system of wealth maximization. The average wealth of the existing population will increase as a result of immigration so long as any negative externalities of immigration are fully internalized to the immigrants.[58]

The measurement problem that so plagues utilitarianism is easily solved if the domain of the wealth-maximization criterion is restricted to actual markets that are free from serious problems of monopoly or externality. Any voluntary transaction that occurs in such a market must increase the wealth of the society. This proposition is not the Pareto principle in the sense discussed earlier, which is a principle of utility, but is an essentially tautologous principle of wealth maximization. Voluntariness is, however, too restrictive a condition, and once the domain of the wealth-maximization criterion is expanded to include hypothetical markets, a problem of measurement arises. But it is a less serious problem than that of measuring happiness. For example, the right of the physician who treats an unconscious accident victim to later claim his regular fee from the victim is founded on the reasonable assumption that if the victim could have negotiated with the physican for such service at such price he would have done so. It is easier to guess people's market preferences in areas where the market cannot be made to work than to guess what policies will maximize happiness.

The "interpersonal comparison of utilities" is anathema to the modern economist, and rightly so, because there is no metric for making such a comparison. But the interpersonal comparison of values, in the economic sense, is feasible, although difficult, even when the values are not being compared in an explicit market. At least this is so where, as in my example of the physician treating someone who is unconscious, there is a background of market transactions that can be referred to for help in estimating the values involved in the involuntary transaction. The problem of determining values when there is no such background—when, for example, we are considering values at a stage of human society before any explicit markets have come into being—is postponed to the next chapter.

58. Conflicts between maximizing the wealth of a nation and that of the world will also be rare, because most trade restrictions hurt both parties to them.

The perils of instrumentalism are also less acute in a system of wealth maximization than in a utilitarian system. In the wealth-maximization approach the only basis for interference with economic and personal liberty is such a serious failure of the market to operate that the wealth of society can be increased by public coercion, which is itself costly. Although economists differ as to when markets fail to operate effectively and how costly it is to rectify those failures, at least these are empirical rather than value questions. Some libertarians worry that the economist will exploit the measurement problems inherent in the use of a hypothetical-market criterion to impose all sorts of duties on people in the name of efficiency. But to repeat, imposing duties is appropriate in the economic view only in the exceptional case where market transaction costs are prohibitive. Professor Epstein has suggested that the wealth-maximization principle would entail forcing a surgeon to travel across India if he were the only physician who could save some individual.[59] I disagree. This is not a case of high transaction costs. If the individual can meet the surgeon's price, the surgeon will travel to treat him; if not, the surgeon will maximize the social wealth by staying home.

As this example suggests, the economic approach is less hospitable than the utilitarian to redistribution. Many utilitarians, it will be recalled, derive an income-equalization goal from a combination of the principle of diminishing marginal utility of money income and the hunch that people's utility functions are pretty much alike (or at least not positively related to wealth). But in a system of wealth maximization, the fact that A has a greater capacity for enjoying a given amount of money than B is no reason for taking money away from B and giving it to A. The transfer might increase the happiness of society but it would not increase its wealth. However, the conclusion that any coerced transfer payment is unproductive must be qualified in two respects. First, some presumably modest efforts to achieve a more

59. Epstein, supra note 14, at 199; but see Landes & Posner, supra note 42, at 126–127.

equal distribution of income and wealth may be economically justifiable, because such a distribution may reduce the incidence and hence costs of crime, both by increasing the opportunity costs of the criminal (that is, his forgone income from legitimate activity) and, less probably, by decreasing the potential revenues from crime.[60] Second, insofar as people are altruistic and hence willing to transfer some of their income to those worse off than they, the public-good aspects of charitable giving (that is, the fact that the alleviation of poverty will benefit a nongiver) may justify public efforts to reduce poverty. Even this ground for redistribution is clearly more limited than the grounds available to the utilitarian: few people are so altruistic that they wish to be leveled down to the point where none are poorer than they.[61]

Quite apart from these (limited) grounds for public redistribution of wealth, it would be a mistake to criticize the wealth-maximization principle as indifferent to distributive considerations; rather, it resolves them automatically. Earlier I showed how a system of rights could be deduced from the goal of wealth maximization itself. Once these rights (to one's body, labor, and so forth) are established, they will be sold, rented, or bartered to yield income to their owners. In general, the wealthier people will be those who have the higher marginal products, whether because they work harder, or are smarter, or for whatever reason. In a system whose goal is to maximize society's wealth, the distribution of wealth that results from paying people in (rough) proportion to their contribution to that goal is not arbitrary. The main point, however, is that the specific distribution of *wealth* is a mere by-product of the distribution of *rights* that is itself derived from the wealth-maximization principle. A just distribution of wealth need not be posited.

60. The economic model of crime that generates these implications is developed in Isaac Ehrlich, "Participation in Illegitimate Activities: An Economic Analysis," in *Essays in the Economics of Crime and Punishment* 68 (Gary S. Becker & William M. Landes eds. 1974). Of course, whether income redistribution is an efficient method of crime control depends on its costs and benefits relative to those of alternative methods, such as more severe or certain punishment.

61. See Arnold Harberger, "Basic Needs versus Distributional Weights in Social Cost Benefit Analysis" (unpublished paper, U. Chi., Dept. Econ.).

Nor is the justice of this reward system undermined when some people live off inherited wealth and make no personal contribution to augmenting the wealth of society. The expenditure of inherited wealth represents simply the deferral of part of the accumulator's consumption beyond his lifetime. To be sure, if heirs work as well as spend their inheritance, the rest of society will be richer. We dislike the idle heir, as we do the lazy man, not because he is a parasite—he isn't—but because he does not produce a surplus for the rest of us to enjoy.

This point suggests an important redistributive aspect of wealth maximization. Because people do not receive their full social product, in effect some (often much) of the wealth they produce is "taxed away" by consumers. In general, the more wealth a person produces, the higher the "tax" he pays (in absolute, not relative, terms).

Let us consider now whether the economic approach, like the utilitarian, yields results violently inconsistent with our moral intuitions (assuming equality of wealth is not one of those intuitions). The "utility monster" has no place in a system of ethics founded on wealth maximization. The fact that I might derive so much gusto from torturing people as to exceed their misery in a felicific weighing would not make me a good man or give me the right to torture people. I would have to *buy* my victims' consent, and these purchases would soon deplete the wealth of all but the wealthiest sadists. Critics of the market system tend to think of the opportunities created by wealth rather than of the constraints a market system places on the fulfillment of individual desire. In a thoroughgoing utilitarian system no budget constraint exists to cramp the style of the utility monster. But in a system of wealth maximization his activities are circumscribed by the limitations of his wealth, and his victims are protected by the rights system, which forces the monster to pay them whatever compensation they demand.

The problem of envy further illustrates the moral differences between utilitarianism and wealth maximization. In a society where envy was widespread and intense, the achievement of maximum happiness might require that government adopt drastic policies of income equalization even though they reduced the total wealth of the society. But in a society devoted to wealth maximization, envy provides no ground for public intervention. There is no basis for arguing that redistribution of wealth from the envied to the envious is necessary to rectify a market failure.

The difference between utilitarian and economic morality, and the source, I believe, of the "monstrousness" of the former, is that the utilitarian, despite his professed concern with *social* welfare, must logically ascribe value to all sorts of asocial traits, such as envy and cruelty, because these are common sources of personal satisfaction and hence of utility. In contrast, lawfully obtained wealth is created by doing things for other people— offering them advantageous trades. The individual may be completely selfish but he cannot, in a well-regulated market economy, promote his self-interest without benefiting others as well as himself. This may be why laziness is a disfavored trait in our society. The lazy person substitutes leisure—which does not produce any consumer surplus for the rest of society to enjoy— for work, which does.[62]

The Kantian may not be convinced that the pursuit of wealth can never lead to monstrousness. He may want to amend Smart's sheep example, discussed earlier, as follows. Let there be 100,000 sheep worth in the aggregate more than any money value that can reasonably be ascribed to a child: is the driver therefore a good man when he decides to sacrifice the child? The economic answer is yes—and it is the answer given all the time in our (and every other) society. Dangerous activities are regularly permitted on the basis of a judgment that the costs of avoiding the danger exceed the costs to the victims. Only the fa-

62. It may not be completely coincidental that nineteenth-century English thought, which in its philosophical aspect was dominated by utilitarianism, in its literary aspect celebrated idleness—escaping from "trade" to the genteel pottering of the country squire's life. These seemingly opposed tendencies are united by a preoccupation with the pursuit of happines, in which productive activity need not figure. The man who leads a contemplative, withdrawn rural life may be happier than the captain of industry, but he will also produce a smaller surplus for the rest of society to enjoy

natic refuses to trade off lives for property, although the difficulty of valuing lives is a legitimate reason for weighing them heavily in the balance when only property values are in the other pan.

As further evidence that a moral system founded on economic principles is congruent with, and can give structure to, our everyday moral intuitions, consider the close correspondence among (1) the ordinary person's concept of carelessness, (2) the tort law's definition of negligence, and (3) the economist's concept of negligence, as elucidated by John Brown and others.[63] Carelessness means creating non-cost-justified—wasteful or wealth-reducing—risks. The ordinary man, as well as the judge applying the negligence rule and the economist explicating it, distinguishes the careless accident from the "unavoidable" accident that could not have been prevented at a cost less than the expected accident cost.

The other form of moral monstrousness, which derives from the sacrifice of individual to aggregate interests, is a less serious problem in the economic than in the utilitarian approach. To be sure, one can imagine a successful nuisance suit against the owner of a brick plant because unforeseen changes in the character of the neighborhood occurring after the plant was built have made it a suboptimal land use. This looks like a case of sacrificing individual to group welfare, but probably the owner of the plant was compensated for the risk of such a suit.[64] And what Dworkin has called "external preferences"[65]—an aversion to a group not based on some palpable intrusion (noise, pollution, or whatever)—will rarely provide grounds for public intervention in a system of wealth maximization. If Nazi Germany wanted to get rid of its Jews, in a system of wealth maximization it would have had to buy them out. There would be no more

---

63. See John Prather Brown, "Towards an Economic Theory of Liability," 2 *J. Legal Stud.* 323 (1973).

64. See discussion of ex ante compensation in Chapter 4.

65. Dworkin, supra note 14, at 232–238, 275–277, and see discussion in Chapter 13.

economic basis for coercion here than there is in the usual (that is, low-transaction-cost) eminent-domain context.[66]

But one must not overlook the possibility of extending the logic of certain nuisance cases to Jews, blacks, and other racial, religious, or ethnic minorities. If a funeral parlor can depress land values, because people living near it are upset to be reminded of death, and on this ground can be condemned as a nuisance, likewise the presence of Jews or blacks in a neighborhood might so upset their neighbors as to depress land values by an amount greater than the members of the minority would be willing to pay to remain in the neighborhood. In these circumstances some form of segregation would be wealth maximizing. The example seems rather far-fetched, however. It is unlikely that ostracism, expulsion, or segregation of a productive group would actually increase a society's wealth.

We saw in the last chapter that Bentham thought the disutility created by the appearance and importunings of beggars justified enslaving them. The economic analysis of begging parallels that of the funeral parlor. To compel the funeral parlor to relocate will impose costs on its customers but confer benefits on third parties, namely people averse to having a funeral parlor in the neighborhood. A ban on begging would impose costs on the beggars and those who derive utility from giving to beggars, while conferring benefits on those who find the beggars' presence offensive. But it is unlikely that the benefits would outweigh the costs. While the costs of relocating the funeral parlor, merely moving it from a residential to a nonresidential area, are likely to be small, beggars cannot be "relocated" to places where they will not offend any passers-by, for the beggar's success depends precisely on being in a place where there are many passers-by. Begging can be "zoned" only by being banned alto-

---

66. See Posner, supra note 13, at 40–44, for an economic argument that the eminent-domain power is unjustifiable in most of the instances in which it is used and should be confined mainly to right-of-way takings—but that in any event compensation should be required.

gether, which would be like banning advertising on the ground that some people who read an advertisement or see a commercial are not potential customers and find the advertising offensive. The costs of an advertising ban would surely exceed the benefits, and the same is probably true of a ban on begging.

Another touchy issue is that of negative population externalities. In a society where the ratio of people to resources was so high that the social cost of additional population would exceed its social product, a case could be made for forcibly limiting the birth rate—depending, of course, on the costs of implementing such a policy by the inherently imperfect instruments of government. Although the economist prefers, on strictly economic grounds, taxing births to prohibiting additional births beyond some fixed quota per family, one can imagine cases in which the optimal tax would be prohibitive for many people. This would be especially likely if the optimum population was smaller than the existing population, in which event merely limiting the birth rate to the replacement level would not be sufficient to maximize the society's wealth.

Another area where wealth maximization may yield results at variance with common moral intuitions involves the economist's relentless insistence on freedom of contract in contexts free from fraud, externality, incapacity, monopoly, or other sources of market failure. Suppose A, perhaps to provide money for his family (but the reason is unimportant), sells himself into slavery to B; or C borrows money from D with a penalty clause that in the event of default D can break C's knees. From a wealth-maximization standpoint there is no economic basis for refusing to enforce either contract unless some element of fraud or duress is present. Nor would the economist think either contract so irrational as to create an irrebutable presumption that it was procured by fraud or duress or is vitiated by insanity or other incapacity.[67] Or. if some white person categorically refuses to associate with blacks because prior experience with some black

---

67. See "Note on Paternalism," in *The Economics of Contract Law* 253 (Anthony T. Kronman & Richard A. Posner eds. 1979).

people has caused him to form an unfavorable impression of them in general, and the costs to him of individualized consideration of blacks exceed the expected benefits, there is no basis in economic theory for criticizing his conduct; as we shall see in Chapter 12, it is wealth maximizing.

To summarize, I have attempted to develop a concept of justice based on wealth maximization as distinguished from utility maximization in the Benthamite sense. The chapter has, however, only introduced a complex subject. I have been more concerned with elucidating the concept of wealth maximization and contrasting it to utilitarianism than with justifying it systematically. So far the case has rested mainly on the somewhat narrow and negative ground that wealth maximization avoids some of the ethical difficulties posed by utility maximization. If one views wealth maximization as constrained utilitarianism (the constraint being that society seeks to maximize the satisfaction only of those whose preferences are backed up by a willingness to pay), one can defend it by whatever arguments are available to defend utilitarianism; but one can do better than that, as the next chapter shows.

4

The Ethical and Political
Basis of Wealth Maximization

The Consensual Basis of Efficiency

Terminological Clarification

Pareto superiority—the principle that one allocation of resources is superior to another if at least one person is better off under the first than under the second and no one is worse off[1] —was thought, by Pareto himself, to solve the traditional problem of practical utilitarianism—that of measuring happiness across persons to determine a policy's effect on total utility.[2] As is well known, the Pareto solution is apparent rather than real.[3] Since it is impossible to measure utility directly, normally the only way of demonstrating the Pareto superiority of a change in the allocation of resources is to show that everyone affected by the change consented to it. If A sells a tomato to B for $2 and no one else is affected by the transaction, we can be sure that the utility to A of $2 is greater than the utility of the tomato to him, and vice versa for B, even though we do not know how much A's and B's utility has been increased by the transaction. But because the crucial assumption in this example, the absence of

1. For a recent and lucid discussion of Pareto ethics by a philosopher, see Jules L. Coleman, "Efficiency, Exchange, and Auction: Philosophic Aspects of the Economic Approach to Law," 68 *Calif. L. Rev.* 221 (1980). Discussions of Pareto criteria by economists are, of course, very numerous. A good recent textbook treatment is Catherine M. Price, *Welfare Economics in Theory and Practice* (1977). See also references in note 12 infra.

2. See Vincent J. Tarascio, *Pareto's Methodological Approach to Economics* 79–82 (1968).

3. For a recent statement see Guido Calabresi & Philip Bobbitt, *Tragic Choices* 83–85 (1978).

third-party effects, is not satisfied with regard to *classes* of transactions, the Pareto-superiority criterion is inapplicable to most policy questions: for example, whether a free market in tomatoes is Pareto superior to a market in which there is a ceiling on the price. The removal of such a ceiling would result in a higher market price, a larger quantity produced, higher rents to owners of land specialized to the growing of tomatoes, a reduction in the output of substitute commodities, and many other effects. It would be impossible to identify, let alone to negotiate for the consent of, everyone affected by the move from a price-controlled to a free tomato market.[4]

I have described the concept of Pareto superiority as an attempt to solve the utilitarian's problem of the interpersonal comparison of utilities. But it is also possible to locate Pareto ethics in the Kantian philosophical tradition. Consent, an ethical criterion congenial to the Kantian emphasis on treating people as ends rather than means, in a word, on autonomy,[5] is the operational basis of Pareto superiority. It is not the theoretical basis, so long as Pareto superiority is viewed as a tool of utilitarian ethics. If the utilitarian could devise a practical utility metric, he could dispense with the consensual or transactional method of determining whether an allocation of resources was Pareto superior—indeed, he could dispense with Pareto superiority itself.

4. The revealed-preference approach (see, e.g., Paul Anthony Samuelson, *Foundations of Economic Analysis* 146–156 [1947]) offers a method, unfortunately not very practical either, of determining whether a change is Pareto superior without requiring consent. Imagine that C is a third party affected by the transaction between A and B. Before the transaction, C's income is X, which he uses to purchase commodities $a \ldots n$. The transaction may affect C's income as well as the prices of $a \ldots n$. However, if after the transaction C's income, now Y, is large enough to enable him to purchase $a \ldots n$ at their current prices, then we may say (without having to consult C) that the transaction between A and B did not make him worse off. But the information necessary to apply this approach is rarely available, in part because some of the commodities that C buys (love, respect, etc.) may not be priced in any market, and his ability to obtain them may be adversely affected by the transaction between A and B.

5. Consent and autonomy are not identical concepts, however. For example, one might think the status of a slave inconsistent with being an autonomous human being, even if the status had been voluntarily assumed to increase the welfare of one's children.

If one considers consent an ethically attractive basis for permitting changes in the allocation of resources on grounds unrelated to the fact that a consensual transaction is likely to increase the happiness of at least the immediate parties, one will be led, in the manner of Nozick and Epstein,[6] to an ethical defense of market transactions that is unrelated to their promotion of efficiency in either the Pareto or the wealth-maximization sense. To be sure, in a market free from third-party effects, forbidding transactions would reduce the wealth of society and at the same time would reduce liberty or autonomy; hence the goals of maximizing wealth and of protecting autonomy would coincide. But the assumption of no third-party effects is stringent, and when it is abandoned, a wedge between consent and wealth maximization appears. Suppose a company decides to close a factory in town A and open a new one in B, and in neither location are there significant pollution, congestion, or other technological externalities from the plant. The move may still lower property values in A and raise them in B, making landowners in A worse off and those in B better off. Therefore the move will not be Pareto superior.[7] In this example the third-party effects are merely "pecuniary" externalities, meaning that they result simply from a change in demand rather than from the consumption of some scarce resource (such as clean air, in the case of pollution, which is a technological externality), or, stated otherwise, that they have no net effect on the wealth of society; but this fact is irrelevant from the Pareto-superiority standpoint. All that matters is that the plant move will make some people worse off—the landowners in A and doubtless others, such as workers who have skills specialized to the plant being closed and positive costs of relocating in B.[8]

6. See Robert Nozick, *Anarchy, State, and Utopia* (1974); Richard A. Epstein, "Causation and Corrective Justice: A Reply to Two Critics," 8 *J. Legal Stud.* 477, 488 (1979).

7. I ignore for the time being the possibility of ex ante compensation of the affected landowners.

8. It is no answer that the externalities could be internalized by the cities' offering tax inducements to the plant's owner. That would not make the plant's moving (or remaining) Pareto superior, because those people who paid the higher taxes necessary to finance the inducements would be worse off than before.

Yet the move must increase the wealth of society, since the plant owners are better off, and the pecuniary externalities cancel out. Accordingly, the wealth-maximization criterion proposed in the last chapter would allow the move. And as Jules Coleman has pointed out,[9] so would the Kaldor-Hicks criterion (sometimes called "Potential Pareto Superiority"), which requires not that no one be made worse off by a change in allocation of resources but only that the increase in value be sufficiently large that the losers can be fully compensated.[10] Since the decrease in land values in A is matched by the increase in B, in principle (that is, ignoring transfer costs) the landowners in A could be compensated, and then no one would be worse off. But in the absence of compensation, not only is full consent to the plant move lacking, total utility may be lower than before the move, because there is no way of knowing whether the utility to the winners of not having to pay compensation exceeds the disutility to the losers of not receiving compensation.[11]

The Kaldor-Hicks criterion is much criticized, even by economists, precisely because it does not ensure that utility will be maximized.[12] Nevertheless, it is incorrect to state that the Pareto criterion is the only "normal professional sense" of the term efficiency.[13] For example, when economists say that monopoly is inefficient, they mean inefficient in the Kaldor-Hicks or wealth-

9. See Coleman, supra note 1, at 239–242.

10. See Nicholas Kaldor, "Welfare Propositions of Economics and Interpersonal Comparisons of Utility," 49 *Econ. J.* 549 (1939); J. R. Hicks, "The Foundations of Welfare Economics," 49 *Econ. J.* 696 (1939); T. de Scitovszky, "A Note on Welfare Propositions in Economics," 9 *Rev. Econ. Stud.* 77 (1941).

11. Suppose the landowners in A incurred a loss of 100 utiles (an arbitrary measure of utility) because of the $1 million fall in property values in A resulting from the move, while the landowners in B obtained only 80 utiles from the $1 million increase in their property values. Then the Kaldor-Hicks criterion would be satisfied, but total utility would be reduced.

12. See, e.g., William J. Baumol, *Economic Theory and Operations Analysis* 378–380 (2d ed. 1965); Amartya Sen, "The Welfare Basis of Real Income Comparisons: A Survey," 17 *J. Econ. Lit.* 1, 24–25 (1979). For a good recent discussion of alternative criteria of economic efficiency, see Jack Hirshleifer, "Evolutionary Models in Economics and Law: Cooperation versus Conflict Strategies" 7–13 (U.C.L.A., Dept. Econ., Working Paper no. 170, March 1980).

13. Ronald M. Dworkin, "Is Wealth a Value?" 9 *J. Legal Stud.* 191, 194 (1980).

maximization, not the Pareto, sense. Figure 2 depicts the standard economic analysis of the welfare effects of monopoly. By reducing output and raising price, the monopolist transfers to himself the part of the consumer surplus[14] labeled B in the figure. Part A remains with the consumers. Consumers lose the part labeled C, but the monopolist does not gain it. C is the traditional welfare loss of monopoly.[15] The loss is clear from a wealth-maximization standpoint: the sum of consumer and producer surplus is less under monopoly than under competition (A + B compared to A + B + C). Thus a move from monopoly to competition would satisfy the Kaldor-Hicks or wealth-maximization criterion for a gain in efficiency. But it would not satisfy the criterion of Pareto superiority, because the monopolist would be worse off. And it would not be utility maximizing unless the utility of B + C to consumers exceeded the utility of B to the monopolist. Yet most economists would not hesitate to pronounce monopoly inefficient if it has the effects depicted in Figure 2. Indeed, most economists say Pareto but use Kaldor-Hicks in making welfare judgments.

Wealth Maximization and the Principle of Consent

The use of the word "efficiency" in the Kaldor-Hicks sense can be defended simply as an analytical convenience that enables issues of allocation to be discussed separately from issues of distribution. Kaldor himself defended it in this way, and he also offered an ethical argument that in retrospect seems naive. He argued that the government could always transform a wealth increase into a Pareto improvement by compensating the losers out of the gains to the winners. Whether or not it would do so was "a political question on which the economist, *qua* economist, could hardly pronounce an opinion."[16] Kaldor seems to have been suggesting that if the losers from some policy deserve compensation, the government will award it to them, and hence that a wealth increase will be transformed into

14. See note 57 in Chapter 3, supra.
15. See, e.g., F.M. Scherer, *Industrial Market Structure and Economic Performance* 17–18 (2d ed. 1980).
16. Kaldor, supra note 10, at 550.

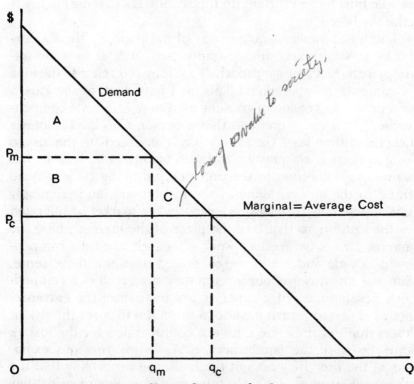

Figure 2. The welfare effects of monopoly. Q = output; q_m = monopoly output; q_c = competitive output; P_m = monopoly price; P_c = competitive price. A = part of consumer surplus kept by consumers; B = part of consumer surplus appropriated by the monopolist; C = welfare loss of monopoly.

a Pareto improvement unless there is some independent and compelling ethical reason for not following the Pareto principle. But this is a satisfactory approach only if it is assumed that the government makes decisions on ethical grounds. If instead government is viewed as an arena in which interest groups struggle for advantage with no regard for ethical considerations,[17] it cannot be presumed that the failure to compensate

17. See the section of this chapter, "Implications for the Positive Economic Analysis of Law," infra.

people hurt by an efficient (in the Kaldor-Hicks sense) policy is ethically based.

There is, however, another way of harmonizing the Kaldor-Hicks or wealth-maximization approach, at least in some settings, with the Pareto approach. That is by reference to the idea of consent, the operational basis, as I have said, of the Pareto criterion. The version of consent used here is ex ante compensation.[18] It is my contention that a person who buys a lottery ticket and then loses the lottery has "consented" to the loss so long as there is no question of fraud or duress; at least he has waived any objection to the outcome, assuming there was no fraud in the lottery. Many of the involuntary, and seemingly uncompensated, losses experienced in the market or tolerated by the institutions that take the place of the market where the market cannot be made to work effectively are fully compensated ex ante and hence are consented to in the above sense. Suppose an entrepreneur loses money as a result of a competitor's development of a superior product: since the entrepreneur's expected return includes a premium to cover the risk of losses due to competition, he was compensated for the loss ex ante. So were the landowners in A, in my previous example, at the time they bought the land: the probability that the plant would move was discounted in the purchase price they paid.[19]

The concept of ex ante compensation provides an answer to the argument that the wealth-maximization criterion, applied

18. The argument that follows is sketched in Richard A. Posner, "Epstein's Tort Theory: A Critique," 8 *J. Legal Stud.* 457, 460, 464 (1979). A similar argument is made independently in Frank I. Michelman, "Constitutions, Statutes, and the Theory of Efficient Adjudication," 9 *J. Legal Stud.* 431, 438–440 (1980). Both arguments resemble a position taken by many welfare economists: that the Kaldor-Hicks criterion for deciding whether to undertake a public project satisfies the Pareto-superiority criterion provided there is a sufficient probability that an individual will benefit in the long run from such projects, though he may be a loser from a particular one. See A. Mitchell Polinsky, "Probabilistic Compensation Criteria," 86 *Q. J. Econ.* 407 (1972), and references cited there.

19. A parallel but more difficult case, because of possible information costs, is that of the worker who loses his job (and incurs positive relocation costs) when the demand for his services collapses as a result of the development of a superior substitute for the product.

unflinchingly in market settings such as my plant-relocation example, would violate the principle of consent. A more difficult question is raised by the attempt to similarly base nonmarket but arguably wealth-maximizing institutions, such as the negligence system of automobile accident liability, on the principle. If a driver is injured by another driver in an accident in which neither was at fault, in what sense has the injured driver consented, or waived any objection, to not being compensated for his injury, which is the result under the negligence system?

To answer this question, we must consider the effect on the costs of driving of insisting on ex post compensation, as under a system of strict liability. By hypothesis the costs would be higher. Otherwise the negligence system would not be wealth-maximizing, and the issue of justifying wealth maximization by reference to the principle of consent would not arise. Would drivers be willing to incur higher costs in order to preserve the principle of ex post compensation? Presumably not. Any driver who wanted to be assured of compensation in the event of an accident, regardless of whether the injurer was at fault, need only buy first-party, or accident, insurance—by hypothesis at lower cost than he could obtain compensation ex post through a system of strict liability.

This point can be most easily grasped by imagining that everyone involved in traffic accidents is identical—is the same age, drives the same amount, and so forth. In these circumstances everyone will pay the same rates for liability and accident insurance. The difference between negligence and strict liability will be that under negligence, liability-insurance rates will be lower and accident-insurance rates higher because fewer accidents will give rise to liability, while under strict liability the reverse will be true. If, as I am assuming, negligence is the more efficient system, the *sum* of the liability and accident insurance premiums will be lower under negligence,[20] and everyone will prefer this.

20. This assumes that all accident costs are reflected in insurance rates. Some accident-prevention costs (e.g., the value of time lost in driving more slowly) are not. Presumably these costs would also be higher under strict liability if that is the less efficient liability rule.

I have used the example of negligence versus strict liability because it has been used to argue that the wealth-maximization approach is inconsistent with an approach based on notions of personal autonomy.[21] If a requirement of consent in the sense in which I am using the term is deemed an adequate safeguard of the autonomy interest, this argument must fail unless it is shown that a strict liability system would be cheaper than a negligence system.

My analysis may be questioned on the ground that the consent on which I am prepared, in principle at least, to justify institutions such as the negligence system is fictitious because it is not express.[22] But this objection founders precisely on the unavailability of a practical method for eliciting express consent, not so much to individual market transactions—though even there, as I have noted, the consent of third parties affected by those transactions often cannot feasibly be elicited—as to *institutions,* such as the negligence system or indeed the market itself. If there is no reliable mechanism for eliciting express consent, it follows not that we must abandon the principle of consent but that we should be satisfied with implied (or more precisely, perhaps, hypothetical) consent where it exists. Its existence can be ascertained by asking the hypothetical question whether, if transaction costs were zero, the affected parties would agree to the institution. The procedure resembles a judge's imputing the intent of parties to a contract that fails to provide expressly for some contingency.[23] Although the task of imputation is easier in the contract case, that case is still relevant in showing that implicit consent can be meaningful. The absence of an underlying contract affects one's confidence in making an inference of implicit consent but not the propriety of drawing such inferences.

To be sure, "A proposal is not legislation simply because all

---

21. See Richard A. Epstein, "A Theory of Strict Liability," 2 *J. Legal Stud.* 151 (1973).

22. I do not regard the political survival of negligence for automobile accidents as evidence of such consent.

23. Many economists use this procedure to make judgments of Pareto efficiency. For a recent example see Steven Shavell, "Accidents, Liability, and Insurance" 5–7 (Harv. Inst. Econ. Res., Disc. Paper no. 685, June 1979; forthcoming in *Am. Econ. Rev.*).

the members of the legislature are in favor of it."[24] But that is because there is a mechanism by which legislators can express actual consent. Sometimes the mechanism is inoperative, as when a question arises as to the scope or meaning of a past legislative enactment, and then courts are allowed to infer the legislative intent. This is an example of implicit, or hypothetical, but still meaningful consent.

Another objection to using consent to justify institutions that maximize wealth is that consent is rarely unanimous. Contrary to my earlier assumption, people are not identical ex ante. Why should the fact of higher driving costs (I am assuming for the sake of argument) under a system of strict liability than under a negligence system persuade people who do not drive to accept negligence? To the extent that such people could actually be identified, one might grant them the protection of a strict liability system if one placed a great value on autonomy[25] and if one could settle the threshold question of whose autonomy prevails in a case of conflict—a question I address below. But most people who do not drive do not stay at home either. They use other modes of transportation—taxis or buses or subways (or perhaps their spouses drive them)—whose costs would by assumption be higher under a system of strict liability; and those costs, or a large fraction of them at least, would be borne by the users. Even the nondrivers might therefore consent to a negligence system for transport accidents if it were cheaper than a system of strict liability.[26] No institution, of course, will command even the implicit or hypothetical support of everyone, but only a fanatic would insist that unanimity be required to legitimize a social institution such as the negligence system.

Professor Coleman argues that I am using the word "consent" in a linguistically eccentric way.[27] A person may consent to an

24. Epstein, supra note 6, at 496.

25. An approach suggested in George P. Fletcher, "Fairness and Utility in Tort Theory," 85 *Harv. L. Rev.* 537 (1972).

26. This leaves open the possibility of further subdividing the transport industry for liability purposes and of having one rule for buses, another for autos, etc.

27. See Jules L. Coleman, "Efficiency, Utility and Wealth Maximization," 8 *Hofstra L. Rev.* 509, 531–540 (1980).

institution under which he has no right to be compensated in the event of a particular kind of injury, but if the injury occurs he does not "consent" to the injury. But go back to the lottery example with which I began. If I freely enter a fair lottery and lose, my claim of "unfairness" at losing will fall on deaf ears. Likewise if I agree to build a house for a fixed price and to assume the risk that my labor and materials costs will rise during the period of the contract, I cannot complain, if those costs do rise, that it is "unfair" to hold me to the contract. In both cases I have freely agreed to a course of action carrying with it certain risks, the risks are compensated, and the materializing of those risks is thus within the scope of the agreement. I have waived any objection to the outcome. The idea of consent seems to me broad enough to embrace the concept of waiver. But no matter: so long as my usage of "consent" is understood, even if it is unorthodox, there should be no confusion.

My approach may be thought to raise the following question: why should not society's ruling principle be the protection and enhancement of personal autonomy, the value that underlies the principle of consent, rather than the maximization of wealth? The answer is that just as literal adherence to the Pareto-superiority criterion would be paralyzing, so the ethics of personal autonomy, interpreted and applied without regard for the consequences for human welfare, would, as noted in the last chapter and as conceded by Kant's followers in contemporary legal thought,[28] yield a great deal of misery. Wealth maximization as an ethical norm gives weight both to utility, though less heavily than utilitarianism does, and to consent, though perhaps less heavily than Kant himself would have done.

Another objection to using autonomy directly as an ethical norm, an objection well illustrated by the choice between strict liability and negligence, is that it requires an arbitrary initial assignment of rights. I assumed that the victim of an accident had some kind of moral claim to compensation (whether ex post or ex ante) even though the injurer was not at fault. But one could

28. See Charles Fried, *Right and Wrong* 10 (1978); Richard A. Epstein, "Nuisance Law: Corrective Justice and Its Utilitarian Constraints," 8 *J. Legal Stud.* 49, 75, 79 (1979).

equally well assume that people have a right not to be hampered in their activities by being made liable for accidents that they could not have prevented at reasonable cost. No liability denies the autonomy of the victim; strict liability, the autonomy of the injurer. To differentiate the two *when neither is at fault* is no simple task.[29]

Comparison to Rawls's Approach

My discussion of the choice between negligence and strict liability systems that the individual is assumed to make before an accident occurs—a choice under uncertainty from which is inferred consent to a social institution—may seem derivative of Rawls's analysis of justice.[30] In fact, both Rawls's and my analyses have common roots. The "original position" approach was pioneered by economists seeking to establish the consensual foundations of utility maximization in a fashion somewhat similar to my approach here.[31] As Kenneth Arrow has explained, they

> start[ed] from the position . . . that choice under risky conditions can be described as the maximization of expected utility. In the original position, each individual may with equal probability be any member of the society. If there are n members of the society and if the ith member will have utility u_i, under some given allocation decision, then the value of that allocation to any individual is $\Sigma u_i(1/n)$, since $1/n$ is the probability of being individual i. Thus, in choosing among alternative allocations of goods each individual in the original position will want to maximize this expectation, or, what is the same thing for a given population, maximize the sum of utilities.[32]

29. For the divergent views of Kantian legal philosophers on this question see note 22 in Chapter 3. And cf. Jules L. Coleman, "The Morality of Strict Tort Liability," 18 *Wm. & Mary L. Rev.* 259, 284–285 (1976).

30. See John Rawls, *A Theory of Justice* (1971).

31. See Kenneth J. Arrow, "Some Ordinalist-Utilitarian Notes on Rawls's Theory of Justice," 70 *J. Philos.* 245, 250 (1973).

32. *Id.*

The twist that Rawls gave to choice in the original position was to argue that people would choose to maximize the utility of the worst outcomes in the distribution rather than expected utility. Again in the words of Arrow:

> It has, however, long been remarked that the maximin theory has some implications that seem hardly acceptable. It implies that any benefit, no matter how small, to the worst-off member of society, will outweigh any loss to a better-off individual, provided it does not reduce the second below the level of the first. Thus, there can easily exist medical procedures which serve to keep people barely alive but with little satisfaction and which are yet so expensive as to reduce the rest of the population to poverty. A maximin principle would apparently imply that such procedures be adopted.[33]

If, with Arrow, one finds expected utility a more plausible maximand than maximin is, one is driven to the startling conclusion that utilitarianism has a firmer basis in the principle of consent than Rawls's "justice as fairness"! But any theory of consent based on choice in the original position is unsatisfactory, not only because of the well-known difficulties of describing the preference functions of people in that position but also because the original-position approach opens the door to the claims of the nonproductive. In the original position, no one knows whether he has productive capabilities, so choices made in that position will reflect some probability that the individual making the choice will turn out to be an unproductive member of society—perhaps one of Nozick's "utility monsters." The original-position approach thus obscures the important moral distinction between capacity to enjoy and capacity to produce for others. I prefer therefore to imagine actual people, deploying actual endowments of skill and energy and character, making choices under uncertainty. This is choice under conditions of

33. *Id.* at 251.

natural ignorance rather than under the artificial ignorance of the original position.

Limitations of Wealth Maximization as an Ethical Norm Founded on Consent

The argument that consent can supply an ethical justification for social institutions that maximize wealth requires qualification in two respects.

First, where the distributive impact of a wealth-maximizing policy is substantial and nonrandom, it is difficult to elicit or impute broad consent without actual compensation. I mentioned this possibility in connection with the choice between negligence and strict liability to govern traffic accidents, but it seemed unimportant there. Suppose, however, the issue were whether to substitute a proportionate for a progressive income tax. The substitution would increase the wealth of society if the increase in output (counting both work and leisure as output) by upper-bracket taxpayers, whose marginal tax rate would be lowered, exceeded the reduction in output caused by raising the marginal tax rate of lower-bracket taxpayers. But unless the net increase in output was sufficiently great to increase the after-tax incomes even of those taxpayers who would be paying higher taxes—and let us assume it was not—the lower-bracket taxpayers could hardly be assumed to consent to the tax change, even though it would be wealth maximizing.

I was first stimulated to investigate the ethical foundations of wealth maximization by the suggestion that it was too unappealing a value to ascribe to common law judges.[34] Yet it is precisely in the context of common law adjudication, as contrasted with the redistributive statutory domain illustrated by my tax example, that the consensual basis of wealth maximization is most plausible. The rules that govern the acquisition and transfer of property rights, the making and enforcement of contracts, and liability for accidents and for the kinds of naked aggression that

---

34. For a recent statement of this view see Frank I. Michelman, "A Comment on 'Some Uses and Abuses of Economics in Law,'" 46 *U. Chi. L. Rev.* 307 (1979).

were made crimes at common law are supported by a broad consensus and distribute their benefits very widely. For example, it is naive to think that refusing to enforce the leases poor people sign with richer landlords would make the poor better off. Landlords would charge higher rentals because of the greater risk of loss or would shift their property into alternative uses, with the result that the housing supply available to the poor would be smaller and the price higher.[35] If from this example we generalize that the choice among common law rules usually does not have systematic distributive consequences, then it is reasonable to suppose that there is (or would be, if it paid people to inform themselves in these matters) general consent to those common law rules that maximize wealth. If so, a common law judge guided by the wealth-maximization criterion will be promoting personal autonomy at the same time.

Second, the initial assignment of property rights may seem a fertile area for generating conflicts between wealth maximization and consent. What if A's labor is worth more to B than to A? Then it would be efficient to make A the slave of B but this result would hardly comport with the principle of consent. I suggested in the last chapter that such cases are rare, but I would hesitate to say that they are nonexistent. One can imagine situations in which the costs of physical coercion were lower than the costs of administering employment or other contracts; in such situations slavery might be wealth maximizing, but it presumably would not be consented to.[36] There are modern examples, such as parental (and public) authority over children and military conscription. We do not use the term slavery to describe these examples, where it can be argued that efficiency in the sense of wealth maximization is allowed to override notions of autonomy. We reserve the term for those palpably exploitative forms of involuntary servitude that rarely can be justified on efficiency grounds. These distinctions suggest that efficiency

35. See Neil K. Komesar, "Return to Slumville: A Critique of the Ackerman Analysis of Housing Code Enforcement and the Poor," 82 *Yale L. J.* 1175 (1973).

36. On the costs of organizing economic activity through contract in primitive societies see Chapter 6.

as I have defined the term retains considerable moral force even when it is in conflict with notions of autonomy and consent.

Implications for the Positive Economic Analysis of Law

Why the Common Law Is Efficient

Scholars like myself who have argued that the common law is best explained as an effort, however inarticulate, to promote efficiency have lacked a good reason why this should be so. We may seem to be naive adherents of the outmoded "public interest" theory of the state.[37] This is the theory that the state operates, albeit imperfectly, to promote widely shared social goals—of which efficiency as I have defined it is one (we need not worry how important a one). The state promotes efficiency through providing or arranging for the provision of "public goods," goods that provide benefits not limited to those who pay for them and hence that are produced in suboptimal amounts by private markets. One of these public goods is a legal system that corrects sources of market failure such as externalities.

The public interest theory of the state is under severe attack from the proponents of the "interest group" or, more narrowly, "producer protection" theory of the governmental process,[38] which assigns primacy to redistribution as the object of public policy. The emphasis on redistribution results from treating government action as a commodity that is allocated in accordance with the forces of demand and supply. The characteristics that enable an industry or group to overcome free-rider problems and thereby outbid rival claimants for government protection and largesse have been studied, and the conclusion has been reached that compact groups generally outbid diffuse ones for government favor.

37. For a review of the rival theories of government discussed in this part of the chapter see Richard A. Posner, "Theories of Economic Regulation," 5 *Bell J. Econ. & Mgmt. Sci.* 335 (1974).

38. The seminal paper in the economic theory of interest group politics (as distinct from the earlier political science theory) is George J. Stigler, "The Theory of Economic Regulation," 2 *Bell J. Econ. & Mgmt. Sci.* 3 (1971).

The interest group theory is an economic theory because it links government action to utility maximization by the people seeking such action. The public interest theory is a description rather than a theory because it does not show how utility maximizing by individuals results in government action that promotes the interest of such diffuse groups as the "public," consumers, taxpayers, or some other broad category. And the implication of the interest group theory that diffuse groups are likely to lose out in competition with more compact groups for government protection undermines the plausibility of the public interest theory even as description.

However, common law doctrines that satisfy the Pareto-superiority criterion in the form of the "principle of consent" (no common law doctrine would satisfy a literal interpretation of the Pareto criterion) are plausible candidates for survival even in a political system otherwise devoted to redistributive activities. A rule or institution that satisfies the principle of consent cannot readily be altered, at least by the tools (damages, injunctions) available to common law judges, in a way that will redistribute wealth toward some politically effective interest group. This is particularly clear in cases, such as the landlord-tenant case discussed earlier, where the parties to litigation have a pre-existing voluntary relationship. Then all the court is doing is altering one term of a contract, and the parties can make offsetting changes in the remaining terms.[39] Even if the dispute does not arise from a contract, the parties may be interdependent in a way that largely cancels any wealth effects from a change in the rule of liability. For example, in the nineteenth century, farmers were major customers of railroads, so it would not have made much sense then to attempt to transfer wealth from railroads to farmers or vice versa simply by broadening or narrow-

---

39. It is noteworthy that Professor Ackerman, a leading advocate of using tort law to force landlords to improve the quality of housing, couples this with a proposal for a public subsidy to prevent tort liability from leading to a reduction in the supply of housing for the poor. See Bruce Ackerman, "Regulating Slum Housing Markets on Behalf of the Poor: Of Housing Codes, Housing Subsidies and Income Redistribution Policy," 80 *Yale L. J.* 1093 (1971).

ing the liability of railroads for damage to crops growing along railroad rights of way.

The potential for using the common law to redistribute wealth systematically is not great even in a case where there is no prior dealing among the parties to the redistribution. For example, it is hard to see how moving from a negligence system of automobile accident liability to a system of strict liability would increase the wealth of a compact, readily identifiable, and easily organizable group in the society. No one knows in advance whether he will be an accident victim. The principal effect of the move would simply be to reduce most people's wealth a little (always assuming that strict liability would indeed be less efficient than negligence in that setting).

This analysis does not deny the importance of interest groups in shaping public policy. The point is rather that by supporting the efficiency norm in areas regulated by common law methods, they are likely to promote their self-interest. By doing so they increase the wealth of the society, of which they will get a share; no alternative norm would yield them a larger share. To be sure, none of them will devote substantial resources to promoting the efficiency of the common law, because the benefits that each group derives will be small and because each will be tempted to take a free ride on the others. But for the efficiency norm to survive, few resources have to be devoted to promoting it; its distributive neutrality operates to reduce potential opposition as well as support.

This analysis implicitly treats judges simply as agents of the state and hence does not confront the difficulties that judicial independence from political control poses for any self-interest theory of judicial behavior. That is a problem in the economics of agency. The point of the present analysis is to relate the efficiency theory of the common law to the redistributive or interest group theory of the state, albeit some of the links in the chain are obscure. Also, the theory implies that where legislatures legislate within the area of common law regulation—legislate, that is, with respect to rights and remedies in torts, contracts, property, and related fields—they too will try to promote efficiency. It is not the nature of the regulating institution but the subjects and methods of regulation that determine whether the government will promote efficiency or redistribute wealth.[40]

The relationship of this analysis to my earlier ethical analysis should be clear. The principle of consent that I extracted from the Pareto-superiority criterion is another name for absence of systematic distributive effects. The probabilistic compensation discussed in connection with the negligence system of automobile accident liability allowed me to ignore ex post distributive effects in evaluating that system. By the same token, no group can hope to benefit ex ante from a change in the system (assuming the system is the most efficient one possible), and those who lose out ex post, being few and scattered, are not an effective interest group.

Is the Common Law Efficient or Utilitarian?

Can one distinguish empirically between the efficiency theory of the common law and the theory that in the heyday of the common law the judges subscribed to the dominant ideology, which was utilitarianism? In the last chapter I showed that some influential figures in the legal scholarship of that period described the common law as utilitarian. It is unlikely that they meant utilitarian in contrast to economic. I know of no instances where utilitarian deviated from economic teaching and the common law followed the utilitarian approach. For example, income equality, protection of animals, and prohibition of begging are all policies advocated by Bentham, the most thoroughgoing utilitarian, yet there are no traces of these policies in the common law. Bentham also believed in imposing a legal duty to be a "good Samaritan," but the common law, perhaps on economic grounds, rejected such a duty.[41] Nor is there any trace in

---

40. In this analysis, the features of the judicial process that I have argued elsewhere (e.g., Richard A. Posner, *Economic Analysis of Law* 404–405 [2d ed. 1977]) tend to suppress distributive considerations are thus viewed as effects rather than as causes of the judicial emphasis on efficiency.

41. Compare Jeremy Bentham, *Theory of Legislation* 189–190 (R. Hildreth ed. 1894), with William M. Landes & Richard A. Posner, "Salvors, Finders, Good Samaritans, and Other Rescuers: An Economic Study of Law and Altruism," 7 *J. Legal Stud.* 83, 119–127 (1978).

the common law of sympathy for the thief, rapist, or any other criminal who seeks to defend his crime on the ground that he derived more pleasure from the act than his victim suffered pain. Utilitarianism is a sufficiently flexible philosophy to accommodate arguments that allowing such a defense would not really maximize happiness in the long run, but this is just to say that enlightened utilitarianism incorporates the sorts of constraints that make wealth maximization an attractive ethical principle.

Dworkin's Critique of Wealth Maximization

My views on wealth maximization have been criticized by a number of philosophers and philosophically minded lawyers.[42] One of these critics, Ronald Dworkin, seems to me fairly representative, and I shall address here his most important criticisms.

First Dworkin argues that wealth is not "a component of social value"—not the only component and not even "one component of social value among others."[43] This may seem a bold challenge to conventional wisdom, which holds that wealth is *a*

---

42. See, e.g., Jules Coleman, supra note 27; Ronald M. Dworkin, "Is Wealth a Value?" 9 *J. Legal Stud.* 191 (1980); Anthony T. Kronman, "Wealth Maximization as a Normative Principle," 9 *J. Legal Stud.* 227 (1980); Ernest J. Weinrib, "Utilitarianism, Economics, and Legal Theory," 30 *U. Toronto L. J.* 307 (1980); Joseph M. Steiner, "Economics, Morality, and the Law of Torts," 26 *U. Toronto L. J.* 227, 235–239 (1976).

I should like to comment briefly on what I take to be the central, or at least the most powerful, criticisms of Professors Weinrib and Steiner. Weinrib argues that the concept of the hypothetical market, which plays such a large role in the theory of wealth maximization, is critically different from that of an actual market in that in an actual market both parties to a transaction are made better off by the transaction, and this element of compensation is absent in a hypothetical market transaction (e.g., A runs down B and injures him, and is absolved from liability because the cost of precautions to A exceeded the expected accident costs of his conduct). Weinrib's objection is obviated if my argument from ex ante compensation is accepted. Moreover, he fails to note that even actual market transactions frequently have a noncompensatory element, in that adverse effects of such transactions on nonparties are not compensated. Professor Steiner objects that the hypothetical-market approach violates the economist's strictures against interpersonal comparisons of utility, but this point is answered in the last chapter, where I point out that interpersonal comparisons of wealth do not pose the acute measurement problems that have led economists to forswear interpersonal comparisons of utility.

43. Dworkin, supra note 42, at 195.

value, if not the only or the most important value. But his argument is actually a play on words, for Dworkin defines a component of social value as "something worth having for its own sake,"[44] and no one values wealth for its own sake. To argue that wealth is not a social value because it is not an end in itself is, however, to adopt an eccentric definition of "social value." If I say, "Loyalty is a social value because it facilitates the organization of productive activity," I am not misusing the English language by attaching the term "social value" to a mediate rather than an ultimate goal.

Dworkin rests his argument on an example that conceals the instrumental character of wealth maximization. The example is the following. Derek has a book that he would sell for $2 and that Amartya would pay $3 to have. An omniscient tyrant short-circuits the market system and gives the book to Amartya without compensating Derek. As Dworkin argues, it is difficult to see how society is better off as a result. But suppose we change the figures. Let the book be worth $3,000 to Amartya and $2 to Derek. Then the transfer probably will increase the amount of happiness in society, even if Derek is not compensated. This is especially likely if Derek might receive one of these delicious windfalls sometime. Of course, in arguing along these lines I am hitching wealth maximization to utility maximization, but I am willing to do this because, as stressed in the last chapter, happiness is one of the ultimate goods to which wealth maximization is conducive. The relationship between wealth and utility is obscured by the particular numbers Dworkin uses in his example.

Another feature of the Amartya-Derek example requires comment: the absence of a plausible reason for taking the transaction away from the market and putting it into the hands of a "tyrant." Suppose we change the example as follows. Derek owns a home, and Amartya owns an airline. An airport is built near Derek's home, and Amartya's airline produces noise that reduces the value of the home by $2,000. Derek sues the airline, alleging a nuisance. The evidence developed at trial shows that

44. *Id.*

it would cost the airline $3,000 to eliminate the noise and thereby restore Derek's home to its previous value; on these facts the court holds that there is no nuisance. This example is analytically the same as Dworkin's, but it illustrates more realistically than his how a system of wealth maximization would operate in a common law setting, and it makes less plausible his argument that wealth is not a "component of social value" in a reasonable sense of this expression.

Dworkin discerns a problem of circularity in my attempt to derive a system of rights from a goal of maximizing wealth. It is the familiar problem of "wealth effects," to which I referred briefly in the last chapter. In asserting that a rise in the price of some good will lead to a fall in the quantity demanded of the good, the economist normally ignores the effect of the price change on incomes even though the income effect may feed back into price. The rise in price will reduce the incomes of consumers, and a consumer's demands may change with a change in his income. Since the demand for some goods may actually rise as incomes fall (potatoes in Ireland is the conventional example), an increase in the price of a good could, as a result of the feedback effect mentioned above, result in an increase in the demand for the good, rather than, as normally assumed, a decrease. Empirical study has failed to discover a good that behaves in this way, but it is theoretically possible that there is one. Similarly, it is theoretically possible that the initial assignment of a good might determine its ultimate assignment, even if transaction costs were zero, especially where the good was a very large part of the individual's wealth—like a glass of water in the desert.[45] This has long been known, but again no one has come up with a realistic example.

Dworkin offers an example.[46] Agatha is assumed to have a tal-

45. In the desert setting as usually described, the glass of water is the only thing of value; someone who lacks it has zero wealth and therefore cannot buy it from someone who has it. This is an extreme example of how the distribution of wealth can affect resource use, but it is parallel to the example of a price increase that affects resource use via its effect on incomes and, through that effect, on consumer demands.

46. Dworkin states that the example was offered for another purpose; see Dworkin, supra note 42, at 224, but see *id*. at 208–209.

ent for writing brilliant detective stories but a preference for some less remunerative activity (call it gardening). If Sir George, a publisher, owns her labor, he will compel her to write detective stories, and she will be able to buy her freedom only by promising to continue writing detective stories, because that is the only activity in which she could hope to earn a sum large enough to induce Sir George to free her. If he is initially assigned the right to her labor, therefore, she will remain a slave —whether to him or to whomever she borrows money from to buy her freedom. If she is initially assigned the right to her labor, however, she will not write detective stories, or not so many, and Sir George will not be able to buy the right to her labor. Thus it seems that economic analysis does not yield a determinate initial assignment of rights.

But this ignores the fact that if Agatha were free she almost certainly *could*—not would—write more detective stories than she would write if she were a slave. People have an incentive to work harder when they work for themselves than when they work for other people. As a slave, Agatha has no incentive to work hard, because the fruits of her labor inure to Sir George rather than to her. He will try to prevent her from shirking, but this will be difficult to do; it is especially difficult to establish and enforce output norms for such a nonroutine activity as writing stories. Suppose the value of her output to Sir George is $1 million, but if she were free she could produce detective stories worth $1.2 million in the same amount of time. Then presumably she could produce detective stories worth $1 million in less time and have time left over for gardening. If so, she could and would buy her freedom. Having done so, she will be worse off than if she had been free from the outset (she owes $1 million, plus interest, to whoever financed the purchase of her freedom). But that is not the point. The point is that wealth maximization leads to a determinate solution in the Agatha–Sir George case once it is assumed that she could produce more if she were free than if she were a slave. Since she would retain her freedom if given it from the first and would purchase it if she began as Sir George's slave, the initial assignment does not determine the final assignment. Transaction costs are therefore minimized by making her free in the first place.[47]

A problem of indeterminacy may arise, however, if rights are being assigned when a society first comes into existence. In the Agatha–Sir George example it was easy to obtain a determinate rights assignment, because only one good in society was un-owned—Agatha's labor. With every other good having a market or shadow price, one could compute, in principle at least, the effects on aggregate wealth of assigning Agatha's labor to herself or to Sir George. But suppose no goods are yet owned: land, labor, sexual access—everything is up for grabs. How can each good be assigned to its most valuable use when no values—no market or shadow prices—exist? This is the problem of wealth effects with a vengeance. All rights have yet to be assigned; assignment of rights on so massive a scale is bound to affect prices; and prices in turn will affect the question of whom the rights should be assigned to.

The problem is exaggerated in two respects. First, we need not be troubled in any case where the particular issue of policy that we are concerned with is marginal to the society as a whole. Even moving from negligence to strict liability for automobile accidents would not have so large an effect on prices as to prevent a comparison of the total wealth of society before and after the change. Second, the assignment of rights at the outset of social development is unlikely to determine the allocation of resources many generations later. Suppose at the beginning one man owned all the wealth in a society. To exploit that wealth, he would have to share it with other people—he would have to pay them to work for him. His remaining wealth would be divided among his children or other heirs at his death. Thus, over time, the goods and services produced and consumed in the society would be determined not by his preferences but by those of his employees and heirs. Probably after several generations most prices in this society, both market and shadow prices, would be

---

47. Dworkin states "that a theory that makes the moral value of slavery depend on transaction costs is grotesque." *Id.* at 211. He does not elaborate.

similar to those in societies in which the initial distribution of wealth was more equal. If so, it means the initial distribution of wealth will eventually cease to have an important effect on the society's aggregate wealth. In that event we can ask the question: what initial assignments of rights would most quickly move the society to its eventual wealth level? The answer suggested in the last chapter is that assigning labor rights to their "natural" owners and splitting up land into the smallest parcels in which the available economies of scale can be exploited will minimize transaction costs and thus move the society more rapidly to the level it would eventually reach anyway, even if all rights were initially assigned to one man.[48]

Dworkin makes the separate argument that wealth maximization is unlikely to "produce more total welfare-for-others activity than other, more compromising, economic and political structures."[49] Granted, that if the social objective is to maximize the transfer of wealth from the more to the less productive, setting a proximate goal of wealth maximization may be the wrong approach (although the amount of wealth transferred is in general positively related to the wealth of a society). But I do not argue that wealth maximization would *maximize* transfers (or protection of rights, or happiness), only that it would give us some of all of these things. Dworkin thinks we could get more of all three by aiming directly at each. But because there is no common currency in which to compare happiness, sharing, and protection of rights, it is unclear how to make the necessary trade-offs among these things in the design of a social system. Wealth maximization makes the trade-offs automatically. If there is a better approach, it is not obvious and Dworkin has not described it.

Dworkin states that production for others "has no inherent moral value if [the producer] acts with the intention of benefiting only himself."[50] He reaches this conclusion as a matter of

48. An implication of this analysis is that it is possible to speak of efficient rights assignments in premodern, premonetary societies, an issue considered further in Chapter 6.

49. Dworkin, supra note 42, at 211.

50. *Id.* at 211–212.

definition: moral value consists solely "in the will or intentions of the actor."[51] That is a narrow definition. If the effect of encouraging wealth maximization is to yoke selfish desires—which in most people are their strongest desires—to the service of other people, and to do so without coercion, these features of wealth maximization should commend it to the altruistic designer of a social system.

Dworkin argues that judges could promote utility more effectively by aiming directly at its maximization than by trying to maximize wealth as a proxy for it. He therefore invites the (utilitarian) judge to consider, for example, that although "the community will pay more for candy than for medical care lost through the noise of a candy machine, . . . the candy will be bad for its health and therefore its long-term utility."[52] He thinks a utility-maximizing judge faced with a decision to either "protect the workers of an ailing and possibly noncompetitive industry or hasten their unemployment by structuring rights in favor of a developing new industry" might choose the former.[53] Logically, Dworkin's utilitarian judge should also consider, in deciding a criminal case, whether the criminal derived more pleasure from the criminal act than the victim suffered pain. But even an extreme utilitarian would hesitate to turn judges loose from all moorings in ascertainable fact by inviting them to consider happiness in the manner suggested by Dworkin. Wealth maximization is, to be sure, imperfectly correlated with utility maximization, but the costs—in uncertainty, in protracted litigation, and in error—of using utility as a legal standard support using wealth as a proxy for it. The case for wealth maximization in common law adjudication is even stronger when the objections to utilitarianism discussed in the last chapter, besides the difficulty of measurement, are brought into play. A rule utilitarian might use wealth maximization as his rule; this is the practice of many economists.

Turning to positive analysis, Dworkin argues for rejection of the finding that common law rules are best explained as if

51. *Id.* at 211.
52. *Id.* at 218.
53. *Id.*

judges sought to maximize wealth, no matter how well that explanation conforms to the facts, unless and until there emerges a generally accepted theory of why this should be so. He illustrates with an example that can be simplified as follows. Imagine that in the last ten cases decided by the Illinois Supreme Court, the sequence of affirmances and reversals (affirmance = 1 and reversal = 0) was 1101100111. Would we say that this sequence explained the pattern of affirmances and reversals? No, it simply describes it. Now let a group of people make up their own sequences—0011001100, 0001110101, and so on. Suppose one of these sequences accurately described the next ten decisions of the Illinois Supreme Court. Would we say that the person who suggested that sequence had succeeded in explaining the pattern of decisions? Again the answer is no. It would be odd to suggest, however, that the reason the sequence fails as an explanation is that it has not been related to the motivations or biology of judges; it fails because it does not tell us anything interesting about the world. Suppose instead we found that the pattern of affirmances and reversals in all appellate courts in the United States over the last hundred years conformed perfectly to the formula $R_t = \sqrt{A_{t-1}}$; that is, the number of reversals (R) in any period (t) is the square root of the number of affirmances (A) in the previous period. If this "law" were found to be highly significant in repeated testing on different bodies of data, we would feel that we had made an exciting, if puzzling, discovery. We would say that we had "explained," in a meaningful sense of the term, the pattern of affirmances and reversals by appellate courts, although we would be troubled if we could suggest no reason why the pattern should take such a form.

If the common law can best be explained as if the judges were trying to maximize social wealth, this is a less mysterious fact than my hypothetical "law" of affirmances and reversals. The common law assumed its modern shape in the nineteenth century, a period when economic values were an important part of the prevailing ideology. Also, as mentioned earlier in this chapter, the common law tends to regulate behavior in areas where redistribution is difficult to accomplish and where, therefore, the only way for a group to increase its wealth is to support policies that lead to an increase in the wealth of society as a whole, in which the group will share. There are also the evolutionary models of the common law that Dworkin mentions.[54] No doubt it is an embarrassment to the supporters of the economic theory of the common law that there are so many explanations of why the common law is efficient. But the empirical regularity found by the economic theorists is not so arbitrary and improbable that it should be disregarded until we have a generally accepted theory tying this regularity to the motivations or the biology of judges, litigants, or legislators.

To summarize briefly this part of the book, I have tried to develop a moral theory that goes beyond classical utilitarianism and holds that the criterion for judging whether acts and institutions are just or good is whether they maximize the wealth of society. This approach allows a reconciliation among utility, liberty, and even equality as competing ethical principles. The approach seems to have played an important role in the growth of the common law, which is not surprising when the limitations of common law as a means of redistributing, as distinct from creating, wealth are taken into account. Wealth maximization is not, however, the only conception of the good or the just that has influenced law, as I show in Part IV of this book.

---

54. See *id.* at 220; these theories are discussed in William M. Landes & Richard A. Posner, "Adjudication as a Private Good," 8 *J. Legal Stud.* 235, 259–284 (1979).

II
THE ORIGINS OF JUSTICE

5

The Homeric Version
of the Minimal State

The general question examined in the next four chapters is whether and to what extent economic theory can explain the legal and other social institutions of primitive societies.[1] In this chapter, recurring to the issue of social order touched on in Chapter 2, I ask how minimum order is maintained by primitive institutions. Through an examination of the society depicted in the Homeric epics,[2] I hope to challenge the assumption, largely unquestioned since Hobbes, that a state (if only a minimal, "nightwatchman" state) is necessary to maintain the internal and external security of society. I am not advocating anarchy. My argument is that a state is not a precondition of social order in the circumstances depicted in the Homeric epics—and even there, it is just barely not. In our circumstances we could not do without a state.

This chapter is a case study. A number of the matters discussed here (gifts, honor, custom, and so on) receive a broader treatment in Chapter 6, and in Chapter 7 I return to ancient Greece to discuss some aspects of the law of fifth- and fourth-century Athens.

1. For reasons discussed in the next chapter, I define primitive as preliterate, and hence include in my analysis the early, largely preliterate societies out of which modern Western civilization evolved, such as the societies depicted in the Homeric epics and the Norse sagas.

2. Some evidence that the society depicted in the Homeric poems is realistic (and hence a proper source of data for scientific study), albeit fictive in many of its details, is presented in the section "Homeric Individualism" of this chapter, infra. I assume the reader knows at least the broad outline of the plots of the *Iliad* and the *Odyssey;* no more than that is needed to follow my argument.

A Taxonomy of Limited Government

I will sketch a model of limited government—government that conceives its function to be the establishment of a minimal framework of public order within which private energies can enjoy the greatest possible scope—and then compare it to the government described (or implied) in the Homeric poems. Although many ancient societies had highly bureaucratic and intrusive rather than limited governments (a pertinent example being the Mycenaean palace state revealed by the Linear B tablets),[3] and although the Homeric poems are set in the Mycenaean era, there are no traces in Homer of the bureaucratic, centralized, regulatory state revealed by the Linear B tablets.[4] The "governments" depicted in the Homeric poems are uniformly of a highly limited type.[5]

Functions

Truly limited government has only one function—to assure physical security in both its internal and external aspects. The internal aspect has to do with securing the individual's person and property from coercive invasions such as murder or steal-

3. See T. B. L. Webster, "Polity and Society: Historical Commentary," in *A Companion to Homer* 452 (Alan J. B. Wace & Frank H. Stubbings eds. 1962); John Chadwick, *The Mycenaean World* 69–83 (1976).

4. With the doubtful exception of Agamemnon's overlordship; see note 12 infra. In fact, although *demos* means approximately "district," *gaia* "land," and *patris gaia* "fatherland," there is no specific word in Homeric Greek for (nation) state. In Homer, the primary meaning of *polis* is simply "fortified town" (see John L. Myres, *The Political Ideas of the Greeks* 69–70 [1927]), but *polis* can also include the rural areas ruled by the city's ruler. A state may contain more than one *polis* (Agamemnon's realm evidently contained a number of cities, since he proposed to give seven to Achilles), but there is no specific word for such a state, although *demos* may be used in this sense in book 2 of the *Iliad*.

5. Unless one equates "government" with "governance" and treats the Homeric household, the *oikos*, as a state, which I decline to do. Although the Homeric *oikos* is more extensive than the modern family (the *oikos* might include not only a man's immediate family but his adult married children, unrelated adults serving as retainers, such as Patroclus in Peleus's household, and numerous slaves), it would trivialize the concept of state to include the *oikos*.

ing. Without some minimal internal public order, community welfare would be diminished. This is not to say that without a state people would run amok, killing and stealing from each other. They would take measures to protect themselves from coercion, whether by going around armed, maintaining a retaliatory capability, living in extended family groups, concealing their possessions, or switching to activities (such as hunting compared to agriculture) that require less of the kind of investment that can be readily appropriated by someone else. But these are costly measures, and it is generally believed—on the whole correctly but perhaps not in the conditions of Homeric society—that basic protection can be provided more efficiently publicly than privately.

External security—protection against predation from outside the community—could also, in principle, be left to the private sector, but again this is generally thought more efficiently done by the state. A logical extension of this function of the state is predation against other communities.

Structure

Even the very limited purposes of government sketched above would seem to presuppose a fairly complex governmental structure. Besides an executive authority to assure internal and external security, presumably composed of a chief executive (king, president) assisted by subordinate officials and functionaries (soldiers, police, tax collectors), there must be some machinery for determining the guilt of people accused of violating the rules against coercion. Some kind of consultative body is also necessary, but it need not be a legislature. The consultative organs may be informal and of little power, and in the limiting case (Stalin's politburo?) purely decorative or vestigial. But it is extraordinarily rare for a single man to be so powerful that he can govern without the assistance of some other men who are not mere lackeys. And questions of power to one side, the head of government will want the advice of the outstanding men of the state in matters of importance.

Problems

Two problems that a limited government must overcome if it is to function effectively are particularly important in Homeric society. One is control: the government must be sufficiently well administered to accomplish its (modest) goals. The other problem is succession, of assuring an orderly transition when the chief executive is long absent or dead. The solution normally entails having a successor designated in advance of any vacancy so that when the chief executive dies or leaves, there is no ambiguity as to his successor and therefore no interregnum. A third problem—tyranny—is strangely absent from the Homeric world, where the problem is weak, rather than excessively strong, government.

Values

The task of government is made easier if most citizens' personal values are supportive of the governmental mission. The organization of defense is facilitated by patriotic feeling; the control of murder is easier if people internalize a regard (appropriately qualified) for the sanctity of human life. My term for the social or civic virtues is "altruism," defined as a positive regard for the welfare of people outside of one's immediate family and close friends. Patriotism, public-spiritedness, trustworthiness, and adherence to promises illustrate the altruistic disposition.[6]

An important element of sympathy or altruism is perceptual rather than ethical—the ability to put oneself in the other fellow's shoes, to feel as he does. Adam Smith argued that this perceptual ability is the foundation of the ethical, of the caring for or sense of duty toward others: one does not care what happens to other people unless one is able to enter imaginatively into

6. A qualification is necessary: in order for the concept of altruism to denote the kind of values that make governing easier, the concept must embody an ordering of sympathies in which the interest of the community as a whole is ranked ahead of sympathetic regard for a narrower group. Loyalty, for example, could reduce rather than enhance the effectiveness of government if it were to one's fellow conspirators in a plot against the government.

their thoughts and feelings.[7] But empathy, as I shall call the perceptual dimension of sympathy, is also politically relevant because it facilitates the resolution of conflict. The individual who understands how two contending parties feel is better able to compromise their dispute than one who cannot empathize with the disputants. But empathy is not enough; detachment, the ability to disentangle personal and emotional stakes in an issue, is also very important to the successful exercise of political authority.

Government and Political Values in Homer

The governments depicted in the *Iliad* and *Odyssey* are even more limited than the model of minimal government sketched above. Moreover, what government there is in the Homeric world generally does not work.[8]

Functions

The only well-defined and generally accepted governmental function in the world depicted in the Homeric poems is defense

7. See Adam Smith, *The Theory of Moral Sentiments* (1759; reprint ed. 1969); Ronald H. Coase, "Adam Smith's View of Man," 19 *J. Law & Econ.* 529 (1976).

8. Homeric governments fall into three broad classes: (1) those of Greek states (Mycenae, Pylos, and Ithaca, for example); (2) those of foreign states (primarily Troy and Scheria); and (3) various ad hoc or quasi-governments such as those of the Olympian gods, the Greek alliance against Troy, and smaller fighting or raiding parties. There are some functional and structural differences among, and sometimes within, these classes, but the problems and values are similar and the classes are best discussed together. My descriptions of these governments owe much to previous studies. See George M. Calhoun, "Polity and Society: The Homeric Poems," in *A Companion to Homer,* supra note 3, at 431 n.2, 432–440; M. I. Finley, *The World of Odysseus* (2d rev. ed. 1978), especially ch. 4; P. A. L. Greenhalgh, *Early Greek Warfare: Horsemen and Chariots in the Homeric and Archaic Ages* 156–172 (1973); A. M. Snodgrass, *The Dark Age of Greece: An Archeological Survey of the 11th to 8th Centuries B.C.,* at 392–394, 435–436 (1971); and, with reference to the society of the gods, Martin P. Nilsson, *A History of Greek Religion,* ch. 5 (2d ed. 1949). See also A. W. H. Adkins, *Moral Values and Political Behaviour in Ancient Greece: From Homer to the End of the Fifth Century,* ch. 2 (1972); G. S. Kirk, "The Homeric Poems as History," in *The Cambridge Ancient History,* vol. 2, pt. 2, at 820–850 (I. E. S. Edwards, C. J. Gadd, G. L. Hammond, & E. Sollberger eds., 3d ed. 1975); Myres, supra note 4, at 64–82; T. A. Sinclair, *A History of Greek Political Thought,* ch. 1 (2d ed. 1967).

(for example, of Troy) against foreign invaders; even as to this, as we shall see, there is some question. Murder, stealing, and other violations of internal public order are not public offenses. No public machinery of adjudication, enforcement, or punishment is maintained for the security of person or property. The sanction for murder is retaliation by the victim's family, operating outside of any public framework of rights or remedies. In the shield scene in the *Iliad* and elsewhere, it is suggested that the victim's family might accept a price (*poinē*) in lieu of killing the murderer and that the price might be determined by some form of private arbitration, but at no stage in the process is the state involved.[9]

This is true even if the victim is the king. There is no distinct concept of regicide as political murder or treason: the murder of Agamemnon is an offense not against the Mycenaean *polis* but solely against Agamemnon and his family. Moreover, because a son has no superior legal claim to his father's throne, when Orestes revenges Agamemnon he does so in a purely personal capacity—he is neither the king nor the crown prince but an aspirant with no greater jural right than Aegisthus.

As mentioned, the state does have responsibility for defense against foreign invasion. Priam's authority over the conduct of the Trojan defense is unquestioned—he (or his field commander Hector) decides whether to open or close the gates, to parley, to return Helen.[10] Yet the public character of the Trojan defense is compromised by the prominence of Priam's immediate family in the origin and conduct of the war, which has no public purpose. It is fought simply to allow Paris, one of Priam's sons, to keep a foreign woman whom the rest of the Trojans hate. The principal combatants are Priam's sixty-two sons and sons-in-law, and—with the exception of Aeneas—the most con-

9. There are, however, a few hints of public judges (though they play no part in the action of the poems)—e.g., in Odysseus's first visit to Hades, the reference to judging by Minos, the king of Crete.

10. The technology of defense, especially the great walls of Troy, would imply some anterior public defense activity, were it not that the *Iliad* says Poseidon and Apollo built the walls of Troy. The wall and ditch built to protect the Greek ships were constructed in wartime.

spicuous fighters on the Trojan side who are not members of Priam's family, Glaucus and Sarpedon, are not even Trojans. The Greeks are fighting not so much the Trojan state as Priam's *oikos*.

Offensive warfare seems not to be a public activity at all. Odysseus and the other kings accompany Agamemnon and Menelaus to Troy not to enrich or otherwise aggrandize their states nor to enhance their states' security against potential Trojan aggression,[11] but to honor obscure, perhaps wholly personal, obligations to Agamemnon and Menelaus and to obtain booty and fame, conceived of as purely personal assets and emoluments.[12] For Ithaca as a whole (or Pylos, or Mycenae, or Phthia) there is nothing to be gained from the war. The same is true of the piratical raids described in the *Odyssey*.

The usual civilian functions of government seem not to be governmental in Homeric society. There is no public road building or harbor improvement (the port at Scheria may be an exception), no coinage, no record keeping, no regulation of foreign commerce, no police, and no courts. Some sort of taxation is suggested in a few places,[13] along with the king's reciprocal obligation to defend the state.[14] But it is significant that no tax

11. However, there is a hint of a potential concern with Trojan aggression in Achilles' statement in book 1 of the *Iliad* that he has nothing to fear from the Trojans because of the remoteness of Phthia.

12. It is unclear how Agamemnon induces the other Greek kings to accompany him and Menelaus on the expedition to Troy. It is implied that they do so under some kind of obligation to him. See G. S. Kirk, *Homer and the Oral Tradition* 47 (1976). But the nature of the obligation—whether resulting from gift-guest relations or reflecting some authority of Agamemnon over the other Greek states—is not explained. Agamemnon is *primus inter pares* and commander-in-chief of allied forces, but he is not a Greek emperor (he wields a scepter as symbol of his authority, but he is not alone in this—see note 18 infra). For a contrary view, see Georges C. Vlachos, *Les Sociétés politiques homériques* 303–317 (1974).

13. Notably in Alcinous's suggestion of a levy on the people of Scheria to recompense him and his nobles for the gifts they gave Odysseus, but also in Agamemnon's reference to the gifts Achilles will receive from the people of the cities that Agamemnon is offering to give him. For some briefer references to war taxes, see *Iliad* 13.663–669, 23.296–298.

14. Mentioned in Sarpedon's speech to Glaucus: see James M. Redfield, *Nature and Culture in the Iliad: The Tragedy of Hector* 99–100 (1975).

collectors are mentioned; in general, not even a rudimentary public finance can be discerned.

Perhaps the most telling evidence of the absence of governmental functions is in the twenty-year vacancy in the kingship of Ithaca. Mentor, the nominal regent, is completely powerless and ineffectual. To the extent that anyone has authority, it is the suitors hanging about Odysseus's residence, pestering his wife, and (toward the end) plotting against Telemachus. But never are they reported as conducting public business. Apparently, in twenty years not a single item of public business arose.[15]

Structure

Homeric society seemingly presents the paradox of a government that has a structure but virtually no functions. Each state has a "king" (*basileus*) advised by a council (*boulē*) of nobles (*aristoi*), plus a subordinate public official (*kērux*, "herald"), whose principal functions are to deliver the king's messages and commands and to summon and regulate the *agorē*, a kind of popular assembly. There is also (perhaps) a kind of superking, the *anax andrōn*. The divine polity on Olympus has a supreme king, Zeus; the other Olympian gods (as distinct from lesser immortals) constitute his informal *boulē*.

Such executive authority as one finds in the Homeric state is exercised by the *basileus*. Priam is one, as are Menelaus, Idomeneus, Achilles, Odysseus, and the other Greek leaders at Troy. Agamemnon is *basileus* of Mycenae but also the leader of the Greek forces at Troy. The term *anax* in the Homeric poems, as distinct from the Linear B tablets, is an honorific title of high nobility rather than a functional position in a chain of command (a god is never called a *basileus* but often an *anax*). The term *anax andrōn* (*anax* of warriors) seems to denote Agamemnon's position as chief of the Greek alliance, although it is occasionally

15. To be sure, when Telemachus summons an assembly of Ithacan notables he is asked whether the assembly is to consider a private or public (*demios*) matter, but it seems that by "public" the speaker means not a political question but simply a matter of widespread interest such as the return of Odysseus and his men from Troy.

used of much lesser figures, such as the Trojan Anchises. The position seems, however, more a wartime expedient than a well-defined governmental role. Agamemnon is the mightiest Greek *basileus* and therefore commander of the host (with the other *basilées* making up his *boulē*), but he is not the king or emperor of the Greeks.

The conventional translation of *basileus* as king is misleading.[16] The Homeric *basileus* is more like a medieval English baron. He is the most powerful man in a district, he has the largest *oikos,* and if there is a raid to be conducted or if the district is attacked he will be in command and apportion any booty. But in the normal course he does not perform governmental functions because normally in the Homeric world there are none to perform.

Where the medieval parallel breaks down is in the absence of an authority higher than these local magnates. There is no word in Homer to describe an entity to which Odysseus's polity might be subordinate. Nor can Odysseus's own position be conceptualized as one of genuine kingship by identifying a lower tier of barons. Below Odysseus and the other *basilées* are simply households, *oikoi*—some fairly extensive, to be sure, but none that are agglomerations of households.[17]

Given the absence of governmental functions except in the intermittently active area of external security, it is not surprising to find that Odysseus's concerns upon his return relate solely to his *oikos*—to his wife and son, his slaves, and his goods. There is no hint either that he might have public business to attend to or that the suitors might have designs on the polity of Ithaca as distinct from Odysseus's household. Although the suitors fear an

16. Quite apart from the fact that the term is sometimes applied to people who are not kings, such as Priam's sons (who do not even have their own *oikoi*) and the suitors of Penelope. The poverty of the political vocabulary is a clue to the rudimentariness of Homeric political institutions.

17. An exception is Scheria. Alcinous's *boulē* is composed of *basilées*, each of whom seems to have his own domain, not just an *oikos*. But Homer marks Scheria in so many ways as foreign, indeed fantastic; perhaps this is one of its foreign traits. A more important exception may be the reference in book 9 of the *Iliad* to Phoenix as "ruling" (*anassōn*) a part of Peleus's kingdom.

adverse public reaction if they kill Telemachus openly, Odysseus makes no effort to rouse public opinion or to enlist the people of Ithaca in the fight to restore him to the kingship. Nor, finally, is there any suggestion that if Odysseus had appealed to the Ithacan populace they would have rallied to him because he is the legitimate occupant of the throne,[18] because he is remembered as having been a good king, or for any other reason.

The most clearly delineated political institution in Homeric society is the *agorē*. The people who count—be they the suitors' kinsmen, the *basilēes* of the various Greek contingents at Troy, or the members of Odysseus's force during the wanderings— come together frequently in *agorai* to deliberate common problems, to iron out disputes, and to plan future action. At the *agorē* people sit, and rise only to speak; the *kērux* hands the scepter to the speaker. Rank and file are present but do not speak (save for Thersites' unmannerly eruption in the *Iliad*), though they may express their views by shouting assent or dissent to a proposed course of action.

The *agorē* is generally a deliberative rather than a governing body. The members have a right to be heard but no decision-making authority. The *agorē* wants Agamemnon to return Chryses' daughter, but he refuses, and although he is a minority of one and flat wrong to boot, there is no suggestion that in ignoring the wishes of the *agorē* he is exceeding his legal authority. The nearest thing to a vote in the *agorē* occurs in the last book of the *Odyssey*. The relatives of the suitors are deliberating whether to fight Odysseus. The majority decides to fight and the minority simply leaves. But in this case there is no one in command. The most powerful *agorē* in the poems is that of the suitors, precisely because there is no *basileus* or equivalent. Although Antinous is the suitors' principal ringleader, major deci-

---

18. It is perhaps significant that there is no concept of the royal "throne" in Homer (*thronos* is just a chair), nor any other symbol of kingship with the occasional exception of the scepter—and scepters are used to mark other sorts of authority as well, such as a priest's or herald's, or the speaker's inviolability in the *agorē*. Agamemnon's scepter, however, is apparently special. See *Iliad* 1.277–279, 2.100–108, 9.99.

sions are made by consensus, and Antinous does not persist in proposals that the *agorē* disapproves.

In the traditional or embedded value structure of the poems, the *agorē* is a sign of civilization.[19] But it does not follow that the *agorē* is an effective institution; as we shall see, generally it is not.

The nature of law in Homeric society is a clue to the paucity of governmental structures. The words in Homeric Greek that come closest to "law," *dikē* and *themis,* mean custom. It is custom that prescribes the methods of sacrificing to the gods, the proper treatment of suppliants and beggars, and other legal and nonlegal aspects of social behavior. Reliance on custom is inevitable in a society that lacks formal institutions, such as courts and legislatures, for promulgating laws. In the absence of such institutions, the only rules are those practices which, because they satisfy a social need, are adhered to over a long period of time. Though we think of law as preeminently an emanation of the state—though law is indeed often defined as a command backed by public force—lawmaking in Homeric society is not a governmental function at all.

Problems

Such government as does exist in Homeric society doesn't work well. The main problems are absence of settled procedures for succession and lack of control. There are no rules of succession in the Homeric world. When Odysseus leaves Ithaca, the executive authority simply becomes vacant, and it is made clear that if Odysseus should finally be declared dead, no one has a paramount claim to succeed him as king, not even his only son.[20] In fact, Telemachus is just about out of the running, be-

---

19. The Cyclopes are derided as lacking an *agorē,* and the gods' lack of a formal *agorē* may be a clue that Homer regards them as more primitive than human beings.

20. Any claim of a king's son to succeed his father is based on the intensely practical consideration that his relationship to the incumbent may give him an edge over his rivals; there is no legally prescribed succession. Even the king's right to resume the kingship after an absence is contested, in both Odysseus's case and Agamemnon's, though Menelaus and Nestor, at least, have no difficulty in reestablishing themselves on their return from Troy

cause whoever Penelope chooses to be her husband will obtain control over Odysseus's *oikos* and with it the material basis for claiming primacy among the Ithacan nobility. The fact that Penelope (indirectly) controls the succession has sometimes been thought a vestige of a pre-Greek matriarchal society. But the poems themselves imply something quite different: the rules of succession are so unclear that the kingship of Ithaca will go by default—that is, to whomever Penelope happens to choose as her husband. That Penelope might herself exercise the royal power during Odysseus's absence or that an effective regent might be appointed during Telemachus's minority or that Laertes might be recalled to office are never suggested as possible solutions to the leadership crisis.[21]

Lack of control—managerial incapacity—is a major theme in both poems. Agamemnon is temperamentally miscast in the role of the Greek commander-in-chief at Troy.[22] In book 2, the panic in the Greek forces that Agamemnon accidentally touches off and Thersites' disruption of the decorum of the *agorē* are powerful symbols of the loss of control following Agamemnon's revealing, in his quarrel with Achilles in book 1, his incapacity to govern the Greek host effectively. Particularly noteworthy, because it recurs in quite different circumstances with both Priam and Odysseus, is Agamemnon's inability to separate his personal interests from his public responsibilities. He refuses for purely selfish reasons to return Chryseis, not understanding that his position as commander-in-chief requires him, at the very least, to balance his private and the public interest.[23]

21. Perhaps the reason for the weak regents in Ithaca and Mycenae (where Agamemnon's bard is left in charge) is that a strong one would be unlikely to relinquish power to the returning *basileus*. See note 20 supra.

22. As emphasized in Redfield, supra note 14, at 93.

23. See *id.* at 94. The problem with Agamemnon's leadership illustrates the frequent conflict in government between procedural and substantive regularity, a conflict Homeric society is unable to resolve. As Nestor explains in book 1 of the *Iliad*, Agamemnon's claim to be commander-in-chief is based on the accepted principle that the mightiest *basileus*, in terms of the size of the forces he can muster, is commander-in-chief. This is an appealingly simple and clear-cut procedural rule that avoids the uncertainty created by absence of clear succession rules, but it may also entail filling a position with an unsuitable individual.

Lack of political control is also a serious problem on the Trojan side. The Trojans find themselves fighting a hopeless war for the foreign wife (whom they despise) of Paris, the black sheep of Priam's family. The woman was obtained, moreover, by Paris's serious breach of hospitality, which is the cornerstone of the Homeric moral code. The inability of Priam and Hector to avoid or extricate the Trojan state from an unjust war, which even if won would bring the Trojans no tangible gain, indicates a fundamental incapacity to exercise public authority.

The main problem of Trojan political management is that Paris is Hector's brother and Priam's son. Family loyalties come before public duty even if the family member to whom loyalty is accorded is unworthy of it. Like Agamemnon vis-à-vis Chryseis, Priam and Hector have a serious conflict of interest because they have a family stake in a question of public concern; that they doom the entire state for Paris's sake demonstrates an absence of "responsible leadership" in the modern sense.

There is a broader point. Historically the state begins as an agglomeration of households when each household is no longer strong enough, even in (loose) alliance with other households, to ward off powerful enemies. But the transition to political society is a difficult one, because the households, having been so long autonomous and having become in some cases powerful miniature states themselves, resist subordination to a larger entity. For a strong state to emerge, the great households must be broken up. Priam's Troy is the symbol of the struggle. With his fifty sons and twelve sons-in-law, all in residence, Priam has a huge household, and loyalty within this family, as manifested in the mysterious refusal of Priam and Hector to coerce Paris, is in conflict with Priam's responsibilities as head of state. Together with notions of honor—a key, as we shall see, to the stability of a society of autonomous households, but a potentially disruptive factor in a system of political order—family loyalty causes the destruction of the Trojan state.

The *Odyssey* alternates between Ithaca and the wanderings, chronicling in both settings a pervasive failure of leadership and management. Odysseus is incapable of exercising effective au-

thority over his men (the *hetairoi*). His inability to maintain a
consistent view of his leadership responsibilities (reminiscent of
Agamemnon's difficulty in the quarrel over Chryseis) is a recurrent source of disaster.

Odysseus's affection or loyalty for his men, even though they
repeatedly let him down, has been thought evidence of his good
nature. An alternative explanation is that it reflects a consciousness of shared guilt. While the devouring of the Sun's cattle by
the *hetairoi* is the immediate cause both of their own death and
of the postponement of Odysseus's return by seven years, the
ultimate cause of the disaster is Odysseus's own act in taunting
the Cyclops. So it is with letting the wind out of Aeolus's bag:
the men did it, but Odysseus, who was asleep at the critical moment, had by his behavior in the Cyclops episode given them
cause to suspect his motives, and he should have told them what
the bag contained. Yet any question of apportioning guilt for
these misadventures is submerged by a sense that they are or-
ganic to Homeric society rather than contingent and avoidable
mishaps; this is a society in which collective undertakings tend
not to work.

A related point is the difficulty of imagining Odysseus suc-
cessfully destroying the suitors *with* the aid of the *hetairoi*. They
are so ungovernable, and Odysseus so inadequate a governor,
that the suitors would have stood a better chance had Odysseus
been encumbered by any of his men. After all, Homer repeatedly tells us that Agamemnon returned to Mycenae with his
men but was killed anyway (and they were wiped out in an ambush). The lone man succeeds where the group fails because
political management is so elusive an art in the Homeric world.

Odysseus not only succeeds without his men, he succeeds
against a group, and again one feels that the suitors are undone
in part by their very number, which induces a false confidence
in their strength. The group is hopelessly irresolute. The absence of effective leadership, stemming from the consensual nature of the suitors' society, is revealed in their inability to formu-
late a procedure for filling the throne of Ithaca or to force
Penelope to a decision, to kill Telemachus on Ithaca after he

eludes the ambush, to keep the beggar from entering the contest of the bow, or to use their superior number to overwhelm Odysseus despite odds of fifty to one; and this lack is also revealed in the *agorē* of the suitors' relatives, where a substantial fraction break off before the fight begins and go home.

The *Odyssey* ends with a political solution. Athena orders the suitors' relatives to stop seeking revenge, promising in exchange wealth and peace for Ithaca. It is like Hobbes's social compact, breaking what could otherwise have become an endless cycle of vengeance. But Odysseus, rather than participate in the peacemaking, is raging to finish off the relatives; only Zeus's thunderbolt dissuades him from doing so. Odysseus's solution to the political problem presented by the suitors' relatives is to kill them.

The conclusion of the *Odyssey* suggests that political solutions to problems are gifts from the gods. Yet the problem of political management is also conspicuous, in both poems, at the divine level. Zeus is clearly supreme de jure, as it were. Not only can he intervene in human affairs without leaving Olympus (unlike the other gods), but he can bring heavy sanctions to bear on any god who defies him. Yet he exercises rather little real authority. He has no trustworthy staff (except for conveying messages), commands no personal loyalty or affection among any of the gods, lacks plans and purposes, and is easily cozened, manipulated, distracted, and defied. Zeus's plan (*Dios boulē*) in the *Iliad* is derailed repeatedly and in the *Odyssey* succeeds mainly because of Poseidon's momentary inattention. Zeus, like Agamemnon, is invested with great formal power but exercises it on the whole ineffectually because he, like Agamemnon, is temperamentally ill suited to his role. An additional element is Zeus's lack of the supporting structures and personnel without which no one can exercise power effectively.

Values

The lack of effective government in Homer is abetted by a system of values in which the civic virtues are notable mainly for their absence. The lack of any Greek patriotic feeling in the

Trojan War has been remarked.[24] No opprobrium attaches to Achilles for withdrawing from combat and thereby nearly bringing disaster upon the Greek forces. Such altruistic acts as do occur have an ambiguous flavor. Hector seems to be fighting for his state as well as for his family and honor—he repeatedly rejects adverse omens with the slogan "the best omen is to fight for the fatherland"—but the cause for which he is fighting is an unworthy one in the Homeric value structure, and his civic virtue helps to mark him both as a foreigner and as the inferior of his rival Achilles. Achilles twice lapses into altruism, and these lapses prove to be his undoing. Seeing the Greeks fleeing in rout before Hector, he momentarily sympathizes with them in their suffering and sends Patroclus to find out what is going on; this, Homer remarks, is the beginning of the end for Patroclus. Later Achilles recalls the compromise Nestor had suggested— that is, to send Patroclus to fight in Achilles' armor. Again yielding to an impulse of sympathy for the Greeks in their plight and in that moment embracing the "politics of compromise," Achilles sends Patroclus, and symbolically himself, to destruction. When Achilles finally kills Hector, thereby sealing the doom of Troy and assuring the Greek victory, it is for a personal end—to avenge Patroclus. Patroclus is to Achilles as the damsel is to the medieval knight errant. The concept of war, a political enterprise, does not enter.[25]

It is no accident that the compromise which dooms Patroclus was suggested by Nestor. The embodiment in the *Iliad* of political sagacity, Nestor is the only character who has a conception of warfare as organized conflict rather than as a melee of individual champions.[26] Nestor is a symbol not only of political sa-

24. See, e.g., Saul Levin, "Love and the Hero of the *Iliad*," 80 *Transactions Am. Philological Ass'n* 37, 40–43 (1949). There is, to be sure, a strong sense of ethnicity (e.g., vis-à-vis Phoenecians) but that is different from patriotism.

25. Again illustrating the poverty of its political vocabulary, Homeric Greek contains no word for war, as distinct from battle or fight, *polemos* or *mache*. Cf. C. S. Lewis, *A Preface to Paradise Lost* 28 (1942): "The Trojan War is not the subject of the *Iliad*. It is merely the background to a purely personal story."

26. It is Nestor who inveighs against civil war, who proposes building the wall to protect the Greek ships and organizing the Greek forces by tribes and clans (*phula* and *phrē-*

gacity, however, but also of old age. He himself harps incessantly on his extreme age and attendant incapacity for fighting. Political ability is presented as a consolation for old age rather than as the normal endowment of leaders in their prime.[27]

Perhaps one reason why political skills are not valued more highly is that in the Homeric world the mass counts for little. Odysseus destroys the numerous suitors virtually single-handedly, and in the battle scenes in the *Iliad* the individual heroes cut through the mass of warriors as through butter. Absent is the recognition, basic to political society, that a well-organized group of mediocre individuals will almost always defeat the superior but lone individual.[28]

Again with the notable exception of Nestor, the Homeric individual tends to lack the perceptual as well as ethical aspect of altruism (what I have termed empathy). One reason Agamemnon and Achilles clash so violently in the beginning of the *Iliad* is their inability to see that the claim each is asserting with such tenacity has a counterpart in the other's very similar claim.[29] Also conspicuous is Agamemnon's emotionalism, his lack of detachment.

The Homeric Social Order

Although Homeric society seems critically deficient in the structures and supporting values and competencies of even the minimal state, the world depicted by Homer is not the Hobbes-

---

trēs), who observes that if the Greek warriors stop to strip the fallen foe their victory will be less complete, and who devises a battle plan involving the massing of charioteers and foot soldiers.

27. It may be suggestive of the Homeric attitude toward the preeminent political skill of compromise that the critical compromise Nestor proposes to Achilles is short-sighted (though lucky in its ultimate consequences for the Greek cause). It involves the serious if characteristic error in the Homeric world of giving someone a bigger role than he can play, a plight in which not only Patroclus finds himself but Agamemnon, Hector, Telemachus, and many others.

28. See, e.g., Adam Smith, *The Wealth of Nations* 232–233 (Edwin Cannan ed., reprint ed. 1904).

29. However, Achilles demonstrates empathy for Priam in book 24.

ian state of nature. There is a well-developed system of private institutions and values that enables the desired minimum of social interactions to be achieved without a state. The counterpart to the Hobbesian state of nature in the Homeric world is the state of the Cyclopes, who live wholly without refinement or social intercourse. Against that vision of barbaric existence is set one of a civilized society in which the requisite social harmony is attained through patterned interactions among households. People travel and in the course of their travels collect gifts. From these, as well as from household manufacture of clothing, tripods, and the like, the individual amasses a stock from which he can dispense gifts to his visitors. Host and guest (both *xeinos*) are subject to a moral law of hospitality (summarized in the terms *xeinios* and *xenios*), which enjoins the host to be generous and the guest not to abuse the host's generosity. Besides exchanging gifts, the parties to the host-guest relationship—that is, the *xeinoi*—form marriage and other alliances.

Though explicit trade in the Homeric world is limited to transactions with non-Greeks,[30] the gift system is plainly a form of trade in that it is explicitly reciprocal,[31] but it is trade of a special sort. The usual purpose of trade is to facilitate the division of labor, which implies that the things traded will be different from each other—a shoe for a loaf of bread rather than a shoe for a shoe. Yet the exchange of gifts in Homer is largely an exchange of like things, usually ornamental objects. The purpose is not to enable the parties to specialize in the productive activities in which they may have a comparative advantage. Indeed, often the gifts are not even produced by the people exchanging

---

30. See M. I. Finley, "Marriage, Sale, and Gift in the Homeric World," 2 *Revue internationale des droits de l'antiquité* (3rd ser.) 167, 173 (1955). A major exception is the sale of services: the *demioergoi* referred to in the *Odyssey* (singers, physicians, etc.) trade their services for food and other goods.

31. "The word 'gift' is not to be misconstrued. It may be stated as a flat rule of both primitive and archaic society that no one ever gave anything, whether goods or services or honors, without proper recompense, real or wishful, immediate or years away, to himself or to his kin. The act of giving was, therefore, in an essential sense always the first half of a reciprocal action, the other half of which was a counter gift." Finley, supra note 8 at 64.

them but are either booty or a gift received in a former exchange. The Homeric *oikoi* are depicted as largely self-sufficient from a productive standpoint.

To understand the purpose of gift exchange, we must picture a society in which people live in small scattered groups—in households each consisting of little more than a single family. These households face two great problems aside from food and shelter. The first is how to reproduce themselves without committing incest, against which there is a powerful and nearly universal taboo that is apparently of genetic origin. The second is how to survive against human marauders. The incest problem is solved by marriage with members of other households,[32] the defense problem by alliances either with kin living in separate households or with strangers. Gift exchange facilitates both forms of reaching out by enabling the member of one household to inform himself concerning the qualities of someone from a different household who may be a stranger. If I give you a gold tripod and receive in exchange a coarse blanket, I learn something about your suitability as an ally or as a father-in-law: if that is all you have to give me, it probably means you are not a very good fighter, for you have not been able to collect a store of booty from which to give me a good present.[33] The informational function of gift exchange explains why in Homeric society marriages are normally contracted with a *mutual* exchange of gifts rather than with gifts for the bride alone.

What marks the Cyclopes as savages is not the absence of an *agorē* and of *themistes*, though these are the details remarked by the poet, but their abstention from the gift-exchange system. This is the significance of their rudeness (in more than one sense). It is why Odysseus's argument to Polyphemus—that a host who eats his guests will not have many visitors—falls on deaf ears.

32. Finley, supra note 30, at 172, points out that marriages in Homer are almost always between members of geographically distant *oikoi*.

33. The role of war booty in the gift-exchange system helps to explain why, in Homeric warfare, the victor in a fight pauses to strip the fallen foe before engaging another enemy.

The gift-guest morality is central to the events depicted in the *Iliad* and *Odyssey*. The Trojan War is caused by Paris's abuse of Menelaus's hospitality. Agamemnon's initial refusal to "trade" Chryseis for the ransom tendered by her father, his subsequent insistence on taking Briseis in exchange for Chryseis whom he has finally been forced to give up, Achilles' refusal to trade his wrath for Agamemnon's tendered gifts, and later his acceptance of Priam's gifts in exchange for Hector's body are critical turning points in the *Iliad*. In the *Odyssey* Paris reappears, as it were, as the 108 suitors of Penelope; the Cyclops is severely punished for his abuse, as a host, of the guest relationship; and the suitors are found breaking both sides of the moral law—in their behavior as guests in Odysseus's house and as hosts to the disguised Odysseus.

The poems contain not only a moral code centering on the guest relationship but a machinery for enforcing the code, though not a public one. The machinery is vengeance. The ancient Greek word for avenger, *dikēphoros*, means literally "justice-bringer." Paris's abuse of Menelaus's hospitality is revenged by the destruction of Troy, the suitors' abuse of Odysseus's hospitality by their destruction. The emphasis on honor (*timē*) as a central moral virtue can be understood only in relation to the nature of the law enforcement machinery. The hot-tempered man who is quick to avenge a slight plays an important role in a system of deterrence based on retaliation, by making credible the threat to retaliate, which is the essential deterrent to wrongful acts in such a system.[34]

In sum, the Hobbesian state of nature is avoided in the Homeric world by a system of values (hospitality, honor) and implementing practices (revenge, gift exchange) that, while not communitarian or political, fosters the necessary cooperation. The situation resembles the morality of modern international relations.[35] There is no international government, yet extensive

---

34. Revenge is discussed more systematically in Chapters 7 and 8. The word *dikē-phoros* does not actually appear in Homer.

35. On the analogies between international relations and primitive law concerning maintenance of public order, see Michael Barkun, *Law without Sanctions* (1968).

cooperative relationships are established and maintained across national boundaries. People travel and trade more or less securely in most areas at most times. Reciprocity and retaliation maintain a tolerably stable international order that resembles what the Homeric poems present as an attainable ideal of social interactions outside of the *oikos*—a substitute for the "nightwatchman" state.

The decentralized, reciprocal, prepolitical social order of the Homeric world is, however, a fragile one, and the *Iliad* and *Odyssey* depict its disintegration. Its fragility is symbolized by the Trojan War. When Paris spirited Helen away, he did Menelaus a grievous wrong, and Menelaus could be expected to seek revenge. But Paris lives in a walled city, so there is no way Menelaus alone or even with the help of his personal retainers can avenge himself against Paris. True, Menelaus has a brother, and the obligation to avenge a wrong is recognized as a kinship obligation. But even with Agamemnon's aid, Menelaus is not strong enough to get his revenge; the brothers need to enlist the help of numerous nonrelatives, notably Achilles.

Consider the two main incidents in the *Iliad* involving Menelaus: his duel with Paris in book 3 and his wounding by Pandarus in book 4. The duel is the prepolitical solution to offenses against the moral order, but it is aborted. When Menelaus is wounded by Pandarus, and Agamemnon thinks he will die, Agamemnon is particularly upset because he thinks that the siege of Troy will then have to be abandoned. Agamemnon can conceive of the war only as an act of private vengeance that must cease when the wronged individual dies. Even within the value system of the *Iliad* this is an extreme position, since a dead man's relatives have a duty to avenge him. But Agamemnon's characteristically extreme reaction to the possibility of Menelaus's death shows how difficult it is for the Homeric mentality to conceive of a "cause" adequate to sustain an enterprise so political as the Trojan War.

Once one group of households discovers how to organize into a state, the members of the other, scattered households are in great danger—they can no longer protect their interests by making credible threats to retaliate against infringers of those interests. The state begins in response to the problem of external (not internal) security.[36] The Homeric poems depict an intermediate stage in which the individual household either joins with those of kinsmen and guest-friends in uneasy alliance to avenge a specific infringement of the moral code (the Greeks) or expands internally to form the nucleus of a state (the Trojans).

Homeric Individualism

The structure of institutions and values that I have called Homeric will be familiar to anyone who has read accounts of primitive societies. The gift exchanges and rites of hospitality; the blood feuds; the chief who leads in wartime but does not rule in peacetime, who does not even administer the internal criminal law;[37] the loose confederacy that arises to cope with a foreign threat and collapses when the threat is past;[38] the building of alliances through kinship and guest visits;[39] the killing of male captives and the enslavement and "concubinization" of female captives;[40] the succession of the chief's son to the chieftainship as a matter of practice rather than of right;[41] the duel;[42] the

36. This appears to be in fact the basic dynamic according to which societies of scattered households are transformed into states. See Robert Bigelow, *The Dawn Warriors: Man's Evolution toward Peace* 8, 13 (1969); Robert L. Carneiro, "A Theory of the Origin of the State," *Science* 733 (Aug. 14, 1970).

37. See Max Gluckman, *Politics, Law and Ritual in Tribal Society* 86–87 (1965).

38. See Marshall D. Sahlins, "The Segmentary Linkage: An Organization of Predatory Expansion," in *Comparative Political Systems* 89, 95–96 (Ronald Cohen & John Middleton eds. 1967).

39. Gluckman, supra note 37, ch. 3 (aptly entitled "Stateless Societies and the Maintenance of Order"); Lucy Mair, *Primitive Government* 51 (1962).

40. See Edward O. Wilson, *Sociobiology: The New Synthesis* 572–573 (1975). This practice, like the "double standard" mentioned below in the text, evidently has a genetic basis. It is a method of maximizing the spread of the genes of the prevailing group. Genetic aggressiveness is a genetic trait that will tend to be favorably selected in the struggle for survival, since any group that possesses it will tend to spread its genes (including the one carrying the genetic-aggressiveness trait) more widely than a group that does not possess it.

41. See Gluckman, supra note 37, at 88.

42. See Mair, supra note 39, at 41.

highly developed sense of honor;[43] the formally endorsed "double standard" which enjoins chastity on the wife but permits the husband to have all the concubines he can get—all are familiar features of primitive, prepolitical societies. This is powerful evidence that the society described by Homer is "real," albeit not necessarily historical in its details, but it also suggests a puzzle. Homer is the poet of the heroic individual. Yet we do not associate "individualism" with primitive societies even when they lack governmental institutions. We think of people in such societies as imprisoned in a web of custom and caste and kinship that leaves little room for any manifestation of individuality.

But in this we are wrong. A highly individualistic trait documented in the anthropological literature is the sense of personal honor and the readiness to fight for it.[44] As mentioned, this characteristic serves an important deterrent function in a society held together by reciprocity and retaliation rather than by public institutions of coercion. Paradoxically, a highly individualistic personality trait functions as a substitute for communal institutions. That it also impedes the operation of those institutions is an important theme of the *Iliad* (concern with honor both undoes Troy and delays the Greek victory), marking Homer as a chronicler of the transition between prepolitical and political society.

Kinship and class or caste status are present in the Homeric poems but do not deprive the hero of his individual freedom and responsibility. Although it is important to the plot of the *Iliad* that Menelaus and Agamemnon are brothers and that Achilles' mother is a goddess and Hector's is not, these relationships do not create a sense that outcomes are predetermined; the point of Achilles' divine parentage is to give a reason why he is such a powerful fighter.[45] Individuality is compromised, how-

43. See *id.* at 40.
44. See *id.*
45. Homeric man requires the identification of an external cause for every observed phenomenon, and the cause usually assigned is the act of some god. So if one observes a mighty warrior, one infers that there is a god in his family tree. Or if Agamemnon behaves like a fool, it must be because some god blinded him. This does not absolve him of responsibility, however, any more than my saying "I don't know what got into me" is a plea in justification or excuse. See E. R. Dodds, *The Greeks and the Irrational* ch. 1 (1951).

ever, within the *oikos*. The social atom in the Homeric world is not the individual but the household, a collectivity. But the Homeric *oikos* is not a true collective either. It is an extension of the head—of Odysseus or Agamemnon or whomever—and heads of households are the main characters in both poems. Their individuality is not compromised.

The nature of the personal relationships within the *oikos* is suggested by the word *philos,* which combines the notions of "dear" and of "own"; my arm is *philos* and so is my daughter. The members of one's *oikos* are a part of one's being. That is why the treachery of Odysseus's disloyal servants is felt with such a special intensity and why the death of Patroclus—not Achilles' kinsman but a member of his household—affects Achilles so violently. It is why a word like "friendship" has no counterpart in Homeric Greek. The gift relationships are alliances of a pragmatic nature, while relationships within the *oikos* —for example, the relationship between Achilles and Patroclus —have the intensity of close family relationships even when there is no family tie.

Some Modern Parallels

That the Homeric epics should depict principles of social order so different from our own, yet speak to us so movingly across the millenia, suggests that those principles cannot be wholly lacking in our own society; on reflection it is plain they are not. They are simply obscured by the vast public sector, which fills our vision. The coherence of many social institutions —organized religion, international trade, criminal societies, families, clubs, the private arbitration tribunals maintained by many trade associations and stock exchanges—is minimally and sometimes not at all procured by threat of public coercion. An important example is the ordinary commercial contract. Most such contracts would be obeyed even if there were no legal sanctions for breach, simply by the implicit threat of the disappointed party to refuse to engage in mutually beneficial exchanges with the breacher in the future. Gifts are exchanged in our society, and the sense of honor is still a human trait.

These "prepolitical" features of our modern social order can be illuminated by the study of their more distinct counterparts in the society depicted by Homer. Consider the gift that is not money. An economist would point out that since the recipient must know his own wants better than the donor, a gift of money equal to the cost of the gift would enhance the recipient's welfare at no additional cost to the donor.[46] However, as in Homeric gift exchanges, the modern nonpecuniary gift has an informational as well as donative function. It tells the recipient something about the donor's tastes and values, and the response to it tells the donor something about the recipient's tastes and values.

The study of Homeric society reveals not only a set of institutions and values alternative to those of political society but also a systematic linkage among them. Hospitality, reciprocity, honor, gifts, and revenge operate in mutually supportive roles to create a cohesive community. A similar constellation of traits and practices is probably found in those modern settings where, as in Homeric society generally, the coercive power of the state is not the basis of the social order. For example, I conjecture that in trades where, because of cost or other reasons, legal sanctions for breach of contract are ineffectual, businessmen will be extremely sensitive to accusations of sharp dealing because reputation is the only surety of faithful performance between contracting partners. The sense of business honor would be highly developed in such a trade, but less so in trades where merchants looked more to the courts to protect them from sharp dealing.

The Theory of the State

The analysis in this chapter may cast at least an oblique light on an old question in philosophy and anthropology: the origin

---

46. The cost to the donor would actually be less; he would save the time consumed in selecting and purchasing the gift.

of the state. Political philosophers from Hobbes to Nozick have sought to justify the state—the minimal, "nightwatchman" state, at least—as a solution to the problem of internal security.[47] There is, to be sure, a difference between justification and explanation. One can justify the state by imagining its formation as the product of a social contract, or one can explain it as the actual product of such a contract. The former is the approach of Nozick, the latter that of Hobbes.[48] But in either case the view of the state as the solution to the problem of internal security implies that there are no better solutions. This chapter should raise a doubt in the reader's mind as to whether the state is always the only possible solution to the problem of maintaining order within a society. Custom, gift exchange, honor, kinship, and other prepolitical institutions found in the Homeric poems make up an alternative system of order to the state. Probably these institutions would not work well in modern conditions (the reasons for this suggestion are explored in Chapters 7 and 8). But any rigorous theory of the state must explain *why* they would not work well today.

Anthropologists and ancient historians have not made the mistake of thinking that the state originated in the search for public order. Two theories dominate current anthropological-historical speculation on the origins of the state. One emphasizes the role of the state in coordinating large-scale economic projects, such as irrigation; this is the "hydraulic" theory of the state.[49] The other emphasizes conquest and defense against attempted conquest as motivating factors.[50] The analysis in this chapter supports the latter theory. The Homeric poems do not disclose public works on such a scale as would require state supervision, but they do disclose a problem of organizing to retali-

---

47. See Thomas Hobbes, *Leviathan* 202, 223–228 (C. B. MacPherson ed. 1968); John Locke, *The Second Treatise on Government* 70–73 (Thomas P. Peardon ed. 1952); Robert Nozick, *Anarchy, State, and Utopia* 15–17 (1974).
48. See Hobbes, supra note 47, at 189–192; Nozick, supra note 47, at 5–6.
49. See Karl Wittfogel, *Oriental Despotism* 49 (1957).
50. See Franz Oppenheimer, *The State* 15 (1914).

ate against a wrongdoer sheltered by a walled city. Another positive theory of the state should be mentioned: the exploitative. If wealth is unequally distributed in a society, wealthy individuals will have an incentive to hire retainers, and a state may eventually emerge from these armed bands. Thus, the maintenance of a stateless society may require equalizing the distribution of wealth. This issue is considered in the next chapter.

6

A Theory of Primitive Society

In this chapter I argue that many of the distinctive institutions of primitive society, including gift giving and reciprocal exchange, polygamy and brideprices, the size of kinship groups, and the value placed on certain personality traits such as generosity, are best explained as adaptations to uncertainty.[1] However, many important aspects of primitive life, including warfare, religion, and slavery, are omitted or discussed only in passing.[2]

The Costs of Information

The fact that primitive people do not understand the laws of nature well (belief in magic and sorcery is almost universal

1. The antecedents of my theory in the work of Clifford Geertz, Gary Becker, and others, as well as the general question of the applicability of economic concepts to primitive society (the "formalist" versus "substantivist" debate in economic anthropology), are discussed in Richard A. Posner, "A Theory of Primitive Society, with Special Reference to Law," 23 *J. Law & Econ.* 1–4 (1980). My analysis of primitive society is extended in an interesting recent paper by Reuven Brenner, "A Theory of Development, or Markets and Human Capital in Primitive Societies" (N.Y.U. Dept. Econ., Jan. 1980).

Although the analysis in this and the next chapter is limited to "primitive" societies as defined in note 1, Chapter 5, supra, much of the analysis is applicable, *mutatis mutandis*, to somewhat more advanced societies: to "peasant" societies, for example. Compare James C. Scott, *The Moral Economy of the Peasant* (1976), discussing the importance of "hunger insurance" in peasant societies; McCloskey's work on open fields in medieval English literature, referenced in note 28 infra; Samuel L. Popkin, *The Rational Peasant* (1979), a recent and far-ranging effort to apply the economic model to peasant behavior and institutions; Douglass C. North & Robert Paul Thomas, *The Rise of the Western World: A New Economic History* (1973); and the discussion of law enforcement in fifth- and fourth-century (B.C.) Athens in Chapter 8 of this book.

2. Warfare was discussed in Chapter 5, and religion is discussed in Chapter 8. These discussions are fragmentary. No one has yet developed an adequate economic theory of either war or religion.

among primitive peoples), have no system of writing and consequently no records,[3] and lack modern communications technology—with all that these lacks imply—suggests that the costs of obtaining information are higher in primitive than in advanced societies. More precisely, more inputs of time or other resources are required to obtain the same amount of information. This is trivially true of information concerning the many scientific and technical principles unknown to the primitive world. But·it is also true of information concerning the probability that the other party to a contract will perform (there are no courts to coerce his performance) or that the quantity delivered in a sale is the quantity bargained for (there are no scales in primitive markets); the cause of a death (there are no police or autopsies, and the possibility that death was caused by witchcraft cannot be rejected out of hand); and the marginal product of a farm laborer's work.

To be sure, some sources of ignorance are more characteristic of modern than of primitive life. One is specialization of knowledge, which in the twentieth century has advanced to the point where each of us is an ignoramus regarding vast areas of human knowledge. Another is the conditions of life and work in an urbanized society. The anonymity, impersonality, and privacy of such a society result in our knowing less about neighbors, co-workers, and even friends and family members than we would know in a primitive society. Both sources of ignorance, however, far from reflecting high information costs, are actually the product of low information costs, which have enabled knowledge to advance to the point where specialization has become efficient and have enabled social order to be maintained without continuous surveillance of the population.

The second point, relating to surveillance, requires amplification. No matter what the ratio of territory to inhabitants (and often it is very high), primitive people tend to live in crowded conditions where they are denied the preconditions of privacy

3. Like most generalizations about primitive society, this one is not universally valid. Some primitive societies have developed ingenious systems of record keeping that do not involve writing. See A. S. Diamond, *Primitive Law Past and Present* 203 (1971).

—separate rooms, doors, opportunities for solitude or anonymity, a measure of occupational or recreational mobility.[4] Lack of privacy has a number of implications for primitive values and institutions. It helps explain why crime rates in primitive societies are apparently moderate despite the absence of either formal investigative machinery (public or private) or compensatingly heavy penalties. The example of crime suggests, however, that the absence of privacy in primitive societies may itself be an adaptation to the high costs of information in a society that lacks public or private investigatory institutions or any form of press. One way of reducing information costs is to create living conditions in which everyone knows everything about everyone else. The denial of privacy in a primitive society serves to enlist the entire population as informers and policemen.[5]

While the denial of privacy increases the production of information in one respect, it reduces it in another, which may help to explain why the accretion of knowledge, and hence economic development, proceed so slowly in primitive societies. As I discuss more fully in Part III, some measure of privacy is necessary both to create the peace and quiet required for sustained and effective mental activity (which might lead to an improved understanding of the world) and to enable people, by concealing their ideas from other people, to appropriate the social benefits of their discoveries and inventions. In the absence of either formal rights to intellectual property, such as patent laws create, or public subsidization, concealment is the only method of obtaining a reward for developing a new productive technique. The costs of defining and enforcing intellectual-property rights are high even in our society, so that trade secrets remain an impor-

4. For evidence, see references in notes 16 and 31 in Chapter 9 and note 17 in Chapter 10, infra.

5. Marshall Sahlins, in *Stone Age Economics* 204 (1972), remarks on the "publicity of primitive life" as a mechanism for preserving public order. Donald W. Ball, "Privacy, Publicity, Deviance and Control," 18 *Pac. Soc. Rev.* 259 (1975), summarizes a number of cross-cultural studies finding a negative correlation between privacy and severity of punishments in a society and between privacy and the existence of law-enforcement institutions, although his interpretation of these findings is different from that implied in the text. And see the discussion of "shame" versus "guilt" cultures in Chapter 7.

tant method of appropriating the benefits of innovation; presumably these costs are even higher in primitive societies.[6] Public subsidization of inventors is ruled out by the rudimentary public finance in primitive societies, a factor that is itself traceable to the high costs of information in such societies. That leaves secrecy, which lack of privacy makes difficult to obtain.

The information costs that result from the lack of a system of writing require special mention. Complicated mental activity is possible without literacy, including subtle analysis of character and prodigious feats of memorization, both illustrated by the circumstances in which the Homeric poems were composed and originally performed. But what is generally not possible is large-scale organization for production or governance. Bureaucracy is closely associated with record keeping. This is as true of the Mycenaean palace state depicted in the Linear B tablets and the even earlier Egyptian and Sumerian kingdoms as it is of the modern state.[7] Among preliterate peoples government is generally weak[8] and sometimes nonexistent.[9] The absence of effective government, which I tentatively attribute to nonliteracy,[10]

6. To be sure, one finds property rights to a song, a spell, a crest, or a name—see, e.g., Diamond, supra note 3, at 188; Harold E. Driver, *Indians of North America* 269, 285 (2d rev. ed. 1969)—but, so far as I am aware, not to a productive idea or invention.

7. The link between literacy and government has been noted. See Diamond, supra note 3, at 39; Jack Goody, "Introduction," in *Literacy in Traditional Societies* 1, 2 (Jack Goody ed. 1968); Jack Goody & Ian Watt, "The Consequences of Literacy," in *id*. at 27, 36; Maurice Bloch, "Astrology and Writing in Madagascar," in *id*. at 277, 286.

8. An exception, but one that proves the rule, is the Ashanti kingdom in eighteenth-century Africa, which developed a system of record keeping, albeit one that did not involve writing. See Melville J. Herskovits, *Economic Anthropology* 420 (2d rev. ed. 1952).

9. See, besides Chapter 5 of this book, Driver, supra note 6, ch. 17; Herskovits, supra note 8, at 399–405, 416–438; Lucy Mair, *Primitive Government* (1962); Max Gluckman, *Politics, Law and Ritual in Tribal Society* (1965); *African Political Systems* (M. Fortes & E. E. Evans-Pritchard eds. 1940). I. Schapera, *Government and Politics in Tribal Societies* (1956), argues that previous writers exaggerated the weakness of primitive government, at least in African tribal society, though he gives examples of very weak governments in such societies. See *id*. at 38, 85, 88.

10. The causation could, however, go the other way. Primitive societies lack large-scale institutions because they are illiterate, but lacking such institutions they have no need for the kind of record keeping that requires literacy. For other communicative needs, even extremely subtle ones, an unwritten language may be quite adequate, as the Homeric poems attest.

has, as we shall see, profound consequences for the structure of primitive social institutions.

A Model of Primitive Society

Assumptions

I shall propose a simple model of primitive society. Although the model is derived from the assumption of high information costs, it can equally well be viewed and defended as an inductive generalization from the descriptive anthropological literature on primitive societies, unrelated to any underlying premise concerning the conditions of information in such societies.

The purpose of my model is not to deny the variety and complexity of primitive societies or to provide a realistic description of a particular society, but to explain why such institutional characteristics as weak government, ascription of rights and duties on the basis of family membership, and gift giving as a fundamental mode of exchange are found so much more frequently in primitive and archaic societies than in modern ones.[11] I am well aware that virtually any generalization about primitive society can be contradicted by reference to the practices of one or more such society. But if one looks at primitive and early so-

---

11. For archaic societies, the best general account of social institutions remains Henry Sumner Maine, *Ancient Law* (1861), though some of its conclusions are no longer accepted. On the current standing of Maine in light of the findings of modern anthropology, see Robert Redfield, "Maine's *Ancient Law* in the Light of Primitive Societies," 3 *W. Pol. Q.* 574 (1950), especially at 585–587. M. I. Finley, *The World of Odysseus* (2d rev. ed. 1978), is very good on the society depicted in the Homeric poems. On the Norse sagas, see sources referenced in David Friedman, "Private Creation and Enforcement of Law: A Historical Case," 8 *J. Legal Stud.* 399 (1979). The literature of modern social anthropology is of course vast. Some examples of this literature are Driver, supra note 6, on the North American Indian societies; Herskovits, supra note 8; Robert H. Lowie, *Primitive Society* (2d. ed. 1947); Lucy Mair, *African Societies* (1974); Carleton S. Coon, *The Hunting Peoples* (1971); *African Systems of Kinship and Marriage* (A. R. Radcliffe-Brown & Daryll Forde eds. 1950); Elman R. Service, *Primitive Social Organization* (2d ed. 1971). There are innumerable highly readable studies of particular societies, such as E. E. Evans-Pritchard, *The Nuer: A Description of the Modes of Livelihood and Political Institutions of a Nilotic People* (1940); Bronislaw Malinowski, *Crime and Custom in Savage Society* (1926); and Leopold Pospisil, *Kapauku Papuans and Their Law* (1958).

cieties as a whole and compares them with modern societies, one finds recurrent institutional differences, and it is these I seek to account for in my model.

The anthropologist may object to this effort on the further ground that my analytical categories, drawn as they are from modern economic theory, are ethnocentric and do violence to the ways in which primitive people think about their activities and institutions. But this objection could equally well be made to economic studies of modern society. Consumers and businessmen do not describe their activities in the terms that the economist uses, any more than primitive man does. The explanatory power of economics is independent of the consciousness of the economic actor.

The specific assumptions of the model are as follows:

1. There is no (effective) government. This exaggerates the anarchy of primitive life, but for most primitive societies (such as Homeric society, discussed in the last chapter) not critically. There may be a chief who is the leader in wartime but has no functions in peacetime and elders who exercise some intermittent authority; but generally there are no courts, legislatures, police, prosecutors, tax collectors, or other familiar public officials. At this level of abstraction the difference between no government and slight government is too small to matter. As mentioned earlier, I attribute the lack of government to nonliteracy, although the possibility that the causation runs in the opposite direction cannot be excluded.

2. The state of technical knowledge in the society is such that only a limited variety of consumption goods can be produced, with variety measured both by the number of separate goods and by quality variations within a single good. Admittedly, lack of standardization could generate considerable random quality variation, and variety is to some extent in the eye of the beholder.

3. The goods produced in the society are assumed to be traded on only a limited basis for goods produced in other societies. Unlimited trade would enable unlimited variety. But the costs of transportation, plus transaction costs created by lan-

guage differences, lack of currency, and lack of contract-enforcement mechanisms, make foreign trade generally a small part of the primitive economy.

4. The consumption goods produced in the society are assumed to be perishable goods that are consumed as soon as they are produced, which again is an exaggeration. Yet food preservation is a serious problem, and food is the most important product of such societies.[12]

A fifth assumption is necessary to keep the society from adopting more productive techniques:

5. The private gains from innovation—from reducing costs (including transportation), or increasing the variety of goods produced—are assumed to be negligible, either because such gains cannot be appropriated (the privacy problem) or for exogenous reasons.

The Insurance Principle and Its Implementing Institutions and Values

The model sketched above implies the strong if somewhat misnamed "redistributive" ethic that has been noted in innumerable studies of primitive society.[13] One expects insurance, specifically against hunger, to be a very important product in such society. The conditions of production, in particular the difficulty of storing food, create considerable uncertainty with

12. Sahlins, supra note 5, at 11–12, 31–32, explains the interrelationship, in a hunting economy, of lack of variety and lack of storability. Hunting bands must rove widely in search of game. Possessions, including preserved meat, would hamper their mobility, so one observes that the members do not have many possessions and do not preserve meat. Similarly, in primitive cultivation societies most of the members' energies are devoted to crop production, and the crops cannot be stored and are not converted into storable food products. Herding societies produce the most durable consumption goods; their institutions are somewhat different—and in the direction the model predicts.

13. The term "redistribution" as commonly used in economic and ethical discourse implies an effort, through the state, to bring about more (occasionally less) ex post economic equality than the free market would. Anthropologists generally assume that primitive societies are redistributive in approximately this sense (that is, in wanting to equalize wealth ex post beyond what the market would bring about or what would be efficient in the sense of wealth maximizing), but they tend to reserve the word "redistribution" for the allocation of a tribe's surplus agricultural production by the chief.

regard to the future adequacy of an individual's food supply and hence create considerable variance in his wealth.[14] In these circumstances it will be attractive to both parties to make a transaction whereby A, who produces a harvest that exceeds his consumption needs, gives part of his surplus to B in exchange for B's commitment to reciprocate if their roles are ever reversed. The alternative of self-insurance is not open to A because of the assumption that food is not storable.

The attractiveness to A of insurance is further enhanced by the assumed scarcity of alternative goods for which to exchange his surplus food: A will not be so tempted as he otherwise might to exchange his food surplus for other consumption goods rather than to buy hunger insurance with it. To be sure, he may be able to exchange his extra food for production or capital goods, of which the most important are women. But they are another form of "crop insurance," as are children, because of kinship obligations. And, apart from other economic reasons that limit the incidence of polygyny even in societies which permit it, as most primitive societies do, a highly durable and valuable good such as a woman is so much more valuable than one good harvest or one good kill, which are limited and evanescent, that it is difficult to accumulate the purchase price. Hence one expects that, other things being equal, polygyny will be more common in herding than in other primitive societies, because a herding society has durable goods to exchange for women.[15]

14. On the precariousness of primitive life see Manning Nash, *Primitive and Peasant Economic Systems* 22 (1960); M. Fortes, "The Political System of the Tallensi of the Northern Territories of the Gold Coast," in *African Political Systems*, supra note 9, at 239, 249.

15. Some evidence relevant to this prediction can be found in Frederic L. Pryor, *The Origins of the Economy: A Comparative Study of Distribution in Primitive and Peasant Economies* (1977). Eliminating from his sample societies—not primitive in my sense—which he classifies as "economically oriented" or "politically oriented," and then comparing the incidence of polygyny: in societies in which animal husbandry yielded at least 10 percent of all food, polygyny was common in 13, not common in 7; in societies in which animal husbandry yielded less than 10 percent of all food, polygyny was common in 9, not common in 11. (Calculated from Pryor, supra, at 328, variable 5; 333–334, variables 59, 61, 69; 336–339.)

In short, without assuming that primitive people are any more risk averse or less individualistic than modern people, one can nonetheless explain economically the importance of insurance as a product demanded and supplied in primitive society. Indeed, primitive people might be less risk averse than modern people yet still desire more insurance, both because of their riskier circumstances and because of the dearth of alternative goods. But we have yet to consider the institutional form in which insurance will be provided. The first assumption of the model—the absence of a government—rules out the possibility that the food surplus will be taxed away and redistributed by the state to the needy. Also, in combination with the underlying conditions of information in primitive society, which are likely to retard the emergence of formal markets, the absence of an effective government impedes the emergence of a formal private insurance market in which food would be exchanged for an enforceable promise to reciprocate when and if necessary. There is no state to enforce promises. To be sure, even without formal sanctions, most promises will be honored simply because the promisor wants the promisee to deal with him in the future. But not all will be honored: an old man may renege on his promise to share his surplus if it is unlikely that he will live long enough to be "punished" for his breach of contract by the refusal of anyone else to sell him hunger insurance in the future.[16]

However, governmental social insurance and formal market insurance do not exhaust the institutional repertoire. For example, the effectiveness of reciprocity as an incentive to share surplus food with others can be enhanced if people confine their sharing to, or at least concentrate it within, a group whose members know and continually interact with one another and have broadly similar abilities, propensities, character, and prospects. The institution most likely to satisfy these requirements

16. In one primitive society it is reported that the young are reluctant to share their food with the old because it is unlikely that the old will be there to reciprocate in the future. See Allan C. Holmberg, *Nomads of the Long Bow* 151–153 (1969).

On the limitations of self-enforcing agreements, see the interesting paper by L. G. Telser, "A Theory of Self-Enforcing Agreements," 53 *J. Bus.* 27 (1980).

for a satisfactory informal "mutual insurance company" is the family. The family as we know it, however, is too small to create an adequate risk pool for insurance purposes. This may be one reason why primitive societies devote so many of their linguistic, legal, and informational resources to delineating kinship groups much larger than the modern family or, for that matter, the primitive household.[17] The primitive concern with careful definition and determination of the kinship group is based not on some idle genealogical curiosity but on the fact that in a primitive society the legal and moral obligations that we moderns have to support our very close relatives (sometimes only our minor children) extend to all of the members of one's kinship group. I attribute this to a lack of alternative insurance mechanisms in primitive society.

The argument so far establishes only why people might want to limit their insurance arrangements to kinsmen, not why they should be *required* to enter into such arrangements with them. Recent work in the economics of information suggests an answer to this question. Consider modern life insurance. If we assume that individuals know their own life expectancy better than the insurance company, there will be a tendency for the better risks to withdraw from the insurance pool because they do not wish to pay premiums based on average life expectan-

17. The most common system of kinship among primitive peoples is the patrilineal, wherein descent is traced through the male line. In a patrilineal system a man, his sons, their sons, etc., belong to the same descent group, while his daughters' sons will become members of the descent group of the men the daughters marry. But kinship ties often cross the line between different descent groups. For example, a woman upon marriage may remain a member of her father's descent group, entitled to seek assistance from him, although she lives with another descent group. The main point, however, is that the primitive kinship group is larger than the modern or primitive *household,* and where kinship ties cross, descent groups may achieve a measure of geographical diversification. These characteristics of the kinship group are presumably related to its insurance functions, as are the rigid and demanding obligations among kin—for example, a brother's son might be entitled to take a cow from the brother without asking permission, let alone paying. See, e.g., I. Schapera, *A Handbook of Tswana Law and Custom* 219–221 (1938). For excellent introductions to the complexities of kinship definitions and structures in primitive society, see A. R. Radcliffe-Brown, "Introduction," in *African Systems of Kinship and Marriage,* supra note 11, at 1; Robin Fox, *Kinship and Marriage: An Anthropological Perspective* (1967).

cies, which are lower than theirs, and the pool will shrink, conceivably to the vanishing point.[18] One solution to this problem is employee life insurance, whereby insurance is provided as a condition of employment and no one can withdraw from the insurance pool without giving up his job.[19] A similar problem and solution are found in primitive society. If a man knows better than anyone else how likely he is some day to need food from a kinsman, the better risks will tend to select themselves out of the insurance system. This problem would disappear if the customary insurance premium (for example, during his lifetime a nephew can demand one cow from his uncle) could be varied by a negotiation in which the parties would communicate to each other any respects in which their prospects differed from the average. But if this alternative to selection out is assumed to be infeasible because of the high costs of information, then we have a reason to expect the obligations of sharing to be made compulsory within the kinship group.[20]

What determines the size of the kinship group within which an obligation to share is recognized? On the one hand, the larger the group, the smaller will be the covariance in the food production of the individual members and hence the more insurance will be provided. It is essential that the kinship group be larger than the household, since the covariance within the household is likely to be very high; also, the more geographically scattered the kinship group, the lower the covariance will be. On the other hand, the smaller and geographically more concentrated the kinship group is, the less serious will be the "moral hazard" problem—the temptation of a man not to work and to live off his kinsmen.[21] Presumably, there is some opti-

18. See George A. Akerlof, "The Market for 'Lemons': Quality Uncertainty and the Market Mechanism," 84 *Q. J. Econ.* 488 (1970).

19. See Yoram Barzel, "Some Fallacies in the Interpretation of Information Costs," 20 *J. Law & Econ.* 291, 303 (1977).

20. To be sure, this leaves open the possibility that the better risk will simply forswear his kinship membership. But this is a very costly step to take because of the protective functions of the kinship group, discussed in the next chapter.

21. Cf. S. F. Nadel, "Dual Descent in the Nuba Hills," in *African Systems of Kinship and Marriage*, supra note 11, at 333, 358.

mum size and dispersion of the kinship group depending on the circumstances of the particular society. The optimum size is presumably larger the more primitive the society is: the less variety and storage possibilities of consumption goods, the less the wealthy man gives up by producing a surplus to be shared in part with his poor kinsmen, and hence the disincentive effect on him of having to share is smaller. The effects on his incentives may be trivial indeed if, as is plausible, the precise amount of the surplus produced is beyond his control. And, given the nonstorability of food and the uncertainty of the harvest, the poor kinsman who relaxes his own productive efforts in anticipation of sharing in a wealthy kinsman's harvest is acting recklessly.[22]

The obligation of sharing with kinsmen is not the only device by which primitive society, lacking formal insurance contracts or public substitutes, provides hunger insurance for its members. Generosity toward other members of one's village or band as well as toward kinsmen is a more highly valued trait in primitive than in modern society, and the reason appears to be that it is a substitute for formal insurance.[23] The fact that in a primitive society a man obtains prestige by giving away what he has rather than by keeping it has been considered as evidence of the inapplicability of the economic model to such societies. (The potlatch of the Northwest Indians is only the most dramatic example of "buying" prestige by giving away one's goods on a seemingly extravagant scale.[24]) But where consumption goods

22. The optimal size of the group within which income is shared is discussed in another context in John Umbeck, "A Theory of Contract Choice and the California Gold Rush," 20 *J. Law & Econ.* 421 (1977).

23. Compare E. E. Evans-Pritchard, supra note 11, at 85: "This habit of share and share alike is easily understandable in a community where every one is likely to find himself in difficulties from time to time, for it is scarcity and not sufficiency that make people generous, since everybody is thereby insured against hunger. He who is in need to-day receives help from him who may be in like need to-morrow."

24. See Stuart Piddocke, "The Potlatch System of the Southern Kwakiutl: A New Perspective," in *Economic Anthropology: Readings in Theory and Analysis* 283 (Edward E. LeClair, Jr. & Harold K. Schneider eds. 1968). There are also informational and political objectives of dissipating surpluses, and in primitive societies that have the technological capacity to store food, these objectives may interfere with storage of surpluses and thus with the provision of insurance against hunger. For an example see S. F. Nadel, *The Nuba: An Anthropological Study of the Hill Tribes of Kordofan* 49–50 (1947).

are limited in variety and durability, giving away one's surplus (by which I mean simply the difference between production and normal consumption) may be the most useful thing to do with it, at least from society's standpoint. It is not surprising that it should earn the kind of prestige we bestow on a great inventor, scientist, captain of industry, or entertainer.[25]

If prestige is the carrot that encourages generosity, an extreme illustration of the stick is the occasional Eskimo practice of killing ungenerous rich people.[26] In our society such behavior would be shortsighted; as we saw in Chapter 3, a productive individual, however selfish, produces consumer surplus for others to enjoy. But consumer surplus reflects the benefits of division of labor, specialization, and exchange of the resulting output, features that are largely absent from primitive society. The principal good exchanged in the simplest societies, such as that of the Eskimos, is insurance, and the rich man's refusal to share his surplus with others is a refusal to engage in this exchange. He really is of little or no use to the other members of the society, so killing him does not impose costs on them as it would in an advanced society.

The insurance perspective may also help to explain why some primitive societies do not allow interest to be charged on a loan. A "loan" in primitive society often corresponds to the payment of an insurance claim in modern society; it is the insurer's fulfillment of his contractual undertaking, and allowing interest

25. The fact that in primitive, as in modern, society prestige is related to social productivity is (inadvertently) brought out in a passage quoted in Herskovits, supra note 8, at 121, to illustrate his contention that "the prestige drives that have been seen to afford so strong a motivation for labor in other groupings is at a minimum" in nomadic society. The quoted passage reads: "When the immediate needs for food have been supplied, a person is neither much criticized for doing nothing, nor much praised for occupying a better house or a larger garden, both of which may have to be abandoned in the next move." But in these circumstances building a better house or a larger garden is *not* constructive. The society is better off if people conserve their energies (and hence food needs) rather than make investments whose fruits cannot be reaped.

26. See E. Adamson Hoebel, *The Law of Primitive Man: A Study in Comparative Legal Dynamics* 81 (1964). There is little emphasis in Eskimo culture on kinship, probably because their environment forces them to live in very small, widely scattered bands that have little regular contact with one another. See *id.* at 68. The emphasis on generosity to unrelated individuals within the band is a substitute for kin insurance.

would change the nature of the transaction. A related custom is that a man may be required to make a loan when asked.[27] The involuntary loan is another dimension of the duty of generosity noted earlier. Since in my model a man's surplus is assumed to have relatively little value to him (because of storage problems and a lack of goods for which to exchange a surplus), the ordinary resistance that rich people would feel at being required to make loans is attenuated.

The insurance function of loans is especially pronounced in the cattle lending which is so prominent a feature of African tribal society. The main purpose of such loans is not to earn interest but to disperse one's cattle geographically so as to reduce the risk of catastrophic loss from disease.[28]

A loan without interest resembles a gift, especially if (as is common) the society does not provide remedies for default.[29] Yet the moral duty to repay a loan is recognized in primitive societies and is enforced in various ways. Similarly, gifts in primitive society are explicitly reciprocal: a man is under a strong moral duty to repay a gift with a gift of equivalent value.[30] In

27. See R. F. Barton, *The Kalingas: Their Institutions and Custom Law* 132 (1949); Herskovits, supra note 8, at 373.

28. See, e.g., E. H. Winter, "Livestock Markets among the Iraqw of Northern Tanganyika," in *Markets in Africa* 457, 461 (Paul Bohannan & George Dalton eds. 1962); Elisabeth Colson, "Trade and Wealth among the Tonga," in *id.* at 601, 607; Nash, supra note 14, at 50–51. The resemblance to the "open fields" policy in medieval English agriculture, discussed by McCloskey in similar terms, is evident. See Donald N. McCloskey, "English Open Fields as Behavior towards Risk," 1 *Res. in Econ. Hist.* 124 (1976), and "The Persistence of English Common Fields," in *European Peasants and Their Markets* 73 (William N. Parker & Eric L. Jones eds. 1975). McCloskey remarks the presence of open-field policies in some primitive societies. See *id.* at 114. He also notes the possibility of the family's acting as an insurance institution. See *id.* at 117.

29. The absence of such remedies appears to explain why, where interest is permitted, the interest rate is often very high: the probability of default is very high. See Herskovits, supra note 8, at 228.

30. The literature on gift-giving in primitive and archaic societies is immense. For some examples see Finley, supra note 11, at 62; Herskovitz, supra note 8, ch. 8; Bronislaw Malinowski, "Tribal Economics in the Trobriands," in *Tribal and Peasant Economies: Readings in Economic Anthropology* 185 (George Dalton ed. 1967); Marcel Mauss, *The Gift: Forms and Functions of Exchange in Archaic Societies* (Ian Cunnison trans. 1954); V. A. Riasanovsky, *Customary Law of the Nomadic Tribes of Siberia* 144–145 (1938); Sahlins, supra note 5, ch. 5. See also Chapter 5.

these circumstances the term "gift" is a misnomer. Gifts, noninterest-bearing loans (sometimes involuntary), feasts, generosity,
and the other "redistributive" mechanisms of primitive society
are not the product of altruism; at least, it is not necessary to
assume altruism in order to explain them.[31] They are insurance
payments.[32] The principle of reciprocity that commands a man
to repay a loan or a gift when he can or to feast his benefactors
when he can provides some protection against the free-riding
or moral-hazard problems that would otherwise be created by
so inclusive and informal a system of insurance as is found in
primitive societies.

It is sometimes argued that, however reciprocal, the exchange of gifts in primitive society cannot be a form of trade
because so often what is exchanged is the same sort of good and
because there is no time limit on when reciprocation is due. But
these points show only that the exchange of gifts is not the same
kind of trade that arises in a more complex society out of the
division of labor and resulting specialization. Its purpose is to
even out consumption over time rather than to exploit the division of labor and would be utterly defeated if the gifts were exchanged simultaneously.[33]

Nor is it correct to argue, as in the following passage about
gift exchange in early medieval society, that the absence of
"profit motive" distinguishes such exchange from modern commercial transactions:

31. The feast is not only a means of providing food to many people; it is also a form
of "forced saving"—the giver of the feast must accumulate food in order to give it. Of
course, the feast may dissipate the accumulated food prematurely. See note 24 supra.

32 Cyril S. Belshaw, *Traditional Exchange and Modern Markets* 38 (1965), describes a
practice in one tribe which illustrates this point nicely. A creates a gift-exchange relationship by making a gift to B, which B is not free to refuse. Thereafter A can demand
reciprocation of the gift from B at any time. This "on demand" reciprocity gives A a
hedge against uncertainty. Cf., with reference to loans, S. C. Humphreys, *Anthropology
and the Greeks* 152 (1978).

33. The simultaneous exchange of gifts does occur in primitive societies but it has a
different function, discussed in Chapter 5 and also later in this chapter, from either
insurance or exploiting the division of labor.

This mutual exchange of gifts at first sight resembles commerce, but its objects and ethos are entirely different. Its object is not that of material and tangible "profit," derived from the difference between the value of what one parts with and what one receives in exchange; rather it is the social prestige attached to generosity, to one's ability and readiness to lavish one's wealth on one's neighbours and dependents. The "profit" consists in placing other people morally in one's debt, for a counter-gift—or services in lieu of one—is necessary if the recipient is to retain his self-respect.[34]

The author writes as if the typical modern commercial transaction were one-sided—A sells B a good or service knowing that it is worth less than B thinks. Rather, the typical transaction is mutually advantageous because it enables both parties to exploit the division of labor. Giving in the expectation that the gift will some day be reciprocated involves the same "profit motive" as the modern commercial transaction, although its basis is the desire for insurance rather than the desire to exploit the division of labor.[35]

The system of reciprocal exchange, as we may describe the network of institutions described above for allocating a food surplus in a primitive society, would appear to be a fragile one because there are no legal sanctions for failure to reciprocate

---

34. Philip Grierson, "Commerce in the Dark Ages: A Critique of the Evidence," in *Studies in Economic Anthropology* 74, 79 (George Dalton ed. 1971).

35. Another example of the insurance mechanisms of primitive society is the pair of principles that (1) debts never expire—there is no statute of limitations, although in an oral society it would be a considerable convenience—and (2) people inherit their fathers' debts even when the debts exceed the estate. See, e.g., Barton, supra note 27, at 126; Max Gluckman, *The Ideas in Barotse Jurisprudence* 195 (1965); R. S. Rattray, *Ashanti Law and Constitution* 370–371 (1929). The saying is, "Debts never rot." See Walter Goldschmidt, *Sebei Law* 62, 188, 204 (1967). These principles increase the scope of the insurance principle. If you lend money to an old and poor man, you are not permanently out of pocket; his heirs remain obligated to you. Yet the inheritance of debts is not a crushing burden on them. They are obligated to repay the loan only if and when they have a good year and therefore can afford to repay it without lowering their own consumption below its normal level.

promptly and adequately for benefits received.[36] Perhaps, therefore, a sixth assumption should be added to the model:

6. The population is immobile, in the sense that a member of one village, band, or tribe cannot readily join another and distant unit. Mobility would make the incentive to free ride and the reluctance to share without an enforceable promise to reciprocate very great. Mobility is in fact quite limited in most primitive societies, as the conditions of information in such societies would lead one to expect. Where mobility is great, the system of reciprocal exchange tends to break down.[37]

Some quantitative evidence bearing on the foregoing analysis is presented in Table 1. The table shows that the less developed

Table 1. Relative frequency of modes of distribution at different levels of economic development.

	Relative frequency of distribution mode	
Type of distribution	15 societies at lowest level	15 societies at highest level
Goods		
Market exchange	7	14
Sharing	13	3
Reciprocal exchange	13	3
Centralized redistribution	3	10
Labor		
Market exchange	2	14
Reciprocal exchange	10	9
Centralized redistribution	0	5
Other		
Presence of interest	2	9.5

Source: Pryor, supra note 15, at 309 (tab. 11.1).

36. For some examples of attempts to evade the obligations of reciprocal exchange see Sahlins, supra note 5, at 125, 128–129, and note 16 supra.

37. For evidence of this in an Eskimo village see Pryor, supra note 15, at 91. A similar point is made in the biological literature on reciprocal altruism. See David P. Barash,

a primitive society is—and the more, therefore, its economy approximates the conditions of my model—the more likely it is to distribute goods through gift exchange, noninterest-bearing loans, and sharing, and the less likely it is to rely on market exchange. Pryor also found that reciprocal exchange is more important in hunting, fishing, and agricultural societies than in gathering and herding societies: consistently with the spirit of my model, he remarks that in the first three types of society the food supply is more uncertain, which increases the demand for a principle of reciprocal exchange.[38]

The rows in Table 1 labeled "centralized redistribution" refer to redistribution by a public authority such as a chief or king. The paucity of centralized redistribution among the least developed societies is a clue to the weakness of government in those societies.[39]

Political Aspects of Insurance and Polygamy

Insurance tends to equalize the ex post distribution of wealth, and there is evidence that this is an effect of the insurance arrangements of primitive society.[40] But equality of wealth is not only a by-product of insurance; it is also a precondition of the maintenance of a pregovernmental political equilibrium. A man who has a food surplus year after year—a wealthy man—would be an inviting target to other members of the society. He could use his wealth to hire retainers to protect him, trading part of his surplus for their loyalty, and other members of society could

---

Sociobiology and Behavior 314 (1977). The biological concept of reciprocal altruism seems, in fact, indistinguishable from the economic concept of self-interested but reciprocal exchange that I use to explain primitive social institutions.

38. See Pryor, supra note 15, at 195. For references to discussions in the anthropological literature of the insurance function of reciprocal exchange in primitive societies see Posner, supra note 1, at 18–19 n. 51.

39. Pryor's sample includes peasant as well as primitive societies. The predominance of market exchange and public redistribution in the second column suggests that the columns are comparing primitive societies (column 1) with what in my terminology would be nonprimitive societies (column 2).

40. Pryor, supra note 15, at 200–201, finds reciprocal exchange to be positively correlated with socioeconomic equality. See also *id*. at 261, 276.

try to undermine the retainers' loyalty by promising them a bigger share of his surplus if they turned against him and appropriated his wealth. In the resulting struggle, either the wealthy man or someone else might emerge with such a following that he could overawe the other individuals and families in the society: could, in short, establish a state, with himself as its head. Thus, observing a society that has little or no government despite the limited variety of consumption goods (and hence an incentive to use any surplus to hire thugs and henchmen), one may assume that there are institutions that limit the ability of the abler or more energetic people to use their surplus food for political ends. The insurance institutions of primitive society have this effect by tending to dissipate surpluses.[41]

The political function of insurance in primitive societies is illuminated by comparison with the feudal system. Feudalism is one response to a situation in which some people are able to produce an agricultural surplus but there are few goods to buy with it. They use the surplus to hire retainers and thus enhance their political power.[42] Most primitive societies are not feudalistic. The poor man has rights to the goods of his (wealthy) kinsman without corresponding duties to serve him. This one-sided

41. Consistently with this analysis, Pryor, supra note 15, at 426–427, finds a negative correlation between socioeconomic equality and amount of government, as do several earlier studies referenced in Edwin E. Erickson, "Cultural Evolution," 20 *Am. Behavioral Scientist* 669, 673 (1977). And Robert A. LeVine, "The Internalization of Political Values in Stateless Societies," 19 *Human Organization* 51, 53 (1960), finds a negative correlation between equality and sharing on the one hand and the possession of political values on the other hand.

In discussing the institutions that support a pregovernmental equilibrium in primitive society, I make no judgment as to whether those institutions are efficient in an economic sense. Probably government is more efficient than alternative institutions of public order. But effective government may not be feasible in a preliterate society, in which event the substitute institutions may represent efficient second-best solutions to the problem of public order. On the efficiency of primitive institutions see further the conclusion to Chapter 7.

42. This is approximately Adam Smith's theory of feudalism. See *The Wealth of Nations* Bk. 3, ch. 4 (1776). Cf. Mair, supra note 9, ch. 4, especially p. 67. On the importance of armed retainers in at least the early stages of medieval European feudalism see 1 Marc Bloch, *Feudal Society* 154, 169 (L. A. Manyon trans. 1961). For a recent economic analysis of feudalism, stressing other factors, see North & Thomas, pt. 2, supra note 1.

relationship would be intolerable under conditions of great and persistent inequality of wealth—a class system. But the emergence of such a system is forestalled by the vagaries of the harvest and the hunt, which are extreme in the primitive economy, and by the difficulty of storing an agricultural surplus or an animal's carcass without decay, or of exchanging these things for durable goods. Because of these factors, everyone in the society has a large variance in his expected wealth and is therefore willing to subscribe to an elaborate set of insurance arrangements despite his current wealth position. The result is to equalize wealth ex post.

Polygamy, superficially a source of great inequality, may actually promote the economic equality and resulting political stability of primitive society. To be sure, in its usual form—polygyny (many wives)—polygamy presupposes some inequality of wealth.[43] Given diminishing returns (not offset by opportunities for greater division of labor) from having additional wives, a supply of women more or less fixed at the number of men, and a strong desire by most men to have at least one wife, one man would have to be much wealthier than another to be willing and able to pay more for his second, third, or nth wife than a rival suitor seeking his first. The amount of polygyny is often small even where it is permitted,[44] which indicates either that the inequality of wealth is not great (as appears to be true in most primitive societies) or that the returns from having a second wife are indeed much lower than those from the first (or that both factors are at work). In any event, while polygyny presupposes some inequality in wealth, it need not increase it. Where polygyny is common, generally the bridegroom or his kin must pay a substantial brideprice to the bride's kin.[45] More impor-

43. See Gary S. Becker, *The Economic Approach to Human Behavior* 240 (1976).

44. See, e.g., *id.*, and references cited; A. S. Diamond, supra note 3, at 246 n.2.

45. Since the brideprice is divided among the bride's kin, this is a further example of the insurance principle at work. Lucy Mair, *Marriage*, ch. 4 (2d ed. 1977), is a good introduction to the complex subject of brideprice. Polygyny seems strongly associated with payment of substantial brideprice. See Amyra Grossbard, "Toward a Marriage between Economics and Anthropology and a General Theory of Marriage," 68 *Am. Econ.*

tant, polygyny has a tendency to reduce inequality over time by increasing the number of dependents (wives and children) who must be provided for when the husband dies.[46] Because his estate is divided in more ways,[47] the inequality of wealth in the next generation is less. Where polygyny is not permitted, inheritance by primogeniture would tend to perpetuate inequalities of wealth across generations, so one would expect to find rules of equal inheritance, or other equalizing departures from primogeniture, in primitive societies where polygyny is forbidden. There is some evidence for this correlation.[48]

To be sure, polygyny tends to increase inequality across families, assuming that the polygynous offspring remain within the father's family, as would be true of the male offspring in a patri-

---

Rev. Papers & Proceedings 33, 36 (1978); Pryor, supra note 15, at 364 (tab. B3). Pryor's statistical study of brideprices (see *id*. at 348–368) goes some way toward resolving the old debate over whether the payment of brideprice is a real exchange or merely some kind of symbolic gesture—in favor of the exchange model. On the prevalence of bride purchase in archaic societies see Diamond, supra note 3, at 57, 69. Diamond is here speaking of the "early codes," i.e., the laws of societies which have just become literate. Presumably these codes largely codify the preexisting body of oral law. For further discussion of primitive marriage customs, see Chapter 7.

46. See M. Fortes, supra note 14, at 250; Jack Goody, "Bridewealth and Dowry in Africa and Eurasia," in Jack Goody & S. J. Tambiah, *Bridewealth and Dowry* 1, 13, 17–18, 32 (1973); Robert A. LeVine, "Wealth and Power in Gusiiland," in *Markets in Africa*, supra note 28, at 520, 522–523; Frederic L. Pryor, "Simulation of the Impact of Social and Economic Institutions on the Size Distribution of Income and Wealth," 63 *Am. Econ. Rev.* 50, 54 (1973). See also Jack Goody, *Production and Reproduction: A Comparative Study of the Domestic Domain* (1976), arguing for an association between polygamy, brideprice, equality of wealth, and weak government, on the one hand, and monogamy, dowry, inequality of wealth, and strong government, on the other. For some evidence that monogamy is positively and polygamy negatively correlated with strong government, see Mary Douglas, "Lele Economy Compared with the Bushong: A Study of Economic Backwardness" in *Markets in Africa*, supra note 28 at 211.

47. See discussion of family law in the next chapter.

48. Of the seventeen societies classified by Pryor, supra note 15, at 327–339, as ones in which a positive political orientation was lacking but in which polygyny was also uncommon, information contained in the Human Relations Area Files indicates that only one had primogeniture as the method of inheritance, one had no inheritance at all, and the other fifteen divided property more or less equally on death (though sometimes only male offspring inherited). In contrast, primogeniture is common in primitive polygynous societies, meaning that the eldest son of each wife inherits the estate allocable to that wife. See note 14, Chapter 7.

lineal society. Because of the important role of the family in the maintenance of public order, such a disequalizing force could upset the political equilibrium of a primitive society. But usually in primitive societies authority in kinship groups is not tightly centralized; and since the groups tend to fission when they grow large,[49] beyond some point an increase in the number of members may not significantly increase the group's power— the added strength may be offset by reduced cohesion. The contrast with the hierarchical structure of feudalism (or of the modern corporation) is evident.

Polygyny disperses political power in another way, by increasing the opportunity costs of retainers.[50] Wealth is thereby diverted into a politically harmless channel, because women are useless as fighters in primitive societies.[51] Consistently with this analysis, it is reported that in one African tribe where government had emerged to the extent that the chief was claiming a monopoly of the right to redistribute the tribe's food surplus to the needy members of the tribe, the chief encouraged the wealthy men of the tribe to buy additional wives. He was con-

49. See, e.g., Daryll Forde, "Double Descent Among the Yako," in *African Systems of Kinship and Marriage*, supra note 11, at 285, 294.

50. That is, to hire a retainer, the wealthy man forgoes the opportunity to buy another wife instead. An alternative use of wealth would be to rent one's extra land or hire laborers to work it. But this alternative appears to encounter information costs greater than primitive society can cope with. See notes 12 and 13 and accompanying text in Chapter 7.

51. Thus, is it completely accidental that feudalism flourished in medieval Europe, which was strongly monogamous? My analysis suggests that, other things being equal (obviously a vital qualification), feudalism is less likely to emerge in a society where polygyny is permitted than in one where it is forbidden. Diamond, supra note 3, at 376, states that brideprice diminished with the growth of feudalism. This finding makes sense because the opportunity cost of a wife is higher in a feudal than in a prefeudal system.

The value of additional wives, it should be noted, is not only or mainly to provide sexual variety; it is to provide additional insurance, especially by increasing the number of sons to whom, as members of his kin group, the father can look for support in his old age. Accordingly, where women are the principal capital good in a society, it is understandable why a man who sells women for other goods should be despised—as he is among the Tiv, for example (see Paul Bohannan, "Some Principles of Exchange and Investment among the Tiv," in *Economic Anthropology*, supra note 24, at 300, 304): he is dissipating his capital.

cerned that if they did not use their wealth in that way they might use it to feed the needy and thereby undermine his position.[52]

Table 2 cross-tabulates two of Pryor's variables: polygyny and the society's political orientation. The table shows that polygyny is more common in a society that is negatively politically oriented (that is, tending toward statelessness) than in one that is positively oriented. This evidence is consistent with my suggestion that polygyny operates to disperse political power and thereby support the pregovernmental political equilibrium of primitive society.

Other Primitive Adaptations to High Information Costs

1. Concerning the most conspicuous primitive institution explicable by reference to the high costs of information—the belief in and practice of magic, sorcery, and witchcraft—I shall content myself with noting how frequently superstitions appear to promote the economic well-being of the society. For example, in many societies a man who gets too wealthy—who fails, in other words, to carry out his social duty of sharing his surplus— is likely to be considered a witch.[53] This result may be thought

Table 2. Political orientation and polygyny.

Political orientation	Number of societies	
	Polygyny common	Polygyny uncommon
Positive[a]	4	12
Negative[b]	7	1

Source: Calculated from Pryor, supra note 15, at 318, 333–334 (variables in 6, 69), 336–339.
a. Marked 1 in col. 61, p. 339 of Pryor.
b. Marked −1 in *id.*

52. See I. Schapera, "Economic Changes in South African Native Life," in *Tribal and Peasant Economies,* supra note 30, at 136, 142.
53. See, e.g., Driver, supra note 6, at 444.

an example of the primitive's envious resentment of anyone who lifts himself above the average—and envious resentment may in fact describe his feelings—but it can equally well be viewed as a rational response (judged by consequences, not state of mind) to the demand for insurance and the lack of the conventional modern mechanisms for supplying it. Or consider the belief of one tribe that misfortune will befall anyone who sells his goods on the way to the market.[54] This seems a silly belief until it is remembered that a market's efficiency is increased if as many buy and sell offers as possible can be pooled in it. Or consider the common practice in primitive and archaic societies of burying people with their personal possessions or destroying those possessions at their death.[55] These are methods of equalizing wealth in the next generation,[56] yielding benefits that have already been discussed.

2. Age grading—the assignment of tasks or roles on the basis of age—is more common in primitive than in modern societies. For example, all males seven to ten years of age in a primitive community might be assigned as herdsmen, all those eleven to fourteen as junior warriors, all fifteen to thirty-year-olds as senior warriors, all those above thirty as tribal elders. Sex is also used more than in modern societies to determine work assignments. One explanation for this kind of age and sex grading is simply that the tasks in such societies are so simple that individual differences are unimportant to the quality of performance. Another explanation, drawing on recent work in the economics of information, notes that age and sex are proxies for individual fitness for a particular job. They economize on the information required to make an assessment of individual strength, skill, and character.[57] Despite the superior knowledge of each other's character that primitive people possess because of their lack of

54. See Herskovits, supra note 8, at 205.
55. See, e.g., *id.* at 491–492.
56. See T. Scarlett Epstein, *Capitalism, Primitive and Modern* 31 (1968).
57. See, e.g., Edmund S. Phelps, "The Statistical Theory of Racism and Sexism," 62 *Am. Econ. Rev.* 659 (1972). This point forms the heart of my analysis of racial discrimination in Part IV.

privacy, difficulties of evaluation and supervision may make the measurement of an individual's marginal product more costly in primitive than in modern societies, leading the former to rely more heavily on crude but cheap proxies for individual capacity.

3. As mentioned earlier, gifts play a larger role in primitive than in advanced societies. While their role is partly explained in terms of mutual insurance, they also have the direct informational aspect discussed in the last chapter. Gifts within the kin group or village are generally an aspect of the insurance system described earlier, for within the small group all is known about everyone's character and nothing remains to be communicated by gift. But an exchange of gifts between strangers, as accompanies betrothal to the member of another kin group living in another village, probably has an informational function.[58] (These betrothal gifts, it should be noted, are distinct from the brideprice, which is the purchase price.) Viewed as a signaling device, a gift need not actually be received or enjoyed by the donee. The form of Northwest Indian potlatch, sometimes regarded as pathological, in which goods are destroyed rather than given away can be interpreted as an especially credible method of signaling the possession of wealth and of whatever qualities are correlated with its possession.[59]

4. With regard to trade in the ordinary sense—trade of unlike articles between strangers—in primitive society, transaction costs are high because of the costs of information regarding the reliability of the seller, the quality of the product, and trading alternatives (the market price). However, institutions have arisen that reduce these transaction costs. One is gift exchange, which communicates information about one's character and intentions. The exchange of gifts is a common accompaniment to primitive trade.[60] For example, the *kula* ring of the Trobriand

58. See, e.g., Barton, supra note 27, at 40. The principle of exogamy (see Chapter 7), the size of the kinship group, and the likelihood that most people in the village are kin combine to create a situation in which a spouse often must be sought in another village —which is likely to mean among strangers.

59. See Edward O. Wilson, *Sociobiology* 561 (1975).

Islanders, an elaborate system of gift exchange between members of different communities, although not trade in the usual sense (it consisted essentially of the exchange of like ornamental objects), facilitated trade. As Cyril Belshaw explains:

> The *kula* itself was not oriented to individual trade in its ceremonial activities. But alongside the *kula* persons visiting their partners took advantage of the opportunity to engage in trade. Malinowski makes the point that *kula* part-ners would exchange gifts of a trade character in addition to *vaygu'a* [the ornamental objects exchanged in the *kula* ring], and that the security afforded by the partnership would make it possible for the visitor to make contact with other persons in the village and trade with them.[61]

In addition, many primitive societies have "customary" prices for the goods involved in trade rather than prices determined by negotiation between the parties.[62] Customary prices do not change as quickly as the conditions of demand and supply and are therefore a source of inefficiency. But given the high costs of markets in primitive societies, such prices may be more efficient than freely bargained prices, especially because people have claims on the goods of their kin.[63] Multiparty transactions are generally more costly than transactions between two parties; this is probably one reason why trade is relatively rare in primi-

---

60. See, e.g., Herskovits, supra note 8, at 196. A related practice is the solemnization of a formal debt by the exchange of gifts. See Gluckman, supra note 35, at 197–198.

61. Belshaw, supra note 32, at 16. For an interesting recent economic analysis of the *kula* ring, see Janet T. Landa, "Primitive Public Choice and Exchange: An Explanation of the Enigma of the Kula Ring" (U. Toronto, Dept. Pol. Econ., n.d.).

62. See examples in Herskovits, supra note 8, at 206–210; Sahlins, supra note 5, at 295, 299–300, 308–309, and Pospisil, supra note 11, at 121–122. Notice that both haggling (see Clifford Geertz, "The Bazaar Economy: Information and Search in Peasant Marketing," 68 *Am. Econ. Rev. Papers & Proceedings* 28 [1978]) and the fixing of customary prices, though seemingly at opposite ends of the spectrum of price flexibility, are explicable in terms of the high information costs in primitive societies. Neither method of price setting is as common in modern societies.

63. This is presumably the reason why, in at least one society, it is customary for a buyer to give gifts to the seller's kin. See Barton, supra note 27, at 107..

tive societies.[64] To the extent that there is trade, however, it can be facilitated by customary prices, which reduce transaction costs by eliminating the need for a many-sided negotiation over price.

Another response to market transaction costs is the transformation of an arms-length contract relationship into an intimate status relationship. In some primitive societies if you trade repeatedly with the same man he becomes your blood brother and you owe him the same duty of generous and fair dealing that you would owe a kinsman.[65] This "barter friendship" is a way of bringing reciprocity into the exchange process and thereby increasing the likelihood that promises will be honored despite the absence of a public enforcement authority.[66]

5. The formality and decorum of primitive speech and manners are well documented, and Chapters 9 and 10 will relate these characteristics to the lack of privacy in primitive societies. The argument, briefly, is that people who lack conversational privacy must learn to express themselves precisely and circumspectly, since many of their conversations are bound to be overheard, creating abundant possibilities of recrimination and misunderstanding. The economic analysis of primitive rhetoric can be carried further, though I shall only sketch the argument.

The art of rhetoric, so highly developed in primitive and early cultures, so neglected (except by politicians) in modern

64. See *id.* at 110–111; Maine, supra note 11, at 271 (Beacon ed. 1970); and Table 1, supra.

65. See Gluckman, supra note 35, at 174. Raymond Firth speaks of the "personalization" of economic relations in primitive society, *Primitive Polynesian Economy* 315, 350 (1939). Nash, supra note 14, at 49, describes the use of an "idiom . . . of fictive kinship" in market transactions.

66. Marshall Sahlins has noted still another device by which security of primitive trade is enhanced—what he calls economic "good measure," that is, the buyer's deliberately overpaying a seller in order to induce the seller to deal fairly with him in the future. See Sahlins, supra note 5, at 303–304. The overpayment increases the cost to the seller of a breach of trust that would induce the buyer to withdraw his patronage. On the economic basis of such a practice, see Gary S. Becker & George J. Stigler, "Law Enforcement, Malfeasance, and Compensation of Enforcers," 3 *J. Legal Stud.* 1, 6–13 (1974).

Finally, the bazaar itself may be viewed as an adaptation to the high costs of information and communication. Those costs make it difficult to pool offers to buy and offers to sell except by bringing all of the buyers and sellers face to face.

ones, appears to be a response to high costs of information.[67] In the words of one of the few modern textbooks on the subject:

> In dealing with contingent human affairs, we cannot always discover or confirm what is the truth . . . But frequently, in the interests of getting on with the business f life, we have to make decisions on the basis of uncertainties or probabilities. The function of rhetoric is to persuade, where it cannot convince, an audience. And in matters where the truth cannot be readily ascertained, rhetoric can persuade an audience to adopt a point of view or a course of action on the basis of the merely probable.[68]

Consider the familiar rhetorical device known as the "ethical appeal," with which a speaker tries to ingratiate himself with his audience. As Corbett points out, "All of an orator's skill in convincing the intellect and moving the will of an audience could prove futile if the audience did not esteem, could not trust, the speaker."[69] However, if the truth of the speaker's words were readily verifiable, there would be no interest in his character, no occasion for trust. Character is a proxy for credibility that becomes important only where the costs of information are high. Thus I conjecture that the importance attached to rhetorical skill in primitive and early cultures reflects not only the absence of privacy in those cultures but also the high costs of information, which make it necessary for speakers to use rhetorical techniques to make their utterances credible.[70]

---

67. J. L. Hermessen, "A Journey on the River Zamora, Ecuador," 4 *Geo. Rev.* 434, 446 (1917), compares the Jivaro Indians' roundabout style of speaking to "our guarded phraseology noticeable amongst politicians when delicate matters are being discussed."

68. Edward P. J. Corbett, *Classical Rhetoric for the Modern Student* 73 (2d ed. 1971).

69. *Id.* at 35.

70. Another signaling device in the primitive repertoire is the sense of honor (less grandly, touchiness), discussed in the last chapter. See also Gluckman, supra note 35, at 232; E. E. Evans-Pritchard, supra note 11, at 151; Mair, supra note 9, at 40. The readiness to retaliate signaled by a highly developed sensitivity to affronts is an important deterrent to aggression in a society that lacks formal institutions of law enforcement. For some evidence see Robert A. LeVine, supra note 46, at 54, who finds a negative correlation between possession of political values and a strong sense of honor.

7
The Economic Theory of Primitive Law

In this chapter I extend my analysis of primitive society to legal institutions, with special emphasis on the system of strict liability that dominates primitive tort and criminal law.[1] The reader is warned again of a certain overgeneralization in the discussion; I am interested in explaining the central tendencies of primitive law rather than every variation in it.

The Legal Process

Dispute Resolution

Suppose there is a rule (for the moment we need not worry where it comes from) that a man may not take his neighbor's

---

1. For early societies my major sources are Henry Sumner Maine, *Ancient Law* (1861; Beacon ed. 1970); A. S. Diamond, *Primitive Law Past and Present*, pt. 1 (1971). See also Harold J. Berman, "The Background of the Western Legal Tradition in the Folk-law of the Peoples of Europe," 45 *U. Chi. L. Rev.* 553 (1978). For primitive societies my major sources are R. F. Barton, *The Kalingas: Their Institutions and Custom Law* (1949); Max Gluckman, *The Ideas of Barotse Jurisprudence* (1965), and his *Politics, Law, and Ritual in Tribal Society* (1965); Walter Goldschmidt, *Sebei Law* (1967); P. H. Gulliver, *Social Control in an African Society: A Study of the Arusha: Agricultural Masai of Northern Tanganyika* (1963); E. Adamson Hoebel, *The Law of Primitive Man: A Study in Comparative Legal Dynamics* (1954); P. P. Howell, *A Manual of Nuer Law: Being an Account of Customary Law, Its Evolution and Development in the Courts Established by the Sudan Government* (1954); Leopold Pospisil, *Anthropology of Law: A Comparative Theory* (1971); Valentin A. Riasanovsky, *The Customary Law of the Nomadic Tribes of Siberia* (1965); John Phillip Reid, *A Law of Blood* (1970); Simon Roberts, *Order and Dispute* (1979); I. Schapera, *A Handbook of Tswana Law and Custom* (1938); *Ideas and Procedures in African Customary Law* (Max Gluckman ed. 1969); *Law and Warfare* (Paul Bohannan ed. 1967); *Readings in African Law* (E. Cotran & N. N. Rubin eds. 1970).

yams without the neighbor's permission. However, he does take the yams, or at least the neighbor alleges that he has. How is the dispute to be resolved and a sanction applied if the rule is found to have been violated? One possibility is retaliation by the neighbor. But that may be a costly procedure, given the organization of primitive society into kin groups that provide mutual protection, and given other limitations of retaliation as a method of maintaining social order (discussed in the next chapter). The aggrieved neighbor may therefore decide to engage a passerby, a village elder or wise man, or another presumptively impartial third party to adjudicate his dispute.[2] The alleged violator also has an incentive to submit to adjudication—or "arbitration" as we should probably call it in view of its private nature— lest his refusal to do so trigger retaliation by the neighbor. To be sure, the alleged thief who is clearly guilty and expects to be so adjudged by an impartial arbitrator may prefer not to submit to arbitration or not to comply with the arbitrator's adverse judgment, but his kin group is a restraining influence. They may urge him to submit to arbitration to avoid getting involved in a feud over his deed, as they are likely to do because of their collective responsibility. And he will probably submit to their urging; otherwise they may desert him when the neighbor or the neighbor's kin retaliate for his refusal to submit to arbitration or to comply with the arbitrator's award.

The system just described is completely informal, but some primitive societies, for example the Yurok Indians of California, had more formal systems of primitive arbitration.[3] A Yurok who wanted to prosecute a legal claim would hire from two to four men, who could not be his relatives or residents of his village, and the defendant would do the same. These arbitrators, who were called "crossers," would go between the litigants to ascertain claims and defenses and to collect evidence. After hearing all of the evidence, the crossers would render a judg-

2. See, e.g., Maine, supra note 1, at 364.
3. See William M. Landes & Richard A. Posner, "Adjudication as a Private Good," 8 *J. Legal Stud.* 235, 242–245 (1979).

ment for damages. Each crosser would be compensated for his work by receiving some shell currency from the litigants.

Requiring each party to pick at least two crossers who could not be relatives or neighbors presumably reflected a concern with obtaining impartial adjudication. The requirement reduced the probability that the arbitrators would have a conflict of interest. Refusing to abide by the crossers' judgment was punished in the following way: the defaulting defendant became the wage slave of the plaintiff, and if he refused to submit to this punishment he became an outlaw and could be killed by anyone without the killer's incurring any liability for the deed.

Fact-finding Procedures

High information costs are reflected in the reliance on oaths, ordeals, and other dubious or irrational methods of factual determination that are sometimes used in primitive adjudication. Yet the superstitious element in primitive fact-finding is easily exaggerated. There was less reliance in African tribal society than in medieval European adjudication on the ordeal, the wager of battle, and similarly bizarre methods of finding facts.[4] Observers of tribal justice have been generally well impressed by the competence of the tribunals and by the distinctions made —sometimes more intelligently than under modern American rules of evidence designed to control juries—among hearsay, circumstantial, direct, and other categories of evidence.[5] Yet the ability of primitive tribunals to find the facts is limited because of the absence of police and other investigatory machinery and techniques (such as autopsies) and because of the assignment of supernatural causes to natural phenomena (such as a death from natural causes ascribed to the witchcraft of an enemy). We

4. See Diamond, supra note 1, ch. 21. Even the bizarre methods are perhaps rational in a setting where transaction costs are so high that people are unwilling to attempt factual determinations on their own, i.e., without divine assistance.

5. See Max Gluckman, *The Judicial Process among the Barotse of Northern Rhodesia*, ch. 3, 107–108 (1955); and his "Reasonableness and Responsibility in the Law of Segmentary Societies," in *African Law: Adaptation and Development* 120 (Hilda Kuper & Leo Kuper eds. 1965); Pospisil, supra note 1, at 236–238.

shall see that these costs of information appear to have shaped primitive substantive law in important ways.

The Source of Norms

Two of the common sources of legal norms, legislation and executive decree, are ruled out by the assumption introduced in the last chapter that there is no state. Since the arbitrators, though private, are a sort of judge, it may seem that the third common source of law—judicial decisions viewed as precedents guiding future conduct—could operate in primitive society. But even putting aside the problem that illiteracy would create for any system of precedent similar to the Anglo-American common law (primitive man's ingenuity might be able to overcome the problem[6]), one has still to ask what incentive the arbitrator has to issue opinions that will stand as precedents. Even our society does not attempt to create property rights in rules or precedents. Our judges receive salaries from the state, and appellate judges are expected to write opinions setting forth their grounds of decision; such opinions are precedents. But the typical primitive judge, like the modern arbitrator, must look to the disputants rather than to the society at large for his compensation, since he is a private citizen.[7] Modern arbitrators usually do not write opinions, because the parties to a dispute generally obtain only a trivial fraction of the benefits generated by a precedent—those benefits accrue to all those whom the precedent enables to shape their future conduct better—and hence are unwilling to pay for the arbitrator's creating precedents. Similarly, primitive judges are unlikely to provide oral opinions usable as precedents.

6. See discussion of "remembrancers" in I. Schapera, "The Sources of Law in Tswana Tribal Courts: Legislation and Precedent," 1 *J. Afr. Law* 150 (1957).

7. See, e.g., Barton, supra note 1, at 164–167. A famous example is the "shield scene" in book 18 of the *Iliad*. Maine's interpretation, that the two talents of gold referred to in the scene are a fee for the judges, has been widely accepted. See Maine, supra note 1, at 364; Robert J. Bonner and Gertrude Smith, *The Administration of Justice from Homer to Aristotle* 38–40 (1930). Even in a primitive society that has some rudimentary government, the judges tend to be at best quasi-official figures and to be paid, if at all, out of litigant fees. See, e.g., Riasanovsky, supra note 1, at 12.

The remaining source of law, and the one that dominates primitive law, is custom. It is custom that prescribes the compensation due for killing a man, the formalities for making a contract, the rules of inheritance, the obligations of kinship, the limitations on whom one may marry, and so forth. Custom (including customary law) resembles language in being a complex, slowly changing, highly decentralized system of exact rules. Their exactness is a substitute for a system of broad standards particularized by judges through the creation of precedents. The exactness of those customary rules that are designed to price an act (like killing) can also be explained in terms of the high costs of negotiation where, as is typically the case, an entire kin group (or more likely two groups) is affected by the negotiation, thus making it a multiparty transaction.

The more exact a rule is, the less adaptable it is to changing circumstances. We would therefore expect a system of exact rules to provide some method for changing the rules quickly. A system of customary law has no such method, but this is not a serious problem in a static society. There is little danger that legal change will lag behind social change in such a society and produce the sorts of anachronisms which in the case of English common law and Roman law created a demand for legal fictions, equity, and legislation to keep the law up to date. These devices are found less often in primitive legal systems.[8] Evidently Roman and English society were changing faster than a system of purely customary law (no fictions, no equity) could

---

8. On legal fiction in Roman and English law see Maine, supra note 1, ch. 2. Equity and legislation require a more elaborate governmental structure than is found in the usual primitive society. Legal fictions, too, appear to be rare in primitive societies. For a good discussion see T. O. Beidelman, "Kaguru Justice and the Concept of Legal Fictions," 5 *J. Afr. Law* (1961). However, fictive kinship is sometimes found. And one often finds artificial, "legalistic" reasoning. For example, in one African tribe if a man kills a member of his clan he pays less compensation than if he kills a stranger, on the ground that as a member of the clan he is entitled to share in any compensation it receives. See Robert Redfield, "Primitive Law," in *Law and Warfare,* supra note 1, at 3, 12. The reasoning is absurd but the rule makes economic sense. Where killer and victim are members of the same clan, the probability of detection is higher and hence the optimal penalty lower. But this is not an example of legal fiction in the sense here, of a device for getting around an anachronistic, dysfunctional rule.

keep up with—which means faster than the typical primitive society.

Property

A study by Harold Demsetz of the property rights systems of North American Indians pointed out that the appropriateness of recognizing a property right in a resource is a function of its scarcity, and hence market value, relative to the costs of enforcing such a right.[9] Where land is so abundant relative to population that its market price would be less than the cost of fencing the land or otherwise enforcing a property right to it, individual rights to the land will not be asserted; it will be treated as common property. As land becomes scarcer—because of a rise in the ratio of population to land owing to the introduction of Western medicine or a rise in the demand for some crop or animal grown on the land because of access to Western markets—a system of individual property rights tends to develop.[10] But even in a very primitive agricultural society, some land is bound to be more valuable than other land because of superior fertility, workability, or location (proximity to the camp or village, making it safer from enemy attack) and would command a positive market value if it could be bought and sold. Moreover, enforcement of a property right to such land would not be costly if it was a purely possessory right (a usufruct) which allowed the possessor to exclude people from the land only so long as he was actually working it. In fact, such possessory rights are common in primitive law. They have two additional elements: (1) the possessor can transfer his right to members of his family or pass it to his heirs, but (2) he cannot sell the land.[11]

9. See Harold Demsetz, "Toward a Theory of Property Rights," 57 *Am. Econ. Rev. Papers & Proceedings* 347, 351–353 (1967).

10. See, e.g., David E. Ault & Gilbert L. Rutman, "The Development of Individual Rights to Property in Tribal Africa," 22 *J. Law & Econ.* 163 (1979). Cf. Douglass C. North & Robert Paul Thomas, *The Rise of the Western World: A New Economic History* (1973).

11. See, e.g., Melville J. Herskovits, *Economic Anthropology* 368–370 (2d rev. ed. 1952); Barton, supra note 1, at 89–98; Schapera, supra note 1, at 201, 205, 207; Maine, supra note 1, ch. 8.

My model of primitive society is helpful in explaining this structure of property rights. The benefits are both political and economic. The man who has a good harvest is not permitted to use his surplus to buy another's land and reduce the other to dependency on him—which would be a politically destabilizing transaction in a pregovernmental society—but is led instead to give the surplus to the other. The effective demand for land is thereby reduced as well, making it more likely that a poor man will be able to find tolerably good land somewhere else in the community. At the same time, possession (in the sense of actually working a piece of land or killing and seizing a wild animal) provides clear evidence of the fact and extent of ownership. The alternative is either fencing or a record system. The former could be quite costly in a society that has only simple tools, and the latter is ruled out by the assumption of illiteracy.

The costs of the primitive possessory system of land rights, in impeding the marketability of land and in distorting the intertemporal allocation of resources to land development, are lower than they would be in an advanced society. To begin with, the sale of land in primitive societies would be difficult in any event because of the network of kinship obligations. A man could not sell land on whose output some kinsman depended, or sell cows needed to buy his younger brother a wife, without consulting the affected kinsmen or at least allocating the proceeds of the sale among them; this would increase the effective number of transacting parties and so the costs of transacting. Thus, the primitive land market would probably operate poorly even if land were freely alienable. Furthermore, while in an advanced society inalienability would prevent the concentration of land into holdings large enough to enable the exploitation of economies of large-scale production, such exploitation is largely infeasible in primitive society. It entails a capacity for organization, for coordinating the work of many people under central direction, that is precluded by the high costs of information.[12]

---

12. Some empirical support for this proposition is provided by Pryor's findings that land-rental and labor contracts generally emerge late in the development of a society,

The social benefits of allowing a man to assemble more land than he could personally work would therefore be slight. Moreover, some opportunity for expanding one's holdings is created by polygyny, which enables a man to buy several wives to work a large estate.[13] The potentially destabilizing effect of polygyny on the equality of wealth and power is offset, as noted in the last chapter, by the increased number of children, which leads to a greater division of the land in the next generation.[14]

When ownership rights in a resource can be obtained only by capture or use (that is, when only possessory rights are recognized), there is a tendency to take too much too soon, but again this is not a frequent problem in a simple society. It is cheaper for a band of hunters to move on when the game in an area is depleted than to regulate the game population by creating fee-simple rights to hunting territories. It is cheaper for the primitive agricultural community to abandon worn-out land for several years until its fertility is naturally restored than

relative to markets in goods. See Frederic L. Pryor, *The Origins of the Economy: A Comparative Study of Distribution in Primitive and Peasant Economies* 126–127, 141 (1977). And notice in Table 1 in Chapter 6 how reciprocal exchange of labor persists after reciprocal exchange of goods has largely given way to market exchange of goods. Presumably the costs of market transactions in renting land or hiring labor (to work the land or do any other work) are higher than the costs of simply selling goods, because of the difficulty of either measuring the tenant's or worker's marginal product or monitoring his effort. Cf. M. I. Finley, *The Ancient Economy* 65 (1973).

13. Consistently with this suggestion, Pryor, supra note 12, at 137, found a negative correlation between the existence of land rentals and the presence of polygyny. The reason why the costs of supervising wives might be lower than those of supervising (other) field hands is that the food that the wife grows in part to feed her son is a form of joint consumption of husband and wife; thus the feeding of his son is a benefit to the husband that the latter obtains without having to monitor the wife's efforts.

14. Under South African tribal law, for example, the land worked by each of a polygynist's wives is a separate estate which on his death passes to the eldest son of that marriage, so that his total holdings are broken up on his death. See A. J. Kerr, *The Native Law of Succession in South Africa* 35, 54 (1961); 4 N. J. van Warmelo, *Venda Law* 815, 899 (1949). Notice that the combination of polygyny and primogeniture achieves similar results to a rule of equal inheritance, which would be less efficient because it would often force the division of estates into inefficiently small units. Among nomads, where the principal wealth (herds) is almost perfectly divisible, a rule of equal inheritance is often found. See Austin Kennett, *Bedouin Justice: Law and Custom among the Egyptian Bedouin*, ch. 10 (1925).

to enforce fee-simple rights in the hope of encouraging the owners to regenerate the land more quickly, if regeneration techniques are unknown. Where investment is feasible in primitive society—the setting of traps is an example—it is often protected by the grant of a nonpossessory property right. The man who sets a trap is entitled to the trapped animal even if someone else finds it in the trap and thus "possesses" it first.[15]

Contracts

In primitive as in modern law, exchange and contract are not synonymous. The formation of marriages, exchanges within the household or kin group, and gift giving are the most important forms of exchange (or, the same point, the role of explicit markets in organizing production and distribution is smaller in primitive than in modern economies); therefore, the potential domain of the law of contracts—the law, that is, governing trade with strangers—is limited.

Several features of primitive contract law recur with sufficient frequency to be regarded as typical. (1) Executory contracts (those that neither party has begun to perform when the breach occurred) are not enforced. (2) Damages are not awarded for loss of the expected profits of the transaction; instead, the standard remedy is restitution. (3) A breach of contract where the other party has completed performance—that is, breach of a half-executed as distinct from an executory contract—is often treated as a form of theft from the promisee. (4)

---

15. See, e.g., Diamond, supra note 1, at 189; Goldschmidt, supra note 1, at 157. Cf. Vernon L. Smith, "The Primitive Hunter Cultures, Pleistocene Extinction, and the Rise of Agriculture," 83 *J. Pol. Econ.* 727, 742–743 (1975).

The analysis in this section has been of land rights. The position with respect to other kinds of property is closer to that of modern law—always subject to the "cloud over title" cast by the rights of kinsmen. One of the few goods to which a kinsman usually cannot assert a claim is a man's wives (though he may, if in need, be able to claim a share of her or her children's agricultural surplus which might otherwise go to the husband-father). Women's (comparative) immunity from the claims of kinsmen is another reason why they are such a highly valued good in primitive societies, as measured by the brideprice they command.

The seller is liable for any defect in the product sold (*caveat venditor*).

These features taken together suggest that contract law barely exists even in the limited sphere in which it applies. A law of contracts is not needed to generate the rule that a buyer who refuses to pay for goods he has already taken possession of must return them to the seller. Yet apart from liability for defective products, that seems to be the only important duty that primitive contract law imposes. The reason becomes apparent once it is realized that the economic function of modern contract law is to facilitate transactions in which the performance of one or both parties takes considerable time. Such an interval opens up the possibility both that unforeseen events will disrupt performance and that one of the parties will be tempted to exploit the strategic opportunities that nonsimultaneous contractual performance may create. The interval over which contract performance occurs is presumably a positive function of the complexity of the economic activity being regulated by the contract. The economic activity of primitive societies is simple, so if the transactions governed by the law of contracts usually involve simultaneous (or virtually simultaneous) performance, the scope for that law is reduced to assigning liability for defects that show up later. If we assume just one element of nonsimultaneity, namely that payment sometimes follows transfer of the good sold, then all that is needed is a principle of restitution that will make the buyer return the good to the seller. This would not be an adequate remedy in a modern economy, where contracts are often made long before performance is due, where prices may change rapidly, and where, therefore, an important purpose of contracts is to assign the risk of price changes to one party or the other.[16] Prices change slowly in primitive societies,

16. For example, if A agrees to sell B widgets for $2 apiece and makes delivery as agreed, and B then refuses to pay because immediately after delivery the price of widgets falls to $1, a purely restitutionary remedy (e.g., A gets his widgets back) would not carry out the risk-shifting function of the contract. On the basic economics of contract law, see *The Economics of Contract Law* (Anthony T. Kronman & Richard A. Posner eds., 1979); Richard A. Posner, *Economic Analysis of Law*, ch. 4 (2nd ed. 1977).

partly because so many prices are customary, and contracts need not be made long in advance of performance.

One type of risk-shifting contract that primitive society could use, of course, would be a contract allocating the risk of hunger. Such contracts would facilitate what the last chapter showed was one of the most important products in a primitive society, insurance against hunger. However, the information requirements of an explicit insurance contract are formidable, and in a small-scale society informal kin insurance may provide an acceptable, and administratively cheaper, alternative.

The rule of *caveat venditor* in primitive sales law can be derived from the costs of information in primitive markets. To be sure, the products tend to be simple, and this fact in isolation would suggest that the costs of inspection are the same to buyer and to seller. Such reasoning has been used to explain the rule of *caveat emptor* in nineteenth-century Anglo-American common law, a rule now giving way to *caveat venditor* under pressure of growing complexity of products and hence increasing costs of inspection to buyers relative to sellers. An important difference between primitive and nineteenth-century markets, however, is the infrequency of trading in the former. Because exchange with strangers is exceptional, individuals may not develop the skills of the experienced and knowledgeable consumer, so the costs of inspection to the buyer relative to the seller may be high despite the simplicity of the product. In addition, the seller is the superior insurer of a product defect because he can spread its costs over his entire output. Although this argument is also made in modern discussions of the relative merits of *caveat venditor* and *caveat emptor*, it is superficial in the modern extent because the buyer has a variety of insurance options open to him which may be as good as or better than seller's self- or market insurance. The insurance options of the primitive consumer are more limited.

Family Law

In most primitive societies, the law relating to the family is the most elaborate body of legal principles. This is not surprising.

The rules governing relations within the household correspond in function and importance to the law of corporations and of agency in modern societies; and since women are the principal goods exchanged in most primitive societies, the rules governing marriage and divorce overshadow the contract law. I will discuss four aspects of primitive family law: the level of detail in that law, brideprice, the liberality of primitive divorce law, and exogamy.[17]

Level of Detail

One can imagine a system of primitive family law consisting of a few fundamental principles (the right of kin to payment for giving a girl in marriage, the right to buy more than one wife, and so forth) that would leave the details to negotiation by the affected parties. But one is more likely to find a vast number of family transactions regulated by custom in minute detail,[18] often including prices, with the scope for individual variation, whether by testamentary will or by agreement, limited and sometimes nonexistent. Among the reasons suggested in the last chapter for exactness in primitive law, the most important in the family-law context is the high costs of voluntary transactions that involve a large number of parties—potentially, all the members of two kinship groups. For example, since brideprice is the property of the bride's kinship group, if the price and its allocation among the kin were left to negotiations within the kin group, the transaction with the bridegroom would be extremely costly. Protracted negotiations are in fact reported where the brideprice and its allocation are not fixed by custom.[19] Primitive family law will often seek to avoid these costs by specifying not only the brideprice but how it is to be split up among the bride's kin. One expects that, other things being equal, the larger the kinship group that is entitled to share in the brideprice, the

17. Polygamy and inheritance were discussed in Chapter 6 and will not be examined further here.

18. For a sense of the complexity that is common in primitive family law see 5 N. J. van Warmelo, *Venda Law* (1967).

19. See Lucy Mair, *Marriage* 57 (2d ed. 1977).

more likely it is that the level and allocation of the brideprice are fixed by custom rather than left to negotiation.[20]

Brideprice

Commonly one finds in primitive society a positive brideprice (rather than no price or a negative price—dowry) paid to the bride's kin rather than to the bride herself. This pattern is perhaps related to a (conjectured) three-stage historical evolution in the methods of obtaining a wife: from capture or stealing, to payment, to the modern system of promising to cherish and support.[21] The reason why in each stage the male takes the initiative appears to be genetic.[22] Because of the female's limited reproductive capacity, submission to sexual intercourse imposes a substantial opportunity cost on her from the standpoint of

20. For some evidence bearing on this point, compare A. R. Radcliffe-Brown, "Introduction," in *African Systems of Kinship and Marriage* 17 (A. R. Radcliffe-Brown & Daryll Forde eds. 1950), on large kin groups and fixed compensation and shares, with Max Gluckman, "Kinship and Marriage among the Lozi of Northern Rhodesia and the Zulu of Natal," in *id.* at 166, 194, on flexible brideprice and small number of involved kin, and with S. F. Nadel, "Dual Descent in the Nuba Hills," in *id.* at 331, 341–342. Cf. Günter Wagner, "The Political Organization of the Bantu of Kavirondo," in *African Political Systems* 197, 222–223 (M. Fortes & E. E. Evans-Pritchard eds. 1940), on optimum clan size.

The relationship between the communalizing of property rights and the fixing of price or shares by custom is a general one. For example, where hunting is done in groups, or (an even closer parallel to the brideprice case) where the insurance principles of the society require that the kill be shared among the kin group or in some cases the entire band or village, primitive law often prescribes the exact division, thus avoiding a multiparty negotiation. See, e.g., Barton, supra note 1, at 85–86. It would also be avoided if each kin group or village had a chief who negotiated on behalf of the group and distributed the proceeds among the members. Such figures do emerge in primitive societies, but when this happens it may mean that the society is on its way to becoming a state. Where leadership is weak even at the kinship-group and village levels, customary prices and shares play an important allocative role.

21. The first stage is speculative; for some evidence regarding it see Mair, supra note 19, at 110–111. Several forms of nonpecuniary exchange generally precede brideprice historically, including sister exchange, working for one's prospective father-in-law, and going to live with the bride's kin. And some marriages involve payment of dowry (generally a preinheritance distribution to the bride by her kin) without brideprice. Some of these variants will be taken up later.

22. See, e.g., David P. Barash, *Sociobiology and Behavior* 147–150 (1977); Edward O. Wilson, *On Human Nature* 125–126 (1978).

perpetuating her genes. Male fecundity is so great that the corresponding opportunity cost to him is trivial. Hence, the woman tries to conserve her reproductive capacity through careful screening of eligible mates while the man is much more indiscriminate. Where wives are obtained by capture, the woman's efforts to elude capture operate to screen out the less enterprising males, who are also less likely to produce numerous offspring that will survive to maturity. Brideprice is an alternative screening device. It is less costly in real resources than fighting yet is effective from the female's standpoint so long as there is a good correlation between the male's willingness and ability to pay for a wife on the one hand and the likelihood of his producing and protecting her children on the other.[23] Since my analysis is premised on the assumption that human beings were rational throughout prehistory, I attribute to growing wealth rather than to growing rationality the transition from capture to barter: bride purchase requires production sufficiently beyond subsistence needs to yield a stock of goods that can be exchanged for a woman.

Consistently with this analysis, one observes in some societies that the man who is too poor to raise the brideprice can obtain a bride by going to work for her father for a period of time.[24] He demonstrates by his habits of work his fitness to marry the girl. A related solution is "matrilocal" marriage: the husband remains with the wife's family without payment of brideprice.[25] The bride's family have less need to screen his fitness for the marriage in this case. Instead of leaving the entire protective function to the husband and his kin, as in patrilocal marriage, they are present to help protect the offspring.

This analysis does not explain why brideprice rather than, as

23. Cf. Barash, supra note 22, at 294. This is not to say that it is necessarily women who take the initiative in establishing a brideprice system; I assume they do not. But males benefit in a genetic sense from an institution that assures fitter mates for their daughters.

24. See, e.g., Harold E. Driver, *Indians of North America* 225 (2d rev. ed. 1969).

25. See Harold K. Schneider, *Economic Man: The Anthropology of Economics* 145 (1974).

today, dating or courtship is used as a screening device. Generally in primitive societies, girls are married at puberty—at an age when they lack mature judgment—so dating may not be an efficient method of choosing among suitors. The marriage could be arranged by the girl's parents without brideprice, but it may be difficult for the parents to inform themselves about the qualities of a stranger who is often (because of the exogamy rule) from a different village, save through the information conveyed by his capacity to make a substantial payment.

Another way of interpreting brideprice, also based on the costs of information, is as a device for compensating the wife in advance for her services in the household. A wife in a primitive society may have limited ability to enforce fair compensation by her husband for her services, so she demands payment in advance, in the form of brideprice. However, this explanation is plausible only where the brideprice is paid to the bride. More commonly it is paid to her kin, which, it has been suggested, is a security device.[26] The bride's kin have an incentive to encourage her satisfactory performance as a wife (as by refusing to harbor her should she run away from her husband), because if she misbehaves, the husband may have a claim to the return of the brideprice. He has an incentive to treat her well because if he mistreats her she may have a right to leave him, and her kin will have no obligation to return the brideprice.[27]

Notice the tension between having a detailed and exact family law and using brideprice as a device for screening suitors. If brideprice is fixed by custom, the costs of the multiparty negotiation between the suitor and girl's kin group are reduced, but

26. See Becker, "Marriage: Monogamy, Polygamy, and Assortative Mating" (mimeo., U. Chi. Dept. Econ., Oct. 1978).

27. Still another possible explanation for brideprice is that it compensates the girl's kin for either (1) the cost of screening suitors for her, since, as mentioned, she is normally a young girl not obviously competent to compare the offers she receives, or (2) their investment in training her to be a good wife.

The payment of dowry, or negative brideprice, remains unexplained by my analysis. Perhaps dowry is often a gift to the bride by her (well-to-do) parents. This is consistent with the fact that payment of dowry is associated with wealthier societies than payment of brideprice is. See Pryor, supra note 12, at 357, 364–366.

the use of brideprice as an allocative device is weakened, because direct bidding of the suitors against one another is prevented.

Divorce Law

Primitive law is on the whole more liberal toward divorce by either husband or wife than Western law was until very recently,[28] and divorce is common in many primitive societies.[29] This liberality may reflect the fact that the cost of divorce to the children is less where there are alternative child-rearing institutions to the nuclear family. The children of primitive people grow up amid numerous kin who have an interest (based on having common genes) in protecting the children to whom they are related. This ready-made "day-care center" reduces the importance of having both parents attend to raising the child.[30]

The frequency of divorce in primitive society may also reflect the inferiority of brideprice as a sorting device relative to courtship of a mature woman who makes her own choice of husband.[31] The costs of information may be so high in primitive society that there is no good way of sorting the females to the males, so that matching is poor and marital instability high. Alternatively, because the parents spend less time with their children (since other kin share in the rearing of the children), there is less demand for a sorting device that will mate people with similar genetic endowments (positive assortative mating). One value of positive assortative mating is in reducing the variance of traits between parent and child, thereby promoting a harmonious household.[32] If such harmony is relatively unimportant in

28. See Diamond, supra note 1, at 183, 249; Mair, supra note 19, at ch. 11. Until the middle of the nineteenth century, divorce was possible in England only by act of Parliament. In Roman Catholic countries divorce on any grounds was traditionally impossible, though annulment was sometimes available as a substitute.

29. See, e.g., *id.* at 189; Pryor, supra note 12, at 430.

30. See Barash, supra note 22, at 295, 308.

31. Also, since women in primitive societies usually do some work outside the home (especially agricultural work), they are in a better position to support themselves than many women in modern societies.

32. See Gary S. Becker, *The Economic Approach to Human Behavior* 225–226 (1976).

primitive society, so will be a sorting device designed to produce it, and a crude and cheap sorting device such as brideprice may be an efficient substitute.[33] Furthermore, positive assortative mating fosters inequality between families,[34] which could undermine the primitive social equilibrium. Hence the fact that brideprice is not a very efficient method of positive assortative mating may be not a shortcoming but an advantage.

Another possible factor in the relative instability of primitive marriage is that the insurance function of marriage itself is less important than at later stages of social development. This insurance function arises from the fact that the correlation of spouses' health and other welfare factors is less than one, so given a mutual obligation of support and assistance, marriage serves as a form of health, hunger, and life insurance (if one spouse dies the other will take care of the children). The network of primitive kinship obligations makes this particular form of insurance less important, and hence marital dissolution less costly, than at a later stage of social development in which kinship obligations have receded but market and social insurance is not yet common. In principle, the insurance function of marriage is compatible with consensual (though not with unilateral) divorce, because a spouse will agree to a divorce only if he or she is fully compensated for any forgone benefits, including insurance, of the marriage. However, if we assume that at this intermediate stage of social development the costs of monitoring the voluntariness of the wife's agreeing to a divorce are great,[35] we

33. Brideprice is not cheap to the groom's kinship group, of course, but it is cheap to society as a whole because it is simply a transfer payment between the two kinship groups—the loss to one is the gain to the other. Notice that where brideprice takes the form of cattle or some other edible product, it serves the incidental purpose of inducing the accumulation of such products, which in turn provides an important form of hunger insurance. See Marguerite Dupire, "Trade and Markets in the Economy of the Nomadic Fulani of Niger (Bororo)," in *Markets in Africa* 333, 338–339, 359 (Paul Bohannan & George Dalton eds. 1962), on cattle "hoarding" as insurance.

34. See Becker, supra note 32, at 241.

35. The husband could make the wife's life unbearable in an effort to force her to "agree" to a divorce. Determining voluntariness is difficult, which is one reason why legal standards based on state of mind tend to emerge late in the evolution of a legal system.

can see why requiring grounds for divorce or even forbidding divorce altogether might be a rational social measure.[36]

Exogamy

Requiring a man to marry outside his group, normally his kinship group, is usual in most primitive societies. Unlike the incest taboo, exogamy appears to be cultural rather than genetic. This is shown by the facts that (1) the rules of exogamy vary greatly across cultures—and some cultures encourage endogamy, whereas none to speak of encourage incest; (2) often the rules prohibit marriage with relatives who are quite remote in a genetic sense and sometimes with nonrelatives (that is, adopted members of the kinship group), while some incestuous unions (for example, between a man and his sister's daughter) may not be forbidden by the rules of exogamy although contrary to the tribe's incest taboo; and (3) the incest taboo prohibits sexual intercourse without regard to marriage, while exogamy is a limitation on marriage rather than on intercourse as such.

A cultural explanation of exogamy thus seems indicated. Exogamy serves an insurance function in those cases, which are common, where kinship obligations cross the boundary between the intermarrying groups. Thus, in a patrilineal system a man is not a member of his mother's kinship group, but he may still have a claim to assistance from her relatives.[37] Exogamy thus broadens the insurance pool. This effect is particularly important where, as is again common, each kinship group resides in a compact area, so that exogamy enables geographical diversification of risk. Exogamy also facilitates trade and alliances by creating personal relationships between families and villages. Finally, it may reduce the ferocity of retaliation for wrongs

36. Stringent divorce laws reduce marital instability, and hence increase the insurance function of marriage, in another way. They increase the optimal level of investment in screening prospective marriage partners for compatibility, since the costs of incompatibility are greater when divorce is unobtainable.

37. See, e.g., Robin Fox, *Kinship and Marriage: An Anthropological Perspective* 132–133 (1967) on "complementary filiation"; Daryll Forde, "Double Descent among the Yakö," in *African Systems of Kinship and Marriage*, supra note 20, at 329.

done by a member of one kinship group against a member of another.

The System of Strict Liability in Tort

The tort law of modern societies embraces a variety of accidental and intentional injuries—killing, wounding, taking property, slandering, and so on. Generally, liability is imposed only if the injury was inflicted intentionally or negligently. If the accident could not have been avoided by the exercise of reasonable care, there is no liability. The intentional injurer may be guilty of a crime as well as of a tort. Primitive law typically (though not invariably) deals with this class of harms in a manner very different from that of modern societies, which can be summarized in the following propositions:[38]

1. *Virtually the entire burden of deterrence is placed on the tort (private) law.* There is no criminal law to punish acts such as murder or theft,[39] because there is no state; criminal law as we know it is a branch of public law.

2. *The remedy for a wrong evolves from retaliation to compensation.* The earliest remedy for tort—retaliation, often leading to a feud—yields in time to a system of compensation (bloodwealth, composition, wergelds) paid to the victim or his kin by the injurer or his kin. Acceptance of compensation is at first optional, and the right to retaliate against the injurer instead is recognized. But later it becomes customary to accept compensation and improper to retaliate. From the standpoint of society as a whole, compensation is a cheaper remedy than retaliation, be-

---

38. For sources, besides those listed in note 1 supra, see L. T. Hobhouse, "Development of Justice," in 2 *Evolution of Law* 128 (Albert Kocourek & John W. Wigmore eds. 1915); Richard R. Cherry, "Primitive Criminal Law," in *id.* at 122; Austin Kennett, *Bedouin Justice*, ch. 6 (1925); T. P. Ellis, *Welsh Tribal Law and Custom in the Middle Ages* (1926); David Friedman, "Private Creation and Enforcement of Law: A Historical Case," 8 *J. Legal Stud.* 399 (1979); Marc Bloch, *Feudal Society* 123–130 (L. A. Manyon trans. 1961); Sally Falk Moore, *Law as Process*, ch. 3 (1978); *The Lombard Laws* 7–11 (Katherine Fischer Drew trans. 1973). Some of the issues discussed here are also discussed in Chapter 8.

39. But see the section on criminal law, infra.

cause it involves simply a transfer payment rather than the destruction of a person or his property. As before, I attribute the transition from retaliation to compensation not to growing rationality, diminishing bloodthirstiness, or other factors that assume fundamental differences in intelligence or tastes between primitive and modern man, but simply to growing wealth. A system of compensation will not work unless injurers and their kin have a sufficient stock of goods in excess of their subsistence needs to be able to pay compensation for the injuries they inflict on others.[40]

The idea that the only sanction for a personal injury or death should be a payment of money damages is consistent with economic theory. The economic analysis of crime recommends greater reliance on the fine relative to imprisonment and other nonmonetary punishments than is found in modern penal systems, on the ground that the fine is a cheaper punishment from a social standpoint. A fine is simply a transfer payment, whereas imprisonment involves net resource costs, including the forgone legitimate production of the defendant during the period of incarceration.[41] To be sure, reliance on monetary sanctions is feasible only under certain conditions; we shall see to what extent these conditions are found in primitive society.

3. Responsibility is collective. If one person injures another, in the retaliation stage of social order the victim's kinsmen have a duty to him which they can discharge only by killing or injuring the injurer or one of his kinsmen. In the compensation stage the injurer's kinsmen must come up with the required compensation if the injurer himself cannot or will not do so. If neither the injurer nor his kinsmen pay the required compensation, the

---

40. Thus in some societies an injurer who cannot afford the wergeld is allowed to give a child instead. See Diamond, supra note 1, at 265.

An intermediate stage between the feud and compensation is the duel, a means of redress that economizes on the expenditure of resources on fighting. See Redfield, supra note 8, at 9. In primitive liability law, the duel is to the feud what matrilocal marriage is to marriage by capture in family law.

41. See Gary S. Becker, "Crime and Punishment: An Economic Approach," 76 *J. Pol. Econ.* 169 (1968); Richard A. Posner, "Optimal Sentences for White Collar Criminals," 17 *Am. Crim. L. Rev.* 409 (1980).

victim's kinsmen then have a duty to retaliate against the injurer —or his kinsmen—for their refusal to compensate.

The importance of the kin group in the enforcement of primitive tort law derives from the absence of effective government. Where the threat of retaliation is the only deterrent to misconduct, it is important that the threat be credible, and often it would not be if there were only one potential retaliator. Even after compensation is substituted for retaliation, there must still be a credible threat of retaliation in the background to coerce payment of the compensation. The need to maintain a credible retaliatory capability is another reason, besides the need for a risk pool, why the recognized kin group is larger in primitive than in modern societies.

The principle of collective responsibility—so abhorrent to modern sensibilities—may be efficient in the conditions of primitive society. The fact that any of a killer's kinsmen is fair game to the victim's kinsmen avenging his death, or, in the later stage of development, that the killer's kinsmen are collectively liable to the victim's kinsmen should the killer fail to pony up the compensation that is due from him, gives his kinsmen an incentive to police his conduct. They may decide to slay him themselves to avert the danger to them. They also have an interest in weeding out the potential killers in their midst in order to avoid the costs in retaliation or compensation should they be harboring a killer.[42] Thus the fact that the killer may not be the initial target of retaliation, rather than reducing the probability that the sanction will ultimately come to rest on him, increases it by giving his kinsmen an incentive to "turn him in."[43] Collective responsibility is another ingenious device, like denial of privacy,

---

42. See, e.g., Barton, supra note 1, at 244; Diamond, supra note 1, at 264–265; Moore, supra note 38 at 120; Reid, supra note 1, at 83–84; Wagner, supra note 20 at 218–219.

43. There are analogies in modern law. For example, under the doctrine of *respondeat superior,* an employer is liable for the torts committed by his employees in the furtherance of their employment. The (economic) explanation of this liability is that it gives the employer an incentive to monitor the employees' behavior. See Richard A. Posner, "A Theory of Negligence," 1 *J. Legal Stud.* 29, 42–43 (1972).

by which a primitive society creates substitutes for the public investigatory machinery that it lacks.[44]

4. *The relevant collectivity is the kin group.* The preceding discussion assumed that the collective rights and duties in the primitive tort system should be kinship rights and duties. This assumption now has to be examined. Why do we not find, instead of kinship groups, voluntary groups—the protective associations discussed by Robert Nozick?[45] First, the transaction costs of organizing a large group of people for common ends are presumably lower where the members are relatively homogeneous and already bound together in a system of reciprocal rights and duties by virtue of the insurance function of the kinship group. Self-defense becomes just another one of these rights and duties. Second, use of kinship as the organizing principle limits the size of the self-defense group. A purely voluntary system of protective associations would be unstable because of the great advantages accruing to any association that, by overcoming the problems of internal coordination and control, grew to where it overshadowed any other association. Such an association would become the state. This is a reason to expect self-defense to be a kinship obligation in a society that has managed to survive without effective government. Third, when an individual is injured or killed, the action injures all of the members of the recognized kinship group, because they have a claim on his income, which has now been reduced. They are therefore the proper parties plaintiff.

What form of kinship is optimal for law enforcement? Compare a unilineal system, such as the patrilineal system, with an ambilineal or cognatic system. In a patrilineal system a man's kinship group includes his relatives in the male line for some designated number of generations. This system automatically assigns every individual to a nonoverlapping kin group. A cognatic kinship group, where a man is the kin of his relatives in both the male and female line, does not yield a neat pattern of

44. Cf. J. C. Vergouwen, *The Social Organization and Customary Law of the Toba-Batak of Northern Sumatra* 365 (1964).

45. See Robert Nozick, *Anarchy, State, and Utopia* 118–119 (1974).

nonoverlapping kinship groups. This creates problems in using the group to assign collective responsibility for law enforcement.[46] If A kills B, a relative of his wife, in a patrilineal system B's kinship group would not include A and would have a duty to take action against A or A's kin. But in a cognatic system A and B would be kinsmen, and there would be no clear basis for action against A.[47] In tribal Africa, the compensation system was based on patrilineal kin groups and was stable.

As noted in the last chapter, a patrilineal kinship group is not ideal from the insurance standpoint. There is likely to be a high covariance in the wealth of the members where, as is common, they live in the same village. Exogamy with complementary filiation, or some similar concept of obligation to relatives by marriage, provides a solution. The insurance principle is broadened to embrace groups living in different locales and therefore having a lower covariance of wealth, but the kinship groups remain distinct for purposes of law enforcement.

5. *The compensation for killings and other injuries is prescribed in an exact schedule.* The customary law will specify, for example, that forty head of cattle is the compensation required for killing a freeman, twenty for killing a slave, two for putting out a man's eye, and so forth.[48] This pattern, very common in primitive law, is different from that of modern tort law, where damages are assessed on an individual basis in every case. At the stage of social development where acceptance of compensation by the victim's kin is optional, it is easy to see why a fixed level of compensation would be preferred to a multiparty transaction among the members of both kin groups. Even when acceptance of compensation becomes compulsory, the information costs of an individualized determination of damage may make adherence to the fixed-compensation approach optimal for the primitive society.

46. See Fox, supra note 37, at 47–49, 150.

47. See Bloch, supra note 38, at 137–138, 142.

48. See, e.g., Diamond, supra note 1, at 58–59, 65, 66, 269–270; Howell, supra note 1, at 70; Charles Dundas, "The Organization and Laws of Some Bantu Tribes in East Africa," 45 *J. Royal Anthro. Inst.* 234, 279–283 (1915).

Exclusive reliance on monetary (or monetary-equivalent) penalties may seem questionable on the ground that many of the people in a primitive society must be too poor to pay a sum equal to the value of a life in such society, even if that value is low because of short life expectancy. However, the principle of collective responsibility enables the society to set a level of compensation higher than the average individual can pay, because his kinsmen are liable for the judgment debt.[49] Even if solvency limitations reduced the effective severity of monetary punishments below that of the physical punishments inflicted in the retaliation stage, it would not follow that the expected cost of punishment to offenders was lower. Although the severity of punishment would be less, the probability of its being imposed would be greater, because compensation gives the kinsmen of the slain man (or the victim himself if he survives) an incentive besides revenge for seeking to punish the injurer.

Thus far I have assumed that a fine is an adequate deterrent if it is equal to the cost of the violation. However, if the probability of punishment is less than one, the fine must be raised so that the expected cost of punishment will remain equal to the cost of the violation. Since primitive societies have no police or other public investigatory agencies and since the costs of information are generally high anyway, we might expect the probability of punishment to be very low and hence the optimal "blood-wealth" very high. Yet it seems that penalties are not on average higher than in modern societies,[50] that probabilities of punishment are high,[51] and that crime rates—where comparison is possible—seem comparable to those in advanced societies.[52] A number of factors compensate for the lack of a police force and related institutions of public law enforcement:

49. There is again an analogy to the modern tort principle of *respondeat superior*. See Posner, supra note 43.

50. Especially where compensation has replaced retaliation as the characteristic sanction. For some evidence see Friedman, supra note 38, App. I.

51. See Gulliver, supra note 1, at 127–134.

52. See *African Homicide and Suicide* 237, 256 (Paul Bohannan ed. 1960).

a. The lack of privacy makes it difficult to conceal wrongdoing.[53]

b. The principle of collective responsibility creates incentives for the kinship group to identify and eliminate members who show dangerous criminal proclivities.

c. Efforts to conceal a crime are often punished separately.[54]

d. Religious belief often discourages concealment of crime.[55]

e. The widespread "social insurance" of primitive society reduces the gains from acquisitive crimes and so presumably their incidence. If I am free to take the food I need from my kinsmen and forbidden to "hoard" more than I need, there is no purpose in stealing food unless none of my kinsmen, or anyone I might beg from, has any food to spare. Theft seems in fact an unimportant crime in many primitive societies.[56]

The combination of high probabilities of punishment with only moderately severe penalties makes economic sense, as a combination of high probabilities of punishment with very severe penalties would not. Whether it is the *optimal* combination is a different question. Economic analysis suggests that a combi-

53. See also note 5 in Chapter 6, supra.

54. See Diamond, supra note 1, at 63–64, 76.

55. For example, it may be considered unlucky to eat with either the kinsman of a man you have slain or the killer of one of your kinsmen. If you kill a stranger you will not know who his kin are. The only way to be sure of never eating with one of them is by announcing your deed so that the victim's kinsmen will avoid eating with you. See Barton, supra note 1, at 241; Gluckman, *The Ideas of Barotse Jurisprudence,* supra note 1, at 219. In another society it is believed that a person who does not submit to a (public) ritual cleansing after killing someone will develop an itch which he will scratch until he dies. See Goldschmidt, supra note 1, at 97. Devices for inducing the killer to reveal his identity are especially important because if the killer's identity is unknown there is no basis for bringing the collective responsibility of his kinship group into play—the identity of the responsible group is also unknown.

56. See Diamond, supra note 1, at 222. However, this appearance may be to some extent an artifact of the communal nature of much of the property in primitive societies: the loss to any one co-owner is too slight to move him to vigorous efforts to apprehend and punish the thief.

nation of low probabilities with very severe penalties frequently is optimal because, so long as the costs of collecting fines or damages are low, a reduction in the probability of punishment, which enables a saving of resources devoted to investigation and prosecution, can be offset at low cost by increasing the severity of the punishment for those (few) offenders who are caught.[57] However, solvency problems to one side, the low-probability–high-severity approach probably would not be optimal in the conditions of primitive society. Such an approach would increase the variance of punishment compared to systems that combined high probabilities of punishment with low severity; variance or risk is a cost to people who are risk averse; and the prevalence of insurance arrangements in primitive societies suggests that their members, like modern people, are indeed risk averse. The risk factor in a high-severity–low-probability punishment scheme would be especially pronounced in a primitive society because primitive tort law rests on the principle of strict liability. This means that people cannot eliminate the risk of punishment simply by behaving carefully.

6. *Liability is strict.* Strict liability is the normal response of primitive society to acts causing death or injury. If a man injures or kills another, even in an accident that could not have been prevented by the exercise of due care, he must pay compensation to the victim or his kin. In some primitive legal systems the specified compensation is lower if the killing or injuring is accidental, in others not, but almost always some compensation must be paid whether or not the injurer was "at fault" in the sense of modern tort law.[58]

The economic literature has identified four factors bearing on the choice between a strict and a fault approach to liability that

---

57. See Becker, supra note 41.

58. Moore, supra note 38, at 93–94, questions how sharp the contrast is between primitive and modern society so far as strict versus fault liability is concerned, noting that there are many examples of strict liability in modern law. She does not appear to question, however, the proposition that strict liability is more common in primitive than in modern law. An extreme example of primitive strict liability is the refusal in Homeric society to distinguish between accidental and intentional homicide; both are equally culpable. See A. W. H. Adkins, *Merit and Responsibility* 52–53 (1960).

might be important in the primitive setting.[59] First is the costs of information. The determination of fault is more costly, because it involves the consideration of more factors, than the determination simply whether the defendant injured the plaintiff.

The second factor is the ratio of avoidable to unavoidable injuries.[60] If this ratio is very low, a rule of strict liability will be unattractive because it will require a lot of costly legal activity having no allocative effect. The threat of a judgment awarding damages to the victim of an unavoidable injury will not affect the conduct of potential injurers, because by definition the judgment cost is lower than the cost of accident avoidance in such a case.

Third is the cost of accident avoidance to the victim. Strict liability shifts accident-avoidance responsibility wholly from potential victims to potential injurers. If we are confident that injury could not have been avoided by the victim at lower cost than to the injurer, we need not worry that strict liability will reduce the incentive of potential victims to avoid accidents below optimal levels or that it will have to be supplemented by a defense of contributory negligence to take care of cases where the victim is the cheaper accident avoider.

The fourth factor concerns the relative cost of insurance to injurer and injured. Strict liability makes the injurer the insurer of the injured. This may or may not be a cheaper method of insurance than a scheme of liability under which the injured is induced to obtain insurance because he can claim against the injurer only if the latter is at fault.

All four factors suggest that strict liability is probably more efficient than fault liability in primitive society.

The costs of adjudicating fault issues are likely to be high in a society lacking both a professional judiciary and a clear idea of how the natural world works (though a factor pushing in the

59. See Posner, supra note 16, at 137–142, 441–442.

60. By an "avoidable" injury is meant one that could have been prevented at lower cost than the expected cost of the injury. Either an intentionally or a negligently inflicted injury would be avoidable in this sense.

opposite direction is the simpler technologies in primitive societies). Lacking a clear understanding of natural phenomena, a primitive arbitrator would often have difficulty distinguishing intentional from accidental (let alone negligent from unavoidable) conduct.[61] Suppose A and B are members of the same hunting party. They shoot their arrows at a wild boar, but A's arrow is deflected off the boar's back and hits B. It looks like an accident—but A may have procured this "accidental" result by casting a spell. The primitive arbitrator could not reject such possibilities out of hand.

To be sure, uncertainty may bedevil the ascription of causal responsibility as well. This may explain the curious rule of archaic law that makes the punishment more severe if the violator is caught in the act than if he is apprehended later on.[62] The rule is usually explained in psychological terms: the victim or his relatives feel less vengeful after some time has elapsed from the commission of the offense.[63] An economic explanation is also possible. The probability that the wrong man has been apprehended is greater where apprehension is the result of an investigation after the fact, because of the difficulty of determining causal relationships when the act and the injury are not observed at the same time. The reduction in the severity of the penalty when the offender is not caught in the act is thus a method of reducing the punishment costs borne by innocent people.

The widespread use of irrebuttable factual presumptions is further evidence of the high costs of factual determination in primitive society. For example, in some tribes the fact that a man and woman were alone together, for however brief a time, is treated as conclusive proof that sexual intercourse occurred.[64] In another tribe, if extramarital intercourse occurs in an inhabited area and the woman is not heard to scream, her rape

61. See, e.g., J. Walter Jones, *The Law and Legal Theory of the Greeks* 261 (1956); Roberts, supra note 1, at 46, 108–109.

62. See Diamond, supra note 1, at 78; Maine, supra note 1 at 366.

63. See *id.* at 367.

64. See Max Gluckman, *The Ideas in Barotse Jurisprudence,* supra note 1, at 223.

complaint is conclusively presumed to be unfounded.[65] The reliance of primitive law on strict liability may likewise have an information-costs rationale.

This analysis may also explain why, in some societies, if the person killed is a member of the killer's own kinship group there is no liability for the killing.[66] A rule of no liability resembles one of strict liability in dispensing with the need to determine nice questions of motive, duty, and care. There is a presumption that the intrafamilial killing is justifiable—for example, to weed out a killer who might subject the family to retaliation or liability. A costly factual determination is avoided by making this presumption irrebuttable.[67]

The second factor bearing on the choice between strict and fault liability, the ratio of avoidable to unavoidable injuries, also points toward strict liability in the primitive setting. Judging from the reports of anthropologists, most serious injuries caused by people in primitive society are avoidable in the economic sense—most in fact are deliberately inflicted. Thus, a rule of strict liability will rarely shift losses without an allocative gain, for rarely will the injurer's costs of avoidance exceed the expected injury costs.

The large proportion of deliberate injurers also suggests that avoidance costs are higher to victims than to injurers (though no doubt many of the fights that lead to injuries involve an element of avoidable provocation). In these circumstances it is efficient to place all the costs on the injurer, and strict liability does this.

The final factor, insurance, exists in some tension with the last two. If all of the accidents subject to a rule of strict liability were culpable in the sense that they would also give rise to liability

65. See A. L. Epstein, "Injury and Liability in African Customary Law in Zambia," in *Ideas and Procedures in African Customary Law* 292, 300–301 (Max Gluckman ed. 1969).

66. See, e.g., Goldschmidt, supra note 1, at 91, 98, 107–108. This result may also follow simply from the kinship basis of primitive law enforcement.

67. Also, in an intrafamilial killing (or wounding) case, liability is unnecessary for insurance. The victim and his family already have a claim on their kinsmen for assistance.

under a fault system, strict liability would provide no additional insurance. The case for strict liability would still be compelling: the costs involved in making a determination of fault would be completely wasted from a social standpoint because they would not serve to screen out a set of accidents where imposing liability on the injurer would serve no allocative purpose. Assuming that a significant fraction of accidents in primitive society are not due to fault, the system of strict liability does perform a modest insurance function beyond what a fault system would provide. Whether it is an *efficient* insurance mechanism depends on whether the injurer is a better insurer than the victim. Under either of two plausible conditions, the answer is "yes." First, if injurers are on average wealthier than victims, injurer liability will make sense from an insurance standpoint (provided that utility functions are uncorrelated with wealth). Probably injurers are wealthier on average than victims—the man who is stronger, more active, who owns more dogs and cattle and tools, is more likely to be an injurer than a victim (I am speaking of purely accidental injuries here). Second, if compensation is less than completely adequate, injurer liability serves to divide the loss between injurer and victim rather than shift it entirely from the victim to the injurer.[68] For serious injuries, which are the relevant ones from the insurance standpoint, the evidence from our society is that damage awards undercompensate victims,[69] and the same thing is probably true in primitive society.

Criminal Law

I said earlier that primitive peoples have no criminal law because there is no state, but this is an overstatement. Even societies that do not have any governmental organs often regard a few acts, principally witchcraft and incest, as offenses against

68. One tribe splits the cost of an accident fifty-fifty between injurer and victim. See Riasanovsky, supra note 1, at 146–147.

69. See U.S. Dept. Transportation, *Motor Vehicle Crash Losses and Their Compensation in the United States* 90 (1971); Alfred F. Conard et al., *Automobile Accident Costs and Payments* 178–179 (1964).

the community, to be punished even if the victim or his kin do not take action against the offender.[70] The reason for a public sanction seems clear in the case of incest, a "victimless" crime that is harmful to the community. Perhaps witchcraft is deemed a practice whose potential magnitude and difficulty of detection justify a sanction greater than the compensation remedy used in ordinary killing and wounding cases.

With the rise of the state, the criminal law in the strict sense just referred to—that is, a system of punishments separate from the compensation system—tends to expand to embrace murder, assault, theft, and other acts that we conventionally deem criminal.[71] Why does the sovereign consider an act of violence directed against a private citizen an offense against him? A possible reason is that the sovereign in effect sells protection to the citizens in exchange for the taxes he collects. But this overlooks the fact that the citizens are already protected—not badly on the evidence of prepolitical societies—by the compensation system. A reason more solidly grounded in economic theory is that a killing or wounding imposes a cost on the sovereign by reducing the tax revenues he can collect from the victim. The sovereign "owns" an interest in his subjects which is impaired by acts that reduce their wealth. This economic interest is not taken into account by the purely private compensation system, so the sovereign establishes a system of criminal punishment as a method of internalizing this externality.

I close this chapter by addressing two general questions. First, if it is true, as I have argued, that the legal and other social institutions of primitive society are economically rational or efficient, what mechanism drives primitive society to this surprising result?[72] The same question has arisen, as we saw in Chapter 4,

70. See, e.g., Diamond, supra note 1, at 260.
71. See *id.* at 74–75, 85, 92. 273, 293.
72. It will not surprise all anthropologists. See, e.g., Manning Nash, *Primitive and Peasant Economic Systems* 49 (1966). I emphasize once again that, in suggesting that primitive people are economically rational, I am not making any statement about their conscious states. Rational behavior to an economist is a matter of consequences rather than intentions and in that respect resembles the concept of functionality in traditional anthropology. See, e.g., Radcliffe-Brown, supra note 20, at 62, 83; A. R. Radcliffe-Brown, *Structure and Function in Primitive Society: Essays and Addresses*, ch. 9 (1952).

with regard to the finding that the Anglo-American common law is efficient, and in that context the question is far from finally resolved. But it is easier to explain why efficiency would have great social survival value in the primitive world than to explain this for our world. The efficient society is wealthier than the inefficient—that is what efficiency means—and a wealthier society will support a larger population. This effect of greater wealth can be decisive in the competition among primitive societies, where the methods of warfare are simple and numbers of people count for more than in modern warfare. Archaic societies sufficiently durable to have left substantial literary or archaeological remains, and primitive societies sufficiently durable to have survived into the nineteenth century (when serious anthropological study began), are likely, therefore, to be societies whose customs are efficient.

An additional factor is that a primitive society is one that by definition has had a long time to adapt to its environment. The interval within which adaptation can occur depends on the rate of change of the environment. If that rate is very slow, the society has plenty of time to evolve efficient adaptations.

Clearly, however, the primitive social equilibrium is less efficient, at least in the long run, than that of advanced societies: consider the very small proportion of the world's population that lives in primitive societies today. This situation is caused in some part by coercion by the advanced societies rather than peaceful competition (dramatically so in the case of the North American Indians, for example), but probably in greater part by the adaptive responses of primitive society to its economic environment. These responses include practices, such as denying people privacy and preventing them from amassing wealth, which are inimical to economic progress and in turn to population growth.

This brings me to my second general point. An evaluation of whether a society's institutions are efficient or, in the equivalent terminology of Part I, wealth maximizing, depends on what factors are treated as exogenous—that is, treated as factors to which social institutions must adapt as best they can because they cannot change them—and what factors are treated as endogenous, that is, as factors that can be altered by the choice of institutions. In analyses of whether the common law is efficient, invariably a considerable background of constitutional and statutory constraints and social and economic institutions is treated as fixed, and the question is asked whether the common law is an efficient adaptation to that background. For example, Professor Landes and I have argued that the common law rules governing nonmaritime rescues are efficient given the elaborate public infrastructure of rescue services on land, but conceivably one could devise an even more efficient system consisting of different common law principles coupled with a different pattern of public services.[73] Similarly, if high information costs are treated as an unalterable part of the primitive environment, then the primitive institutions described in this chapter and the last are probably efficient; but different institutions might enable the primitive society to surmount the high costs of information and move to a higher plane of efficiency. I believe that one can speak meaningfully of both the common law and the counterpart institutions of primitive society as efficient, while recognizing that alternative institutional arrangements might be even more efficient.

73. See William M. Landes & Richard A. Posner, "Salvors, Finders, Good Samaritans, and Other Rescuers: An Economic Study of Law and Altruism," 7 *J. Legal Stud.* 83, 118–119 and n.88 (1978)

8

Retribution and Related Concepts of Punishment

This chapter examines several related concepts of punishment that are associated primarily with primitive and early societies. The retributive concept of punishment is that

punishment is justified on the grounds that wrongdoing merits punishment. It is morally fitting that a person who does wrong should suffer in proportion to his guilt, and the severity of the appropriate punishment depends on the depravity of his act. The state of affairs where a wrongdoer suffers punishment is morally better than the state of affairs where he does not; and it is better irrespective of any of the consequences of punishing him.[1]

1. John Rawls, "Two Concepts of Rules," 1 *Philosophical Rev.* 3, 4–5 (1955). For a similar definition see A. C. Ewing, *The Morality of Punishment* 13 (1929); and for other discussions of the meaning and ethical basis of the retributive theory, by both supporters and opponents, see K. G. Armstrong, "The Retributivist Hits Back," 70 *Mind* 471 (n.s. 1961); Max Atkinson, "Justified and Deserved Punishment," 78 *Mind* 354 (n.s. 1969); Sidney Glendin, "A Plausible Theory of Retribution," 5 *J. Value Inquiry* 1 (1970); H. L. A. Hart, *Punishment and Responsibility* 230–237 (1968); Donald Clark Hodges, "Punishment," 18 *Philosophy & Phenomenological Research* 209 (1957–1959); John Kleinig, *Punishment and Desert* (1973); John Laird, "The Justification of Punishment," 41 *The Monist* 352 (1931); Herbert Morris, "Persons and Punishment," 52 *id.* 475 (1968); C. W. K. Mundle, "Punishment and Desert," 4 *Philosophical Q.* 216, 221 (1954); Lisa H. Perkins, "Suggestion for a Theory of Punishment," 81 *Ethics* 55 (1970); John Plamenatz, "Responsibility, Blame, and Punishment," in *Philosophy, Politics & Society* 173 (Peter Laslett & W. C. Runcimann eds. 3d ser. 1967). For an especially spirited defense of the retributive approach, see C. S. Lewis, "The Humanitarian Theory of Punishment," in *Theories of Punishment* 301 (Stanley E. Grupp ed. 1971). I know of only one economic analysis of retribution: Donald Wittman, "Punishment and Retribution," 4 *Theory & Decision* 209 (1974). Wittman argues that many features of contemporary penal law reflect the persistence of the retributive concept.

The retributive view has a long history in law and philosophy. It is found in the *lex talionis* of early Roman law, the "eye for an eye" precept in the Old Testament (and a virtually identical precept in the Koran) and in many other early codes, and its philosophical exponents include Immanuel Kant.[2]

The concept of punishment as retaliation or revenge is similar to the retributive concept in that punishment is treated as a form of recompense paid by the offender, but it differs in viewing punishment from the standpoint of the victim. Whereas retribution focuses on the offender's wrong, retaliation focuses on the impulse of the victim (or of those who sympathize with him) to strike back at the offender. A concept more familiar to classicists and anthropologists than to lawyers and philosophers is "pollution." This is the belief that punishment is visited through supernatural agency on the neighbors or descendants of the offender when he himself manages to escape punishment. Although some retributivists have argued that a proper concept of retribution precludes imposing liability on anyone but the offender, concepts of retribution and pollution are frequently conjoined. The Old Testament, for example, states both that the offender shall repay an eye for an eye and a tooth for a tooth and that the sins of the father shall be visited upon the sons.

From Revenge to Retribution, and Beyond

We have seen that the threat of retaliation is the basic mechanism by which public order is maintained in primitive societies. Here I inquire into the incentive or motivation of an individual or of a member of his kinship group to retaliate for a wrong done to him. Deterrence could be a motivation. The vigor with which the victim or his kinship group avenge the present wrong

2. Kant's views on retribution are discussed in Hodges, supra note 1. The literature describing the actual retributory practices of primitive and early societies is very extensive. Some examples are Paul Bohannan, *Law and Warfare* (1967) *passim;* David Daube, *Studies in Biblical Law,* ch. 3 (1969); E. Adamson Hoebel, *The Law of Primitive Man* (1954), *passim.*

may influence the probability of future aggression against them. One reason why vengeance is a family obligation in primitive societies may be precisely to involve in the enforcement process an entity with a sufficiently long future to have a substantial interest in deterrence.

In some cases, however, deterrence may not be a sufficient motivation for a rationally calculating individual to incur the costs of retaliation. An example would be where the conditions of information did not allow a prospective wrongdoer to know in advance the vigor of the victim's (or his family's) retaliation. There might still be a motivation to retaliate, though not a deterrent motivation: retaliation might involve getting something of value from the wrongdoer, which would yield a private benefit separate from deterrence. We saw in the last chapter that a primitive society may prescribe pecuniary or equivalent compensation for wrongs (including criminal offenses such as murder), much as in modern tort law; and probably an important reason for such customs, and for their survival, is that they motivate people to retaliate and hence enhance the credibility of the threat of retaliation and with it public order. But the feasibility of a compensation scheme depends on the possession of wealth by the wrongdoer—or by his family or village, if a principle of collective responsibility is followed—commensurate with the gravity of the wrong; and throughout most of human history people probably lacked sufficient wealth, at least in transferable form, to make the hope of compensation a motivation for a victim or his family to incur the costs of retaliating.

Another instance where conscious or calculating concern with deterrence will not motivate revenge is where the costs of taking revenge are less than the benefits in reducing the expected cost of future aggression. The aggressor might be well protected, so that the avenger would have to incur great risk and other costs to injure him. Or the aggression might have so impoverished the victim and his family as to reduce to negligible levels the value to them of deterring future aggression (there is nothng more to steal).

In cases where the benefits from retaliation are less than the costs, retaliation might seem to be an irrational act from the individual's standpoint. Yet it might not be irrational for the individual to have ex ante, and to be known to have (perhaps from gestures or bearing that express his temperament), an unshakable *policy* of retaliation that is not reexamined or changed each time he suffers some aggression. Knowledge that a victim will retaliate when attacked without making a fresh cost-benefit analysis will discourage aggression more effectively than knowledge that the victim will respond "rationally" to each act of aggression by weighing the costs and benefits of retaliation as they then appear. To be sure, the policy yields greater costs as well as greater benefits, for if an aggressive act does occur, retaliation will be pursued regardless of risks and other costs. But the gains of the policy may exceed the losses, ex ante.

The problem with such a policy is credibility. The individual must somehow bind himself in advance not to yield to the temptation to behave opportunistically when attacked (by weighing the costs and benefits of retaliation as they then appear). The problem of commitment has been discussed in many other contexts,[3] but the commonest methods of commitment, such as a legally enforceable promise, are not available in a primitive society. Two methods of commitment may be available in that setting, however. One is genetic. If an unshakable policy of retaliation would increase the fitness of the individual who adhered to such a policy, there could evolve through natural selection psychological traits that guaranteed retaliation regardless of the benefit-cost ratio at the time the aggressive act took place, traits that put the victim in a towering rage precluding cool calculation. The second method of commitment is cultural—according social approval to the "man of honor," the man ready to retaliate against the slightest affront. As noted in previous chapters, this cultural characteristic is more pronounced in societies that lack strong public enforcement institutions than in those that have them. But the direction of causation may be a

---

3. See, e.g., Thomas C. Schelling, *The Strategy of Conflict,* ch. 5 (1960); Richard A. Posner, "Gratuitous Promises in Economics and Law," 6 *J. Legal Stud.* 411 (1977).

problem here: the presence of highly individualistic, touchy, quick-to-anger individuals may make it more difficult to create and maintain effective public institutions.

A desire to retaliate not motivated by hope of compensation or by desire to establish a reputation that will deter future wrongdoing is a form of negative altruism. The victim or his family incurs the costs (including risks to personal safety) of avenging a wrong because injuring the wrongdoer increases the avenger's utility. To emphasize the effects of retaliation on the victim's utility is not, however, to offer a utilitarian *justification* of retribution. Such a justification would require that the increase in the victim's (or his family's) utility exceed the reduction in the wrongdoer's utility brought about by the punishment, and the measurement problem is intractable. My point is only that the avenger must derive utility from his act in order to be motivated to do it in the absence of compensation.

The assumption of interdependent utilities is not a new one in economics; it lies behind much of the work on the economics of the family.[4] What is somewhat new is the assumption of interdependent *negative* utilities.[5] The ultimate basis of both types of interdependence would appear to be biological. Just as biologists have related (positive) altruism within the family to genetic fitness, even using the term "familial solidarity,"[6] so they have remarked the survival value of a gene for retaliation against aggression.[7] The analysis is more complex where retaliation is "irrational" judged by the costs and the deterrence benefits of the retaliatory act as they appear when the act is committed. But

4. See Gary S. Becker, "Altruism, Egoism, and Genetic Fitness: Economics and Sociobiology," 14 *J. Econ. Lit.* 817 (1976).

5. It is not entirely new. Economists have sometimes discussed envy. For a recent and rigorous analysis of envy within the family, see Gary S. Becker, "Altruism in the Family" (U. Chi. Dept. Econ., June 1979).

6. Donald T. Campbell, "On the Genetics of Altruism and the Counter-Hedonic Components of Human Behavior," 28 *J. Soc. Issues* no. 3, at 21, 27 (1972). See also references in Becker, supra note 5.

7. See Robert L. Trivers, "The Evolution of Reciprocal Altruism," 46 *Q. Rev. Biology* 35, 49 (1971); J. Hirshleifer, "Natural Economy versus Political Economy," 1 *J. Soc. & Biological Structures* 319, 332, 334 (1978). Hirshleifer speaks of "reactive responses whose delivery is guaranteed by emotion." *Id.* at 332.

even here, as we have seen, the act may be rational and may contribute to survival when viewed not in isolation but as the price the individual pays for having a genetically programmed policy of retaliation.[8] If this point is accepted, then it is easy to see how a disposition to retaliate for a wrong done not to oneself but to a member of one's family might also contribute to survival.

The vengeful component in our genetic makeup remains an important element in deterring aggression. Nuclear deterrence is premised on the belief that a nation's leaders will retaliate in circumstances (the complete destruction of the nation) where retaliation could yield no tangible benefits. Another example is the belief that people will terminate trading relations with those who have cheated them without calculating the costs and benefits of continuing those relations—without, that is, treating the costs to them as sunk. One recent article suggests that the discovery of fraud may result in the seller's losing future business from the defrauded buyers because of negative altruism.[9] Another states: "Although it may not always be in one's narrow self-interest to punish the other party to . . . a reciprocal relationship since termination may impose a cost on both, it may be rational for one to adopt convincingly such a reaction function to optimally prevent cheating."[10] This statement seems to be talking about the deliberate adoption of a retaliatory posture, but deliberateness is unnecessary if the desire to retaliate has a genetic basis.

The sort of "retribution" I have described in the consumer case is not called by such ominous names as retribution or vengeance and is not looked at askance as something primitive or

8. Thus Trivers, supra note 7, at 49, notes that retaliation "often seems out of all proportion to the offenses committed. Friends are even killed over apparently trivial disputes. But since small inequities repeated many times over a lifetime may exact a heavy toll in relative fitness, selection may favor a strong show of aggression when the cheating tendency is discovered."

9. See Benjamin Klein & Keith B. Leffler, "The Role of Price in Guaranteeing Quality" 35 n.40 (n.d., Disc. Paper no. 149, U.C.L.A., Dept. Econ.).

10. Benjamin Klein, Robert Crawford, & Armen A. Alchian, "Vertical Integration, Appropriable Rents, and the Competitive Contracting Process," 21 *J. Law & Econ.* 297, 305 n.18 (1978).

irrational. Yet people who seek to predicate criminal punishment on the desire for revenge are thought bloodthirsty and archaic. There appear to be two reasons for the different reactions in these two cases. First, we rely on the state to enforce the
criminal laws to a greater extent than we rely on it to protect
consumers from getting cheated. Although there is a Federal
Trade Commission, the prospect of losing future business probably deters more consumer fraud than the expected costs of
FTC proceedings. Until the nineteenth century the criminal
area, too, was largely private.[11] But today the primary responsibility for bringing criminals to justice rests on civil servants
rather than on the victims of crime or their families. The
smaller the private role in law enforcement, the less functional
is revenge. Police officers and other civil servants employed by
the criminal justice system are not motivated by vengeful feelings. They are paid to administer a criminal justice system based
primarily on a deterrent rationale. To be sure, even a public enforcement system relies to some extent on the "thirst for revenge" to motivate victims and sometimes bystanders to assist
the police. That a victim of crime is quite likely to complain to
the police and appear as a witness at the trial of the offender, all
without compensation, is some evidence that a genetic disposition to retaliate has survived, for his cooperation is unlikely to
have a significant effect in deterring future crimes against him.
Nevertheless, because its role in criminal justice has shrunk,
vengeance has come to seem an archaic emotion in the context
of criminal punishment.

The second reason that people reject the idea of vengeance as
the basis of criminal punishment today is the wedge between
crime and punishment that is created when the probability of
imposing punishment is less than one. This wedge is based on
sound economic considerations[12] but has the collateral effect of
making the punishment for a crime more severe, ex post, than

---

11. See, e.g., Douglas M. MacDowell, *The Law in Classical Athens*, ch. 4 (1978); 2 Leon
Radzinowicz, *A History of English Criminal Law and Its Administration from 1750* (1957).
12. Discussed in the section on strict liability in Chapter 7.

the crime itself. In a system where punishments are often more severe than the crimes for which they are imposed, someone who tries to justify those punishments by the equality or proportionality between the suffering of the victim and the suffering of the criminal when he is punished will indeed sound bloodthirsty; for he is, unwittingly, advocating that the criminal receive a punishment disproportionate to the crime. It is possible to justify the disproportion, but not on retributive grounds.

This difficulty tends not to arise in primitive societies, which have devices for pushing the probability of apprehension and punishment near to one. Considerations of solvency and of risk aversion may, as we saw, make this pattern optimal for such societies. Its side effect is to make the optimum punishment equal in severity to the crime. This may explain why early theorists of retribution, such as the authors of the Old Testament and of the Koran, describe retribution as an equality between the crime and the punishment. It may explain why being punished was traditionally compared to paying a debt.[13] In a modern system of punishment, there need be no exact correspondence between the gravity of the crime and the severity of the punishment; a less serious crime might be punished more severely than a more serious one if the former was easier to conceal. The debt analogy therefore becomes strained.

A more sophisticated version conceives retribution not as a consequence of the victim's desire for revenge but as a substitute for, or limitation on, vengeance. The idea is that without some customary or legal constraints, people might react to a wrong by retaliating against the wrongdoer disproportionately, leading him or his family to retaliate in turn against the retaliator or *his* family. To avoid an endless cycle of injury, retaliation, and counterretaliation—a costly system for controlling aggression—custom may prescribe that the retaliator may inflict no

13. See, e.g., Lucien Lévy-Bruhl, *The "Soul" of the Primitive* 104 (Lilian A. Clare transl. 1928); Morris, supra note 1, at 478; Friedrich Nietzsche, "On the Genealogy of Morals," in Friedrich Nietzsche, *On the Genealogy of Morals and Ecce Homo* 63 (Walter Kaufmann trans. 1967).

more severe injury than the wrong (a tooth for a tooth rather than an eye for a tooth) and that the wrongdoer may not seek vengeance against the retaliator in turn. Retribution in this view limits the severity of punishment under a pure system of retaliation[14] and is distinguished from the latter both by notions of proportionality, which limit the level of retaliation, and by notions of justice, which preclude counterretaliation by the original wrongdoer (if the victim-avenger observes the proportionality constraint).

This view is important because it reveals a serious deficiency, or inefficiency, in a simple vengeance approach to punishment. There is nothing in the concept of vengeance or in its emotional (genetic) underpinnings to suggest a limitation on the magnitude of retaliation. Once a man is injured, triggering a desire to retaliate, why should he want to inflict *no greater* injury on the aggressor? In at least one case he will surely want to inflict a greater injury on the wrongdoer than the wrongdoer inflicted on him. That is the case where the cost of inflicting a greater injury is less than the cost of inflicting a lesser injury, as it often will be. For example, in many cases it is cheaper to kill a wrongdoer than to wound him. Killing him reduces the probability that *he* will retaliate (although it increases the probability of his family's retaliating) and, by removing a witness, reduces the probability that the retaliation will be detected.

Thus there can be no assurance that a pure system of retaliation or revenge would result in the imposition of optimal penalties. But this is not to say that there would be too much crime. There might rather be too little. In a society in which a person may be killed in revenge for having spat at another, the incidence of spitting will probably be lower than in a society where it is forbidden to kill in revenge for being spat on. However, a

14. For some representative statements of this view see M. J. L. Hardy, *Blood Feuds and the Payment of Blood Money in the Middle East* 32 (1963); Geoffrey MacCormack, "Revenge and Compensation in Early Law," 21 *Am. J. Comp. Law* 69, 74 (1976); Perkins, supra note 1, at 56; Leopold Pospisil, "Feud," in 5 *International Encyclopedia of the Social Sciences* 389 (1968). Compare Armstrong, supra note 1, at 487.

punishment scheme in which the punishment is far more serious than the crime will not be optimal unless the probability of
detection and punishment is very low, and I have suggested that
typically in primitive societies it will be high. The closer that
probability is to one, the more closely should the severity of the
punishment approach the gravity of the crime. This condition
would often not be fulfilled in a system of pure vengeance.

While there is a possible genetic basis for retaliation, there is
no similar basis for the limitations on it that are imposed by the
proportionality component of retribution. These limitations are
presumably cultural, with one possible, partial exception. The
common primitive practice of exogamy has the effect of creating family relationships across potentially retaliating groups.
Because of the gene of family altruism, this effect may mitigate
the ferocity with which one group will retaliate against the other
for a wrong done to one of its members. That is, it may introduce the proportionality required by the concept of retribution.

To summarize, in circumstances where law enforcement is
private and the probabilities of detecting and punishing offenses are high, conditions widely encountered in primitive and
early societies, a pure vengeance system is unlikely to be optimal, because it will result in excessive punishment. The age-old
disapproval of feuding has an economic basis after all, though it
is not the conventional basis, that allowing feuds produces too
much violence. Similarly, the view that the retributive theory of
punishment represents an advance in social thought about
crime over a pure vengeance theory is economically correct, because retribution, implying proportionality, is superior to vengeance as a basis for punishment under the conditions stated
above. But retributive justice is not functional when those conditions are not fulfilled—when enforcement is not private and
probabilities of detection and punishment are not high—
and this explains why the retributive theory of punishment has
declined with the rise of modern governments and with the increased concealability of criminal activity resulting from the
growth of privacy.

Pollution: Retribution against Neighbors and Descendants

I have thus far spoken of retaliation against the wrongdoer himself, but the customs of primitive and early societies often allow retaliation against someone else, such as his neighbor or a member of his family (collective responsibility). My interest here is in the special form of collective responsibility known as "pollution."[15] In ancient Greece a murderer polluted his city, and if he wasn't expelled or killed the citizens would suffer plague or other misfortune. Sophocles' play *Oedipus Tyrannus* describes the pollution of Thebes as a result of Oedipus's murder of his father. In Greek thought, murder or other wrongdoing also polluted a man's descendants. For example, in Aeschylus's play *Agamemnon* we are given to understand that Atreus's wrongdoing contaminated several generations of his descendants.[16] There are parallels to these Greek beliefs in the Old Testament, and one can find similar beliefs in primitive cultures in Africa and elsewhere.[17]

15. On pollution in ancient Greece (*"miasma"*), see Arthur W. H. Adkins, *Merit and Responsibility*, ch. 5 (1960); 1 Robert J. Bonner & Gertrude Smith, *The Administration of Justice from Homer to Aristotle* 53–55 (1930); E. R. Dodds, *The Greeks and the Irrational* 35–37 (1951); J. Walter Jones, *The Law and Legal Theory of the Greeks: An Introduction* 254–257 (1952); Douglas M. MacDowell, *Athenian Homicide Law* (1963), especially ch. 14; Erwin Rhode, *Psyche* 176–179, 294–297 (1925). On pollution in a variety of primitive and early societies see Mary Douglas, *Purity and Danger* (1966). My discussion of pollution in fifth- and fourth-century (B.C.) Athens expands the scope of this part of the book beyond the primitive and early society as defined in Chapter 5, for Athens at that time was not a preliterate society.

16. For a skeptical view of hereditary guilt in *Agamemnon*, see Michael Gagarin, *Aeschylean Drama* 62–64 (1976).

17. See Douglas, supra note 15, for examples; also Elizabeth Colson, *The Plateau Tonga* 107–109 (1962); Meyer Fortes, "The Political System of the Tallensi of the Northern Territories of the Gold Coast," in *African Political Systems* 239, 253 (Meyer Fortes & E. E. Evans-Pritchard eds. 1940); E. Adamson Hoebel, *The Law of Primitive Man* 156–159 (1954); E. H. Meek, "Ibo Law," in *Essays Presented to C. G. Seligman* 221 (E. E. Evans-Pritchard et al. eds. 1934); E. L. Peters, "Some Structural Aspects of Feud among the Camel-Herding Bedouin of Cyrenaica," 37 *Africa* 261, 264–265 (1967); J. M. Powis Smith, *The Origin and History of Hebrew Law* 49 (1931). For some Biblical examples see Num. 35:31–33; Deut. 19:13, 21:8–9; II Kings 24:4.

Pollution differs from family collective responsibility in two ways. First, the punishment operates without human agency; rather than a member of the victim's family taking revenge, the gods visit misfortune on the neighbors or relatives of the wrongdoer. Second, pollution is often "vertical" instead of "horizontal," in the sense of hurting the descendants rather than contemporaries of the wrongdoer. This difference is connected with the first, because human vengeance is usually more or less contemporaneous with the wrongdoer's act; therefore, if directed against a relative of the wrongdoer, it tends to hit a living relative rather than an unborn descendant. Supernatural punishment need not act so quickly.

My explanation of this curious form of collective punishment, and its salience in ancient Athens, emphasizes (1) the reliance on the family to initiate criminal proceedings against a wrongdoer; (2) the small size of Athenian families and the absence of strong kinship groups; and (3) a scarcity of alternative devices for maintaining a high expected punishment cost of crime.

Pollution is mentioned most often in connection with a murder within the family, such as Oedipus's murder of his father. A related point is that the pollution resulting from killing a kinsman is harder to cleanse than that resulting from killing a stranger[18]—the chorus in Aeschylus's play *Seven against Thebes* says it is impossible to cleanse. The association of pollution with murder of kin has been noted by both classical scholars and anthropologists, and an explanation has been suggested that is congenial to economic analysis. Where a murder or other wrong occurs within the family, the mechanism for revenge, which relies on a member of the victim's family taking action, breaks down: the son who murders his father is the natural avenger of his father's murder.[19] Even in fifth-century Athens,

18. See Hubert J. Treston, *Poinē* 307, 316, 318 (1923).
19. See Adkins, supra note 15, at 110–111 n.18; Colson, supra note 17; Douglas, supra note 15, at 133–134; Lévy-Bruhl, supra note 13, at 93; MacCormack, supra note 14, at 81–82; Peters, supra note 17; Treston, supra note 18, at 339; Meek, supra note 17.

when the earlier system (visible in Homer) of direct vengeance by the victim or his family had given way to a system of public adjudication and punishment, the victim's family had the exclusive authority to initiate criminal proceedings for most acts that we regard as criminal, including murder.[20] This system could not work effectively in the case of crime within the family, so an alternative remedy was devised—the automatic punishment brought about by pollution.[21] To the extent that people believed in pollution, and many must have, their belief served to deter crimes which the ordinary machinery of criminal punishment would not have deterred.

A second point about pollution, one especially important in explaining its extension to crimes outside the family, is that the most highly developed conception of homicide pollution is found in the society of ancient Athens, which is noted for its small families.[22] A system of family collective responsibility presupposes that the wrongdoer's family is sufficiently large that its members can be readily located, for the risk of being the target of retaliation gives each of them an incentive to police the others' conduct. But a striking fact about ancient Greece is the small size of families by primitive, or for that matter nineteenth-century, standards. I am speaking, to be sure, of the household, and kinship groups larger than the household—the gene and the phratry—were recognized. But they were loose and dispersed compared to the kinship groups of African tribal so-

20. See MacDowell, supra note 11, at 110–111. Homicide was regarded as a private rather than public wrong. See, e.g., George M. Calhoun, *The Growth of Criminal Law in Ancient Greece* 109 (1927). MacDowell has argued, contrary to the traditional assumption of Greek scholars, that someone other than a relative (or in the case of a slave, his master) could prosecute for murder. See MacDowell, supra note 15, at 95; cf. *id.* at 17–18, 133–134. However, since no compensation was paid for prosecuting a murder case, prosecutions by nonrelatives must have been rare, and MacDowell offers no example of such a prosecution.

21. See 1 Bonner and Smith, supra note 15, at 55.

22. For indirect but cumulatively persuasive evidence of the small size of fifth-century Athenian families, see W. K. Lacey, *The Family in Classical Greece* 130, 165 (1968); Zygmunt Niedzielski, *The Athenian Family from Aeschylus to Aristotle* 4, 60, 106 (1955) (unpublished Ph.D. diss., U. Chi.). Compare L. P. Wilkinson, "Classical Approaches to Population & Family Planning," *Encounter* 22 (April 1978).

ciety.[23] The members of the gene or phratry were not in a good position to monitor each other's conduct, as the members of African kinship groups are. The principle of family collective responsibility is well established in African tribal societies, and generally, a murderer is *not* thought to pollute his descendants. The small size of the effective kinship group in Athens was a reason to impose family responsibility vertically, since aggregating a man with his descendants created a large group of potential targets of retaliation, human or divine, for wrongdoing.[24]

The interesting point has been made that the belief in pollution is associated with the abolition in Athens of the right of a murder victim's family to seek compensation (the *poinē* referred to by Homer) from the murderer.[25] Abolition reduced the probability of punishment; belief in pollution offset (in part at least) the resulting reduction in expected punishment costs, by increasing the severity of punishment.

A parallel to pollution found in many primitive societies is the principle that ordinary debts are inherited. As is sometimes said, "debts never rot."[26] The difficulty of collecting debts in a society that has no judges or police or sheriffs requires that a debtor's heirs be made the guarantors of his debt. The heritability of criminal responsibility may also be pragmatic. To be sure, a man's young children and unborn descendants could not be expected to police his conduct no matter how heavily they might be punished for his misdeeds. But their liability to punishment served to check him in another way, by increasing the costs to him of misconduct. As Arthur Adkins explains: "If one threatens a man that, if he does wrong in certain ways, his family will be blotted out, one is threatening him with a miserable existence after death, since there will be no one to perform the

---

23. See Dodds, supra note 15, at 34; Victor Ehrenberg, *The People of Aristophanes* 156 (1943); G. Glotz, *The Greek City and Its Institutions* 122 (N. Mallinson trans. 1930).

24. Consistently with this point, one finds a strong sense of *tribal* homicide pollution among the Cheyenne Indians, where kinship ties were very loose compared to tribal Africa. See K. N. Llewellyn & E. Adamson Hoebel, *The Cheyenne Way*, ch. 6 (1941).

25. See Treston, supra note 18, at 143–145. On the abolition of *poine* see also Mac-Dowell, supra note 11, at 110.

26. See note 34 in Chapter 5, supra.

rites. Hence in threatening his descendants one is threatening the man himself: a sufficient guarantee of good behavior, provided that the theory is believed."[27] In other words, the "superstitious" belief that the dead enjoy the rites performed in their memory by the living[28] gives a man an incentive not to do anything that will jeopardize the safety of his descendants (for who else will perform the rites for him?). This in turn makes the threat of pollution an effective sanction against misconduct in cases where the ordinary family-initiated criminal processes would not work effectively.[29]

The idea that a murder polluted an entire city may, like the idea of pollution of descendants, also have been related to the small size of the Greek family. Where people do not live in large families, a different unit of collective responsibility from the (living) family must be used—if not descendants, then the neighborhood, town, or city. In Athens "the genes had ceased to mean anything beyond the more or less irrelevant wider family circle. Its members or those of the phratry met only on rare occasions. The communities were therefore of less importance in everyday life *than the neighbors with whom a man lived in direct contact.*"[30] Notice that whereas pollution of descendants raised the *cost* of punishment to the wrongdoer, pollution of neighbors

27. Adkins, supra note 15, at 68–69.

28. See also Robert Flacelière, *Daily Life in Ancient Greece* 57, 196–197 (Peter Green trans. 1965); Wesley E. Thompson, "The Marriage of First Cousins in Athenian Society," 21 *Phoenix* 273, 280–281 (1967).

29. A somewhat similar device was long employed in England to punish traitors. Not only was the traitor executed, but his property was confiscated by the state. Confiscation would impose a cost on him, and thus contribute to deterring treason, if the utility of his heirs entered positively into his utility function. But this method of punishing a man through punishing his heirs requires that he have property. In a poorer society, belief in homicide pollution might be a superior substitute for confiscation, especially since in primitive and early societies the high costs of information concerning the natural world make divine punishment more credible than it would be in modern societies. Another difference between the Greek and the English forms of vertical punishment is that the English relied for its efficacy on the interdependence of the ancestor's and descendant's utility functions; the Greek, more "pragmatic" in this regard, relied on the services that descendants perform for ancestors to motivate the ancestor's concern for the descendants' welfare.

30. Ehrenberg, supra note 23 (emphasis added).

raised the *probability* that he would be punished by increasing the incentives of his neighbors to turn him in.[31] As mobility grows, law enforcement by neighbors can be expected to yield in turn to enforcement by police.[32]

The above analysis may help to explain why, although the society depicted in the Homeric poems is more primitive than that of fifth-century Athens, there is little suggestion in those poems of a belief in pollution.[33] This has puzzled classical scholars. It has been suggested that Homer may have deliberately suppressed references to pollution.[34] But it is generally agreed that there was less belief in pollution in Homeric society, and perhaps the reason is that in so primitive a society there was no need to supplement the vengeance system with such a belief. To be sure, as in fifth-century Athens, nuclear families in Homer are generally small and larger kinship groups seemingly unimportant. But Homeric society did not face the problem of "urban anonymity" that might have made it difficult to apprehend a wrongdoer in fifth-century Athens unless his neighbors could be turned against him by fear of pollution.[35] Also, by the fifth century there was a good deal of migration among Greek cities, so that a murderer who escaped could relocate elsewhere. Self-exile was more perilous (though not uncommon) in the Homeric period. Finally, as mentioned earlier, in Homeric society the victims of crime (or their families) had monetary incentives to seek redress, which had disappeared by the fifth century. In short, it is possible that the expected punishment cost of crime would have been higher in the society depicted by Homer than in fifth-century Athens—except for a belief in pollution, which may have arisen precisely to prevent that cost from falling.

---

31 "For neighbors have sharper eyes than foxes." *Id.* at 157. See also T. B. L. Webster, *Athenian Culture and Society* 40 (1974).

32. See Joel Feinberg, *Doing and Deserving* 238–241 (1970).

33. See, e.g., Gagarin, supra note 16, at 188 n.27.

34. See, e.g., Adkins, supra note 15, at 91.

35. The population of fifth-century Athens has been estimated at 52,000. See Webster, supra note 31.

Consistently with this analysis, some classical scholars have attributed the rise of belief in pollution to a decline in security between the period depicted in Homer and the later, archaic period when the belief flourished.[36] A decline in personal security can also be described as a decrease in the probability that crimes will be punished, and such a decrease can be expected to incite a search for ways of raising the probability, or increasing the level, of punishment. Pollution operated on both variables.

The retributive theory of punishment has been defended on the ground that it precludes the imposition of collective punishment,[37] of which pollution is a form. But analyzed from an economic standpoint, retribution—the view that punishment is just only when it is imposed on and is commensurate with the guilt of a criminal—presupposes that the probability of punishment is already high. If it is not high, devices must be found for increasing either the probability or the severity of punishment. Pollution is such a device. If retributive theory cannot explain it, that is evidence that retribution is not an adequate explanation for punishment.

I do not want to leave the impression that one can expect to find a belief in pollution in every society that has emerged from the rural, large-family state of the typical primitive society. The particular feature of Athenian social organization that may explain the importance of pollution, especially in intrafamilial crimes, is that although criminal adjudication and punishment were public, the society continued to rely on family responsibility to institute punishment. That responsibility was not limited to notifying the prosecutorial authorities; the family had to prosecute the wrongdoer to judgment.[38] And unlike later systems of private enforcement (including the Roman, and the English system until the nineteenth century), there was no free entry into the enforcement business—the enforcer had to be a

36. See Dodds, supra note 15, at 44. Dodds himself regards this as only part of the explanation. The rest he ascribes to changes in the family, but those changes appear to me to be the effects rather than the causes of social change.

37. See Laird, supra note 1, at 373–374.

38. See MacDowell, supra note 15, at 29.

relative of the victim—and no bounties or other compensation were paid to the succesful enforcer.[39] But the small size of families meant that family responsibility for punishing wrongdoers would often fail to work, because there might not be a family member competent to shoulder the duty of bringing the wrongdoer to bar. One can understand in these circumstances a felt need for some other method of punishment, something automatic; it was met by the concept of pollution.[40]

Guilt versus Responsibility

In vengeance visited upon an innocent person—a murderer's descendants or neighbors—we encounter once again that characteristic feature of the "primitive" mentality, the divorce between guilt and responsibility or between culpability and liability. Modern people tend to regard as appropriate for punishment those harmful acts that are either deliberate or negligent, where negligence can be taken to refer to an act that is not cost-justified. There are areas of strict liability in modern law—in fact a growing number. But pollution is a moral rather than legal concept, and the idea of strict liability is more difficult to understand in morality than in law. In law, whether modern or primitive, the rationale of strict liability has to do with the costs of using the legal system. In the last chapter we saw that the economic circumstances of primitive society, in particular the high costs of information, appear to explain the preference for strict liability. But do information costs also shape moral belief? A striking feature of the moral code of the ancient Greeks is precisely the frequent divorce between guilt and responsibil-

39. On private enforcement in Rome, see Alan F. Westin, *Privacy in Western History: From the Age of Pericles to the American Republic* 51 (Rep. to Assn. of Bar of N.Y. Special Comm. on Science and Law, Feb. 15, 1965); in England, 2 Leon Radzinowicz, supra note 11. Bounties for private enforcers were available for lesser crimes in Greece, however. See MacDowell, supra note 11, at 62, 64.

40. My analysis does not, of course, explain those common forms of pollution in primitive society that attach to acts which are not dangerous or criminal as we understand these terms. See Mary Douglas, "Pollution," 12 *International Encyclopedia of the Social Sciences* 336 (1968).

ity.[41] Moral responsibility is repeatedly ascribed to people on the basis of acts neither deliberate nor negligent, and sometimes totally unavoidable. In *Seven against Thebes,* Eteocles and Polyneices come to grief, we are told, because their father, Oedipus, had cursed them. Oedipus himself had come to grief, despite his best efforts to avoid the curse that had been pronounced on him, because of an ancestor's misdeed. Indeed, the categories of misfortune and punishment frequently seem conflated in Greek (and other primitive) thought; at least, consequences count much more than intention in early societies compared to ours. It is the fact that Oedipus killed his father and married his mother rather than the state of mind in which these acts occurred that condemns him and brings suffering to his city.

This difference in moral conceptions may reflect a difference in the costs of information. Intention and negligence do count in an assessment of conduct, because they determine whether the conduct is deterrable. Punishing people for conduct they cannot avoid at reasonable cost will have either no effect or a bad (inefficient) effect. Therefore, as the costs of information fall with increasing knowledge of the laws of nature and with the creation of effective institutions for determining facts, we can expect both the moral and legal concept of responsibility to move away from strict liability, or at least the very simple type of strict liability in which no excuses or justifications are recognized. There is evidence of such a trend in ancient Greece itself. While the society depicted in Homer did not even distinguish between voluntry and involuntary homicides,[42] by the fifth century that distinction was well established in Greek criminal law; but it was still far cruder than in modern law.[43] A secular trend

41. See, e.g., Adkins, supra note 15, at 88–91, 120 ff., 129 n.8; Gagarin, supra note 16, ch. 1. Adkins questions whether pollution is a moral category; clearly, however, it is an unpleasant consequence visited upon people for their conduct, albeit not always culpable conduct. Adkins's doubt suggests how closely modern people associate moral responsibility with blameworthiness.

42. See, e.g., Calhoun, supra note 20, at 16–17; Treston, supra note 18, at 75.

43. See MacDowell, supra note 11, at 114–115. Jones, supra note 15, ch. 14, is a good discussion of the mental element in Greek criminal law.

away from strict liability is especially to be expected in areas of criminal, and perhaps moral, condemnation, where punishment may exceed simple damages. Requiring a person to pay someone who is injured by his activity merely an amount equal to the cost of the injury will not deter an activity that confers benefits greater than its costs including injury costs.[44] But if the punishment is set above simple damages,[45] as is characteristic of criminal punishment, strict liability will deter too much; and so will moral condemnation, if experienced as a substantial cost to those so condemned, visited on conduct that is blameless.

Aeschylus's play *The Eumenides* provides an apt vehicle for tying up the threads of this analysis. Orestes has killed his mother Clytemnestra in revenge for her murder of his father (and her husband) Agamemnon; she in turn was revenging her daughter Iphigeneia, whom Agamemnon (her father) had sacrificed on the way to Troy. Now the Furies are tormenting Orestes for the murder of Clytemnestra. Orestes takes refuge in Athens, is tried by the court of the Areopagus, and is acquitted by one vote.

The play illustrates various problems of retaliation, retribution, pollution, and strict liability. Because Clytemnestra was murdered by her only son (with the assistance of her only surviving daughter, Electra), there is no natural human avenger of the crime,[46] and the role of "law enforcer" falls to the Furies, a supernatural agency. They in turn are commited to a rigid principle of strict liability. Orestes is guilty of murder even though he had a duty to avenge his father;[47] the homicide is justifiable, yet in the eyes of the Furies it is inexcusable.

Orestes' acquittal by the Areopagus, though disingenuously

44. See Richard A. Posner, *Economic Analysis of Law* 137–138 (2d ed. 1977).

45. By more than is just necessary to offset a probability less than one that punishment will be imposed. For an explanation of why punishment for crime should exceed simple damages even if the probability that punishment will be imposed is one, see Guido Calabresi & A. Douglas Melamed, "Property Rules, Liability Rules, and Inalienability: One View of the Cathedral," 85 *Harv. L. Rev.* 1089, 1125–1127 (1972).

46. As stressed by Gagarin, supra note 16, at 65.

47. As stressed in *Choephoroi*, the previous play of the *Oresteia*. It is relevant to note once again that the Greek word for revenge, *dikēphoros*, means literally "justice bringer."

based on Apollo's argument that the woman's role in childbearing is less important than the father's, suggests how a doctrine of excuses can mitigate a principle of strict liability and at the same time transform pure retaliation into retributive justice. Retaliation is a striking back at someone who has harmed one, regardless of the reasons for the harm, and therefore resembles a system of strict liability without excuses. Retribution—the principle that a wrongdoer, not a mere doer, should be punished—is a step toward a system of justice in which responsibility is based on fault and a system of morality in which condemnation is based on blameworthiness. This step could not be taken until there were institutions for determining culpability—for distinguishing justifiable from unjustifiable homicide. It is thus highly appropriate that the court of the Areopagus should be presented in *The Eumenides* as having been created for the express purpose of determining Orestes' guilt. Homeric society lacked such institutions, and that is why the incipient feud between Odysseus and the relatives of the suitors whom he has killed has to be terminated by Zeus's thunderbolt rather than by the judgment of a court inquiring into the justification for Odysseus's deed. Society moves from retaliation to retribution, and relatedly from strict liability to liability based on fault, as the costs of finding and evaluating facts related to the justifications for harmful acts fall.

To summarize Part II very briefly, I have argued that economic analysis yields significant insights into the institutions and behavior of primitive and ancient societies. The underlying economic concepts are those of uncertainty and information costs. These factors explain why primitive and ancient societies place such heavy emphasis on insurance; the forms the insurance takes; why such societies place heavier emphasis than modern societies do on strict liability; and many other values and institutions of primitive society. Although much work remains to be done to consolidate and expand the insights in these chapters, they provide, I believe, evidence of the range and power of the economic model to explain human behavior and social institutions.

III

PRIVACY AND RELATED INTERESTS

9
Privacy as Secrecy

The three chapters in Part III deal with the law and economics of privacy and economically related interests.[1] While the shift from primitive law and society may seem abrupt, a bridge is provided, especially to this chapter, by the economics of information, which plays a fundamental role in my theories of privacy and of primitive society.

"Privacy" is a richly ambiguous and highly charged word.[2] I shall discuss three distinct meanings of it: secrecy, seclusion, and autonomy. The first is the most interesting and is the subject of this chapter. Provisionally, privacy means the withholding or concealment of information, particularly personal information, but business information will be discussed briefly. After developing the economics of privacy as secrecy, I will inquire to what extent the common law of privacy is consistent with the economics of the subject.

1. Apart from a study by Greenawalt and Noam of business privacy, which is discussed and criticized below, and two studies, referenced in Richard A. Posner, "Privacy, Secrecy and Reputation," 28 *Buff. L. Rev.* 1, 2 n.7 (1979), that define privacy as an individual or nuclear family living alone (and find that it has risen very rapidly since World War II), I am aware of no economic analysis of privacy prior to the articles from which these chapters are drawn. Since their publication, several papers on the economics of privacy have appeared in a special issue of *J. Legal Stud.* (vol. 9, no. 3, Dec. 1980), and I shall refer to some of these papers in this chapter and the next.

2. For efforts at definition see, e.g., Hyman Gross, "The Concept of Privacy," 42 *N.Y.U. L. Rev.* 34 (1967); Judith Jarvis Thomson, "The Right to Privacy," 4 *Philos. & Pub. Aff.* 295 (1975).

The Economics of Private Information and Communications

Concealment of Personal Facts

The question whether and to what extent people should have a legally protected right to conceal personal information arises only because some people want to uncover such information about others—to pry, in a word. The first question I address, therefore, is why people want to pry. Is it a matter purely of idle or prurient curiosity, or is a functional, that is to say an economic, explanation possible?

I believe such an explanation is possible, most clearly where an actual or potential relationship, whether business or personal, creates opportunities to profit (monetarily or not) from possessing information about someone else. This is what motivates the demand for personal information by the tax collector, fiancé, partner, creditor, and competitor. Less obviously, much of the casual prying (a term used here without any pejorative connotation) into the private lives of friends and colleagues, such a common feature of social life, may also be motivated by rational considerations of self-interest. Prying enables one to form a more accurate picture of a friend or colleague, and the knowledge gained is useful in social or professional dealings with him. For example, in choosing a friend one wants to know whether he will be discreet or indiscreet, selfish or generous, and these qualities are not always apparent on initial acquaintance. Even a pure altruist needs to know the approximate wealth of a prospective beneficiary of his altruism in order to gauge the value of a transfer to him.

The other side of the coin is that social, like business, dealings present opportunities for exploitation through misrepresentation. Psychologists and sociologists have pointed out—what everyone knows—that even in everyday life people frequently resort to misrepresentation (of their income, prospects, opinions, and so forth) in order to manipulate other people's opinion of them.[3] The "wish for privacy expresses a desire . . . to control others' perceptions and beliefs vis-à-vis the self conceal-ing person."[4] Even the strongest defenders of privacy describe the individual's right to privacy as the right to "control the flow of information about him,"[5] and it is only fair to add that this may be information concerning past or present criminal activ-ity, or moral conduct at variance with the individual's professed moral standards, and that often the motive for concealment is to mislead those with whom he transacts. Other private infor-mation that people wish to conceal, while not discreditable in a moral sense, would if revealed correct misapprehensions that the individual is trying to exploit, as when a worker conceals a serious health problem from his employer, or a prospective husband conceals his sterility from his fiancée. It is not clear why society should assign the property right in such informa-tion to the individual to whom it pertains; the common law, as we shall see, generally does not. (A separate question, to which I return later, is whether the decision to assign the property right away from the possessor of guilty secrets implies that the law should countenance any and all methods of uncovering those secrets.)

We would think it wrong (and inefficient) if the law permitted a seller in hawking his wares to make false or incomplete repre-sentations of their quality. But people "sell" themselves as well as their goods by professing high standards of behavior to in-duce others to engage in advantageous social or business deal-ings with them, while concealing facts that these acquaintances

3. Erving Goffman makes this point, referring explicitly to "misrepresentation" but using the term without any pejorative connotation, in his book *The Presentation of Self in Everyday Life* 58 (1959). See also Roger Ingham, "Privacy and Psychology," in *Privacy* 35 (John B. Young ed. 1978).

4. Sidney M. Jourard, "Some Psychological Aspects of Privacy," 31 *Law & Contemp. Prob.* 307 (1966).

5. Geoffrey R. Stone, "The Scope of the Fourth Amendment: Privacy and the Po-lice Use of Spies, Secret Agents and Informers," 1976 *Am. Bar Found. Research J.* 1193, 1207. See also references cited there, and Edward A. Shils, *The Torment of Secrecy: The Background and Consequences of American Security Policies* 26 (1956).

need in order to evaluate their character. There are practical reasons for not imposing a general legal duty of full and frank disclosure of one's material personal shortcomings. But shouldn't a person be allowed to protect himself from disadvantageous transactions by ferreting out concealed facts about individuals which are material to the implicit or explicit representations that those individuals make concerning their moral qualities? It is no answer that people have "the right to be let alone,"[6] for few people want to be let alone. Rather, they want to manipulate the world around them by selective disclosure of facts about themselves.

To be sure, some private information that people desire to conceal is not discreditable. In our culture, for example, most people do not like to be seen naked, quite apart from any discreditable fact that such observation might reveal.[7] Since this reticence, unlike concealment of discreditable facts, is not a source of social costs, and since transaction costs are low, there is an economic case for assigning the property right in this area of private information to the individual; and this is what the law does. But few people have a *general* reticence that makes them want to conceal nondiscrediting personal information. Anyone who has sat next to a stranger on an airplane or a ski lift knows the delight most people take in talking about themselves to complete strangers. Reticence is more likely in speaking to friends, relatives, acquaintances, or business associates who might use a personal disclosure to gain an advantage (or avoid being disadvantaged) in a business or social transaction.

People's reluctance to reveal their incomes may seem a good example of a desire for privacy that cannot be explained in purely instrumental terms. But I think that people conceal an

6. Olmstead v. United States, 277 U.S. 438, 478 (1928), dissenting opinion of Justice Brandeis. It is a good answer if the question is whether people should have a right to be free from unwanted solicitations, noisy sound trucks, or obscene telephone calls. These invade a privacy interest different from the one discussed in this chapter, since they involve no effort to obtain information.

7. Such reticence seems to be of comparatively recent origin, even in Western society. On medieval European attitudes toward nudity, see Norbert Elias, *The Civilizing Process: The History of Manners* 163–165 (Edmund Jephcott trans. 1978).

unexpectedly *low* income mainly because being thought to have a high income has value in credit markets and elsewhere, and they conceal an unexpectedly *high* income to avoid the attention of tax collectors, kidnappers, and thieves; fend off solicitations from charities and family members; and preserve a reputation for generosity that might be impaired if others knew what fraction of their income they gave away. (The first and second points may explain anonymous gifts to charity.) One must distinguish, however, between concealing one's income from kidnappers and other criminals, on the one hand, and from the tax collector, family members, and creditors, on the other; the former concealment serves a perfectly legitimate self-protective function.

To my argument that people conceal facts about themselves in order to mislead others, one could reply that such concealment may on balance foster efficient transactions, because many of the facts that people conceal (homosexuality, ethnic origins, aversions, sympathy toward Communism or fascism, minor mental illnesses, early scrapes with the law, marital discord, nose picking) would if revealed provoke irrational reactions by prospective employers, friends, creditors, lovers, and so on. This objection overlooks the opportunity costs of shunning people for stupid reasons, or, stated otherwise, the gains from dealing with someone whom others shun irrationally. If ex-convicts are good workers but most employers do not know this, employers who do know will be able to hire them at a below-average wage because of their depressed job opportunities and will thereby obtain a competitive advantage over the bigots. In a diverse, decentralized, and competitive society, irrational shunning will be weeded out over time.[8]

A commercial analogy will help to bring out this point. For many years the Federal Trade Commission required importers

8. This process has been analyzed extensively in the context of racial discrimination; see e.g., Gary S. Becker, *The Economics of Discrimination* (2d ed. 1971); Harold Demsetz, "Minorities in the Market Place," 43 *N.C. L. Rev.* 271 (1965); and Chapter 12. It would seem to be equally at work in the case of discrimination against convicts, homosexuals, and so on.

of certain products, especially those made in Japan, to label the product's country of origin. The reason was a widespread belief, whose rationality the commission was not prepared to confirm or deny, that certain foreign (especially Japanese) goods were inferior. It was also believed that there was some residual anger over Pearl Harbor. But as is well known, Japanese products proved themselves in the marketplace, the prejudice against them waned and eventually disappeared, and today Japanese origin is a proudly displayed sign of quality and good value. This is an example of how competition can, over time, dispel prejudice. A similar example, that of Japanese-American people rather than Japanese products, illustrates the competitive process at work in the realm of employment and personal relationships.

The different treatment of past criminal conduct in the law of torts and the law of evidence provides further insight into this point. Except in California, there is no right of action against someone who publicizes an individual's criminal record, no matter how far in the past the crime occurred; but the use of past crimes to impeach the testimony of a witness in a criminal trial is limited (in the judge's discretion) to relatively recent crimes.[9] In both cases, it is arguable that people can be trusted to discount negative personal information by its recency. But in the tort case the people doing the discounting—friends, creditors, employers, and other actual and potential transactors—pay a price, in the form of lost opportunities for advantageous transactions, if they attach excessive weight to information about the remote past. They thus have an incentive not to react irrationally to such information. Jurors, in contrast, incur no cost from behaving irrationally; the market analogy therefore fails, and a paternalistic approach to the question of the rationality of their decisions may be warranted.

Irrational prejudices, which a market system tends to weed out, must not be confused with acting on incomplete informa-

---

9. See Charles T. McCormick, *McCormick's Handbook of the Law of Evidence* §43 (Edward W. Cleary ed., 2d ed. 1972).

tion. The rational individual or firm will stop searching for a social or business partner at the point where the marginal gain in knowledge from additional search is just equal to the marginal cost in time or money. Consequently, if the value of transacting with one individual rather than another is small or the cost of additional information great, the process of rational search may end at what some would consider a very early stage. If ex-convicts have on average poor employment records, if the cost is high of correcting this average judgment for the individual ex-convict applying for a job, and if substitute employees without criminal records are available at not much higher wages, it may be rational for an employer to adopt a flat rule of not employing anyone who has a criminal record.[10]

There is no evidence that people are in general less rational about how far to carry their search for employees, spouses, and friends than they are in traditional market activities (of which employment is one). A growing empirical literature on nonmarket behavior, including marriage, procreation, and crime, finds that people behave as rationally in these areas as do firms and consumers in explicit markets.[11] These findings argue for allowing people to make their own determinations of how much weight to attach to discreditable facts that other people try to conceal. This "free market" approach suggests that whatever rules governing fraud are optimal in ordinary product markets ought, as a first approximation, to govern labor markets, credit markets, and "markets" for purely personal relationships as well. Thus, if economic analysis would deem it fraudulent to

10. Notice how minimum-wage laws retard the process by which members of different groups obtain access to the employment market. This observation invites the familiar argument that public intervention is warranted to correct the consequences of a previous ill-advised intervention. But the new intervention may turn out to be ill-advised too. For this reason, government's previous failures provide an insufficient basis for urging additional public intervention.

11. See, e.g., Gary S. Becker, *The Economic Approach to Human Behavior* (1976); and Chapter 1 of this book. Part II contains many striking illustrations of economic behavior in nonmarket settings. Because there is no minimum wage in the nonmarket sector, it may be that irrational antipathies are more likely to be weeded out there than in the market sector. Cf. note 10 supra.

refuse to disclose a particular type of fact in the market for goods, such refusal should equally be deemed fraudulent when made by someone seeking a job, a personal loan, or a wife. Annulment of a marriage because of fraud is thus a strict analogue to rescission of a fraudulent commercial contract. Of course, in many areas of personal relations the costs of fraud are too slight to warrant formal legal remedies. And in some where they are high, notably marriage, alternative remedies are available. Courtship provides a period in which prospective spouses can learn enough about each other to cure any misrepresentations. This may be why evidence of more serious fraud is required in annulment cases than in cases seeking rescission of ordinary commercial contracts.[12]

I have suggested that much of the demand for private information about others is really a form of self-protection. But self-protection does not explain the demand, supplied by newspaper gossip columns, to learn about the private lives of complete strangers. Gossip columns provide valuable information of a different sort, however. They recount the personal lives of wealthy and successful people whose tastes and habits offer models to the ordinary person in making consumption, career, and other decisions. The models are not always edifying. The story of Howard Hughes, for example, is a morality play warning of the pitfalls of success. Tales of the notorious and the criminal—of a Profumo or a Leopold—have a similar function.

Why is there less curiosity about the lives of the poor, as measured, for example, by the frequency with which poor people are central characters in novels, than about those of the rich?[13] The reason, I conjecture, is that the lives of the poor do not provide as much useful information in patterning our own lives. What interest there is in the poor is focused on people who are (or were) affluent but who become poor, rather than on those

---

12. See, e.g., Bilowit v. Dolitsky, 124 N.J. Super. 101, 304 A.2d 774 (1973).

13. Surely not because writers know the lives of the rich more intimately than those of the poor: Shakespeare's protagonists are kings and nobles, but he was not an aristocrat.

who were always poor; the cautionary function of such information should be evident.

Warren and Brandeis, in a famous article on privacy, attributed the rise of curiosity about people's lives to the excesses of the press.[14] The economist does not believe, however, that supply creates demand.[15] A more persuasive explanation for the rise of the gossip column is the secular increase in personal incomes. There is little privacy in most poor societies,[16] and consequently people can easily observe at first hand the intimate lives of others. Personal surveillance is costlier in wealthier societies, both because people have greater privacy and because the value (and hence opportunity cost) of time is greater[17]—too great to make it worthwhile to allot a generous amount of time to watching neighbors. In societies where the costs of obtaining information have become too great for the Nosy Parker, the press provides, among its other functions, specialization in prying. The press also unmasks the misrepresentations that people employ to deceive others into transacting with them on advantageous terms. I use "transaction" in a broad sense to include, for exam-

14. "The press is overstepping in every direction the obvious bounds of propriety and of decency. Gossip is no longer the resource of the idle and of the vicious, but has become a trade, which is pursued with industry as well as effrontery . . . To occupy the indolent, column upon column is filled with idle gossip, which can only be procured by intrusion upon the domestic circle." Samuel D. Warren & Louis D. Brandeis, "The Right to Privacy," 4 *Harv. L. Rev.* 193, 196 (1890).

15. "In this, as in other branches of commerce, the supply creates the demand." *Id.*

16. See David H. Flaherty, *Privacy in Colonial New England* 83 (1972); Thomas Gregor, *Mehinakui: The Drama of Daily Life in a Brazilian Indian Village* 89–90, 360–361 (1977); Alan F. Westin, *Privacy and Freedom*, ch. 1 (1967); note 31 infra; and discussion and references in Chapter 10. Gregor's findings on privacy are summarized in Marvin Harris, *Cannibals and Kings: the Origins of Cultures* 12 (1977), as follows: "The search for personal privacy is a pervasive theme in the daily life of people who live in small villages. The Mehinacu apparently know too much about each other's business for their own good. They can tell from the print of a heel or a buttock where a couple stopped and had sexual relations off the path. Lost arrows give away the owner's prize fishing spot; an axe resting against a tree tells a story of interrupted work. No one leaves or enters the village without being noticed. One must whisper to secure privacy—with walls of thatch there are no closed doors."

17. See Staffan Burenstam Linder, *The Harried Leisure Class*, ch. 7 (1970).

ple, the individual who wants to be vice-president without disclosing his history of mental illness (Thomas Eagleton in 1972).

The idea that gossip columns have an informational function
is one of the most strongly resisted implications of the economic
analysis of privacy. But how else is one to explain why "prurient" interest in the private lives of the wealthy and celebrated
apparently is positively correlated with physical privacy? Gossip
columns and movie magazines flourish more in the United
States than in Europe, where there is less physical privacy
(space, anonymity) than in the United States. And although gossip columns, movie magazines, and other vehicles of public gossip are considered the province of the vulgar and uneducated,
their rise in popularity in this country coincides with a rising
level of education—because, I suggest, the growth of physical
privacy has shut off direct observation of how strangers live.[18]

The element of misrepresentation in the concealment of personal information is important, but there are other elements.[19]
First, concealment sometimes promotes rather than impedes
the transmittal of accurate information. At any moment one's
mind is likely to be brimming over with vagrant, half-formed,
and ill-considered thoughts that, if revealed to others, would
provide less information about one's intentions and capacities
than the thoughts one chooses to express in speech. Concealing
one's "inner thoughts" is just the other side of selecting certain
thoughts for utterance and thus communicating one's intentions and values. Similarly, wearing clothes serves not merely to
protect one against the elements but also to make a public statement about one's values and tastes. If we went around naked,
babbling the first thing that came into our minds, we would be
revealing less of ourselves than we do by dressing carefully and

18. Compare Westin's description of the houses of the wealthy in ancient Rome
cheek by jowl with the tenements of the poor. Alan F. Westin, *Privacy in Western Society:
From the Age of Pericles to the American Republic* 44 (Report to Assn. of Bar of City of N.Y.
Spec. Comm. on Sci. and Law, Feb. 15, 1965). This pattern persists to this day in many
European cities but is rare in the United States.

19. I have already discussed reticence unrelated to misrepresentation, and self-protection, as motives for concealment.

speaking with reticence. This is not the point that hypocrisy is the essential lubricant of social relations, which has no obvious economic interpretation. The point is, rather, that if A values B as a potential business associate, telling B he looks like a frog will obscure rather than elucidate A's sincere view of B—which is that he values him as a potential business associate.[20] (The borderland between concealment as information and as misrepresentation is illustrated by the dyeing of hair. The purpose may be to communicate something about the kind of person one is, or it may be to conceal one's age, or it may be both.)

That clothing, adornment, cosmetics, accent, and the like serve not only to communicate but also to misrepresent[21] may conceivably explain some of the sporadic efforts to regulate luxury in dress. In the fourteenth century,

> nothing was more resented by the hereditary nobles than the imitation of their clothes and manners by the upstarts, thus obscuring the lines between the eternal orders of society. Magnificence in clothes was considered a prerogative of nobles, who should be identifiable by modes of dress forbidden to others. In the effort to establish this principle as law and prevent "outrageous and excessive apparel of diverse people against their estate and degree," sumptuary laws were repeatedly announced, attempting to fix what kinds of clothes people might wear and how much they might spend.[22]

A second qualification of the analysis is that the competitive provision of information may lead to its overproduction from

20. If the above analysis is correct, efforts to improve social interactions through nudism, extreme frankness of speech, and other fashionable techniques of group therapy are fundamentally confused. On clothes as signals see Irwin Altman, *The Environment and Social Behavior: Privacy, Personal Space, Territory, Crowding* 36–37 (1975).

21. In this connection see Laurel Leff, "A Secret of Success: Be Good at Getting Wrinkles Ironed Out," *Wall St. J.*, Nov. 15, 1979, p. 1, on face lifts for male business executives.

22. Barbara W. Tuchman, *A Distant Mirror: The Calamitous 14th Century* 19 (1978).

an efficiency standpoint.[23] A firm's advertising serves partly to offset a rival firm's advertising, and the same point can be made of truthful signaling through dress, manners, and other forms of self-advertising. Even where the signal is true, the effort of each individual to signal loud and clear may result in producing more information about personal characteristics than is optimal, in the sense that if transaction costs were zero, all would be better off agreeing to signal less.[24] The dress codes occasionally found in business firms and private schools, though ostensibly intended to raise the standard of dress, may sometimes have the opposite result, to reduce the level and costs of dress. And this may be the real intention; limiting variety in dress reduces the amount of resources devoted to this form of self-advertising.

Secrecy and Innovation

The most important qualifications of the view of privacy as manipulation or misrepresentation involve innovative ideas and private conversations. The public character of information makes its prompt appropriation by others easy. But such appropriation prevents the original producer of the information from recouping his investment in its production and thereby reduces the incentive to make such investments. Two methods of overcoming this problem are compatible with a market system as usually understood. The first is the explicit creation of property rights in information, as in the patent and copyright laws. The second is secrecy, meaning that the information is used by the producer but not disclosed until he has had a chance to profit from his exclusive possession.

The choice between these methods depends on a weighing of relative costs and benefits in particular circumstances. On the benefit side, compare statutory and common law copyright. The former gives the author a property right in his work; no one may copy it without his authorization. Common law copy-

---

23. See Jack Hirshleifer, "The Private and Social Value of Information and the Reward to Inventive Activity," 61 *Am. Econ. Rev.* 561 (1971).

24. On the economics of signaling see A. Michael Spence, *Market Signaling* (1974).

right used the method of secrecy: so long as the author did not publish his manuscript, the law would protect him against unauthorized dissemination by others.[25] Obviously, the method of secrecy would be self-defeating if an author wanted to publish his work or if the practice of an invention would immediately disclose the embodied innovation. And even where secrecy would afford some protection (a publisher might earn substantial revenues before a pirate edition could be printed and distributed), it might be extremely costly. It might entail, for example, accelerated, secretive book publication at higher costs than if the publisher had a property right in the published work. Or a secret process might have valuable applications in another industry, yet the owner of the process would be afraid to sell it because the secret might get out to his competitors.

On the other hand, the costs of enforcing a property right in information would often be disproportionate to the value of the information to be protected: the patent system could not be used to protect a popular host's dinner recipes. And often the costs of tracing information to its origin preclude reliance on a property-rights system: if ideas as such, as distinct from the sorts of concretely embodied ideas protected by the patent and copyright laws, could be patented or copyrighted, the scope of, and difficulty of determining, infringement would be excessive. Consequently, secrecy is an important social instrument for encouraging the production of information, especially in settings where the formal rights system in intellectual property is undeveloped. Thus the law does not require the shrewd bargainer to disclose to the other party the bargainer's true opinion of its value. By a "shrewd bargainer" we mean, in part at least, someone who invests resources in acquiring information about the

25. Common law copyright was not simply an aspect of trespass law. If A, being lawfully on B's premises, made a Xerox copy of B's manuscript but did not remove or damage the manuscript, there was no theft or conversion, but there was an infringement of B's common law copyright.

The recent revision of the copyright law provides statutory protection from the time the work is "fixed in any tangible medium of expression." 1976 Copyright Act, 17 U.S.C. § 102(a).

true values of things. Were he forced to share this information with potential sellers, he would obtain no return on his investment, and the transfer of goods by voluntary exchange into successively more valuable uses would be impaired. So he is not forced to do so, even though the resulting lack of candor in the bargaining process deprives it of some of its "voluntary" character. Similarly, the law does not punish the large purchaser of some company's stock who places a lot of small orders under false names so that his activity will not inform the sellers that they have undervalued the stock.[26] Secrecy is the indispensable method not only of protecting the speculator's investment in obtaining information vital to the prompt adjustment of markets to changed conditions, but also of protecting the investment in information of the great chef or of the housewife who "buys" the esteem of friends with her imaginative cooking. Similarly, the attorney-work-product doctrine is, I think, best understood as the use of secrecy to protect the lawyer's (and hence client's) investment in research and analysis of a case.

I have thus far been speaking as if any information should be the inviolable property of its creator. But this is not what economic theory implies. The purpose of a property right, or of according legal protection to secrecy as a surrogate for an explicit property right, is to create an incentive to invest in the creation of information. Where information is not a product of a significant investment, the case for protection is weakened. This is an important consideration in drawing the line between socially desirable and fraudulent nondisclosure.[27] It may explain why the common law often requires the owner of a house to disclose latent, that is, nonobvious, defects to a purchaser.[28] The ownership and maintenance of a house are productive activities, costly to engage in, but the owner acquires knowledge of

26. A single very large purchase of stock is less likely to be a random event than many small purchases, which could represent portfolio adjustments not motivated by superior information.

27. See Anthony T. Kronman, "Mistake, Disclosure, Information, and the Law of Contracts," 7 *J. Legal Stud.* 1 (1978).

28. See William L. Prosser, *Handbook of the Law of Torts* 698 (4th ed. 1971).

the defects in his house costlessly (or nearly so). Hence requiring him to disclose those defects will not lead him to forgo expending to discover them.

Privacy of Communications

A communication (letter, phone call, face-to-face conversation, or whatever) is a medium by which facts are disclosed. It might seem that if the facts are the sort for which secrecy is desired in order to foster innovation, the communication should be privileged, and if they are discrediting, it should not be. But this approach is too simple. Besides revealing facts about the speaker or listener, a communication may refer to a third party. If that party were privy to it, the speaker would modify the communication. The modification would be costly both in time for deliberation and in reduction of clarity of the communication. For example, if A in conversation with B disparages C, and C overhears the conversation, C is likely to be angry or upset. If A does not want to engender this reaction in C, because he likes C or because C may retaliate for the disparagement, then, knowing that C might be listening, he will avoid the disparagement. He will choose his words more carefully, and the added deliberateness and obliqueness of the conversation will reduce its communication value and increase its cost. To be sure, there is an offsetting benefit if the disparagement is false and damaging to C. But there is no reason to believe that on average more false than true disparagements are made in private conversations, and the true are as likely to be suppressed by the prospect of publicity as the false. If A derives no substantial benefit from correctly observing to B that C is a liar, but stands only to incur C's wrath, the knowledge that C might overhear the conversation may induce A to withhold information that would be valuable to B. This is the reason for, among other things, the practice of according anonymity to referees of articles submitted to scholarly journals.

This analysis implies that eavesdropping is not an efficient way of finding out facts. If the danger of eavesdropping is known, conversations will be modified, at some social cost, in order to reduce their informational content for third parties. The parallel in nonconversational information would be the man who, having a criminal record that the law does not entitle him to conceal, goes to great lengths to avoid its discovery, by changing his name, his place of work and residence, and perhaps even his physical appearance. If the principal effect of refusing to recognize property rights in discrediting information about the individual were simply to call forth an expenditure on some costly but effective method of covering one's tracks, the gains to society would be small and could be negative. But probably that would not be the principal effect. When Thomas Eagleton was nominated for vice-president on the Democratic party ticket in 1972, he could not have concealed his history of mental illness, but he could have concealed his opinions of third parties, given conversational privacy.[29]

Some evidence in support of the above analysis is provided by the experience, well known to every academic administrator, under the Buckley Amendment.[30] This statute gives students access to letters of recommendation written about them unless they waive in advance their right of access. Almost all students execute such waivers, because they know that the information value of a letter of recommendation to which the subject has access is much less than that of a private letter.

Additional evidence for my analysis of conversational privacy is the fact that discourse becomes less formal as society evolves. As noted in Chapter 6, the languages of primitive peoples are more elaborate, more ceremonious, and more courteous than the language of twentieth-century Americans. One reason may be the lack of privacy in primitive societies. Few really private conversations take place, because third parties are normally present and the effects on them of the conversation must be taken into account. (Even today, people speak more formally

29. An intermediate case is the impact of pretrial discovery on corporate record-retention policies. Fewer and less candid records are kept, but an organization (especially a large one) cannot function without keeping *some* documents.

30. Family Educational Rights and Privacy Act of 1974, §513, 20 U.S.C. § 1232g (1974).

when there are more people present.) The growth of privacy has facilitated private conversation and thereby enabled us to economize on communication—to speak with a brevity and informality apparently rare among primitive peoples.[31] Allowing eavesdropping would undermine this valuable economy of communication.[32]

The analysis can readily be extended to any efforts to obtain other people's notes, letters, and other private papers; these efforts inhibit communication. One purpose of common law copyright was in fact to protect the secrecy of diaries and correspondence.[33] The case for privacy against photographic surveillance—for example, of the interior of a person's home—is also strong. Privacy enables a person to dress and otherwise disport

31. Clifford Geertz writes: "In Java people live in small, bamboo-walled houses, each of which almost always contains a single nuclear family . . . There are no walls or fences around them, the house walls are thinly and loosely woven, and there are commonly not even doors. Within the house people wander freely just about any place any time, and even outsiders wander in fairly freely almost any time during the day and early evening. In brief, privacy in our terms is about as close to nonexistent as it can get . . . Relationships even within the household are very restrained; people speak softly, hide their feelings and even in the bosom of a Javanese family you have the feeling that you are in the public square and must behave with appropriate decorum. Javanese shut people out with a wall of etiquette (patterns of politeness are very highly developed), with emotional restraint, and with a general lack of candor in both speech and behavior . . . Thus there is really no sharp break between public and private in Java: people behave more or less the same in private as they do in public—in a manner we would call stuffy at best." Unpublished paper quoted in Westin, supra note 16, at 16–17.
Additional evidence of the relationship between linguistic formality and publicity is that written speech is usually more decorous, grammatical, and formal than spoken speech. In part this is because speaking involves additional levels of meaning—gesture and intonation—which allow the speaker to achieve the same clarity with less semantic and grammatical precision. But in part it is because the audience for spoken speech is typically smaller and more intimate than that for written speech, which makes the costs of ambiguity lower and hence lowers the cost-justified investment in achieving precision through the various formal resources of language. This potential for ambiguity is one reason why people who speak to large audiences normally do so from a prepared text.
32. To be sure, some communication, as among criminal conspirators, may not be related to socially productive activity. In these cases, where limited eavesdropping is indeed permitted, its effect in reducing communication is, from society's standpoint, not an objection but an advantage, because it makes the criminal activity more costly.
33. As emphasized by Warren & Brandeis, supra note 14, at 200–201.

himself in his home without regard to the effect on third parties. This informality, which conserves resources, would be lost if the interior of the home were in the public domain. People dress not merely because of the effect on others but also because of the reticence, remarked earlier, concerning nudity; that reticence is an additional reason for giving people a privacy right with regard to places in which it would be costly to avoid occasional nudity.

Legislative Trends in the Privacy Area

Recent years have witnessed a spate of state and federal statutes relating to privacy, which I examine in Chapters 10 and 11. Here I want only to note an irony in the legislative movement.

My economic analysis implies that privacy of business information should receive greater legal protection, in general, than privacy of personal information. Secrecy is an important method for the entrepreneur to appropriate the social benefits he creates, but in private life secrecy is more likely to operate simply to conceal discreditable facts. And communications within business and other private organizations (the case of government is special, as I show in Chapter 11) seem entitled to as much protection as communications among individuals; in either case the effect of publicity would be to encumber and retard communication. Yet with some exceptions discussed in Chapter 11, the legislative trend, state and federal, has been to give individuals more and more legal protection of the privacy of both facts and communications, and to give business firms and other private organizations less and less. While facts about individuals—arrest record, health, credit-worthiness, marital status, sexual proclivities—increasingly are protected from involuntary disclosure,[34] facts concerning business corporations increasingly are thrust into public view by the expansive disclosure requirements of the federal securities laws (to the point where some firms are "going private" to secure greater con-

---

34. The Buckley Amendment discussed earlier illustrates this trend. Other such statutes are discussed in the next chapter.

fidentiality for their plans and operations), civil rights laws, line of business reporting, and other regulations.

The trend toward elevating personal and downgrading organizational privacy is mysterious from an economic standpoint. The economic case for privacy of communications is unrelated to whether the communicator is a private individual or the employee of a university or corporation; and concerning privacy of information, the case for protecting business privacy is stronger that that for individual privacy.

Greenawalt and Noam reach the opposite conclusion.[35] They make two distinctions between a business firm's (or other organization's) interest in privacy and an individual's interest. First, they argue that the latter is a matter of rights, while the former is based merely on instrumental, utilitarian considerations. However, their reasons for recognizing a right of personal privacy are utilitarian—that people should have an opportunity to "make a new start" by concealing embarrassing or discreditable facts about their past and that people cannot preserve their sanity without some privacy. Inconsistently, they disregard the utilitarian justification for secrecy as an incentive to investment in productive activity—a justification mainly relevant in business contexts.

Their second distinction between business and personal claims to privacy is a distorted mirror of my argument for entrepreneurial or productive secrecy. They argue that it is difficult to establish property rights in information and even remark that secrecy is one way of doing so. But instead of approving of secrecy as a means of creating property rights in information, they use the fact that there are imperfections in the market for information to justify the government's coercively extracting private information from business firms. They do not explain how the government could, or show that it would, use this information more productively than firms. Nor do they consider

---

35. See Kent Greenawalt & Eli Noam, "Confidentiality Claims of Business Organizations," in *Business Disclosure: Government's Need to Know* 378 (Harvey J. Goldschmid ed. 1979).

what impact this form of public prying has on the incentive to produce the information.

Other Privacy Theories

A brief and perhaps partisan review of some other theories of privacy will place the economic theory in perspective. I begin with the most famous theory, that of Warren and Brandeis, who wrote:

> The press is overstepping in every direction the obvious bounds of propriety and of decency. Gossip is no longer the resource of the idle and of the vicious, but has become a trade, which is pursued with industry as well as effrontery. To satisfy a prurient taste the details of sexual relations are spread broadcast in the columns of the daily papers. To occupy the indolent, column upon column is filled with idle gossip, which can only be procured by intrusion upon the domestic circle. The intensity and complexity of life, attendant upon advancing civilization, have rendered necessary some retreat from the world, and man, under the refining influence of culture, has become more sensitive to publicity, so that solitude and privacy have become more essential to the individual; but modern enterprise and invention have, through invasions upon his privacy, subjected him to mental pain and distress, far greater than could be inflicted by mere bodily injury. Nor is the harm wrought by such invasions confined to the suffering of those who may be made the subjects of journalistic or other enterprise. In this, as in other branches of commerce, the supply creates the demand. Each crop of unseemly gossip, thus harvested, becomes the seed of more, and, in direct proportion to its circulation, results in a lowering of social standards and of morality.[36]

Narrowly focused on justifying a right not to be talked about in a newspaper gossip column, the Warren-Brandeis analysis is

---

36. Warren & Brandeis, supra note 14, at 196.

based on a series of unsupported and implausible empirical propositions: (1) newspapers deliberately try to debase their readers' tastes; (2) the gossip they print harms the people gossiped about far more seriously than bodily injury could; (3) the more gossip the press supplies, the more the readers will demand; (4) reading gossip columns impairs intelligence and morality.[37]

Edward Bloustein is representative of those theorists who relate privacy to individuality:

> The man who is compelled to live every minute of his life among others and whose every need, thought, desire, fancy or gratification is subject to public scrutiny, has been deprived of his individuality and human dignity. Such an individual merges with the mass. His opinions, being public, tend never to be different; his aspirations, being known, tend always to be conventionally accepted ones; his feelings, being openly exhibited, tend to lose their quality of unique personal warmth and to become the feelings of every man. Such a being, although sentient, is fungible; he is not an individual.[38]

At one level, Bloustein is saying that if people had no privacy, they would behave more in accordance with customary norms of behavior. That is (to oversimplify slightly), people would be better behaved if they had less privacy. This result he considers objectionable, apparently because greater conformity to socially

37. This last point is elaborated in a passage of Victorian prissiness: "Even gossip apparently harmless, when widely and persistently circulated, is potent for evil. It both belittles and perverts. It belittles by inverting the relative importance of things, thus dwarfing the thoughts and aspirations of a people. When personal gossip attains the dignity of print, and crowds the space available for matters of real interest to the community, what wonder that the ignorant and thoughtless mistake its relative importance. Easy of comprehension, appealing to that weak side of human nature which is never wholly cast down by the misfortunes and frailties of our neighbors, no one can be surprised that it usurps the place of interest in brains capable of other things. Triviality destroys at once robustness of thought and delicacy of feeling. No enthusiasm can flourish, no generous impulse can survive under its blighting influence." *Id.* at 196.

38. Edward J. Bloustein, "Privacy as an Aspect of Human Dignity: An Answer to Dean Prosser," 39 *N.Y.U. L. Rev.* 962, 1003 (1964).

accepted patterns of behavior would produce (by definition) more conformists, a type he dislikes for reasons he must consider self-evident since he does not attempt to explain them.

Bloustein does suggest that publicity reduces not only deviations from accepted moral standards but also creative departures from conventional thought and behavior. While the possession of some privacy may indeed be a precondition to intellectual creativity, these qualities have flourished in societies, including ancient Greece, Renaissance Italy, and Elizabethan England, that had much less privacy than people in the United States have today.

Charles Fried argues that privacy is indispensable to the fundamental values of love, friendship, and trust; love and friendship are inconceivable "without the intimacy of shared private information,"[39] and trust presupposes an element of ignorance about what the trusted one is up to: if all is known, there is nothing to take on trust. But rather than being something valued for itself and therefore missed where full information makes it unnecessary, trust is an imperfect substitute for information. And love and friendship flourish in societies where there is little privacy. The privacy theories of Bloustein and Fried are ethnocentric.

Even within our own culture, some people question whether privacy is more supportive than destructive of treasured values. If ignorance is a prerequisite to trust, it is equally true that knowledge, which privacy thwarts, is a prerequisite to forgiveness. The alleged anomie, impersonality, and lack of communal feeling of modern society may, to the extent that it is real, be related to the high level of privacy our society has achieved.

Fried is explicit in not wanting to ground the right of privacy on utilitarian considerations, but the quest for nonutilitarian grounds has thus far failed. It is doubtful whether the kind of analysis that seeks to establish rights on nonutilitarian or non-economic grounds can even be applied to privacy. It makes no

39. *An Anatomy of Values: Problems of Personal and Social Choice* 142 (1970). For a partial retraction of Fried's views, see his paper "Privacy: Economics and Ethics: A Comment on Posner," 12 *Ga. L. Rev.* 423 (1978).

sense to treat reputation as a "right." Reputation is what others think of us, and we have no right to control other people's thoughts.[40] Equally we have no right, by controlling the information that is known about us, to manipulate the opinions that other people hold of us. Yet it is just this control that is sought in the name of privacy.

Greenawalt and Noam mention additional grounds for valuing privacy: the "fresh start" and "mental health." The first holds that people who have committed crimes or otherwise transgressed the moral standards of society have a right to a fresh start, which requires that they be allowed to conceal their past misdeeds. The second states as a fact of human psychology that people cannot function effectively unless they have some private area where they can behave very differently, often scandalously differently, from their public self; an example is the waiters who curse in the kitchen the patrons on whom they fawn in the dining room. The first point rests on the popular but unsubstantiated assumption that people do not evaluate past criminal acts rationally; only if they irrationally refused to accept evidence of rehabilitation could one argue that society has unfairly denied the former miscreant a fresh start. The second point has some intuitive appeal but seems exaggerated and ethnocentric and is offered as pure assertion; as the next chapter shows, the evidence is against it.

Similarly unsupported is Steven Shavell's suggestion[41] that people operating behind a Rawlsian "veil of ignorance"[42] might agree to the concealment of discreditable personal facts, not knowing whether they *would* do discreditable things but wanting some insurance against the consequences if they should. It is possible that people would make that choice, but without further specification of the preference functions of people in the original position and the alternative forms of private and social

40. See Walter Block, *Defending the Undefendable: The Pimp, Prostitute, Scab, Slumlord, Libeler, Moneylender, and Other Scapegoats in the Rogue's Gallery of American Society* 60 (1976).

41. In unpublished comments delivered at a recent conference on privacy.

42. See discussion of Rawls in Chapter 4.

insurance, one cannot conclude that such an agreement is a likely outcome of choice in that position.

The Tort Law of Privacy

Although the Warren-Brandeis article stimulated the development of the tort law of privacy, the law has evolved very differently from the pattern they suggested, and Bloustein offered his theory of privacy as a criticism of Prosser's authoritative article describing the privacy tort.[43] Could the tort law perhaps be closer to economic than to noneconomic thinking about privacy? The rest of the chapter explores this question.

Commercial Privacy

The broad features of the tort law are those implied in my discussion of an economically sound right of privacy: (1) substantial protection of the confidentiality of creative ideas; (2) liberty to "pry" into most private facts about individuals; but (3) a limitation on eavesdropping to obtain those facts. The first of these is the domain of trade secrets law, a branch of the tort law of unfair competition. Although the best-known kind of trade secret is the secret formula or process, the legal protection is broader—"almost any knowledge or information used in the conduct of one's business may be held by its possessor in secret."[44] In a well-known case the court held that aerial photography of a competitor's plant under construction was tortious and used the term "commercial privacy" to describe the interest protected.[45] This decision illustrates the judicial willingness to protect those secrets that enable firms to appropriate the social benefits that their activities create.

What should be the outer bounds of the commercial-privacy tort? It is accepted that a firm may buy its competitor's product and take it apart with a view to discovering how it was made, even though such "reverse engineering" may reveal secrets of a

---

43. William L. Prosser, "Privacy," 48 *Calif. L. Rev.* 383 (1960).

44. Smith v. Dravo Corp., 203 F.2d 369, 373 (7th Cir. 1953).

45. E. I. duPont de Nemours & Co. v. Christopher, 431 F.2d 1012, 1016 (5th Cir. 1970). See also Smith v. Dravo Corp., supra note 44

competitor's production process. How is this type of prying to be distinguished from aerial photography? One difference is that if the law permitted aerial photography of a competitor's plant under construction, the principal effect would be not to generate information but to induce the competitor to expend resources on trying to conceal the interior of the plant. These resources, as well as those devoted to the aerial photography which they offset, would be socially wasted. (Compare the earlier discussion of photographic surveillance of the interior of the home.) In contrast, the possibility of reverse engineering is unlikely to lead a manufacturer to alter his product in costly ways. Another difference is that aerial photography might disclose secrets that would be more difficult to protect alternatively through the patent system than the kinds of secrets that reverse engineering is likely to reveal.

Personal Privacy

The tort of invasion of personal privacy has four aspects: appropriation, publicity, false light, and intrusion.[46]

Appropriation. In the earliest cases involving a distinct right of privacy, an advertiser uses someone's name or photograph without his or her consent.[47] The classification of these as "privacy" cases is sometimes criticized on the ground that often what the law is protecting is an aversion not to publicity but to lack of remuneration for it: many of the cases involve celebrities avid for publicity. But this fact is an embarrassment only to a tort theory that seeks to base the right to privacy on an alleged social interest in concealment of personal information. There is a good economic reason for assigning to the individual the property right in a photograph of him used for advertising purposes: this assignment assures that the photograph will be purchased by the advertiser to whom it is most valuable. Making the photograph the communal property of advertisers would not achieve this goal.

46. For a good summary of the legal principles in this area see Prosser, supra note 28, ch. 20.

47. See, e.g., Pavesich v. New England Life Ins. Co., 122 Ga. 190, 50 S.E. 68 (1905).

Professor Bloustein does not recognize an economic basis for the "right of publicity" and tries to make this branch of privacy law a criticism rather than vindication of the market place. He writes: "Use of a photograph for trade purposes turns a man into a commodity and makes him serve the economic needs and interests of others."[48] But this is not the theory of the tort law. The law does not forbid a man to use his photograph "for trade purposes"; it gives him a property right in such use. For example, in *Haelan Laboratories v. Topps Chewing Gum,*[49] the court held that when a baseball player had licensed to one manufacturer of bubble gum the exclusive right to use his picture in advertising, no other bubble gum manufacturer could use the picture without the licensee's permission. "A man has a right in the publicity value of his photograph, i.e., the right to grant the exclusive privilege of publishing his picture."[50]

It may seem inconsistent that the law should allow a magazine to sell its subscriber list to another magazine without obtaining the subscribers' consent.[51] However, the costs of obtaining subscriber approval would be so high relative to the value of the list as to make the transactional solution of the *Haelan* case impractical.[52] Moreover, the multiple use of a subscription list does not reduce the value of the list, whereas multiple use of the same photograph to advertise different (especially competing) products could reduce its advertising value to zero. Hence it is important that the individual photographed have a property right that will enable him to ration the number of users of his photograph; the magazine subscriber does not have a comparable interest.

48. Bloustein, supra note 38, at 988.

49. 202 F.2d 866 (2d Cir.), cert. denied, 346 U.S. 816 (1953).

50. *Id.* at 868. For similar cases see "Note: The Right of Publicity—Protection for Public Figures and Celebrities," 42 *Brooklyn L. Rev.* 527, 534–541 (1976).

51. See Shibley v. Time, Inc., 45 Ohio App. 2d 69, 341 N.E.2d 337 (1975).

52. A few magazines offer the subscriber the option of having his name removed from the list that is sold to other magazines. But this solution is unsatisfactory to the subscribers (presumably the majority) who are averse to receiving *some* magazine solicitations, rather than averse to receiving *any* magazine solicitations.

Publicity. If an advertiser uses an individual's picture without his consent, that individual's legal rights are infringed. But if the same picture appears in the news section of the newspaper there is no infringement (at least if the picture is not embarrassing and does not portray the person in a false light—separate tort grounds discussed later). The difference in treatment seems at first glance arbitrary. If a particular publication of an individual's photograph would represent the most valuable use of his likeness, why not require the newspaper to purchase from him the right to publish it?

A superficial answer is that the news photograph has public-good aspects that are absent when an advertiser uses the same photograph. A newspaper that invests resources in discovering news of broad interest may not be able to appropriate the social benefits of the discovery and hence recoup its investment, because a competitor can pick up and disseminate the news with only a slight time lag and without having to compensate the first newspaper. In other words, the first newspaper's research creates external benefits, and one method of compensating the newspaper for conferring these benefits is to allow it to externalize some of its costs as well (whether it is the best method is a separate question). But while this conceivably may explain why a newspaper does not have to pay the newsworthy people about whom it writes, it does not explain the newspaper's right to print *photographs* without payment. The newspaper can copyright the photograph, and then no competing medium can republish it without the newspaper's permission.[53]

Two other reasons may, however, explain the difference in legal treatment between a photograph used in advertising and

53. This is so even after Time, Inc. v. Bernard Geis Assoc., 293 F. Supp. 130 (S.D.N.Y. 1968), held that the "fair use" exception to copyright encompassed the publication, in a book about President Kennedy's assassination, of detailed, accurate charcoal sketches of the Zapruder film of the assassination. The court emphasized the absence of competition between plaintiff and defendants, who did not publish a magazine. Also, the book did not reproduce the photograph itself. Another economic consideration is that, given the circumstances under which the Zapruder film was made (an amateur who by chance filmed the assassination of a president), it is unlikely that the denial of full property-right protection would have any effect on incentives to make such films in the future.

the same photograph used in the news column. First, the social cost of dispensing with property rights is greater in the advertising than in the news case. As suggested earlier, if any advertiser can use a celebrity's picture, its advertising value may be impaired. Thus, if Brand X beer makes money using Celebrity A's picture in its advertising, competing brands might use the same picture until the picture ceased to have any advertising value at all. In contrast, the multiple use of a celebrity's photograph by competing newspapers is unlikely to reduce the value of the photograph to the newspaper-reading public. Second, in the news case the celebrity might use the property right in his likeness, if he had such a right, to misrepresent his appearance to the public—he might permit the newspaper to publish only a particularly flattering picture. This form of false advertising is difficult to prevent except by communalizing the property right.

The case for giving the individual a property right may seem even more attenuated where the publicity is of the person's offensive or embarrassing characteristics. Publicity here would appear to serve that institutionalized prying function which, as noted earlier, is important in a society in which there is a great deal of privacy, which facilitates the concealment of discrediting facts. This conclusion is correct in general and is the result reached in general in the cases; but there is a class of facts which the individual does not want publicized and of which the social value of publicity is also quite limited. Suppose a person has a deformed nose, which is of course well known to those who have dealings with him. A newspaper photographer snaps a picture of the person and publishes it in a story on human ugliness. Since the deformity is not concealable or concealed from people who have dealings with the individual, publication of the photograph does not correct a false impression that he might exploit. To be sure, readers of the newspaper derive value from being able to see the photograph; otherwise the newspaper would not publish it. But because the individual's desire to suppress the photograph is not related to misrepresentation in any business or social marketplace, there is no basis for a presumption that the social value of disclosure exceeds that of concealment. In such a case, the appropriate social response is to give the individual the property right in his likeness and let the newspaper buy it from him if it wishes to publish a photograph of his nose.[54]

Daily Times Democrat v. Graham[55] was such a case. A woman was photographed in a fun house at the moment when a jet of air had blown her dress up around her waist. The local newspaper later published the photograph without her consent. In holding that the newspaper had invaded her right of privacy, the court stressed that it was undisputed that she had entered the fun house solely to accompany her children and had not known about the jets of air. In these circumstances the photograph could convey no information enabling her friends and acquaintances to correct a misapprehension about her character; if anything, the photograph misrepresented her character.

The foregoing analysis may seem to support recognition of a property right in privacy wherever (1) no element of misrepresentation is involved, and (2) the information is contained in a photograph which a purchaser of the property right could copyright, thereby eliminating any externality. However, an exception to this rule is necessary for the case where the nature of the event photographed makes transaction costs prohibitive. It would be inefficient to assign the property right in his likeness to an individual photographed as part of a crowd watching a parade and unidentified to the photographer, or, perhaps, to the accident victim with whom negotiations would be infeasible, given the time limit within which the photograph must be published if it is not to lose its newsworthiness. In the former case, the propety right is plainly more valuable, as a general matter, to the photographer than to the subject of the photograph. This

54. This hypothetical case was suggested by the facts of Griffin v. Medical Society of State of New York, 11 N.Y.S.2d 109 (Sup. Ct. 1939), where, however, publication was in a medical journal rather than a newspaper, and the suit was based on alleged appropriation of the photograph for advertising purposes. Lambert v. Dow. Chem. Co., 215 So. 2d 673 (La. App. 1968), is closer to the hypothetical case.

55. 162 So. 2d 474 (Ala. 1964).

conclusion is less clear in the latter case, so that putting aside First Amendment considerations, which I will not discuss here, some type of balancing of costs and benefits is required. I shall discuss how this balancing is done a bit later.

The cases discussed above are distinguishable from those where, for example, a newspaper reveals past illegal or immoral activity that an individual has tried to conceal from his friends and acquaintances. Since such information is undeniably material in evaluating an individual's claim to friendship, respect, and trust, legal protection of its concealment would be inconsistent with the treatment of false advertising in the market for goods. Nevertheless, a California case, *Melvin v. Reid*,[56] held that the right of privacy extended to such information. The case was rather special because its posture on appeal required the court to accept as true the plaintiff's allegations, which implied that disclosure of her unsavory past could convey no useful information to anybody.[57] A later California case, *Briscoe v. Reader's Digest Association*,[58] held that the right of privacy does not extend to information concerning recent, as distinct from remote, past criminal activity. This distinction moves the law in the right direction but, from an economic standpoint, not far enough. Remote past criminal activity is less relevant to a prediction of future misconduct than recent—and those who learn of it will discount it accordingly—but such information is hardly irrelevant to people considering whether to enter into or continue social or business relations with the individual; if it were irrelevant, publicizing it would not injure the individual.[59] People conceal past criminal acts not out of bashfulness but because po-

---

56. 112 Cal. App. 285, 297 P. 91 (1931).

57. Among the facts alleged were that "after her acquittal, she abandoned her life of shame and became entirely rehabilitated; that during the year 1919 she married Bernard Melvin and commenced the duties of caring for their home, and thereafter at all times lived an exemplary, virtuous, honorable and righteous life." 112 Cal. App. at 286, 297 P. at 91.

58. 4 Cal. 3d 529, 483 P.2d 34, 93 Cal. Rptr. 866 (1971).

59. Could a right of privacy of past criminal acts be based on a social policy of encouraging the rehabilitation of criminals? There is a hint of this view in the court's opinion in *Melvin v. Reid.* But while rehabilitation may reduce recidivism, it also reduces expected punishment costs; whether there is more or less crime in a system that empha-

tential acquaintances quite sensibly regard a criminal past as negative evidence of the value of associating with a person. In light of this analysis, one is not surprised to find that outside of California the principle of *Melvin v. Reid* is rejected.[60]

An important case in which a court refused to recognize an invasion of the right of privacy despite the absence of potential misrepresentation is *Sidis v. F-R Publishing Corp.*[61] The *New Yorker* magazine published a "where is he now" article about a child-prodigy mathematician who as an adult had become an eccentric recluse. One could argue that the *New Yorker*'s exposé produced information useful to people contemplating dealing with Sidis, but the argument would be rather forced; his craving for privacy was so extreme that he had few dealings with other people. It was so extreme that the *New Yorker* might not have been willing to pay the price Sidis would have demanded for his life story.[62] But a distinct economic reason, alluded to earlier, provides some support for the court's conclusion that the publi-

---

sizes rehabilitation is thus unclear. There is also a question whether concealment is a "fair" method of rehabilitation, since it places potentially significant costs on those who deal in ignorance with the former criminal.

Another factor behind the *Melvin* decision may be a belief, uncongenial to economic analysis, that people react irrationally to information concerning past criminal acts. The *Restatement of Torts* gives the example of a former criminal, Valjean, who, though completely rehabilitated, is ruined when news of his past comes to light. American Law Institute, *Restatement (Second) of Torts* § 652D, illustration 26 (Tent. Draft No. 22, 1976). Assuming *complete* rehabilitation, the suggestion that the information would ruin Valjean's career imputes irrationality to the people dealing with him. Perhaps the *Restatement*'s draftsmen were referring not to irrationality, but to the rational basing of judgments on partial information. It is not irrational or malevolent to attach adverse significance to past criminal acts without conducting the kind of thorough investigation that would in a few cases dispel their significance; it is a method of economizing on information costs. See Part IV of this book, infra.

60. See Rawlins v. Hutchinson Publishing Co., 218 Kan. 295, 543 P.2d 988 (1975); Don R. Pember & Dwight L. Teeter, Jr., "Privacy and the Press since Time, Inc. v. Hill," 50 *Wash. L. Rev.* 57, 81–82 (1974). This result, reached under the tort law, has been reinforced by the decision of the Supreme Court in Cox Broadcasting Corp. v. Cohn, 420 U.S. 469 (1975), which holds that the First Amendment may privilege the publication (or as in that case the broadcast) of any matter, however remote, contained in public records. This decision, questionable on its facts, is discussed in Chapter 11.

61. 113 F.2d 806 (2d Cir. 1940).

62. A fact pointing the other way, however, is that Sidis had granted an interview to the *New Yorker* reporter who wrote the story.

cation did not invade Sidis's legal rights. The story was news-worthy in the sense that it catered to a widespread public interest in child prodigies. But once the *New Yorker* published the story, any other magazine or newspaper could, without compensating it, publish the facts that the *New Yorker* had gathered (perhaps by costly research), so long as the republication did not contain the actual language of the original story. Given the number of potential republishers, there was no market mechanism by which the full social value of the *New Yorker*'s information could be brought to bear in negotiations with Sidis over purchasing the right to his life story. In these circumstances there is an argument for not giving him that right—in other words, for allowing the *New Yorker* to externalize some of the social costs (those imposed on Sidis) of its research—since it must perforce externalize some of the benefits.

This analysis may seem to overlook a simple way of reducing the costs of disclosure to Sidis without substantially impairing the value of publication to readers of the *New Yorker* or other magazines that picked up the story: not using his real name in the story. But the magazine would also have to change other details to conceal his identity effectively, and the changes would substantially reduce the information value of the story—readers would not be certain whether they were reading fact or fiction. In *Barber v. Time, Inc.,*[63] however, the court held that a magazine had invaded an individual's right of privacy by naming her in a story about a disagreeable disease she had; the news value of the story was independent of the use of her true name.

All this is not to say that the result in *Sidis* was necessarily correct, especially in a global economic sense. Merely because the *New Yorker*'s story may have generated external benefits, it does not follow that the sum total of the benefits of the story exceeded the sum of the costs, including the costs to Sidis. Obviously this is a difficult comparison for courts to make. They do, however, try; in deciding whether newspaper publicity is unlawful, they look to the offensiveness of the details publicized

63. 348 Mo. 1199, 159 S.W.2d 291 (1942).

and the newsworthiness of the publication, and offensiveness and newsworthiness serve as proxies for the costs and benefits, respectively, of publication.[64]

These proxies, however, are extremely crude. This raises the question: rather than eliminate property rights in one area (privacy) to offset the inefficient consequences of failing to recognize property rights in another area (news), why has the law not recognized a property right in news? To answer this question would carry us far away from the privacy area and entangle us in difficult questions of copyright law and policy. Nor could one stop there. If practical difficulties preclude extending copyright protection to ideas, there is still to be considered the possibility that Sidis might be given a property right in certain facts about himself, which the *New Yorker,* having purchased from him, could enforce against any newspaper or magazine that published its own version of Sidis's story. This solution would assimilate Sidis's case to that of the man with the deformed nose but would also involve serious practical difficulties that cannot be adequately addressed here. Nor is this the place to evaluate the other privileges the law grants to newspapers in order, perhaps, to offset their lack of property rights in the news. Clearly, however, a complete theory of the legal rights and liabilities of the news media would consider the extent to which news gathering confers external benefits and whether the recognition of property rights in the news might not be more efficient than the many immunities society has extended to the press—at some cost to the Sidises of the world—to compensate it for not having property rights in the fruits of its efforts.

To summarize this section, the law distinguishes in a rough way between discreditable and nondiscreditable private information and accords much less protection to the former, as from an economic standpoint it should—though, in California, from that standpoint, there is still too much protection. Where pri-

---

64. In the language of the *Restatement,* the matter publicized, to be actionable, must be "of a kind which (a) would be highly offensive to a reasonable person, and (b) is not of legitimate concern to the public." *Restatement,* supra note 59, at 20.

vacy does not involve any misrepresentation, the protection is broader, but it is limited by problems of externalities and transaction costs that argue against the complete legal protection of privacy even with regard to nondiscrediting facts, as in the case of magazine subscription lists.[65] In a rough way, the *Restatement's* test, which involves a balance between offensiveness and newsworthiness, captures the essential economic elements of the problem; but it would be a better economic test if it were limited to the class of cases in which publicity serves no unmasking purpose. If what is revealed is something the individual has concealed to misrepresent himself to others, the fact that disclosure is offensive to him and of limited interest to the public at large is no better reason for protecting his privacy than if a seller advanced such arguments for being allowed to engage in false advertising of his goods.

False Light. Sometimes the privacy plaintiff seeks damages because the newspaper or other news medium has distorted the facts about him. The existence of a tort of defamation, which, as the commentators have noted, covers much of the same ground as the false-light privacy tort, may seem to compel the conclu-

---

65. In that case another consideration is that the fact disclosed, i.e., that the person listed is a subscriber to a particular magazine, is not the kind of highly personal fact whose disclosure is offensive to the average person. Offense is possible if the list is sold to a magazine that the subscribers to the first magazine find offensive, but this is unlikely to be a serious problem. No doubt many subscribers to *Christian Motherhood* would be offended if solicited by *Playboy,* but *Playboy's* publisher would be unlikely to want to buy the list of subscribers to *Christian Motherhood.*

A somewhat parallel case involves the taking of the census. Should the Bureau of the Census be required to buy the information it seeks from the firms or households that it interviews? Requiring payment would yield a skewed sample if the price were uniform; to get a representative sample despite the different costs of disclosure (and hence price demanded for cooperating) to the firms and households sampled, the Census Bureau would have to use a complicated system of price discrimination which might still fail to assure a representative sample. Coercion seems a lot cheaper in these circumstances. And the costs of disclosure to the people and firms interviewed are small because the government takes precautions against disclosure of the information to creditors, tax collectors, or others who might be able to use the information to gain an advantage over the individual. This is another case where transaction-cost considerations, combined with the limited injury to the individual from disclosure, argue against legal protection of privacy even if the information does not pertain to discreditable conduct.

sion that portraying someone in a false light should be action-able. There is, however, an economic argument that no legal remedy is either necessary or appropriate, because the law can and should leave the determination of truth to competition in the marketplace of ideas. What this argument overlooks, how-ever, is that competition among the news media may not take into account the full costs of being placed in a false light. Sup-pose a *Life* magazine article about a family held hostage inac-curately shows the captors subjecting the family to beatings, verbal sexual assaults, and other indignities. The article imposes private and social costs by conveying misinformation about the family that may deter others from engaging in social or other relationships with its members. If there is a public demand for the accurate portrayal of the family's characteristics, a compet-ing magazine *may* run a story that will correct the false im-pression created by *Life*'s story, but this is not certain. In consid-ering whether to publish such an article, the competitor will not consider the benefits of correction to the family and to people who might transact with its members—it will consider only its readers' interest in such an article.[66]

The economic argument may not seem decisive in light of the earlier point that the publication of newsworthy articles gen-erates external benefits which might justify allowing the news-paper or magazine to externalize some of its costs. However, en-couraging cost externalization in the form of distortion of the truth would be inefficient since distortion would reduce the so-cial benefits as well as costs of publication.

The analysis in this section suggests, incidentally, an eco-nomic reason why the law limits the right of public officials and other public figures to seek legal redress for defamation. Having the status of a public figure increases an individual's

66. See, e.g., Time, Inc. v. Hill, 385 U.S. 374, 407–408 (1967), separate opinion of Justice Harlan. To be sure, the family could, in principle at least, pay *Life* to run a cor-rection, but this solution has the unfortunate characteristic, compared with tort liability, of encouraging inaccurate reporting. *Hill*, like *Cox* (note 60, supra), illustrates the inva-sion of the common law privacy tort by the First Amendment, a subject discussed in Chapter 11.

access to the media by making his denials newsworthy, thus facilitating a market, as distinct from a legal, determination of the truth of the defamatory allegations. The analysis may also explain on similar grounds the common law's traditional reluctance to recognize a right to recover damages from a competitor for false disparagement of goods;[67] the disparaged competitor can rebut untruthful charges in the same advertising medium the disparager used.

Intrusion. Eavesdropping, photographic surveillance of the interior of a home, ransacking private records to discover information about an individual, and similarly intrusive methods of penetrating the wall of privacy with which people surround themselves are tortious.[68] This result is consistent with economic analysis, but cases involving "ostentatious surveillance," as by a detective who follows someone about everywhere, present a more difficult question. The common thread running through the cases in which the courts have held that ostentatious surveillance was tortious is that the surveillance was more intrusive than was reasonably necessary to uncover private information and became a method of intimidation, embarrassment, or distraction. An example is the case of Mrs. Onassis and the aggressive photographer, Ron Galella.[69] The court affirmed Galella's right to photograph Mrs. Onassis but required him literally to "keep his distance." The methods he was using to obtain the photographs impaired her freedom of movement to a degree impossible to justify in terms of the additional information he could obtain thereby.[70]

Consistently with the economic analysis in this chapter, the common law does not limit the right to pry by means that do not

67. See American Washboard Co. v. Saginaw Mfg. Co., 103 F. 281 (6th Cir. 1900), and discussion of disparagement in Chapter 10.

68. See, e.g., Roach v. Harper, 143 W. Va. 869, 105 S.E.2d 564 (1958); Dietemann v. Time, Inc., 449 F.2d 245 (9th Cir. 1971).

69. Galella v. Onassis, 487 F.2d 986 (2d Cir. 1973).

70. It is no answer that she could have paid him to keep his distance; if she had no property right, paying him to desist would simply invite others to harass her in the hope of being similarly paid off.

interfere with the subject's freedom of movement. Thus in Ralph Nader's suit against General Motors, the court affirmed the latter's right to hire someone to follow Nader about, question his acquaintances, and, in short, pertinaciously ferret out personal information about Nader which General Motors might have used to undermine his public credibility.[71] Yet I would expect a court to enjoin any attempt to use such methods to find out what Nader was about to say on some subject in order to plagiarize his ideas.[72]

71. Nader v. General Motors Corp., 25 N.Y.2d 560, 255 N.E.2d 765, 307 N.Y.S.2d 647 (1970).

72. Edward J. Bloustein, "Privacy Is Dear at Any Price: A Response to Professor Posner's Economic Theory," 12 *Ga. L. Rev.* 429 (1978), criticizes several aspects of my analysis of the privacy tort. First he argues that some of the cases protect a kind of shyness (e.g., about nudity) that is not always motivated by a desire to conceal discreditable facts about oneself. See *id*. at 442–447. That the cases protect such shyness is not inconsistent with the economic theory of the privacy tort. It is shyness itself that presents a puzzle from the economic standpoint. Bloustein's larger point, which I accept, is that the term "privacy" embraces more than just concealment of information; the other meanings are discussed in the next chapter. Bloustein also criticizes my discussion of the appropriation cases. See *id*. at 447–449. His criticism is difficult to understand, because he concludes by making a point that is at once an economic point and the heart of my analysis of the appropriation cases: "Once one establishes a personal right to a name and likeness . . . a commercial market in the name and likeness can grow and flourish. A name and likeness can only command a commercial price in a society that permits a person to control the conditions under which he may use his name and likeness for commercial purposes." *Id*. at 449. Bloustein makes the further criticism that I should have offered empirical evidence to support the proposition that poor people figure as central characters in novels less frequently than wealthy ones. *Id*. at 451. Since Bloustein never offers empirical evidence for any proposition that he advances, his demand has a somewhat hollow ring. But in any event, no one who reads novels would doubt that the rich are overrepresented on the basis of their fraction of the population.

10

A Broader View of Privacy

This chapter, in unavoidably miscellaneous fashion, expands my economic analysis of privacy in a variety of directions. I examine the etymology of the word privacy, with special emphasis on two of its senses, seclusion and autonomy; empirical evidence for the economic approach to privacy; a variety of additional related legal doctrines; the protection of reputation by the tort of defamation; and the recent statutory privacy movement in the states.

The Etymology of Privacy: Seclusion and Autonomy

The last chapter examined only the recent meaning of privacy as concealment of personal information. The original meaning of the word "private" in classical antiquity was "nonpublic" in the sense of uninvolved in matters of state.[1] Its root, moveover, is the same as that of words like "privation" and "deprivation." Originally, to be uninvolved in public affairs was to be deprived, and it would not in those days have been a compliment (as it is in some quarters today) to call someone a "very private person." This etymology is a clue to an important if controversial point: the concept of privacy, in anything like the senses in which we use it today, is a Western cultural artifact. The idea that it might be pleasant to be off the public stage was

---

1. See 8 *Oxford English Dictionary* 1388 (1933) (s.v. "privacy"). See also Edward Shils, "Privacy: Its Constitution and Vicissitudes," 31 *Law & Contemp. Prob.* 281 (1966). It is also noteworthy that our word "idiot" is derived from the Greek *idios*, meaning private.

hardly meaningful in a society in which physical privacy was essentially nonexistent—was not only prohibitively costly, but also extremely dangerous. Privacy then was the lot of the pariah.[2]

Gradually the word lost its unfavorable connotations because, I conjecture, growing differentiation of institutions and increasing wealth and public order made it both economically feasible and physically safe for people to have a measure (though initially a small one) of physical privacy. By the seventeenth century we find a concept of privacy as withdrawal from the cares of public life through physical removal to a secluded garden or country estate. This aspect of privacy may be called seclusion, and its outstanding characteristic is a reduction in the number of social interactions. An equivalent term is retirement in its complex modern senses; we speak of a person being retiring (reticent) and also of a person being retired (from a job).

The sense of privacy as seclusion has been immensely influential in the privacy literature; it is the sense in which Warren and Brandeis used the term in their article on privacy discussed in the last chapter. Yet it is actually a rather archaic concept, belonging to the period when physical privacy was very limited—when people lived in such crowded conditions[3] that getting some privacy required withdrawing to an isolated spot of countryside. The opportunities for physical privacy are so much greater in modern society that few people any longer crave the solitude of Walden Pond. The enormous growth of physical privacy was overlooked by Warren and Brandeis when they wrote (well before the era of electronic eavesdropping) that modern man had less privacy than his forebears.

Seclusion can, however, be given a broader meaning than the fastidious withdrawal suggested by Warren and Brandeis. The

2. The original sense of "private" is, incidentally, a further clue to the undifferentiated character of primitive institutions, as discussed in Part II. The public and private sectors are not distinct in primitive and ancient societies. One can view these societies as prepolitical or pregovernmental, but equally one can view them as lacking a clearly defined "private sector."

3. On the paradox of crowding in eras (or areas) of low population density, see next section of this chapter.

word "retire" is again helpful in expressing my meaning. One can retire from the cares of life to some pastoral retreat, or one can retire to one's study to write an article or plan a sales campaign. The first sense implies a reduction in the number of social interactions and therefore in market and nonmarket production; retirement in the second sense is, on the contrary, part of the creative or preparatory stage of production. To illustrate the distinction, one can resent telephone solicitations either because one does not like to have anything to do with people or because one is engaged in or preparing for a more valuable social interaction than the telephone solicitor has to offer.

This "gregarious seclusion" seems more important than seclusion in the sense of solitude. It is doubtful that solitude is a precondition of mental stability or even happiness, for at most times and in most places people have lacked it. It is only very recently, taking the whole course of human evolution, that it was safe for people to be alone for even short periods of time. Even today, while intellectuals fancy themselves leading or wanting to lead retired, contemplative lives, the vast mass of people continue, by preference, to live, work, travel, recreate, and be entertained in groups; even when "alone," the average person is usually listening to the radio or watching television. Most solitude is involuntary, and mental illness is associated with solitude rather than its absence.[4]

However, people whose work is mental rather than physical do require a more tranquil environment than others, and this often entails greater solitude. That is why people engaged in mental work generally have private offices and those engaged in physical work generally do not. The analysis carries over to leisure as well: people whose leisure activities involve intellectual activity (not necessarily of a high order) need a tranquil environment.

As a detail, I note that if there is a taste for pure solitude—that is, for seclusion unrelated to social interaction—it is a *selfish*

4. See, e.g., Cary L. Cooper & Martin C. Green, "Coping with Occupational Stress among Royal Air Force Personnel on Isolated Island Bases," 39 *Psych. Rep.* 731 (1976). See also references in note 30 infra.

emotion in a sense that should be clear from the discussion of the ethics of wealth maximization in Chapter 3. Solitary activity (or cessation of activity) benefits only the actor. Work, and nonmarket interactions such as love, child care, and even casual socializing, confer benefits on others. Production for the market yields consumer surplus, while nonmarket interactive activities presumably yield a form of nonmarket consumer surplus.[5] There is thus a sense in which the person who works is "unselfish" no matter how exclusively motivated by greed he is, while the individual who retires from the world, like the lazy man (who trades market income for a reduction in the disutility of work), reduces his contribution to the wealth of other people in the society.

Creative or gregarious, as distinct from solitary or reclusive, seclusion is a privacy interest of increasing importance because of the growth of education, office work, information, and other factors that have increased the cerebral component in both work and leisure. Yet when people today decry lack of privacy, what they want, I think, is mainly something quite different from seclusion: they want more power to conceal information about themselves that others might use to their disadvantage. This is the meaning of privacy underlying the federal Privacy Act,[6] which limits the retention and dissemination of discrediting personal information contained in government files. I emphasize how far this meaning of privacy is from its early meanings up to and including the idea of seclusion stressed by Warren and Brandeis.

5. For example, the "output" of a social game of tennis is presumably greater than the opportunity costs (or prices) of the activity to the players. Each player confers a net benefit on the other. See George C. Homans, "Social Behavior as Exchange," 63 *Am. J. Soc.* 597 (1958), for a sociological perspective on the element of "trade" involved in nonmarket social behavior. I am not arguing that the individual who chooses solitary over gregarious activity thereby reduces the wealth of society; presumably, he increases it, because he must derive greater (nonpecuniary) income from solitude than from interacting with people, or he would not have chosen it. But his choice confers no benefits on others; no consumer surplus is generated by this type of nonmarket production. The analogy in market economics is to the conversion of the entire consumer surplus in a market into producer surplus through perfect price discrimination.

6. 5 U.S.C. § 552(a) (1976).

Advocates of a broad right of privacy in the sense of secrecy have conflated the two concepts, seclusion and secrecy. They have sought to appropriate the favorable connotations that privacy enjoys in the expression "a very private person" to support the right to conceal one's criminal record from an employer. Yet, as I show in the next chapter, they have not protested against expansive interpretations of the First Amendment that sanction invasions of real seclusion, for example by Jehovah's Witnesses' sound trucks. As Professor Freund pointed out some years ago, "On the whole, the active proselytizing interests have been given greater sanctuary than the quiet virtues or the right of privacy."[7]

Concealment is closely related to another concept, and the linkage indicates the continuity between defamation and invasion of privacy as torts. I refer to "reputation." A person's reputation is other people's valuation of him as a trading, social, marital, or other kind of partner. It is an asset of potentially great value which can be damaged both by false and by true defamation. These possibilities are the basis of the individual's incentive both to seek redress against untruthful libels and slanders and to conceal true discrediting information about himself—the former being the domain of the defamation tort and the latter of the privacy tort. The concept of reputation is not similarly intertwined with that of privacy as seclusion. Indeed, to an individual who is seeking to reduce his interactions with other people, what others think of him is of reduced significance.

To summarize the discussion to this point, the word "privacy" seems to embrace at least two distinct interests. One is the interest in being left alone—the interest that is invaded by the unwanted telephone solicitation, the noisy sound truck, the music in elevators, being jostled in the street, or even an obscene theater billboard or shouted obscenity. This interest is invaded even if the invader is not seeking and does not obtain any information, private or otherwise, about the individual whose peace or quiet—whose seclusion in the broad sense in which I use the

7. Paul A. Freund, *The Supreme Court of the United States: Its Business, Purposes, and Performance* 40 (1961).

term here—is invaded. The individual may be, but certainly need not and typically will not be, a recluse. He may be a full participant in society and even gregarious, yet he may desire freedom from certain interruptions in order to engage in or to prepare (by thinking or resting) for social interactions, whether of a working or leisure nature.

The other privacy interest, concealment of information, is invaded whenever private information is obtained against the wishes of the person to whom the information pertains. Whether or not the invasion impairs the individual's peace and quiet is irrelevant. Sometimes it will, as where the police stop and search a man for evidence of a crime; sometimes it will not, as where a telephone tap is installed without any entry on the premises of the telephone subscriber, or mail is opened without disturbing the contents or delaying its receipt by the addressee. To be sure, knowledge that private information has been or might be disclosed could disturb a person's peace and quiet. But that is just to say that people value secrecy as much as they value being left alone—not that secrecy is identical to peace and quiet.

The above discussion is an effort to identify reasonably definite interests that the concept of privacy may be thought to embrace. But such a discussion cannot do justice to the persuasive or emotive uses of the word "privacy." From its original unfavorable connotation of being off the public stage, the word has come in modern thought to connote a value that civilized people treasure. To be sure, this modern approbation has not gone entirely unchallenged. Critics of a collectivist persuasion rename privacy "anxious privatism" and contrast it with traits of openness, candor, and altruism allegedly encouraged by a more communal style of living.[8] This criticism has value in reminding

8. This is the view of the "humanistic psychology" movement. See Mordechai Rotenberg, " 'Alienating Individualism' and 'Reciprocal Individualism': A Cross-Cultural Conceptualization," 17 *J. Humanistic Psych.* 3 (1977). See also Richard A. Wasserstrom, "Privacy: Some Arguments and Assumptions," in *Philosophical Law: Authority Equality Adjudication Privacy* 148, 162–166 (Richard Bronaugh ed. 1978); Michael A. Weinstein, "The Uses of Privacy in the Good Life," in *Nomos XIII: Privacy* 88, 89–93 (J. Roland Pennock & John W. Chapman eds. (1971). Cf. Edward A. Shils, *The Torment of Secrecy* 102 (1956).

us that privacy is a cultural artifact rather than an innate human need. Most cultures have functioned tolerably well without either the concept or the reality of privacy in either its seclusion or secrecy senses, and this fact must be considered before one concludes that privacy is a precondition to valued human qualities such as love and friendship, let alone (as sometimes argued) a prerequisite of sanity. But the skeptical view of privacy is not widely shared or even understood. Writing recently about the articles on which this chapter and the last are based, Ruth Gavison groups me with the "reductionist" writers on privacy who, in her words, "are united in denying the utility of thinking and talking about privacy as a legal right."[9] I am the "most extreme" of the reductionists because I deny the "utility of all 'intermediate' values."[10] These characterizations are inaccurate. I consider the right of privacy a meaningful legal right; I attempted to describe its contours in the last chapter. I consider privacy itself an intermediate value, as does Gavison,[11] but like her I do not consider that intermediate or instrumental values lack utility. The question is the aptness of the instrument.

Gavison's inaccurate and pejorative characterization of my views, coupled with her conclusion, which is "that the law should make an explicit commitment to privacy,"[12] suggests that her fundamental purpose is to promote reverence for, rather than understanding of, the concept of privacy. But she does, at least, resist the temptation to exploit the favorable connotations that privacy enjoys today by attempting to expand its meaning. In contrast, the Supreme Court,[13] some constitutional scholars,[14] and now a distinguished economist[15] concur in regarding privacy as a synonym for liberty or autonomy. We already have

9. "Privacy and the Limits of the Law," 89 *Yale L. J.* 421, 422 (1980).

10. *Id.* at 422 n.9.

11. *Id.* at 423 n.11.

12. *Id.* at 459.

13. See Chapter 11.

14. See, e.g., Edward J. Bloustein, "Privacy Is Dear at Any Price: A Response to Professor Posner's Economic Theory," 12 *Ga. L. Rev.* 429, 447 (1978).

15. See Jack Hirshleifer, "Privacy: Its Origin, Function, and Future," 9 *J. Legal Stud.* (1980).

perfectly good words—liberty and autonomy and freedom—to describe the interest in being allowed to do what one wants without interference. We should not define privacy to mean the same thing and thereby obscure its other meanings.

The polemical character of the privacy debate is further illustrated by the arbitrary contraction of the term to exclude business privacy, despite the strong economic case for such privacy. Not only is the word privacy rarely used with reference to the private information of corporations or universities, but privacy interests are rarely thought implicated when information is concealed, even if by an individual, in the context of commercial activities.

I want to glance briefly at the concept of *physical* privacy, which refers to the conditions of life, not purely architectural, that afford people a greater or lesser measure of distance from others. Doors, private apartments, unattached single-family houses, and private automobiles facilitate privacy in its less tangible senses of seclusion or secrecy. So do broader social conditions such as urbanization and occupational mobility, which by reducing repetitive contacts between people also reduce opportunities for observation, imposition, and other intrusions. Modern advances in electronic surveillance operate in the opposite direction. Although they probably do not use electronic eavesdropping, modern communards are careful to remove the physical preconditions of privacy, sometimes even to the point of removing doors![16]

An implication of this discussion is that it is inappropriate to limit the concept of physical privacy to activities carried out in a private place such as one's home or office. When a person is walking down the street, he is surrounded by a "private space" in the sense that, although he is visible and audible to other users of the street, he can carry on an uninterrupted conversation with a companion or, if he is alone, think about a problem, observe his surroundings, or concentrate on getting where he is

16. I am told that the faculty offices at Governors State University, in Park Forest South, Illinois, have neither doors nor ceilings, because such barriers to sight and sound would be inconsistent with the university's creed of "openness."

going. A person who accosts or jostles or shouts at him disturbs his privacy in the same way that a loud knock on the door or a sound truck disturbs the privacy of a person ensconced in his home or office. The intrusion in the street may be less significant, and to the extent that it is an unavoidable by-product of the congestion of the street it may be unobjectionable. But there is no reason to deny the applicability of the concept of privacy to activities that are carried on in public but with as much seclusion as conditions permit.

Evidence for the Economic Theory of Privacy

The theory of privacy developed in this and the last chapter is deductive, and this raises the question: what is the empirical basis of the theory? Some evidence, relating mainly to the Buckley Amendment and to the rhetoric of primitive peoples, was presented in Chapter 9 and a bit in Chapter 6. Here I shall review the evidence for the economic model of privacy contained in comparative and psychological studies.

1. Although there is no convenient metric for ranking societies by the amount of privacy they afford, some gross distinctions are possible and suggestive. As I have shown, there is little privacy in primitive societies.[17] This implies, if my economic analysis is correct, that speech in primitive and ancient societies will tend to be more formal and circumspect than in modern societies, in just the same way (another bit of evidence of the economic model) that modern people speak more formally the

17. See, besides references in Chapters 6 and 9, John Beard Haviland, *Gossip, Reputation, and Knowledge in Zinacantan* (1977); John M. Roberts & Thomas Gregor, "Privacy: a Cultural View," in *Nomos XIII: Privacy*, supra note 8 at 199; E. E. Evans-Pritchard, *The Nuer: A Description of the Modes of Livelihood and Political Institutions of a Nilotic People* 15 (1940).

For example, the Yanoama Indians live in large collective dwellings of up to 100 yards in diameter, with as many as 250 people in each dwelling, grouped in families that cluster around their own hearth. There are no walls within the dwellings. The Yanoama villages are surrounded by thousands of miles of virgin forest, but it is considered dangerous to leave the village. See Napoleon A. Chagnon, *Yanomamo: The Fierce People* (2d ed. 1977); William J. Smole, *The Yanoama Indians: A Cultural Geography* (1976).

larger the audience.[18] The Homeric epics provide the most striking but not the only evidence of the precision and decorum of primitive speech—so at variance with the crudeness of primitive technology.[19] Rhetoric was an important field of education and study in Aristotle's time (and indeed long before) but has virtually disappeared today. There seems to be a secular trend, coincident with and arguably related to the growth of privacy, toward informality in speech and writing and away from insistence on lexical and grammatical precision and rhetorical craft.

Another implication of the economic analysis of privacy is that mendacity will be less reprobated in a primitive than in an advanced society. Where people, lacking privacy, know each other very well, telling lies is less likely to serve a manipulative purpose (and more likely to serve a dramatic, diplomatic, or metaphorical function) than in a modern, highly differentiated society where relatively little is known about the people with whom one transacts and much, therefore, must be taken on trust. The difference in the view of mendacity taken by primitive and modern societies was explained long ago by a distinguished sociologist in terms similar to the above.[20]

The economic analysis of privacy may also explain the transition from "shame culture" to "guilt culture." These terms have been used by anthropologists and classicists to distinguish between cultures in which self-esteem is based solely on conformity to external standards of conduct and those in which it is also (or instead) based on having a clear conscience.[21] Primitive and ancient societies tend to approximate the shame model, more advanced societies (including our own), the guilt model. This

18. And the discussion in faculty meetings is more formal if student observers are admitted.

19. Other evidence is discussed in Chapters 6 and 9. See also Clifford Geertz, *Person, Time and Conduct in Bali: An Essay in Cultural Analysis* (1966); Felix M. Keesing & Marie M. Keesing, *Elite Communication in Samoa: A Study in Leadership* (1956); *Language in Culture and Society*, pt. II (Dell Hymes ed. 1964); *Political Language and Oratory in Traditional Society* (M. Bloch ed. 1975).

20. See G. Simmel, "The Sociology of Secrecy and of Secret Societies," 11 *Am. J. Soc.* 441, 446, 450 (1906).

21. See, e.g., E. R. Dodds, *The Greeks and the Irrational* 17–18, 36–37 (1951).

pattern may reflect the lack of privacy in primitive and ancient societies. If one is being watched all the time by one's neighbors and relatives, there is no reason to have a sense of being watched all the time by God. Once people acquire privacy, and with it the opportunity to conceal wrongful conduct, a demand arises for a mode of surveillance that will not be defeated by privacy; the demand is met by the ideas of conscience and guilt and by the religious beliefs that encourage the formation of these ideas.[22]

Two other relations of privacy to primitive culture were examined in Chapter 6. First, in the absence of public law enforcement, privacy will be denied in order to increase the probability of detecting offenses. Second, primitive societies are technologically unprogressive because, in the absence of a well-developed system of property rights in ideas, secrecy is an essential method of enabling people to appropriate the social benefits of their ideas. In a society which denies privacy in order to control crime, there will be few incentives to develop new ideas.

The amount of privacy necessary to sustain innovative activity of a high order may, however, be less than we think. For example, only the very wealthy in ancient Rome enjoyed the physical privacy that most people in advanced countries enjoy today, and their privacy was greatly compromised because they were under continual observation by their servants—many of whom apparently were disloyal (servants were often paid police informers). In the medieval manor the whole household commonly slept together in the great hall, with the lord and lady, perhaps joined by one or two favored guests, in the only bed. As late as the seventeenth century it was common for the well-to-do to have servants sleep in their bedrooms for protection against possible intruders. As late as the eighteenth century, bedrooms opened into each other rather than into a common hallway.[23]

22. Roberts & Gregor, supra note 17, at 212, state: "Perhaps when human surveillance diminishes, supernatural surveillance increases."

23. My main source for the history recounted in this paragraph is the interesting study by Alan F. Westin, *Privacy in Western Society: From the Age of Pericles to the Roman Republic* (Report to Assn. of Bar of City of N.Y. Spec. Comm. on Sci. and Law, Feb. 15,

I conjecture that at some point, reached long ago in Western society, further increases in the amount of personal privacy no longer increased significantly the incentive to innovate but continued to increase the ability of people to conceal their activities for manipulative purposes. Identifying this point of diminishing social returns to privacy is obviously a research task of formidable difficulty; I will not attempt it here but will simply note, both as further evidence of an association between privacy and innovation and as a possible clue to when the point was reached, Lawrence Stone's finding that modern ideas of privacy date from the early rise of capitalism.[24] Stone suggests an ideological affinity between privacy and entrepreneurship; I am suggesting an economic relationship.

Another interesting comparison is between modern-day America and Europe.[25] There is more physical privacy in America. Europeans live in more crowded conditions; single-family houses are rarer; "suburban sprawl" remains largely an American phenomenon;[26] many Europeans still live in villages; and there is greater occupational and geographical mobility in the United States than in Europe. These characteristics bearing on physical privacy are reinforced by the greater in-

---

1965). For an excellent brief discussion, see Lawrence Stone, *The Family, Sex and Marriage in England 1500–1800*, at 253–256 (1977). See also Norbert Elias, *The Civilizing Process: The History of Manners* 163 (Edmund Jephcott trans. 1978); Richard A. Goldthwaite, "The Florentine Palace as Domestic Architecture," 77 *Am. Hist. Rev.* 977 (1972). Stone, at 254, emphasizes the desire to escape prying servants, who were frequent witnesses in criminal proceedings against their masters for adultery, as motivating the demand for privacy. This is further evidence for the instrumental theory of privacy advocated here.

24. See Stone, supra note 23, at 259–260.

25. See Herbert J. Spiro, "Privacy in Comparative Perspective," in *Nomos XIII: Privacy,* supra note 8, at 121; and for the factual basis of this paragraph, Edward T. Hall, *The Hidden Dimension* 123–153 (1966). Follow-up research to Hall's is reviewed in Irwin Altman, *The Environment and Social Behavior: Privacy, Personal Space, Territory, Crowding* 63–64 (1975).

26. The individual who lives in one community, works in another, and commutes between them in a private automobile has much more privacy than the individual who lives and works in a small community and walks or takes public transportation between home and office; there are much greater opportunities for surveillance of the latter person by his neighbors and co-workers.

trusiveness of the state in Europe than in America—the internal passports, and so on. From an economic viewpoint the lack of privacy implies, and one finds, that Europeans are more formal and precise in their use of language, and more reserved and circumspect with strangers—more "private." (The behavior of the Japanese, who also lack privacy by American standards, supports this point.) The American gabbles freely to strangers; the European and the Japanese do not. The American is so favorably situated for concealing discreditable information about himself that he incurs little cost in revealing himself to a stranger. The chance that this stranger will encounter him again or knows people who know him or is otherwise a candidate for significant future interactions is less in the American than in the European or Japanese setting.

This analysis implies that within the United States we should encounter a high level of rhetorical skills among people living in crowded conditions, such as blacks living in slums. Given the educational deficiencies of such people, it would be surprising to find them well equipped with expressive skills. Yet sociolinguists have found that "Nonstandard Negro English," or "Black English Vernacular," while exhibiting important differences in grammar and vocabulary from standard English, is an expressive instrument of considerable subtlety and power.[27] Lack of privacy may explain the emphasis on rhetorical skill in this otherwise deprived culture.

2. Like the comparative studies, the psychological studies reveal greater circumspection where the costs of candor are higher. They show, for example, that a man approached by a stranger will tend to speak less freely to him than a woman ap-

---

27. See, e.g., William Labov, *Language in the Inner City: Studies in the Black English Vernacular* (1972); Edith Folb, *Runnin' Down Some Lines* (1980). For brief discussions see Susan M. Ervin-Tripp, *Language Acquisition and Communicative Choice* 351 (1973), and Peter Trudgill, *Sociolinguistics: An Introduction* 65–83 (1974). Labov states elsewhere: "Our work in the Spanish community makes it painfully obvious that in many ways working-class speakers are more effective narrators, reasoners, and debaters than many middle-class speakers who temporize, qualify, and lose their argument in a mass of irrelevant detail." "A Linguistic Viewpoint toward Black English," in *Language, Society, and Education: A Profile of Black English* 10, 21 (Johanna S. DeStefano ed. 1973).

proached by a stranger.[28] This difference need not be ascribed to biological difference between the sexes. An economic explanation is possible. Men were traditionally involved in more market activities than women and probably derived greater value from concealment of possibly discreditable information than women did. This may explain the greater reticence that traditionally distinguishes men from nonworking women. The same study showed that a man will generally speak about himself with greater candor to a female than to a male stranger. This behavior is consistent with the fact that excepting the occasional Don Juan, a man is more likely to be a candidate for future transactions with another man (who might be a tax collector, a detective, or the employee of a competitor) than with a woman.

Another finding in this study was that when approached by a stranger, out-of-towners at the Boston airport were more likely to confide personal information to the stranger than residents of Boston were. The experimenter offered an explanation that is consistent with the economic approach: "Whereas the Bostonian subject might conceivably expect to run into the experimenter again some day on Beacon Hill or in Copley Square, the out-of-towner could be virtually certain that their paths would never cross again."[29]

The psychological studies relating to privacy tend also to refute the idea that privacy is a psychological necessity. Studies of crowding, a proxy for lack of privacy, indicate that the pure effect of crowding on various measures of mental health or stability is insignificant.[30] Privacy is not something we "need," as we need food or air; it is something we want in order to advance plans far removed from biological imperatives. That people be-

28. See Zick Rubin, "Disclosing Oneself to a Stranger: Reciprocity and Its Limits," 11 *J. Experimental Soc. Psych.* 233 (1975), and studies cited there.

29. *Id.* at 255–256. In the same spirit George Stigler has speculated that the candor, startling to a modern reader, with which the characters in nineteenth-century English novels reveal their incomes reflects the absence of income tax.

30. See, e.g., Jonathan L. Freedman, Stanley Heshka, & Alan Levy, "Population Density and Pathology: Is There a Relationship?" 11 *J. Experimental Soc. Psych.* 539 (1975); Robert Edward Mitchell, "Some Social Implications of High-Density Housing," 36 *Am. Soc. Rev.* 18 (1971); Altman, supra note 25, at 193.

have rationally concerning privacy is also suggested by the way they will substitute reticence for physical privacy when the latter is in short supply,[31] a substitution related to the use of more formal modes of expression with larger audiences (less privacy).[32]

The Common Law and the Economic Theory of Privacy

The last chapter examined the privacy tort and, very briefly, trade secrets and common law copyright. Here I examine briefly three other common law doctrines illuminated by the economic analysis of privacy. They are privileged communications, blackmail, and assault and battery.

Privileged Communications

Suppose that A in conversation with B slanders C, B repeats the slander to C, and C sues A for defamation. Has A the right to sue B to recover any damages paid out to C, on the ground of breach of confidence? The general answer is no, unless A and B have a contract obligating B to respect A's confidences. Such contracts are rarely made, presumably because the costs of a broken confidence are normally low relative to the costs of negotiating and enforcing a contract. Also, effective nonlegal sanctions for breach of promise by a friend or family member are created by the continuing nature of the relationship. An occasional exception is where the confidence is imparted in the course of business dealings, especially if it is a valuable trade secret; here one often finds explicit contracts forbidding breach of confidence.

But if A confesses a crime to B and exacts B's promise not to reveal the confession to anyone, the promise is unenforceable

---

31. See, e.g., Carl I. Greenberg & Ira J. Firestone, "Compensatory Responses to Crowding: Effects of Personal Space Intrusion and Privacy Reduction," 35 *J. Personality & Soc. Psych.* 637 (1977); Altman, supra note 25, at 41–42; and Arab behavior discussed in Hall, supra note 25, at 148.

32. For additional evidence supporting the economic approach see, in Chapter 9, discussion of the Buckley Amendment, Goffman's work on misrepresentation in everyday life, and studies of the growth of single-person households.

no matter what formalities of contractual obligation are employed. There is, however, a set of exceptions to this principle: at common law, information imparted in confidence in conversations between spouses, between client and lawyer, and between certain government officials (executive privilege) is given extraordinary protection.[33] For example, a husband who has confessed a crime to his wife can prevent her from testifying to the confession in a criminal proceeding. This result is puzzling from an economic standpoint. True, the marital and lawyer-client relationships would be impaired if the spouse and the client respectively had to exercise extreme circumspection in communication, because the nature of these relationships makes it easy for the spouse or lawyer to detect guilt from an unguarded remark. But why should society wish to strengthen the bonds of matrimony and of legal representation for criminals?[34]

A possible answer in the case of spousal immunity is that if there is a sufficiently strong social interest in promoting the marriage relationship, the immunity, although it raises the costs of crime, may be justified by the encouragement it offers to spouses to communicate with each other without concern for possible use of the communicated information later in testimony against them. It is not surprising, therefore, in an era when the importance attached to stable marriages has declined, to find a strong movement against the immunity.[35]

Blackmail

Blackmail is the practice of threatening to disclose discreditable information about a person unless he pays the blackmailer to suppress it. If I am correct that the facts about a person (as distinct from his communications) should be in the public domain, so that those who have to decide whether to initiate or

33. See Charles T. McCormick, *McCormick's Handbook of the Law of Evidence*, chs. 9, 10, 12 (2d ed. Edward W. Cleary ed. 1972). The doctor-patient privilege is statutory.
34. A traditional reply in the case of the lawyer-client privilege is that the lawyer's ability to represent his client would be impaired if he were liable to appear in the case as a witness. That reply is unavailable in the case of spousal immunity.
35. See McCormick, supra note 33, at 30 (2d ed. Supp. 1978).

continue social or business relations with him will have full information, does it not follow that the Nosy Parker should be allowed to sell back to the individual the information he obtains? Someone who made it his business to conduct research into people's pasts and sell the results to the newspaper would not be subject to any sanction; why should he be guilty of the crime of blackmail if he tries to sell his research to the subject of it?

If a customer sues a seller for false advertising, his objective is likely to be obtaining a financial settlement rather than publicizing the falsehood. Yet settlement is not considered an improper objective and is freely permitted. Blackmail would seem to serve a function similar to that of the false-advertising suit, as a deterrent to acquiring or concealing characteristics that are undesirable to people with whom one wishes to have social or business dealings.

On the other hand—and this is a closer analogy to blackmail—someone who was neither a customer nor a competitor but was simply in the business of bringing enforcement actions would not be allowed to recover damages for false advertising. The policy against such suits seems to be founded on considerations based on the economics of private law enforcement—unrelated to a judgment that false advertising is less serious in the personal than in the commercial sphere.[36] Where optimal punishment requires a low probability of punishment combined with a high fine,[37] the fine will attract private enforcers (if permitted) into the enforcement "market," with the result that the probability of punishment will rise and the optimal combination of probability and severity of punishment will be thwarted. The solution is to limit private enforcement—of which blackmail is simply one form—or, stated otherwise, to substitute public for private enforcement.

If this analysis is correct, we would expect to find a positive correlation between public enforcement and hostility to black-

36. See William M. Landes & Richard A. Posner, "The Private Enforcement of Law," 4 *J. Legal Stud.* 1, 42–43 (1975), from which this analysis is drawn.
37. See discussion of this model of optimal punishment in Chapter 7.

mail, and we do. Before the nineteenth century, the prohibition of blackmail was limited to what today would be called extortion (threatening to burn down a man's house if he won't pay "protection"); it did not embrace threatening to expose a person's criminal or immoral activities.[38] This was a period when most enforcement of laws, including criminal laws, was private.[39] The prohibition against blackmail in its modern sense dates as expected from the rise of public enforcement in the nineteenth century.

Assault and Battery

To associate assault and battery with privacy may seem to be straining after paradox. Surely these torts protect a more tangible interest than privacy: bodily integrity. I believe, however, that the idea of privacy as seclusion may hold the key to understanding why assault in its strict tort sense and batteries that involve no physical injury (such as spitting in someone's face) are tortious at common law.

In tort law an assault is a gesture, such as raising one's arm to strike, aiming a gun, or drawing a sword on someone, that creates an expectation—"apprehension" in its legal, not everyday, sense—of imminent battery. It is not a battery if there is no actual touching. The threatening gesture might be interrupted or withdrawn before an actual touching occurred, or the assailant might not have intended to actually commit a battery (as where an unloaded gun is pointed at someone who believes it is loaded). If the threatening gesture is used to obtain something from the victim to which the assailant is not entitled, we have a form of theft. But where the gesture is simply an unsuccessful attempt to commit a battery, either because the assailant changes his mind or because he is interrupted, what is the basis for making it actionable?

Perhaps the attempt is punished in order to discourage bat-

38. See Douglas H. Ginsburg, "Blackmail: An Economic Analysis of the Law" (Harv. L. Sch., mimeo., Nov. 4, 1979).

39. See Landes & Posner, supra note 36, at 1–2; and references in Chapter 8, note 45.

teries—punished, that is, under the same theory by which attempted murder is punished, although the intended victim suffers no harm.[40] But that is evidently not the theory of the assault tort. There is no tort unless the victim apprehends an imminent battery,[41] even though apprehension is irrelevant from the standpoint of punishing attempts. Suppose A creeps up behind B and is about to brain him when he is interrupted, and B doesn't find out about A's attempt until afterward. While A may be guilty of a crime, he has not committed a tort.

The difference between this case and that in which there is apprehension of imminent battery is, I suggest, that the latter involves an invasion of the seclusion interest and the former does not. Whether or not the apprehension is a source of fright or, rarely, of actual emotional injury, it is an interruption or distraction, an invasion of peace and quiet.[42]

The idea of privacy as seclusion may also explain why the common law provides a remedy for the victim of a noninjurious battery, such as being spat on, or being struck in anger but not hard enough to be hurt.[43] These are invasions of the "private space" that surrounds a person even in public and enables him to attend to his own thoughts. The offense is not to bodily integrity in any substantial sense but to the seclusion element of one's privacy.

Finally, in the assault that creates an apprehension only of noninjurious battery—as where A makes a gesture to slap B with a glove in an offensive, but not physically injurious, manner—we have the clearest example of the legal protection of a pure interest in seclusion, divorced from physical harm.

---

40. On the economics of punishing attempts, see Steven Shavell, "Harm as a Prerequisite for Liability" (Harv. L. Sch., unpublished Aug. 1979); Donald Wittman, "Prior Regulation versus Post Liability: The Choice between Input and Output Monitoring," 6 *J. Legal Stud.* 193 (1977).

41. See William L. Prosser, *Handbook of the Law of Torts* 38–40 (4th ed. 1971).

42. However, this analysis does not explain why the common law did not, until recently, provide a remedy to someone who is placed in apprehension of imminent bodily harm by negligent as distinct from intentional wrongdoing—someone who, for example, jumps to avoid being hit by a speeding car.

43. See Prosser, supra note 41, at 36.

Defamation and Disparagement

It has long been recognized that the tort of defamation (libel and slander) raises parallel questions to the privacy tort, and economics is useful in clarifying the precise relationship between the two torts. Economics also provides a perspective in which to evaluate the frequent charge that defamation is doctrinally the least satisfactory branch of tort law because it is riddled with arcane and irrational distinctions, such as that between libel *per se* and libel *per quod*.[44] As we shall see, economic theory renders intelligible the general structure, although not all the details, of defamation law.

Reputation—the opinion others hold of one as a candidate for business or social transactions—has important economic functions in a market system, indeed in any system where voluntary interactions are important. It reduces the search costs of buyers and sellers and makes it easier for the superior producer to increase his sales relative to those of inferior ones. In these ways it helps channel resources into their most valuable employments—a process at the heart of the market system. This role is not limited to explicit markets. It is just as vital to the functioning of the "marriage market,"[45] the market in friends, the political market, and so on.

The falsification of reputation is therefore a matter of legitimate social concern. Such falsification can take either of two forms. A firm or an individual—it does not matter which—may try to create an undeservedly good reputation either by affirmative misrepresentation or by the concealment of discreditable facts. The latter is the process that gives rise to the kind of

44. Prosser states: "It must be confessed at the beginning that there is a great deal of the law of defamation which makes no sense. It contains anomalies and absurdities for which no legal writer ever has had a kind word, and it is a curious compound of a strict liability imposed upon innocent defendants, as rigid and extreme as anything found in the law, with a blind and almost perverse refusal to compensate the plaintiff for real and very serious harm." Prosser, supra note 41, at 737 (footnote omitted). Chapter 19 of the Prosser book contains a lucid summary of the rules of defamation law, on which I draw heavily in the following discussion.

45. See Gary S. Becker, *The Economic Approach to Human Behavior* 206 (1976).

pseudo-privacy claim discussed in the last chapter. Or—and here is where the tort of defamation enters—the falsification of reputation can take the form of besmirching another person's or firm's deservedly good reputation.

One can identify in a broad way the factors that make it more or less likely that attempts at defamation[46] will be made. First, if everything is known about an individual, so that his reputation is not an extrapolation from limited knowledge but the sum of all the facts about him, defamation will not pay, because it will not be believed. (Stated otherwise, if the costs of information are very low, any falsity in an aspersion about a person or product will be detected.) This implies that defamation is a problem chiefly of relatively modern as distinct from tribal or village societies. The relative infrequency of references to defamation in accounts of primitive society provides some support for this observation.[47] An additional factor, however, is the inverse relationship between the importance of reputation as a factor in transactions and the existence of well-developed remedies for breach of contract. In the absence of such remedies the parties' interest in preserving their reputations for honoring contracts is the only solid assurance that neither will terminate opportunistically. The less developed the social institutions of contract are, the greater are the potential losses from impairment of one's reputation.

A related but more complex consideration is the difficulty of "living down" one's reputation in a close-knit tribal or village society. In a mobile urban society such as ours, an injury to reputation can often be cured simply by changing one's job or place of residence. However, since a great deal of specific human cap-

---

46. I use the term generally to mean a false aspersion, though the legal approach is to regard the aspersion as the defamation, and truth as a defense to liability.

47. Defamation was a recognized wrong among the Nuer people of the Sudan, but significantly, it was said to be "usually associated with false accusation of witchcraft" (P. P. Howell, *A Manual of Nuer Law: Being an Account of Customary Law, Its Evolution and Development in the Courts Established by the Sudan Government* 70 [1954])—a type of accusation whose falsity is difficult to detect among people who believe in witchcraft, even if they lack privacy. To similar effect, see Walter R. Goldschmidt, *Sebei Law* 131–133 (1967).

ital may be lost in such a move, the cure may be costly. The greater range of defamatory utterances made possible by modern technology must also be considered: television can besmirch an individual's reputation throughout the world.

Weighing the above factors, one might conclude that the problem of defamation is apt to be most serious in a society that has recently emerged from the tribal-village state in which reputations cannot be credibly falsified but that has not yet developed effective institutions of contract that would reduce the importance of reputation as a factor in people's decisions to transact. Consistently with this suggestion, we find the defamation tort broadly defined in late, but not early, republican Rome.[48] Conditions in the early republic were presumably close to those of tribal society, while the late republic may be described as a society recently emergent from the tribal state. Similarly, in medieval England, again a society recently emergent from the tribal state, defamation actions apparently flourished, especially in the ecclesiastical courts. Later, though the tort was more broadly defined in some respects, its practical utility was reduced by the creation of various defenses and in particular by rules strictly construing defamatory utterances against the victim.[49]

Since defaming an individual and disparaging a competing producer or his goods are both fraud, the question arises why the tort of defamation developed earlier and further than that of disparagement.[50] An answer is suggested by the economic literature on fraud.[51] That literature distinguishes among

48. See H. F. Jolowicz & B. Nicholas, *Historical Introduction to the Study of Roman Law* 191, 273 (3d ed. 1972).

49. On the history of defamation in England, see C. H. S. Fifoot, *History and Sources of the Common Law: Tort and Contract* 126–153 (1949); Van Vechten Veeder, "The History and Theory of the Law of Defamation I," 3 *Colum. L. Rev.* 546–547 (1903); R H. Helmholz, "Canonical Defamation in Medieval England," 15 *Am. J. Legal Hist.* 255 (1971); R. C. Donnelly, "History of Defamation," 1949 *Wisc. L. Rev.* 99, 100–101

50. The common law took a very restrictive approach to disparagement, illustrated by American Washboard Co. v. Saginaw Mfg. Co., 103 F. 281 (6th Cir. 1900).

51. See e.g., Michael R. Darby & Edi Karni, "Free Competition and the Optimal Amount of Fraud," 16 *J. Law & Econ.* 67 (1973); Phillip Nelson, "Information and Consumer Behavior," 78 *J. Pol. Econ.* 311 (1970).

"search" or "inspection" goods, whose quality and fitness are ascertainable on inspection before sale; "experience" goods, whose qualities are revealed only in use (such as the durability of a camera); and "credence" goods, whose qualities are so difficult to discover that the buyer is heavily dependent on the seller's good faith. The buyer's need for legal protection rises as we move along the spectrum from search to credence goods. In the formative era of the common law of disparagement (say, up to the enactment of the Federal Trade Commission Act in 1914), most goods were still search goods, and the need for legal protection against disparagement by a competitor was therefore small. But long before then an individual had become a credence good, to be taken on faith rather than inspection, and his need for legal protection of reputation was greater than that of the producer of a disparaged good. If A called B a crook, B's social and business acquaintances probably would not know him so intimately as to be confident that A's claim was false.[52]

To equate defamation with commercial disparagement may seem to give defamation too commercial an air and to ignore the "dignitary" interests that the tort protects. However, the tort is not in fact designed for the protection of peace of mind, self-esteem, or other "private" interests or sensitivities. This is shown by the requirement of "publication." The aspersion must be communicated to someone besides the victim in order to be actionable. That is, it must lower other people's opinion of the victim's character and so impair his opportunities for advantageous social or business transactions.[53] A wounding lie that does

52. A similar argument is made in Ellen R. Jordan & Paul H. Rubin, "An Economic Analysis of the Law of False Advertising," 8 *J. Legal Stud.* 527 (1979).

It is consistent with this analysis that corporations can complain of defamation to the same extent (*mutatis mutandis*) as individuals, for the corporation itself is bound to be a credence good even if its products are search goods. If a competitor says a corporation doesn't pay its bills, prospective creditors of the corporation have no ready basis to contradict the assertion.

53. "A communication is defamatory if it tends so to harm the reputation of another as to lower him in the estimation of the community or to deter third persons from associating or dealing with him." American Law Institute. *Restatement (Second) of Torts* § 559 (Tent. Draft no. 20, 1974).

not impair those opportunities is not actionable. This result is consistent with the fact that the privacy tort does not afford a remedy for an individual's feelings that have been wounded by disclosure of truthful facts that are material to other people in deciding whether to transact with him.

The defamation and privacy torts interact in two other notable ways. First, if A in private conversation with B slanders C, and an eavesdropper overhears the conversation, the slander is not actionable.[54] This is the logical corollary of the social judgment, which I have argued has an economic basis, that the privacy of conversations should be protected in order to foster effective communication. Second, privacy and defamation differ in that a disclosure of private information, to be actionable as an invasion of privacy, must be "publicized"[55]—disseminated widely—whereas defamation is actionable so long as one person reads or hears it. This distinction becomes explicable once the economic relationship between the two torts is grasped. Normally the disclosure that gives rise to a privacy claim is truthful (if it were false, it would be actionable as defamation). When such a disclosure is made in a small circle, normally the circle of people acquainted with the individual whose privacy has been breached, there is a social benefit: the individual is unmasked and his acquaintances can reevaluate their relationships with him in the light of a more complete knowledge of his character.[56] However, if the disclosure is widely publicized, it is likely to reach beyond the circle of his acquaintances to people with whom he has neither present dealings nor any substantial likelihood of dealing in the future. Disclosures to them are less likely to perform an unmasking function and more likely to invade the interest in seclusion (as distinct from manipulation) than more selective disclosure. The publicity requirement thus serves to identify the subset of disclosures most likely to entail inva-

54. See Prosser, supra note 41, at 774.

55. See *id.* at 810.

56. Thus it is not an actionable invasion of privacy for a creditor to write a debtor's employer informing him that his employee has failed to pay the debt when due. See, e.g., Cullum v. Government Employees Fin. Corp., 517 S.W.2d 317 (Tex. Ct. Civ. App. 1974).

sions of legitimate interests. The situation in the case of defamation tends to be reversed. Defamation is likely to inflict its worst social harm precisely in the circle of the individual's friends or acquaintances. It is they whom the lie is most likely to deflect from social transactions, to their own injury as well as the defamed individual's, because it is they with whom he transacts.

Let us consider the economic rationality of some other distinctive features of the defamation tort. First, although defamation is usually classified as an intentional tort, it has a strong flavor of strict liability, because it is not a defense that the defendant may have exercised reasonable care to avoid defaming the plaintiff. In one well-known case, the author of a fictitious newspaper story by sheer fortuity gave a character in the story the name of a real person, Artemus Jones. Jones sued for libel and won upon a showing that his neighbors thought the story was about him.[57] As we saw in Chapter 7, one basis for choosing between strict liability and alternative rules, such as no liability or negligence liability, is the relative ability of injurer and victim to avoid harm. Jones could have done nothing to avoid being defamed, whereas the author or publisher might have checked to see whether there was a real-life counterpart to the fictitious villain, or at least might have included the now-standard disclaimer to the effect that any resemblance to any person living or dead is purely coincidental.[58] Most victims of defamation cannot avoid being falsely defamed, so that casting liability on them would have no beneficial allocative consequences; in contrast, most false defamation can be avoided by reasonable inquiry on the part of the defamer. In these circumstances a rule of strict liability is attractive from an economic standpoint.

57. Jones v. E. Hutton & Co., [1909] 2 K.B. 444, aff'd, [1910] A.C. 20. Although the court treated the choice of the name as pure happenstance, in fact Jones had once been employed by the defendant's newspaper which defamed him.

58. In Washington Post Co. v. Kennedy, 3 F.2d 207 (D.C. Cir. 1925), where the report of a criminal charge against one man was taken to refer to another man having the same first and last names, the court pointed out that the newspaper easily (cheaply) could have avoided the confusion by using the middle initials of the man it was writing about.

Consistently with this distinction, the mere disseminator of a slander or libel—a newspaper distributor, for example—is liable for defamation only if he is negligent in failing to recognize the defamatory or untruthful character of the utterance. Since the costs to the mere disseminator of preventing defamation are often prohibitive, a rule of strict liability would be economically unjustifiable because often it would shift the losses from defamation to people who had no practical ability to prevent it.

Another notable exception to strict liability is the no-liability rule applicable to group defamations—"all lawyers are shysters," for example. Several considerations support this rule. First, the injury to an individual member of the group tends to be trivial. The difference in this respect between group and individual defamation is the difference between the demand facing an individual firm and the demand facing the industry of which it is a part. The substitutability of the products of other firms in an industry is likely to be so great as to make the demand for the individual firm's output almost perfectly elastic. But the industry demand may be highly inelastic, because products of other industries are not close substitutes. If people believe the libel "X is a shyster lawyer," they can and will substitute other lawyers, and X's business will drop sharply. But if they believe that *all* lawyers are shysters, there isn't much they can do about it—there are no close substitutes for lawyers. The loss of business to the profession, and hence to the individual lawyers if they are assumed to share proportionally in the profession's loss of business caused by the defamation, will be small.

A related point is that most group libels, if attributed to *all* members of the group, are inherently incredible and hence do little harm, and if attributed only to some or even to most members, do little harm to any individual. Few people would believe that all lawyers are shysters. But if for the sake of credibility the libel is restated in the form "most lawyers are shysters," then the harm to the individual lawyer must be discounted by the probability that a client or prospective client will view him as included in the shyster majority rather than the nonshyster minority. Finally, when group attributes or tendencies are at issue, the costs of determining the truth or falsity of an utterance are greater than when only a single individual's characteristics are at issue.

Another feature of the defamation tort—that there can be no actionable defamation of a dead person—may also seem to be based on the costs of determining whether the aspersion is true or false There is, however, another possible explanation for this rule. The economic function of reputation is to foster transactions, and once the transactor is dead, any subsequent injury to his reputation can have no market impact. Stated otherwise, personal reputation is a form of nontransferable human capital and hence is extinguished by death. But this point is overstated: being told that your father was a thief or a bankrupt may, if I believe in the heritability of criminal tendencies, affect my willingness to transact with you. The law provides a remedy for the most serious of these cases by allowing a descendant to maintain a defamation action where the deceased ancestor is alleged to have possessed some clearly inheritable defect or disorder.[59]

The best known, and a much criticized, distinction in the law of defamation is that between the standards for proving slander (oral defamation) and those for proving libel (written). Slander is actionable without proof of special damages (that is, without proof of actual pecuniary loss) only if the slanderer alleges conduct falling into one of the four *per se* categories: criminal acts, loathsome disease, female unchastity, and unfitness for one's profession or vocation. Outside of these categories, a slander to be actionable must be shown to have caused an actual monetary loss to the victim. Libel is not so confined. The victim need prove special damages only if his identity is not evident on the face of the libel; if extrinsic facts are necessary for the identification, then special damages must be proved unless the libel alleges conduct falling within one of the four categories defining slander *per se*.

The idea of a *per se* category is not in itself to be criticized. It is a familiar legal technique (widely used, for example, in antitrust law) that can be justified in many areas on the basis of the trade-

---

59. See "Developments in the Law—Defamation," 69 *Harv. L. Rev.* 875, 893–894 (1956).

off between the costs of error and the costs of reducing the probability of error by a more detailed examination of the facts in a particular case. The principal criticism of the *per se* categories in slander is that they have not kept pace with changing times. They made fairly good sense when first established.[60] For a woman to be thought unchaste in traditional societies drastically reduced her opportunities for marriage, a transaction of immense importance for women in such societies. To be thought to have leprosy, syphilis, or plague—the diseases classified as loathsome for purposes of the tort—would greatly reduce one's opportunities for interactions of all sorts, as would being thought a criminal. Finally, to be thought unfit for one's job would have a direct effect upon one's ability to participate in advantageous market activities.

The distinction between a libel that identifies the victim on its face and one where identification requires extrinsic facts makes only superficial economic sense, however. Having to know additional facts in order to link up the libel with the intended victim reduces the potential circle of those who will act on the libel to the victim's (and their own) disadvantage. But the people who know the relevant extrinsic facts are precisely those most likely to be acquainted with the victim, while those ignorant of these facts are likely to be people who have no acquaintance or potential acquaintance with the victim and hence are unlikely to act on the libel anyway. The extrinsic-fact rule smuggles a publicity requirement into defamation—where, as I have explained, it does not belong—by the back door.

These details to one side, the stricter treatment of written than of oral defamation makes economic sense for the following reasons.

1. Perhaps least persuasive today is the traditional ground that written defamations tend to reach larger audiences than spoken ones.[61] There have always been anomalous cases (the

60. On the historical origin of the categories, see Veeder, supra note 49, at 560 n.l.

61. To be sure, the larger audience may often be composed of strangers, so that the incremental harm may seem small. But by the same token, strangers will generally be less capable of detecting the falsity in the defamation than acquaintances, so the added harm may not be small, after all.

private letter versus the public address to a large audience), but it is the growth of radio and television that has sapped the traditional ground of much of its force.

2. Written defamation is more durable than spoken. Even if initially disseminated less widely, it remains in existence to be read later, so its total audience is likely to be larger.

3. As noted in the last chapter, it is costly to avoid occasional casual defamations in speech. To have to choose one's words very deliberately—to have to consider carefully the possible misconstructions that might be placed on what one says about another person—reduces the effectiveness of oral communication. A requirement of deliberateness imposes fewer costs on written communications, because writing is a more deliberate process than speaking anyway.[62]

4. A defamatory writing is more credible than a defamatory oral statement and hence more harmful to the individual who is defamed. Precisely because the costs of attaining accuracy are lower in written than in spoken communication, and the costs imposed by inaccuracy higher because of the greater durability and (probable) greater audience of the written word, the reader has a greater expectation of accuracy and will therefore tend to give greater weight to a libel than to a slander. If damages for defamation were readily computable, this difference would be reflected automatically in the damage awards in libel and slander cases; but since they are not, the lower standard for proof of defamation in libel cases may be sensible. To summarize, the costs to victims of written defamation are higher (points 1, 2, and 4), and the costs of avoiding written defamation are lower (point 3), than in the case of oral defamation.

The defense of truth requires mention, if only because of the frequent criticism that it is "unfair" for the law to treat truth as an absolute defense.[63] The harm to an individual from the revelation of a true but perhaps minor or long-forgotten blemish in

62. Donnelly, supra note 49, at 123–124, calls it "unctuous casuistry" that a defamatory radio broadcast is slander if the speaker is speaking extemporaneously but libel if he is reading from a manuscript. The consideration mentioned here suggests it is not.

63. See, e.g., "Developments in the Law—Defamation," supra note 59, at 932.

his character may, it is argued, outweigh any benefit from correcting the false impression on which his reputation rests. The law has proved stubbornly resistant to the suggested reform, and this is consistent with the analysis in the last chapter. The law provides no protection to people, any more than to sellers of goods, who misrepresent their qualities so that others will enter into advantageous personal or business relationships with them.

Other important defenses to defamation are grouped under the rubric of privilege. There are both "conditional" and "absolute" privileges in defamation law. A conditional privilege entitles the defendant to make a false and defamatory utterance so long as he is not motivated by "actual malice"; in practice this means so long as he honestly, though perhaps unreasonably, believes the utterance to be true. An absolute privilege is effective even if actual malice is shown. An example of conditional privilege is an employer's giving a character reference for a former employee; an example of absolute privilege is a critic's comment on a movie.[64]

The effect of privilege is to reduce the costs of making the statements to which the privilege attaches. Why might the law want to do that? One reason for allowing a person to externalize some of the costs of an activity is that the benefits of the activity are also externalized; if he is forced to bear the full social costs, he may not carry the activity to the socially optimal point. This technique is occasionally employed in the common law.[65] Because the benefit of a character reference inures primarily to the prospective employer rather than to the former employer, if the employer giving the reference were liable for defamation he probably either would not supply one or would omit from it

64. In New York Times Co. v. Sullivan, 376 U.S. 254 (1964), the Supreme Court held that the First Amendment creates a conditional privilege to defame public officials. This privilege, not a part of the common law, is examined briefly in the next chapter.

65. See Chapter 9; and William M. Landes & Richard A. Posner, "Salvors, Finders, Good Samaritans, and Other Rescuers: An Economic Study of Law and Altruism," 7 *J. Legal Stud.* 83, 128 (1978).

any negative references to the employee's character. In principle, the prospective employer could compensate the former
employer for the risk of liability in defamation, or the employee
could waive his right to sue for defamation, but either solution
would involve heavy transaction costs relative to the values involved, and as a practical matter would eliminate most character
references. The law's solution may be the efficient one.

Most conditional-privilege cases are of this general sort, but
not all are. In particular, the conditional privilege that credit
bureaus enjoy to commit the aptly named "slander of credit"[66] is
difficult to justify on economical grounds. There is no externalization of the benefits of a credit bureau's activities—it charges
its clients for its services. The conditional privilege of credit bureaus is a significant anomaly; it set the stage for an important
part of the privacy legislation discussed in the next part of this
chapter.

The critic's absolute privilege rests on a different ground, the
absence of misrepresentation. If I say, "Charlie Chaplin is a
crummy actor," or even, "Chaplin can't act," and this is my hon-
est belief, I am expressing a true if silly opinion rather than stating a false fact. Nor is my opinion any less genuine, or more
misleading, if it is the product of a malicious dislike of the actor.
Misrepresentation comes into play only if the critic makes a false
statement of fact, such as that some author is a plagiarist,[67] or if
he misrepresents his opinion.

To summarize, the basic doctrines of the defamation tort
seem generally consistent with the economics of the problem.
But perhaps because of its bifurcated historical origins (the tort
of slander developed in the medieval ecclesiastical courts, and
that of libel in criminal proceedings in Star Chamber against seditious writings), this field of the common law contains many
curious features,[68] and economics cannot explain every one of

66. See Prosser, supra note 41, at 790.

67. See Fitzgerald v. Hopkins, 70 Wash. 2d 924, 425 P.2d 920 (1967). The other absolute privileges at common law mainly involve governmental (including judicial) officials and are part of the larger tort immunity of governmental figures, a subject outside
the scope of this book.

68. Enumerated and pungently denounced in James C. Courtney, "Absurdities of
the Law of Slander and Libel," 36 *Am. L. Rev.* 552 (1902).

them. In law, as in consumer behavior and every other activity studied by economists, economics is more successful in explaining central tendencies than in accounting for individual decisions.

The Statutory Privacy Movement

Many state and federal statutes relating to privacy, particularly in the sense of secrecy, have been enacted in recent years. Chapter 9 had little to say about these statutes beyond observing that the general trend of legislative activity was to increase the privacy of individuals (meaning here the concealment of personal information) and decrease that of business firms and other organizations. The pattern is actually more complicated. The Freedom of Information Act, ostensibly designed to reduce governmental secrecy, compromises individual privacy as well. Much of the information held by the government and subject to disclosure under the act relates to individuals, and the duty of disclosure yields to the right of privacy only where disclosure would constitute a "clearly unwarranted" invasion of privacy.[69] Similarly, the Bank Secrecy Act, discussed in the next chapter, is only nominally aimed at bank secrecy; its real purpose and effect are to reduce the confidentiality of personal financial data of bank depositors.

I want to take a closer look at the recent statutes designed to protect the individual's privacy against nongovernmental entities (the case for privacy protection against the government is examined in the next chapter). Most of these are state statutes limiting the information that either an employer or a creditor can obtain from any source with regard to a prospective employee or borrower.[70] In the employment context, the emphasis is on limiting the employer's access to the employee's history of arrests and of remote or "irrelevant" convictions; in the credit context, on limiting the creditor's access to the prospective bor-

69. See Frank H. Easterbrook, "Privacy and the Optimal Extent of Disclosure under the Freedom of Information Act," 9 *J. Legal Stud.* 775 (1980).

70. The statutes are listed and discussed in *Report of the Privacy Protection Study Commission, App. I: Privacy Law in the States* (G.P.O. 1977).

rower's credit history. These statutes differ widely in their details, and many states have an employment statute but not a credit statute or vice versa. There is also a federal Fair Credit Reporting Act, which bars creditors from inquiring about or denying credit on the basis of bankruptcies that occurred more than fourteen years earlier, or any other adverse information relating to events (including arrests and convictions) that occurred more than seven years earlier. This is the most important federal statute directly regulating privacy in the private sector.[71]

There are several ways to explain statutes such as the above. One is to suppose that the statutes were enacted in response to some perceived "market failure," justifying public intervention. This approach does not get one very far in the privacy area. There is no reason to suppose that employers would demand from employees and job applicants more information than was justified by the benefits to the employer in screening out unsuitable employees. As noted in the last chapter, the common law courts (except in California) have rejected the idea that a person is entitled to conceal his criminal record, even if it relates to the distant past, because other people might react "irrationally" to its disclosure. Any such argument would be particularly weak in the context of employment, where competition exacts a heavy penalty from any firm that makes irrational employment decisions. Regarding the credit statutes, it is true, as remarked earlier, that the common law courts have unaccountably immunized credit bureaus from slander-of-credit actions. But the sensible way to solve this problem, as routinely done by state legislatures in other areas where the common law goes astray, would be simply to repeal the common law immunity.

If the privacy statutes cannot be explained by reference to a failure of the private market, can they perhaps be explained by reference to heightened public consciousness of the inequity of

---

71. The Buckley Amendment, regulating school records, applies to both public and private schools, so that its major impact falls on public institutions. Many federal statutes, for example those requiring extensive disclosures by corporations to their shareholders, affect privacy indirectly.

discrimination? As I shall show in Part IV, economists have argued that much racial and sexual discrimination may be the product simply of the costs of information, which may lead people to base judgments on very limited data, including the average characteristics of a person's racial group. Could the great national movement against discrimination have increased public sensitivity to other instances in which crude proxies are used to screen out applicants for job or credit? It is the same sort of injustice to deny a person a job because of a flat rule against employing anyone who has a criminal record, when careful investigation would have shown that this individual's criminal record ought not disqualify him from the job,[72] as it is to deny a black a job because of the average qualities of blacks in the relevant employment pool.

The difficulty with a "compassion" theory of the privacy laws is its far-reaching and unacceptable implications. Since the costs of information are always positive and often high, society could not function without heavy reliance on proxies in lieu of full investigation of all relevant facts. If we are sorry for the man whose fifteen-year-old bankruptcy judgment bars him from obtaining fresh credit, we should be equally sorry for the young man who is denied admission to the college of his choice because of his performance on a standardized test that may not accurately reflect his true academic potential.

Perhaps, instead, the privacy statutes are a response to the pressures of some interest group more compact than the public, or the altruistic public, at large. Much legislation has been shown to be of this type.[73] However, with privacy as with other broadly "consumerist" legislation, the benefited groups lack the characteristics of an effective political interest group. They con-

72. An alternative rationale for facilitating the concealment of a criminal record, based on the rehabilitation goal of criminal punishment, was discussed and rejected in the last chapter. See also Richard A. Epstein, "Privacy, Property Rights, and Misrepresentations," 12 *Ga. L. Rev.* 455, 471–474 (1978).

73. See, e.g., William A. Jordan, "Producer Protection, Prior Market Structure and the Effects of Government Regulation," 15 *J. Law & Econ.* 151 (1972); George J. Stigler, "The Theory of Economic Regulation," 2 *Bell J. Econ. & Management Sci.* (1978); and Chapter 4.

sist of people with criminal records and those with poor credit records. The former group is furtive, disreputable, and unorganized. The latter is, if more numerous, not compact in the ways identified by the interest-group theory as favorable to effective political action. And it is probably less numerous than the group of people who will have to pay higher interest rates to compensate lenders for the bad loans made because lenders are unable to obtain sufficient information about the borrowers' credit-worthiness: those who will pay are other marginal borrowers, as the most credit-worthy borrowers will tend to be selected into lower interest-rate categories.

A more plausible candidate for an effective interest group beneficiary of the privacy laws is the blacks, whose political effectiveness in recent years is apparent. Imagine the following sequence. Blacks are discriminated against in credit and employment because (for whatever reason) their performance in these areas is on average poorer than whites'. Some states and the federal government pass laws to prevent discrimination against blacks. Barred from using race as a proxy for employment suitability and credit-worthiness, employers and lenders cast about for other proxies and settle on arrest records, conviction records, bankruptcies, judgments, and the like. They do this not because they are trying to discriminate against blacks but because they want to screen out (or into lower wage or higher interest-rate categories) people who do not meet their qualifications at normal prices. If, however, race is a reasonably close proxy for the underlying characteristics in which the employer and creditor are interested and if the substitute proxies are also reasonably accurate, then the substitute proxies will have almost the same effect on the racial composition of employees and borrowers as explicit use of the racial proxy had. The ban on discrimination will have little impact.

In these circumstances the racial group may seek to bar the substitute proxies as well. It is true that barring arrest records from consideration in employment may result in a black who has no arrest record losing a job opportunity to a black who has one, and barring consideration of past bankruptcies may result in a black who has no record of bankruptcy paying a higher interest rate because creditors are unable to exclude blacks who do (assuming a past bankruptcy increases the probability of a future one—which it must if creditors inquire about past bankruptcies). However, since a disproportionate number of black credit applicants have poor credit records and a disproportionate number of black job applicants have arrest records, laws that wipe out these hurdles to obtaining credit and employment may benefit more blacks than they hurt.

A possible empirical test of this hypothesis is to compare states that have enacted civil rights laws with states that have enacted credit and/or employment privacy statutes. Landes's 1968 study of employment discrimination identified twenty-nine states as having laws (with 'at least some enforcement machinery) forbidding racial discrimination in employment, twenty-one of them before the enactment of the federal Civil Rights Act of 1964.[74] A 1977 study for the Privacy Commission identified eight states as having laws protecting the privacy of private-sector employees and job applicants.[75] Six of these states (75 percent) are among the twenty-nine states identified in Landes's study as having enacted antidiscrimination laws with "teeth," and five (63 percent) are among the twenty-one "early" antidiscrimination states. Thus a state that enacted a nondiscrimination statute was somewhat more likely to adopt an employee privacy statute than one that did not enact a nondiscrimination statute. If it were just as likely to adopt such a statute, the above figures would be 58 percent and 42 percent, respectively.

Regarding credit, the analysis is complicated by the fact that the federal government acted on both discrimination (in the Equal Credit Opportunity Act)[76] and privacy (in the Fair Credit

74. See William M. Landes, "The Economics of Fair Employment Laws," 76 *J. Pol. Econ.* 507, 507 n.1 (1968).
75. See *Privacy Law in the States,* supra note 70, at 17–19.
76. 15 U.S.C. § 1691 (1976).

Reporting Act)[77] before the states did. However, if we continue to use Landes's list as indicative of states having a strong civil rights movement even if they did not legislate specifically with reference to credit, then it is suggestive that of the eleven states[78] that have enacted credit privacy restrictions more stringent than the federal Fair Credit Reporting Act (which was not preemptive in this regard), nine (82 percent) are on Landes's list and six (55 percent) are among the twenty-one early enacting states on that list.

I performed another empirical test using a slightly different body of data, a very recent and thorough compilation by Robert Smith of state and federal privacy statutes. He divides privacy statutes into fifteen categories, of which three categories seem by the earlier analysis clearly related to the interests of blacks —privacy of arrest records, credit information, and employment records—and notes which state (or the District of Columbia or the federal government) has enacted a law in each category.[79] Again using Landes's data and dividing states, including the District of Columbia, into those that enacted fair employment practices laws before 1964, those that enacted them afterward, and those that did not enact them within the period covered by Landes's study, one finds that the average number of categories (in the group of three) in which a state has passed a privacy law is 1.1 for the early-enacting states, 1.0 for the late-enacting states, and .78 for the nonenacting states.

The foregoing results are equally consistent with either the interest-group hypothesis or the hypothesis that both antidiscrimination and privacy statutes are motivated by compassion —but compassion for blacks rather than for poor credit risks

---

77. 15 U.S.C. § 1681 (1976). The legislative history of this important privacy statute indicates a concern that unregulated disclosure of adverse information to creditors could have a disproportionately adverse effect on blacks. See *Fair Credit Reporting,* Hearings on S. 823 before the Subcomm. on Financial Institutions of the Senate Comm. on Banking and Currency, 91st Cong. 1st Sess. 129–132 (May 19–23, 1969).

78. See *Privacy Law of the States,* supra note 70, at n.47.

79. See Robert Ellis Smith, *Compilation of State and Federal Privacy Laws 1978–1979* 2 (1978).

and ex-convicts, as such. A way to distinguish between these alternative hypotheses is to examine the correlation between the presence of a privacy statute and the number of blacks and Hispanics, the two major minority groups that are probably most benefited by the privacy statutes in question. If the correlation is positive, that is evidence for an interest-group explanation; if negative, for a compassion explanation (because the cost of compassion is lower, the smaller the benefited group). If there is no correlation, that is evidence against either interpretation.[80]

By use of multiple-regression analysis, it is possible to embed this correlation in a richer model of the demand for and supply of privacy statutes than one which views them as a function solely of the percentage of blacks and Hispanics in the enacting state. This is done in Table 3. The dependent variable in the regressions reported there takes a value of 0 if the state has no privacy statute in any of the three relevant categories (arrest, credit, and employment), 1 if it has a statute in one of the categories, and so on up to 3. Since most of the statutes were enacted in the early 1970s, I use data from as near to 1970 as possible.

A key independent variable for testing the interest-group theory of these statutes is, of course, the percentage black or Hispanic (in the table, MINO). This variable, however, identifies only the benefits of the statute to the group procuring it and not the costs to other people in the state (who are voters too). The more often people change their residence, the harder it is to obtain information about them that will be useful in deciding whether or not to transact with them, so I have added a variable which measures the amount of migration into the state in recent years (MIG). Its sign is expected to be negative, because the more migration there is, other things being equal, the less likely

80. A complication in the analysis is that the larger the nonwhite population in a state, the more the costs of a privacy statute, in higher crime and interest rates, will be borne by the nonwhites themselves rather than shifted to the whites, and hence the fewer the gains to the nonwhite community as a whole. Perhaps, therefore, states with very large nonwhite populations should be evaluated separately, but I obtained no useful results from this approach.

Table 3. State privacy statute regressions. (Dependent variable equals number of relevant categories in which state has enacted privacy statute.)

Regression	Constant	TAX[a]	PROG	RATIO1	RATIO2	TRAN	LTRAN	INC	LINC	MINO	MIG	R^2
1.	-1.013 (-.940)[b]	-.0002 (-.178)						.0003 (1.323)		.0240 (2.073)	-.019 (-.864)	.12
2	-1.428 (-1.214)	-.0007 (-.594)	.030 (.889)					.0004 (1.550)		.026 (2.210)	-.015 (-.627)	.14
3.	.060 (.051)		.043 (1.322)	-8.292 (-1.554)				.0003 (1.854)		.026 (2.199)	-.003 (-.105)	.18
4.	-1.033 (-1.010)		.020 (.567)		.327 (.034)			.0003 (1.601)		.026 (2.201)	-.020 (-.913)	.13
5.	-4.731 (-2.677)					.023 (2.491)		.0005 (2.992)		.025 (2.284)	-.015 (-.717)	.23
6.	-44.414 (-3.626)						2.539 (2.936)		3.797 (3.477)	.026 (2.450)	-.005 (-.236)	.28

a. Definitions of independent variables:

TAX = state taxes per capita 1976 (*Statistical Abstract of the United States*, 1978)

PROG = maximum state income tax rate minus minimum state income tax rate (same source)

RATIO1 = ratio of per capita state and local expenditures excluding highway expenditures to state per capita income (1972 and 1978 *Statistical Abstract*)

RATIO2 = TAX/INC

TRAN = ratio of total transfer payments to INC, 1976 (1978 *Statistical Abstract*)

LTRAN = natural logarithm of TRAN

INC = state per capita income 1976 (from 1978 *Statistical Abstract*)

LINC = natural logarithm of INC

MINO = percentage black and Spanish heritage in state (from 1970 *Census of Population*)

MIG = percentage of new residents since 1965 (*Census Subject Reports—Mobility for States and Nations*, 1970)

b. t-statistics in parentheses: a t-statistic having an absolute value greater than 2 is statistically significant at the 5 percent level.

a state is to enact a privacy statute. Following Stigler, I include a variable measuring per capita income in the state (INC), which he uses in his test of the altruism or compassion theory of statutes like these privacy statutes.[81] Finally, since a state's resistance to redistributive legislation may be a (negative) function of the amount of redistribution it already engages in, I include several variables that measure the other redistributive activities of the state, such as the per capita tax burden (TAX) and the progressivity of the state income tax (PROG).

The variable measuring minority population is positive and significant in all of the regressions. Income is positive in all of the regressions, too, as predicted by the compassion theory, but significant in only two out of six. The variables measuring the amount of redistributive activity in the state are mostly insignificant, and in one instance have the wrong sign. My measure of the cost of a privacy statute, the amount of recent migration into the state, has the right sign (negative) but is never significant.

These results taken as a whole provide but limited support for the interest-group theory—and none to speak of for the compassionate or altruistic—and other regressions, not reported in Table 3, undermine even these meager results. For example, when I added urbanization and crime as additional measures of the cost of enacting a privacy statute (the former as a proxy for the amount of privacy people have, the latter as a measure of the costs of depriving people of the self-protection afforded by being able to find out about an individual's arrest record and other background characteristics), not only do these variables have the wrong sign (positive), but the minority variable ceases to be significant. A difficulty is that urbanization and crime are positively correlated with percentage black or Hispanic, so it is possible that some of the effect of the minority variable is being picked up in the other two variables.

These results suggest still another theory of state privacy stat-

---

81. See George J. Stigler, "An Introduction to the Economics and Politics of Privacy," 9 *J. Legal Stud.* 623 (1980).

Table 4. State privacy statutes and crime. (Dependent variable equals 1 if state has arrest-record privacy statute, 0 if it does not)

Regression	Constant	TAX[a]	PROG	RATIO1	RATIO2	TRAN	LTRAN	INC	LINC	MINO	MIG	CRIM	R²
1.	-.073 (-.119)[b]	-.0002 (-.298)						-.0000006 (-.004)		-.002 (-.354)	-.014 (-1.200)	.382 (3.928)	.36
2.	-.255 (-.383)	-.0004 (-.607)	.012 (.702)					.00003 (.235)		-.001 (-.192)	-.012 (-1.028)	.377 (3.859)	.37
3.	.110 (.172)	.010 (.570)		-1.016 (-.354)				-.00003 (-.324)		-.002 (-.235)	-.013 (-.997)	.384 (3.943)	.36
4.	.078 (.138)	.012 (.665)			-2.584 (-.523)			-.00001 (-.140)		-.002 (-.260)	-.013 (-1.164)	.386 (3.996)	.36
5.	-1.00 (-.895)					.006 (1.031)		.00005 (.389)		-.001 (-.122)	-.013 (-1.197)	.346 (3.369)	.37
6.	-7.00 (-.686)						.608 (1.509)		.464 (.492)	-.00005 (-.007)	-.011 (-.972)	.325 (3.278)	.37

a. Definitions of independent variables: see footnote a to Table 3; CRIM = State per capita crime rate, FBI index crimes (from *FBI Uniform Crime Reports*, 1970).

b. t-statistics in parentheses: a t-statistic having an absolute value greater than 2 is statistically significant at the 5 percent level

utes—they tend to be enacted in states that are relatively indifferent to the costs of crime, as evidenced by high crime rates which presumably reflect, in part anyway, the operation of the state's criminal justice system. Table 4 explores this hypothesis by rerunning the six regressions in Table 3, adding the state crime rate as an additional independent variable, and changing the dependent variable to whether or not the state has a statute protecting the confidentiality of arrest records (the privacy category most clearly related to criminal activity). In all of these regressions, the crime variable has a positive and strongly significant effect on the dependent variable. These results lend some support to the "soft on crime" theory of privacy statutes.[82] I conclude, however, that the privacy legislation movement remains a puzzle from the economic standpoint.

---

82. There are technical objections to using ordinary-least-squares regression analysis when the dependent variable is dichotomous. However, the regressions in Table 4 were rerun using logit analysis, which is designed for cases where the dependent variable is dichotomous, with no change in the results.

11

The Privacy Jurisprudence
of the Supreme Court

Although the Constitution contains no reference to privacy, notions of privacy have long played an important role in constitutional adjudication as values either protected by specific constitutional provisions, such as the Fourth Amendment, which forbids unreasonable searches and seizures by federal officers, or that must be weighed in the interpretation of other provisions which protect competing values, such as the First Amendment, whose guaranty of freedom of speech might collide with a householder's wish to be free from noisy sound trucks and pesky door-to-door solicitors. And in 1965 the Supreme Court declared a constitutional right of privacy not anchored in any specific provision of the Constitution.

It is hard to quarrel with the proposition that the right of privacy should protect people from invasions by the government as well as from invasions by private individuals and firms. The scope of the right of privacy is a matter of fair debate, and the last two chapters advocated a less generous conception of that scope than is currently fashionable. But with regard to at least one form of privacy—that of secrecy—the economic case for a right against government is stronger than the case against private parties. If creditors, employers, and other private parties who seek information about potential transacting partners to protect themselves against misrepresentation demand more information than necessary for their self-protection, they will pay a price and incur a competitive disadvantage. For example, an employer will have to pay a higher salary to an employee who is required to take periodic lie-detector tests than to one who is

310

not. If the additional information obtained by the tests is not worth the extra salary, the employer is incurring an expense not justified by offsetting benefits, and he will be hurt in competing with firms that do not require such tests. The government is not subject to this market discipline, because in most of its activities it does not face any competition; this is especially true of the federal government. In these circumstances, as Paul Rubin has argued, there is no presumption that the government will strike an appropriate balance between disclosure and confidentiality.[1]

The extent to which the justices of the Supreme Court have perceived and acted on the implications of this analysis is a separate question. We shall see that the Court's protection of privacy has been at best erratic, at worst perverse.

Privacy Cases before *Griswold*

Long before the tort right of privacy came before the Supreme Court, and even before Warren and Brandeis wrote their famous article on privacy, the Court was confronted with claims to the protection of privacy under the Fourth and Fifth Amendments. In most such cases, the explicit constitutional language—search and seizure, probable cause, self-incrimination —could be interpreted without reference to any underlying privacy objectives of the amendments. *Olmstead v. United States*[2] was an important exception. The question in that case was whether wiretapping by federal officers was subject to the Fourth Amendment, and the answer logically depended on the precise privacy interest that is protected by the Fourth Amendment. If it is just the seclusion interest,[3] then wiretapping should not be deemed subject to the amendment; it involves no substantive invasion of physical privacy and often, as in *Olmstead* itself, not even a technical invasion—a trespass. But if a broader concept

1. See Paul H. Rubin, "Government and Privacy: A Comment on 'The Right of Privacy,'" 12 *Ga. L. Rev.* 505 (1978).
2. 277 U.S. 438 (1928).
3. Privacy in the sense of seclusion, or peace and quiet, was discussed in Chapter 10.

of privacy is implicit in the Fourth Amendment, wiretapping might be within its scope.

The Court held that wiretapping was not subject to the Fourth Amendment, in part because there was no trespass on the defendant's premises. The emphasis on trespass was mistaken. If the Fourth Amendment protects only seclusion, an unperceived trespass that does not disturb that interest does not violate the amendment, while if the privacy interests protected by the amendment are broader, it is immaterial that there is no trespass and no invasion of seclusion. The question to be decided in *Olmstead* was precisely what privacy interest the Fourth Amendment was intended to protect, and the Court did not address that question.

If seclusion is not the only interest protected by the Fourth Amendment, the case for bringing wiretapping within its reach is strong even if one lacks enthusiasm for secrecy. As argued in Chapter 9, wiretapping, at least when it is known to be employed on a wide scale, probably is less effective in obtaining information and thus compromising secrecy—which would often be a good thing—than in inhibiting conversation and thus making communication more costly than it would otherwise be. Even this result may be tolerable and conceivably desirable where society wants to discourage communication, as it may when the communication is in furtherance of illegal activity. But law-enforcement officers cannot be trusted to confine their wiretapping to those communications, if only because they do not bear the costs (in less effective communication) imposed on innocent people whose phones are tapped. There should be an external control, whether in the form of a tort remedy, a warrant, or a reasonableness requirement, over the discretion of the executive branch of government to tap phones.

The usual view of *Olmstead* is that it was incorrectly decided because the only difference between conventional police searches and wiretapping is a technological difference that the framers of the Constitution could not have foreseen. I disagree. The difference between the conventional search and wiretapping is the difference between seclusion and secrecy. Conceivably the framers may have been concerned with protecting people's peace and quiet rather than with protecting the secrecy of their conversations.[4] If so, a technological advance that enabled the police to search a man's house with a microwave beam that emitted a loud noise would be subject to the Fourth Amendment, even though the framers had not foreseen this method of search, while wiretapping or "bugging" would not be subject to the amendment at all.

The interest in peace and quiet has long been a factor in objectionable police searches.[5] The importance attached in the early search and seizure cases to the defendant's ownership of the property seized[6] is further evidence that the purpose of the Fourth Amendment is to protect peace and quiet from the disruptive consequences of police searches; the seizure of one's own property is more likely to disturb one's peace and quiet than the seizure of someone else's property. *Hester v. United States,*[7] which held that the Fourth Amendment was not violated

---

4. To be sure, the amendment protects "papers" and "effects" as well as "persons" and "houses," but one cannot engage in ordinary activities uninterrupted while the police are rifling one's papers and effects in the course of a search.

5. See the catalog in United States v. United States District Court, 407 U.S. 297, 326–327 (1972), concurring opinion, of the "gross invasions of privacy" (in the sense of seclusion) resulting from unlawful police searches: "This Court has been the unfortunate witness to the hazards of police intrusions which did not receive prior sanction by independent magistrates. For example, in Weeks v. United States, 232 U.S. 383; Mapp v. Ohio, 367 U.S. 643; and Chimel v. California, 395 U.S. 752, entire homes were ransacked pursuant to warrantless searches. Indeed, In Kremen v. United States, 353 U.S. 346, the *entire contents* of a cabin, totaling more than 800 items (such as '1 Dish Rag') were seized incident to an arrest of its occupant and were taken to San Francisco for study by FBI agents. In a similar case, Von Cleef v. New Jersey, 395 U.S. 814, police, without a warrant, searched an arrestee's house for three hours, eventually seizing 'several thousand articles, including books, magazines, catalogues, mailing lists, private correspondence (both open and unopened), photographs, drawings, and film.' *Id.,* at 815. In Silverthorne Lumber Co. v. United States, 251 U.S. 385, federal agents 'without a shadow of authority' raided the offices of one of petitioners (the proprietors of which had earlier been jailed) and 'made a clean sweep of all the books, papers and documents found there.' Justice Holmes, for the Court, termed this tactic an 'outrage.' *Id.,* at 390–91. In Stanford v. Texas, 379 U.S. 476, state police seized more than 2,000 items of literature, including the writings of Mr. Justice Black, pursuant to a general search warrant issued to inspect an alleged subversive's home."

6. For a review of these cases, see Warden v. Hayden, 387 U.S 294, 303–304 (1967).

7. 265 U.S. 57 (1924).

when officers secretly spied on the defendant, even if they were trespassing on his property, is also consistent with this view.[8] Thus it is possible to explain the result in *Olmstead* on the theory that the only privacy interest protected by the Fourth Amendment is the interest in not having one's solitude broken in on by the police—an interpretation that, whatever its ultimate merits, at least is intelligible and has nothing to do with technological change.

Justice Brandeis, in his dissenting opinion in *Olmstead,* recognized, as the majority did not, that the case properly turned on the nature of the privacy interest protected by the Fourth Amendment. In the central passage of the opinion he explains the concept of privacy he thinks the framers adopted:[9]

> The makers of our Constitution undertook to secure conditions favorable to the pursuit of happiness. They recognized the significance of man's spiritual nature, of his feelings and of his intellect. They knew that only a part of the pain, pleasure and satisfactions of life are to be found in material things. They sought to protect Americans in their beliefs, their thoughts, their emotions and their sensations. They conferred, as against the government, the right to be let alone—the most comprehensive of rights and the right most valued by civilized men. To protect that right, every

8. *Hester* is of additional interest in relation to what might be called the property theory of the Fourth Amendment, e.g., the theory visible in Justice Black's dissent in the *Katz* case, see text infra at notes 25–26, that there must be a trespass to person or property for the Fourth Amendment to be violated. As *Hester* illustrates, the invasion of a property interest is not a sufficient condition to find an invasion of privacy. Is it a necessary condition? An affirmative answer would make sense only if there were no difference between acts of the government and those of private individuals or firms. In that event the same standard should apply, and would apply if the Fourth Amendment were interpreted as requiring a violation of state property or tort law. But the justification and consequences of invasions of privacy by government and by private persons are different and argue for greater restrictions on the former than the latter, and thus for cutting the Fourth Amendment loose from the moorings of state property and tort law. There is nothing in the language or history of the Fourth Amendment to prevent this result.

9. 277 U.S. at 478–479.

unjustifiable intrusion by the Government upon the privacy of the individual, whatever the means employed, must be deemed a violation of the Fourth Amendment. And the use, as evidence in a criminal proceeding, of facts ascertained by such intrusion must be deemed a violation of the Fifth.

But it does not follow that, because the framers wanted to create conditions favorable to certain ideals of human life, they created a "right to be let alone"[10] by government. There is no suggestion of such a right in the Constitution. There are just particular rights to be free from specific forms of invasion of privacy. Moreover, unless privacy is a synonym for freedom—and there is no evidence that Brandeis held such a view—a right to be let alone would protect much more than privacy.[11] For example, conscription would infringe the right to be let alone, though it might be saved from invalidation by the reference to justification in the next sentence of Brandeis's opinion.[12]

The passage quoted above proved to be a harbinger of two important tendencies in contemporary Supreme Court privacy decisions. One tendency is to declare a constitutional right of privacy that has no source in the constitutional text. The other is to broaden the right of privacy beyond seclusion and secrecy, making it a general right (though selectively, nonneutrally applied) to be free from governmental interference. It is surprising that Brandeis was their progenitor. The analytic method in the quoted passage is precisely what he deplored when used by the justices who believed that the due process clause of the Fourteenth Amendment was a charter for the protection of a laissez-faire economy against state legislatures. Those justices

10. The phrase apparently made its debut in the legal literature in Thomas M. Cooley, *A Treatise on the Law of Torts: Or the Wrongs Which Arise Independent of Contract* 29 (2nd ed. 1888), where it was used in reference solely to the torts of assault and battery.

11. See Philip B. Kurland, *The Private I: Some Reflections on Privacy and the Constitution* 14 (1976), The Nora and Edward Ryerson Lecture, University of Chicago, published by The Center for Policy Studies.

12. My objection to the quoted passage is not that Brandeis believed in an unlimited right to be let alone, but that even a limited such right has no constitutional provenance.

had no basis in the text or history of the Fourteenth Amendment for enacting their policy preferences into constitutional law, and neither did Justice Brandeis.

Besides invoking the "right to be let alone," Brandeis's dissent in *Olmstead* relied heavily on *Boyd v. United States.*[13] The Court in that case had held unconstitutional under the Fourth and Fifth Amendments a federal customs statute which provided that if a person refused to produce a document sought by federal authorities he would be deemed, in any penalty suit brought against him under the revenue laws, to admit the truth of any allegations concerning the contents of the document. Brandeis read the following language in *Boyd* as support for the position that wiretapping violates the Fourth Amendment:[14]

> It is not the breaking of his doors, and the rummaging of his drawers, that constitutes the essence of the offense; but it is the invasion of his indefeasible right of personal security, personal liberty and private property . . . which underlies and constitutes the essence of Lord Camden's judgment [in *Entick v. Carrington*]. Breaking into a house and opening boxes and drawers are circumstances of aggravation; but any forcible and compulsory extortion of a man's own testimony or of his private papers to be used as evidence to convict him of crime or to forfeit his goods, is within the condemnation of that judgment. In this regard the Fourth and Fifth Amendments run almost into each other.

This language is pertinent, though somewhat obscurely, to the question whether the Fourth Amendment protects just the interest in seclusion, or whether it goes further and also protects the interest in secrecy or concealment. Lord Camden's opinion in *Entick v. Carrington,*[15] from which the Court in *Boyd* quoted at

---

13. 116 U.S. 616 (1886).
14. 116 U.S. at 630, quoted at 277 U.S. at 474–475
15. 19 Howell's St. Tr. 1029 (1765).

length, treated the violation of the confidentiality of any papers seized in an unlawful search as a circumstance aggravating the basic unlawfulness, which in his view consisted of the unauthorized seizure of property. The intrusion was primary, the compromise of secrecy secondary. *Boyd* appears to reverse the sequence, but the appearance is misleading. For while the breaking in and rummaging are described as secondary, what is primary is the right of "personal security, personal liberty and private property"; and the last surely, the first probably, and the second possibly also relate to the interest in seclusion. Moreover, *Boyd* involved the same kind of aggravating circumstances (though attenuated) as in the traditional police search, for the statute in *Boyd* forced people to spend time sifting through their papers to comply with the production order.

To be sure, one cannot read the above passage from *Boyd* and think that all the Court was concerned about was the inconvenience of having to produce a document. It was also concerned with the analogy between being forced to incriminate oneself by one's testimony and being forced to do so by one's documents. If the Court in *Boyd* was correct that the Fifth Amendment shields a man's documents from use in evidence, why not his phone conversations as well? They are not testimony, but neither was the invoice involved in *Boyd*.

The Fifth Amendment aspect of *Boyd* is no longer good law.[16] But a more important point concerning the bearing of that case on the right of privacy is that the Fifth Amendment seems only tangentially related to the protection of privacy.[17] Not only does the amendment allow a person to be interrogated concerning matters, however private, that do not place him in jeopardy of a criminal prosecution (and thus it does not protect at all the privacy of the innocent); but he can be forced to testify even as to incriminating matters so long as he is granted immunity from

16. See Fisher v. United States, 425 U.S. 391, 408 (1976). See also Andresen v. Maryland, 427 U.S. 463 (1976).

17. See Bernard D. Meltzer, "Privileges against Self-Incrimination and the Hit-and-Run Opinions," 1971 *Supreme Court Review* 1, 21. But see Robert S. Gerstein, "Privacy and Self-Incrimination," 80 *Ethics* 87 (1970), for a contrary view.

prosecution. Thus, even if wiretapping offends privacy, that is not in itself a compelling reason for invoking the Fifth Amendment. Nor does the Court's expansive interpretation of the Fifth Amendment in *Boyd* necessarily support an expansive concept of privacy.

In suggesting that *Olmstead* could rationally have been supported by reference to the difference between privacy as seclusion and privacy as secrecy and that the Brandeis dissent fails to make a persuasive case that the latter is also a protected interest, I do not mean to suggest that *Olmstead* was in fact decided correctly. Colonial Americans were concerned not only with intrusions on their tranquillity and repose but also with the seizure of private information in circumstances where there were few or no elements of interference with peace and quiet—notably the unauthorized opening of mail.[18] Although opening a letter may delay its arrival or increase the chances that it will be lost, these are minor consequences compared with the effect in compromising the confidentiality of the communication—or, in police searches of the home, the interference with peace and quiet. The background of the Fourth Amendment also includes the writs of assistance, which were used primarily to enforce mercantile statutes through searches of warehouses and other commercial buildings.[19] The principal objection to the writs of assistance was probably their effectiveness in ferreting out violations of the unpopular British mercantile statutes rather than the incidental disruptions of business caused by the searches.[20]

18. See David H. Flaherty, *Privacy in Colonial New England* (1972). An early case, Ex parte Jackson, 96 U.S. 727, 733 (1877), mentioned in passing in Brandeis's dissent, had suggested that it would violate the Fourth Amendment for the Post Office to spy on the mails.

19. See, e.g., Jacob W. Landynski, *Search and Seizure and the Supreme Court: A Study in Constitutional Interpretation* 30–38 (1966).

20. Yet it is significant to my basic argument—that the seclusion aspect of privacy has been neglected in discussions of the Fourth Amendment—that the colonists themselves focused on the disruptive effects of the writs of assistance, as in Samuel Adams's *The Rights of the Colonists and A List of Infringements and Violations of Rights, 1772:* "Thus our houses and even our bed chambers, are exposed to be ransacked, our boxes chests and trunks broke open ravaged and plundered by wretches, whom no prudent man

Let us jump ahead to see how *Olmstead* has fared in the modern era. Consistently with the implicit distinction in *Olmstead* between protection of physical privacy and protection of secrecy, the Court in *Goldman v. United States*[21] held that electronic eavesdropping (in the form of "bugging" rather than wiretapping) was not subject to the Fourth Amendment. But in *Silverman v. United States*,[22] the Court reached a contrary conclusion. The bug in *Silverman* was implanted in the wall of the defendant's premises, and the Court distinguished the *Goldman* case, where

---

would venture to employ even as menial servants; whenever they are pleased to say they suspect there are in the house wares & c for which the duties have not been paid. Flagrant instances of the wanton exercise of this power, have frequently happened in this and other sea port Towns. By this we are cut off from that domestick security which renders the lives of the most unhappy in some measure agreeable. Those Officers may under colour of law and the cloak of a general warrant, break thro' the sacred rights of the Domicil, ransack mens houses, destroy their securities, carry off their property, and with little danger to themselves commit the most horred murders." 1 Bernard Schwartz, *The Bill of Rights: A Documentary History* 200, 206 (1971).

It is possible to argue that the privacy interests protected by the Fourth Amendment cannot be very substantial since, in all of the cases I have discussed, the privacy protected is that of wrongdoers. To this argument I would reply that the impression that the Fourth Amendment protects criminals rather than law-abiding individuals is the result of the peculiar remedial scheme for enforcing the amendment. Fourth Amendment claims are rarely advanced except by convicted criminals seeking to have their convictions overturned on the ground that evidence used at trial has been obtained in violation of the amendment. Damage remedies for a violation exist but are rarely invoked. See Bivens v. Six Unknown Fed. Agents of the Bureau of Narcotics, 403 U.S. 388 (1971). Yet a useful way to understand the fundamental purposes of the amendment is to imagine its being enforced exclusively through damage actions. Then police would be deterred from illegal searches by having to make the victim of such a search whole for any injury that the search caused to peace or quiet or to other interests protected by the Fourth Amendment. Whether the victim was later convicted of a crime based on evidence obtained in the search would be a detail. The damage remedy, to the extent that the court was able to assess accurately the damages caused by an illegal search, would protect the privacy of criminals and the law-abiding alike. This would be true whether or not illegally seized evidence was used to convict a person. He would still be entitled to damages measured by the injury to any lawful privacy interest. By "lawful," I mean to distinguish, for example, between the disturbance of the criminal's peace and quiet by an unlawful search and the punishment inflicted on him as a result of illegal activity discovered by the search and later used against him in a criminal proceeding. The punishment would not impair any lawful interest of his.

21. 316 U.S. 129 (1942).
22. 365 U.S. 505 (1961).

the bug had been placed on the outside of the wall of the defendant's premises, as involving no physical penetration. Finally, in *Katz v. United States*,[23] a case that involved tapping a phone in a public telephone booth, the Court, on the authority of *Silverman* and other intervening decisions, overruled *Goldman* and *Olmstead*.

Justice Black, dissenting in *Katz*, was indignant that the majority had relied on *Silverman*, which unlike *Katz* (and *Goldman* and *Olmstead*) had involved a physical penetration of the defendant's premises and hence a trespass. But trespass is irrelevant. The trespass in *Silverman* involved no actual disturbance of the tranquillity of the defendant's premises. As in *Hester v. United States*,[24] where the Court had declined to subject unobtrusive surveillance to the Fourth Amendment even when there was a trespass, the "spike mike" in *Silverman* was unobtrusive and so did not disturb the defendant's physical privacy. If the true basis for *Olmstead* is that the Fourth Amendment protects only the seclusion aspect of privacy, then *Silverman* was indeed inconsistent with *Olmstead* because the Court in *Silverman* used the Fourth Amendment to protect secrecy rather than seclusion.

The Court in *Katz* overlooked the distinction between seclusion and secrecy, treating the meaning of privacy as too obvious to merit extended discussion. Justice Black objected:[25]

By clever word juggling the Court finds it plausible to argue that language aimed specifically at searches and seizures of things that can be searched and seized may, to protect privacy, be applied to eavesdropped evidence of conversations that can neither be searched nor seized. Few things happen to an individual that do not affect his privacy in one way or another. Thus, by arbitrarily substituting the Court's language, designed to protect privacy, for

23. 389 U.S. 347 (1967).
24. See note 7 supra.
25. 389 U.S. at 373.

the Constitution's language, designed to protect against unreasonable searches and seizures, the Court has made the Fourth Amendment its vehicle for holding all laws violative of the Constitution which offend the Court's broadest conception of privacy.

Except for the suggestion, which is not compelled by the language or history of the Fourth Amendment, that only seizures of tangibles are within its scope,[26] it is hard to quarrel with Justice Black. The majority did not attempt to define privacy and was apparently unaware that the result in *Olmstead* could be supported by reference to any principle other than the absence of a trespass.

Justice Black bolstered his asserted distinction between eavesdropping and searches and seizures by noting that eavesdropping had existed at the time the Bill of Rights was adopted— Blackstone's *Commentaries* had mentioned that eavesdropping was a misdemeanor at common law[27]—yet the framers had not sought to prohibit it, either in the Fourth Amendment or anywhere else in the Constitution. This point may not seem decisive, given the difference in effectiveness between personal and electronic eavesdropping and the fact that Blackstone's reference was to eavesdropping by "common scolds" rather than by law enforcers, until one reflects on the importance and effectiveness of one form of personal eavesdropping—the planting of undercover agents in a criminal gang or subversive group. Their use in law enforcement antedates the Bill of Rights by centuries, if not millennia,[28] and their purpose is to eavesdrop.

26. The right declared in the Fourth Amendment "of the people to be secure in their persons" is broadly enough stated to include a right to be free from unreasonable electronic surveillance.

27. See 4 William Blackstone, *Commentaries on the Laws of England* 169 (1769).

28. On the use, by the police of the Roman Empire, of servants to eavesdrop on their masters, see Alan F. Westin, *Privacy in Western Society: From the Age of Pericles to the American Republic* 52–53 (Rep. to Assn. of Bar of City of N.Y. Spec. Comm. on Sci. and Law, Feb. 15, 1965).

The Supreme Court has refused to hold that the use of un-dercover agents to gather leads and evidence of crime is subject to the Fourth Amendment.[29] It has based its refusal on the fic-tion of consent and has adhered to its view even when, as in *Osborn v. United States*,[30] the undercover agent carries a concealed microphone and records the interview with the suspect. The Court's approach was defensible in the *Olmstead* era when, except for the mails, arguably the only privacy right protected by the Fourth Amendment was the right not to be interrupted by police barging in to rifle one's desk or otherwise mess up one's house. But once the Fourth Amendment was held to protect privacy in the sense of secrecy, the step taken in *Silverman* and then in *Katz*, there was no longer a persuasive ground for treat-ing undercover agents as beyond the reach of the Fourth Amendment.[31] The undercover agent clearly invades the pri-vacy-as-secrecy of the people he spies on. It is absurd to say that they "consent" to this invasion of privacy in any sense which the law would elsewhere respect; consent is vitiated by fraud. And it is circular to say that there is no invasion of privacy unless the individual whose privacy is invaded had a reasonable expecta-tion of privacy; whether or not he has such an expectation de-pends on what the legal rule is.[32]

29. See, e.g., Hoffa v. United States, 385 U.S. 293 (1966). For criticism of the Court's approach, see Geoffrey R. Stone, "The Scope of the Fourth Amendment: Privacy and the Police Use of Spies, Secret Agents and Informers," 1976 *Am. B. Found. Res. J.* 1195.

30. 385 U.S. 323 (1966).

31. *Hoffa* and *Osborn* were decided after *Silverman* but before *Katz*, but the Court, in United States v. White, 401 U.S. 745 (1971), expressly declined to overrule the under-cover-agent cases because of *Katz*.

32. See Anthony G. Amsterdam, "Perspectives on the Fourth Amendment," 58 *Minn. L. Rev.* 349, 384 (1974). The problem of circularity was recognized by Justice Rehnquist in his opinion for the Court in Rakas v. Illinois, 439 U.S. 128 (1978), where he stated that the expectation of privacy must be founded on property or other notions outside the Fourth Amendment doctrines themselves. *Id.* at 431 n.12. This is a dam-aging admission so far as the Court's refusal to subject police spies to the Fourth Amendment is concerned. Has not an American citizen a reasonable expectation, based on the customs and mores of a free society, that people who.represent themselves to him as being trustworthy friends are not secret policemen or informers?

The *Griswold* Decision

Katz illustrates the uncritical, but not necessarily incorrrect, expansion in the concept of privacy from the sense of physical privacy or seclusion to the sense of secrecy; similarly, *Griswold v. Connecticut*[33] illustrates a further important expansion in the concept together with a shift in its constitutional foundations. The case involved the prosecution, as accessories in the violation of a state criminal statute prohibiting the use of contraceptives even by married people, of two members of a birth-control clinic who had been dispensing advice on and prescribing contraceptives. In an opinion by Justice Douglas, the Supreme Court held that the statute violated a constitutional right of privacy created by the Bill of Rights.

The relevant portion of the opinion begins apologetically by disclaiming any reliance on notions of "substantive due process" and continues by reminding the reader of how broadly the First Amendment has been interpreted. Although no right of association is mentioned in the First Amendment, such a right has been recognized as a matter of interpretation. On the basis of this example Justice Douglas concludes "that specific guarantees in the Bill of Rights have penumbras, formed by emanations from those guarantees that help give them life and substance."[34] The opinion notes that the First, Third, Fourth, and Fifth Amendments protect privacy and concludes that the "emanations" from these protections create a "penumbral" right of married people to use contraceptives.

The Court's reference to the Third Amendment, which prohibits quartering troops in private homes in peacetime without the consent of the homeowner, was singularly inapt. The Third Amendment is the clearest example in the Constitution of a provision designed to protect privacy solely as seclusion. A

33. 381 U.S. 479 (1965). For a penetrating analysis of the *Griswold* case, see Robert H. Bork, "Neutral Principles and Some First Amendment Problems," 47 *Ind. L. J.* 1, 7–11 (1971).

34. 381 U.S. at 484.

broader objection to this portion of the *Griswold* opinion is that the theory of "emanations" or peripheral rights implies a connection between core and periphery which is lacking in the case of a right to use contraceptives. One can imagine a pamphleteer's right to remain anonymous as being ancillary to his express First Amendment right to disseminate his opinions. But there is no such relationship between the right to use contraceptives and the core rights protected by the Third, Fourth, and Fifth Amendments.[35]

A less spurious invocation of privacy as an ancillary right is found in Douglas's dissenting opinion in *Public Util. Comm'n v. Pollack.*[36] The question in that case was whether the Public Utilities Commission (P.U.C.) of the District of Columbia had violated the due process clause of the Fifth Amendment by allowing the District's trolley company to broadcast (mainly music) on its trolleys and buses. The majority agreed that the broadcasting invaded the passengers' right of privacy in the sense of seclusion but thought the invasion trivial. Justice Douglas disagreed, on the ground not that peace and quiet is itself an aspect of the liberty protected by the due process clause but that allowing the government (which is how he viewed the private trolley company because it was extensively regulated by the P.U.C.) to broadcast music to its captive audiences might lead eventually to sinister efforts by government to propagandize unwilling listeners. In this view the invasion of the passengers' privacy was unconstitutional only because it posed a danger (a rather remote one, to be sure) of violating First Amendment freedoms.

Another example where privacy could be regarded as an ancillary right is *Buckley v. Valeo,*[37] where the Court upheld against privacy objections the provisions of the federal campaign financing law that require public disclosure of the names of con-

35. A feeble effort, abandoned in later cases, was made later in Justice Douglas's opinion to characterize the right to use contraceptives as being ancillary to the Fourth Amendment. See text infra, at notes 40–41.

36. 343 U.S. 451 (1952).

37. 424 U.S. 1, 60–82 (1976).

tributors—of even as little as $100—to candidates for public office. Being allowed to contribute anonymously to a political candidate could have been viewed as a right of privacy ancillary to the First Amendment, which protects freedom of expression primarily to the end of preserving political freedom; but it was not so viewed. The denial of such a right seems inconsistent with the right of anonymity of political pamphleteers[38] and illustrative of the Court's wavering regard for privacy.

Griswold, in contrast, despite the talk of penumbras and emanations, elevates the right of privacy to independent constitutional significance. In doing so it uses privacy in a broad new sense, for the right to use contraceptives is not a right to seclusion—to be free from noise or interruption in home or office—or to conceal information. Perhaps it resembles, or at least has roots similar to, the right of privacy in the sense of seclusion. But the claim of privacy as seclusion is a claim to be allowed to do in private—alone, undisturbed—whatever is allowed by tort or property or criminal law or some other source of rights. It is not a claim to be allowed to do something more than the law allows.[39] The claim in *Griswold* of a right to use contraceptives was a claim to do something a state had forbidden. One cannot conclude that because the Constitution protects the former kind of claim it also protects the latter. To be sure, the right to be free in one's home from noise or other interruptions would be worth little if the state forbade one to do the various things one wanted to do in the privacy of the home. But by the same token, to be free to do what one wants in the privacy of one's home would be worth little if one were poor and unhealthy. There is something wrong with a method of analysis that would allow one to extract from the Fourth Amendment a right to the good

38. The pamphleteer's right to anonymity was upheld in Talley v. California, 362 U.S. 60 (1960); see also N.A.A.C.P. v. Alabama, 357 U.S. 449 (1958). Similar to *Buckley* in spirit is Laird v.Tatum, 408 U.S. 1 (1972), where the Court held that the Army's domestic surveillance program was not unconstitutional under the First Amendment despite its possible effect in "chilling" the expression of unpopular views.

39. See Lorenne M. G. Clark, "Privacy, Property, Freedom, and the Family," in *Philosophical Law: Authority Equality Adjudication Privacy* 167 (Richard Bronaugh ed. 1978).

life. What is wrong is that it equates privacy with the purposes for which people want privacy.

Furthermore, to define the constitutional right of privacy in terms of the ends for which privacy is sought is to ignore the specific limitations of the relevant constitutional provisions. Concluding that the Fourth Amendment is founded on the concept of privacy as seclusion would not justify using that concept as a basis for rights which the language of the Fourth Amendment clearly excludes from its protection. Broadcasting music to captive audiences in the *Pollack* case was an invasion—we will not worry about how serious a one—of the privacy, in the sense of seclusion, of the passengers, some of whose thinking or reading may have been disturbed. But by no contortion of language could it be thought a search or seizure. Similarly, even if the concept of privacy includes the right to use contraceptives, neither the Fourth Amendment nor any other provision of the Constitution can be read to create a right to such use.

This point is further illustrated by the part of Justice Douglas's opinion in *Griswold* in which, perhaps to reinforce his "emanations" approach, he relates the right to use contraceptives to a more conventional notion of privacy by discussing a hypothetical mode of enforcing the Connecticut contraception statute—searching the bedroom for evidence of violations. Such a search would indeed be an invasion of privacy in a conventional sense, but it would be a justifiable invasion if the statute were not otherwise constitutionally objectionable.[40]

Justice Harlan, in his dissenting opinion in *Poe v. Ullman,*[41] which anticipated this part of Douglas's opinion in *Griswold,* had suggested that there was no way to enforce the Connecticut contraception statute without invading privacy. But the facts of *Griswold* show that the state could enforce the statute without invading anyone's privacy—simply by prosecuting, as accessories, the employees of birth-control clinics. It is no novelty for the

40. This can be seen by imagining that the statute in question forbade not contraception but murder and that the police had probable cause to believe that the suspected murderer had secreted the weapon in his mattress.

41. 367 U.S. 497, 548 (1961).

primary violator of a statute to be beyond the effective reach of the law, so that enforcement is possible only against accessories. There are areas of patent and copyright law where only the contributory infringer (the direct infringer's supplier) is ever sued.[42] But even if there were no way to enforce the Connecticut statute without violating a constitutionally protected interest in privacy, it would not follow that the statute violated anyone's right of privacy, but only that the statute could not be enforced, a fate of many statutes punishing "victimless" crimes; and it would not follow that the prosecution of employees of birth-control clinics was a search.

The real objection to the Connecticut contraception statute is not that it invades privacy but that prohibiting contraception, at least by married people, is an undue limitation of freedom of action. This objection is no weightier intellectually by being put in terms of privacy. Perhaps Justice Douglas chose to speak in those terms in order to avoid basing decision explicitly on the concept of "substantive due process."[43] Yet he cited several cases that limited government regulation of the family without reference to privacy, such as *Meyer v. Nebraska*,[44] which held that a state's prohibition of the teaching of foreign, other than classical, languages to children in schools violated (as applied to private schools) a concept of liberty that included "the right of the individual to contract" and "to engage in the common occupations of life."[45] The opinion was by McReynolds, and Holmes dissented.[46] Under the ostensible modern test of substantive due process, whereby a statute is invalid only if it bears no ratio-

42. See, e.g., Aro Mfg. Co. v. Convertible Top Replacement Co., 377 U.S. 476 (1964).

43. This is the concept that the due process clause protects rights not protected by any specific provision of the Constitution—such as the "right to liberty of contract" in the days when the clause was used as a charter of freedom from economic regulation. See Robert G. McCloskey, "Economic Due Process and the Supreme Court: An Exhumation and Reburial," 1962 *Supreme Court Review* 34.

44. 262 U.S. 390 (1923). See also Pierce v. Society of Sisters, 268 U.S. 510 (1925).

45. 262 U.S. at 399.

46. The dissent appears in a companion case, Bartels v. Iowa, 262 U.S. 404, 412 (1923).

nal relationship to a permissible legislative objective,[47] *Meyer* was incorrectly decided.[48] Douglas's citation of *Meyer* (which has been repeated in later privacy cases) is evidence of the survival of substantive due process despite frequent disclaimers. The contemporary Court has simply "deregulated" the family,[49] in the same way that its discredited predecessors prevented states from regulating business. One can agree with the policy preferences of either or both sets of justices while questioning the constitutional basis for their actions.[50]

47. For some examples of the Court's tolerance of statutes attacked as denials of substantive due process, see, e.g., Kotch v. Board of River Port Pilot Comm'rs, 330 U.S. 552 (1947); Williamson v. Lee Optical Co., 348 U.S. 483 (1955). And for denial that there is even a rational-relationship requirement, see Ferguson v. Skrupa, 372 U.S 726, 729 (1963).

48. Holmes, in his dissenting opinion, discussed the "melting pot" philosophy which may have motivated the ban on the teaching of foreign languages to children, and concluded that the statute was not irrational.

49. Besides *Griswold,* see the cases discussed in the text, infra at notes 52–55; Carey v. Population Services Int'l, 431 U.S. 678 (1977); Zablocki v. Redhail, 434 U.S. 374 (1978).

50. Still another objection to Douglas's procedure of extracting a broad right of privacy from a number of constitutional amendments that protect particular aspects of privacy is that such a procedure assumes, what is doubtful, that a statute or constitution is animated by a coherent "spirit" which informs all of its provisions and enables one to decide cases not within the letter of the statute by reference to its spirit. This procedure treats individual statutory and constitutional provisions much like individual cases in a field of common law: from a study of the provisions, as of cases, the judge extracts some ruling principle that can be used to decide a new, previously unforeseen case. But as applied to either a statute or the Constitution, this procedure rests on a failure to understand the difference between legislative enactments, including constitutions, and common-law decisions. See Richard A. Posner, *Economic Analysis of Law* ch. 19 (2d ed. 1977); and Chapter 10 supra (compare "Defamation and Disparagement" with "The Statutory Privacy Movement"). To a greater degree than common-law decisions, legislative enactments are the product of interest-group pressures. Insofar as those pressures prevail, an enactment may lack any "spirit" or rational unity that could provide guidance in areas not specifically covered by the enactment. See Duncan Kennedy, "Legal Formality," 2 *J. Legal Stud.* 351 (1973). Thus the fact that there is one amendment to the Constitution in favor of the press and another against quartering troops in private homes and another establishing a right against being forced to incriminate oneself could be the result of the jockeying of interest groups represented at the Constitutional Convention rather than expressions of a consistent concept of the right to be left alone. At least this possibility should be considered (as Douglas failed to do) before separate amendments are read as if they were common-law decisions expressing a uniform

Privacy in the Supreme Court since *Griswold*

Griswold was the first Supreme Court decision to announce a constitutional right of privacy divorced from the specific privacy-oriented guarantees of the Bill of Rights, as well as the first to interpret privacy in a broader sense than seclusion and secrecy. It appears to have ushered in a new era in the constitutional law of privacy.[51]

Sexual Privacy

In *Eisenstadt v. Baird*[52] the Court was presented with the question whether a state could forbid the distribution of contraceptives to unmarried persons. The Court held that it could not, on the ground that to treat unmarried persons differently in this respect from married people, whose right to use contraceptives had been established in *Griswold,* would be arbitrary and hence violate the equal protection clause of the Fourteenth Amendment. The heart of the opinion is the following passage:[53]

It is true that in *Griswold* the right of privacy in question inhered in the marital relationship. Yet the married couple is not an independent entity with a mind and heart of its own, but an association of two individuals each with a separate intellectual and emotional makeup. If the right of privacy means anything, it is the right of the *individual,* married or single, to be free from unwarranted governmental intrusion into matters so fundamentally affecting a person as the decision whether to bear or beget a child.

principle. Incidentally, if the Constitution has a "spirit," it is one of distrust of government. The modern welfare state is contrary to that spirit, which snould give pause to those who would create constitutional rights based on the Constitution's "spirit."

51. I shall not discuss the Court's nonconstitutional privacy cases. These are mainly cases interpreting various federal privacy statutes, such as the privacy exemption to the Freedom of Information Act, discussed in Anthony T. Kronman's paper of that name, 9 *J. Legal Stud.* 727 (1980). Nor shall I repeat my discussion of the search and seizure cases, some of which were decided after *Griswold.*

52. 405 U.S. 438 (1972).

53. *Id.* at 453.

To say that the right of privacy means *nothing* if it does not allow an unmarried person to obtain contraceptives shows how far the Court had moved by 1972 from any of the usual senses of the word "privacy." The Court in *Griswold* had attempted to relate the right to use contraceptives to familiar notions of privacy by speculating on the intrusive methods by which a statute banning their use might be enforced. This ground was unavailable in *Baird* because the statute forbade not the use but only the distribution of contraceptives. *Baird* is a pure essay in substantive due process. It unmasks *Griswold* as based on the idea of sexual liberty rather than privacy.[54]

Once the Court, in *Baird*, had severed the right to use contraceptives from any concept of privacy as what people do in private, it was perhaps inevitable that the right of privacy would eventually be held to imply the right of any woman to have an abortion, which is an alternative method to contraception for preventing an unwanted birth. To be sure, there are differences between the methods that may be relevant on the issue of the justification for government intervention; in particular, abortion involves the taking of a human (or at least protohuman) life and contraception does not. But on the question whether there is a constitutionally protected interest in being allowed to take measures to avoid giving birth to an unwanted child, as distinct from whether that interest is outweighed by competing interests, there is no difference between contraception and abortion. So perhaps it is not surprising that the Court in *Roe v. Wade*[55] devoted only one sentence to the question whether the right of privacy includes the right to have an abortion.

Baird and *Wade* raise, even more acutely than *Griswold*, the question whether we have a written Constitution, with the limitations thereby implied on the creation of new constitutional rights, or whether the Constitution is no more than a grant of discretion to the Supreme Court to mold public policy in ac-

---

54. This point is recognized in Louis Henkin, "Privacy and Autonomy," 74 *Colum. L. Rev.* 1410 (1974)—and, surprisingly, approved as consistent with "constitutional modernization by the judiciary." *Id*. at 1424.

55. 410 U.S. 113, 153 (1973).

cordance with the justices' personal preferences. Nothing in the language, legislative history, or background of any constitutional provision evinces an intent to limit state regulation of the family, unless the regulation is along racial or otherwise invidious lines. This vacuum of relevant constitutional principle makes the issue in *Baird* and *Wade* quite different from that in *Olmstead* and *Katz*. The Fourth Amendment embodies a concept of privacy that may be broad enough to include the concealment of information. But neither in the Fourth Amendment nor elsewhere in the Constitution is there evidence of a policy of allowing people to engage in sexual activity without fear of giving birth. The Court has tried to bridge this gap by the purely verbal expedient of regarding as an aspect of "privacy" the freedom to engage in activity which the Supreme Court does not think should be regulated. What is private in this view is simply what the Court thinks should not be subject to public control. In this sense, however, the right to follow the occupation of one's choice without hindrance from government could equally well be regarded as an aspect of the right of privacy. The justices who thought that the Constitution protected the right of employer and employee to set the terms of employment without government interference simply lacked the wit to justify their belief in the language of privacy.[56]

Conflicts with Other Rights

Long before *Griswold*, the Court had wrestled with the conflict between the First Amendment right to disseminate ideas by means of sound trucks or door-to-door solicitation and the right of householders to be free from the noise and interruptions caused by these methods. In 1951 the Court upheld a state law forbidding door-to-door solicitation in the absence of advance permission of owners or residents.[57] This ingenious accommo-

56. Justice Marshall believes that there is a constitutional right to be let alone, applicable to the right of a policeman not to cut his hair to meet departmental requirements, that does not need even to be verbalized in right-of-privacy terms. See his dissenting opinion in Kelley v. Johnson, 425 U.S. 238, 253 (1976).

57. Breard v. Alexandria, 341 U.S. 622 (1951). The opinion referred to the householder's interest in "privacy and repose." *Id.* at 625–626.

dation of the rights of privacy and expression was later used to save a statute that ordered the Post Office to stop delivery of direct-mail advertising of a sexual nature to people who filed a statement with the Post Office requesting that they not receive such mail.[58] But this accommodation was not available in the sound-truck cases.

In *Saia v. New York*,[59] the Court invalidated an ordinance requiring a permit for sound trucks, stating: "In this case a permit is denied because some persons were said to have found the sound annoying. In the next one a permit may be denied because some people find the ideas annoying."[60] At first glance the parallel between annoying noise and annoying ideas appears to fail simply because the noise from a sound truck is an invasion of privacy and ideas are not. But this is a superficial distinction. Repose and tranquillity can be disturbed by ideas as well as by sounds. The true difference between noise and annoying ideas is that the former can be controlled without seriously restricting the dissemination of ideas while the latter can be controlled— with some important exceptions[61]—only by forbidding their dissemination altogether. The First Amendment consequences are thus of a very different magnitude. The Court soon realized this and within a year virtually overruled *Saia* in an opinion which recognized that the blare of the sound truck was an invasion of "quiet and tranquillity."[62]

This conclusion was reached without any suggestion that there was a constitutional right to seclusion, although such a right would appear to have firmer roots in the Constitution, and specifically in the Fourth Amendment, than the right to use contraceptives which was asserted in the *Griswold* case. To be

58. Rowan v. Post Office Dept., 397 U.S. 728 (1970).

59. 334 U.S. 558 (1948).

60. *Id.* at 562.

61. See *Rowan*, note 58 supra; *Erznoznik*, note 63 infra; and *Cohen*, note 67 infra.

62. Kovacs v. Cooper, 336 U.S. 77, 87 (1949). Recent cases in the same spirit are Grayned v. City of Rockford, 408 U.S. 104 (1972), upholding an ordinance limiting noise in the vicinity of schools, and Village of Belle Terre v. Boraas, 416 U.S. 1, 9 (1974), upholding single-family-dwelling zoning to protect "quiet seclusion."

sure, constitutional rights in general, and the right of privacy recognized in that case in particular, normally protect against governmental rather than private action; and the distinction is more than technical, since there are good reasons for distinguishing between governmental and private invasions of privacy. But the declaration in *Griswold* of a constitutional right of privacy presumably says something about the Court's view of the importance of the underlying interests protected by the right; and unless the constitutional concept of privacy is to be wholly severed from the traditional meaning of privacy, those interests include tranquillity and repose. Therefore, now that the right of privacy has attained constitutional dignity, one might expect that the type of interest vindicated in *Breard* and *Kovacs* would fare even better in collisions with other constitutional rights. But surprisingly this has not been the case.

Erznoznik v. City of Jacksonville[63] involved a conflict between freedom of speech and, as in the sound-truck and solicitation cases, the right of privacy in the sense of seclusion. The issue was the constitutionality of a city ordinance which forbade the showing of nude scenes on outdoor movie screens visible from a public highway or other public property. The basis of the ordinance was the interest in being able to drive without the distraction of immense nudes looming up before one.[64] The Court, in invalidating the ordinance, gave no weight to the privacy interest. It held simply that the ordinance was overbroad in forbidding the showing of all nude scenes, obscene or not. This approach is wide of the mark. A fifty-foot nude is a distraction whether or not so tastefully done or so integral to a work of substantial artistic merit and intent that it could not be suppressed under the obscenity laws. Some people find nude movie scenes offensive whether or not they violate any obscenity law, and some who do not still prefer not to expose their children to such scenes. One might have thought this interest in seclusion suffi-

63. 422 U.S. 205 (1975).
64. As to whether the seclusion aspect of privacy is applicable to people "in public" (e.g. driving), see Chapter 10, supra.

ciently substantial—to a Court that believes the right of privacy emanates from numerous provisions of the Bill of Rights—to outweigh the minor infringement of the interests of moviegoers caused by the ordinance. The ordinance did not ban the showing of nude scenes either in movie theaters generally or drive-in theaters in particular. It merely required that the screens be so located or shielded as not to be visible from public highways when nude scenes were shown. The necessary adjustments could probably have been made at moderate cost; in contrast, alternative routing for users of the public highways who did not wish to have their sensibilities invaded by nude scenes might well have involved a cumulatively substantial inconvenience.

Some theater owners, to be sure, might have decided not to show movies containing nude scenes rather than shield the movie screen from users of the highways. Even so, since not all drive-in movie screens—and no screens of indoor movie theaters—are visible from the highway, the impact on the audience for nude scenes would probably have been small. In the long run, the impact might well have been negligible, for the screens of drive-in theaters constructed after the ordinance was passed could easily be so located or shielded as to comply with it. The Court seemed aware of this possibility, because it implied that a zoning ordinance regulating the location of drive-in movie theaters might not violate the First Amendment even if motivated by a desire to shield involuntary viewers from nude scenes.[65]

---

65. *Id.* at 212 n.9. The restriction by zoning of the location of "adult" movie theaters was later upheld in Young v. American Mini Theatres, 427 U.S. 50 (1976), though without reference to a possible privacy interest which might support such zoning. Justice Powell was, however, sufficiently concerned with the apparent inconsistency between *Erznoznik* and *Young* to add a concurring opinion in *Young* in which he noted certain technical, and it seems to me trivial, deficiencies of the ordinance invalidated in *Erznoznik*. See 427 U.S. at 73–84. For example, the ordinance contained no limitation on distance—and thus might be violated even if the highway was so far from the movie screen that the screen had the apparent size of a postage stamp. Had such a case, purely hypothetical in the Powell opinion, ever arisen in the enforcement of the ordinance, it would have provided an appropriate vehicle for limiting the scope of its application. But it is too much to expect and require a city council to foresee and provide specifically for every remote application of its ordinances that the judicial imagination might con-

The outcome in *Erznoznik* suggests that the right of privacy as conceived by the Supreme Court does not imply any right to be free from nude movie scenes but does imply the right of unmarried people to use contraceptives. This is an inversion of the values associated with the term "privacy." In this view the Constitution is solicitous of the rights of theater owners to impose nude scenes on an involuntary audience and of couples to fornicate without fear of conception but is not solicitous of the concern for privacy that leads a driver to be offended by the sight of fifty-foot nudes looming at the side of the road.[66]

Erznoznik is particularly interesting because although the invasion of seclusion was mental rather than physical, it would have been possible to protect a right of privacy without doing serious damage to First Amendment interests. A more difficult case is *Cohen v. California*,[67] where the Supreme Court held that a state statute which forbade conduct invading the "peace or quiet of any . . . person" could not constitutionally be applied to the wearing in a courthouse of a jacket on which was printed the legend: "F—— the Draft." Two sorts of invasion of peace and quiet can be distinguished in this case. One is the distress caused by the sentiment behind the legend—opposition to the draft and, by implication, to the American policy in Vietnam at the time. This distress provides an insufficient basis for regulation, even if one rejects the view that it is desirable to force unwanted ideas on people. The basic source of the distress lies not

---

jure up. Perhaps the Court would reply that the doctrine associated with such cases as Thornhill v. Alabama, 310 U.S. 88 (1940), and Smith v. California, 361 U.S. 147 (1959), requires that statutes regulating the expression of ideas be evaluated on their face rather than as applied—that is, by reference to hypothetical rather than actual cases. But if so, refusal to recognize an exception to the doctrine in cases where the challenged legislation is based on a privacy interest is just one more indication that the Court's devotion to privacy is less steadfast than the language of *Griswold* and of the other sexual–privacy cases suggests.

66. In this connection, one notes with alarm Professor Lawrence Tribe's remark, in a section of his treatise dealing with the right of privacy in its very extended modern constitutional sense, that "freedom to have impact on others . . . is central to any adequate conception of the self." Lawrence H. Tribe, *American Constitutional Law* 888 (1978).

67. 403 U.S. 15 (1971).

in seeing opposition to the draft expressed on a jacket but in knowing that people oppose the draft, and that knowledge cannot be stamped out without preventing expression of opposition in any form.

The second affront to privacy comes from the use of the obscene expletive. The offensiveness of the expression is separate from its content, as is shown by the fact that people who oppose the draft might still be offended by the use of the expletive. For people who find public use of obscene language offensive, the invasion of tranquillity and repose is as palpable as in the case of an unwanted telephone solicitation or the blare of a sound truck. Thus the ultimate question in *Cohen* was whether the invasion of privacy was substantial relative to the reduction in the effectiveness of communication brought about by disallowing the favorite term used by the vulgar and the inarticulate to express hostility.

In holding that the invasion of privacy was not substantial, the Court repeated an argument it had made in *Erznoznik,* yet was to reject several years later in *F.C.C. v. Pacifica Foundation.*[68] The argument is that people using the courthouse "could effectively avoid *further* bombardment simply by averting their eyes" and were thus only "briefly exposed" to an offensive sight.[69] This statement ignores every dimension of invasion of privacy except duration. The logic of the argument is that a very loud noise heard for only ten seconds is inherently less invasive of privacy than a softer noise heard for twenty seconds. The Court also disregarded the role of memory in prolonging an offensive sight or sound.

In *Pacifica* the Court upheld, primarily on the basis of the privacy (in the sense of seclusion) interest of the owners of radios and their families, the constitutionality of the Federal Communications Commission's regulation of broadcasting obscene expletives. Since it is no more difficult to change stations on a radio than to avert one's eyes (and one's children's eyes) from a drive-in screen while driving, the result in *Pacifica* is inconsistent with that in *Erznoznik* unless obscene expletives are not entitled

68. 438 U.S. 726 (1978).
69. 403 U.S. at 21–22 (emphasis added).

to constitutional protection—contrary to *Cohen*—or unless the drive-in theater is regarded as a more worthy forum for the expression of opinion than the radio. The last may well be the true if unworthy ground of distinction between *Pacifica* on the one hand and *Erznoznik* and *Cohen* on the other.[70]

Another area of conflict between privacy and the First Amendment is illustrated by *Time, Inc. v. Hill*,[71] which involved a collision between freedom of the press and the branch of the state tort law of privacy that protects people from being portrayed by the media in a "false light." The Court held that a state may constitutionally provide a tort remedy in a "false light" case only if the portrayal was made with "deliberate malice," that is, in deliberate or reckless disregard of the truth. It based this result on its holding in *New York Times Co. v. Sullivan*[72] that defamation suits by public figures were permissible under the First Amendment only if the defamation was deliberately or recklessly false. Although there is a close resemblance between the torts of defamation and of portraying someone in a false light, they are not identical. One difference is that the false-light tort requires publicity—wide dissemination—rather than just publication, which to support a defamation suit need be made to only one other person. Another difference is that in a false-light case, the falsity need not injure the reputation of the plaintiff. One can summarize the difference between the torts in the following way: defamation protects an individual from losing advantageous transactions because his reputation is impaired, while the false-light privacy tort protects a person from unwanted attention—protects privacy in the sense of seclusion.[73]

Since defamation protects reputation, and the false-light tort

70. Radio and television have traditionally been accorded less protection under the First Amendment than other media—compare National Broadcasting Co. v. United States, 319 U.S. 190 (1943), and Red Lion Broadcasting Co. v. F.C.C., 395 U.S. 367 (1969), with Miami Herald Pub. Co. v. Tornillo, 418 U.S. 241 (1974)—on the basis of an economic fallacy discussed in Posner, note 50 supra, at 546–547.

71. 385 U.S. 374 (1967), discussed in Chapter 9, supra.

72. 376 U.S. 254 (1964).

73. Portraying a person in a false light could, of course, impair his ability to make advantageous transactions—could, that is, impair his reputation—but if so it would be actionable as defamation.

privacy, since the Court believes there is a constitutional right of privacy but has never suggested that there is a constitutional right of reputation,[74] and since the plaintiff in *Sullivan* was a public figure and presumably therefore less sensitive to invasions of privacy than the average private citizen, one might have expected the Court to consider the issue whether to require proof of the defendant's actual malice a more difficult issue in *Hill* than in *Sullivan*. Yet the relevant part of the *Hill* opinion does not even mention privacy, and suggests that the case for tort liability was stronger in *Sullivan* because that case involved the "additional state interest in the protection of the individual against damage to his reputation."[75] Reputation is put above privacy, although the latter (one had been told by *Griswold*) has constitutional dignity and the former does not.

Similar misunderstanding and belittlement of the right of privacy under state tort law are evident in *Cox Broadcasting Corp. v. Cohn*,[76] which invalidated a state statute forbidding the publication or broadcast of the names of rape victims. The statute protected that aspect of the tort right of privacy which seeks to shield people from embarrassing, albeit truthful, publicizing of personal information. As we saw in Chapter 9, this aspect of the tort has rightly been interpreted narrowly, because a common motive for a person's concealing information about himself is to induce people to engage in transactions who would not do so if they knew the truth, and because concealment so motivated is a species of fraud entitled *prima facie* to no greater protection than fraud in the market for goods. But not all concealment of personal information is so motivated, as the facts of the *Cox* case illustrate. Since the rape victim in question had been killed by the rapist, knowing she had been raped could not be material to someone contemplating future transactions with her. The motive for suppression of the victim's identity was to spare her parents grief, including unwanted attention from ghoulish members of the public—so that the interest in privacy as secrecy ran

---

74. The Court has stated that there is no constitutionally protected right to a good reputation. See Paul v. Davis, 424 U.S. 693, 711–712 (1976).

75. 385 U.S. at 391.

76. 420 U.S. 469 (1975).

into the older interest in privacy as seclusion. Nor was the name of the victim vital, though it was relevant, to the informativeness of an article or broadcast about the rape.

The Court paid no attention to the particular facts of the case which made it an attractive one for upholding the privacy claim. It invalidated the statute on the ground that the rape victim's identity was contained in court records open to public inspection and that the First Amendment entitles the press to publish any fact contained in such records. The Court suggested that the state might not have violated the First Amendment by denying all public access to the information; but having declined to go that far, the state was not entitled to prevent the information from being publicized in the media.

This reasoning confronts the state with the unhappy choice of conducting rape trials *in camera* (assuming that this could be done without violating the defendant's right to a public trial) or sacrificing the privacy of victims of rape. The state's approach, which the Court invalidated, protected the latter interest at a lower cost in impairment of the public-trial principle than the approach suggested by the Court would have done. The Court seemed to think that the state's willingness to allow the victim's name to appear in the public record of the trial showed that it did not really care about privacy. This misses the fundamental distinction in the tort law of privacy between what is merely public and what is publicized. There is no violation of the tort right of privacy without publicity—wide dissemination—and conversely the right to complain about publicity should not be forfeited merely because the information in question is already known to a few people.[77]

77. Two recent defamation cases, in which the Court has held that the "public figure" rule of New York Times Co. v. Sullivan does not extend to certain "involuntary" public figures, suggest that the *Cox* decision may rest on shifting ground. In Hutchinson v. Proxmire, 443 U.S. 111 (1979), the Court held that a scientist who was ridiculed by a United States senator could sue the senator for defamation because the scientist had not sought publicity for his work outside of the scientific community. And in Wolston v. Reader's Digest Ass'n, Inc., 443 U.S. 157 (1979), the Court held that a man who had been convicted of contempt of Congress sixteen years earlier was not a public figure today. These cases evince a sympathy for the involuntary recipient of media publicity that is lacking in *Cox*. [Footnote continued on next page.]

Record Keeping

Warren and Brandeis's famous article on the right of privacy was a response to the rise of the newspaper gossip column, which they saw as threatening privacy. As pointed out in Chapter 9, they overlooked the possibility that the gossip column was simply a substitute for the type of informal neighborhood surveillance that had been made less efficient by growing urbanization and increases in the value of time, coupled with growing literacy. Those who worry today about loss of privacy focus on the progress of electronics, which has brought us not only efficient devices for eavesdropping (going well beyond the telephone tap) but also efficient techniques of data storage and retrieval, enabling far more information about people to be collected and disseminated. Again, it is possible that these developments have merely offset other factors, notably continued urbanization, which have tended to increase privacy, but that is

---

With regard to one branch of the tort law of privacy, appropriation (see Chapter 9, supra), there is, happily, no conflict between state law and the First Amendment. In Zacchini v. Scripps–Howard Broadcasting Co., 433 U.S. 562 (1977), the issue was whether the broadcast on a news show of the entire act of a "human cannonball" could constitutionally be deemed a tortious appropriation of his property by the broadcaster. The Court held that it could, noting that tort liability was unlikely to limit the dissemination of the human cannonball's act, since, of course, he desired publicity. See *id.* at 573. (The act was broadcast for purposes of entertainment; had the purpose been, say, to question the safety of the act, the broadcaster would have had a stronger First Amendment claim.) The Court could have put the point more strongly. Granting entertainers a property right—the effect of the state tort law in question—should, by encouraging the production of entertainments, increase rather than reduce the production and dissemination of ideas. But recall that in Buckley v. Valeo, note 37 supra, where First Amendment and privacy interests also coincided, the Court rejected the privacy claim.

I want to make clear that even if the notion of a general constitutional right to privacy is rejected, as a proper respect for the written Constitution would seem to require, it does not follow that privacy is not entitled to weighty consideration in First Amendment cases. No one believes the First Amendment should be interpreted literally. It is permissible to limit speech if the reasons for doing so are strong enough, and they need not be reasons found in the Constitution. The interests in liberty and security reflected in state tort law, including the tort law of privacy, are entitled to substantial consideration in determining whether a challenged law violates the First Amendment, whether or not the Constitution itself protects those interests against governmental invasion.

not certain. What is certain is that modern record keeping has been a focus of concern to all those who see themselves as the defenders of privacy—except the Supreme Court.

The Bank Secrecy Act of 1970[78] is an example of the sort of legislation made possible by the progress of information storage that concerns the advocates of privacy. The act, expressly for the purpose of facilitating law enforcement, requires banks to make and retain copies of all checks and other financial transfer instruments (the implementing regulations have limited the copying and retention requirements to large transactions, such as checks in excess of \$10,000) and to make these copies available to law-enforcement agencies. The record-keeping requirements of the act were upheld against privacy and other challenges in *California Bankers Ass'n v. Shultz,*[79] and the production requirements in *United States v. Miller,*[80] where a law-enforcement agency had subpoenaed from a bank copies of the defendant's checks made and kept by the bank pursuant to the Bank Secrecy Act.

The Court emphasized that the records of bank transactions are the property of the bank rather than of the depositor or other bank customer. This would be a relevant consideration if the only aspect of privacy protected by the Constitution were seclusion, for one's physical privacy is not affected by the government's getting access to copies made by a bank. But once privacy is understood to include the confidentiality of private information, property notions become irrelevant, since our confidences are frequently reposed in another's files, those of a physician, an employer, or a bank.[81]

The Court also stressed that checks are not confidential com-

---

78. 12 U.S.C. § 1829b(d).
79. 416 U.S. 21 (1974).
80. 425 U.S. 435 (1976).
81. Or a telephone company: see Smith v. Maryland, 99 S. Ct. 2577 (1979), holding that police use of a "pen register" which records the phone numbers that a telephone subscriber dials does not violate the Fourth Amendment, on the highly artificial ground that the act of dialing discloses the number dialed to the phone company. Or an accountant: see Couch v. United States, 409 U.S. 322 (1973).

munications and that their privacy is in any event compromised by the fact that they are read by the bank's employees. This is the same mistake the Court made in *Cox.* Privacy of information normally means the selective disclosure of personal information rather than total secrecy. (If it meant only the latter, wiretapping would not invade privacy.) A bank customer may not care that the employees of the bank know a lot about his financial affairs, but it does not follow that he is indifferent to having those affairs broadcast to the world or disclosed to the government.

Behind the Bank Secrecy Act cases lie the old required-record cases, which, taken at face value, permit privacy to be invaded with impunity by a simple two-stage procedure.[82] In the first stage the government requires the citizen to provide or make available to the government certain information; in the second the information is supplied to an enforcement agency. The individual has no remedy at either stage. He is entitled to object neither to the requirement of providing the information if the requirement is reasonable, nor to the release of the information by the agency that obtained it from him, since the agency is in lawful possession of the information.

Later cases held, to be sure, that an individual could invoke the Fifth Amendment to justify refusing to supply required information that would incriminate him.[83] But this development makes it all the more surprising that the Court should have brushed aside the constitutional claim in *Miller.* Because the subpoena in *Miller* sought papers rather than an admission and because, as mentioned earlier, the suggestion in *Boyd v. United States* that the Fifth Amendment protects one's papers has been discredited, the claim in *Miller* had to be based on the Fourth rather than the Fifth Amendment. But, as noted earlier, the

82. See, e.g., Shapiro v. United States, 335 U.S. 1 (1948); Robert B. McKay, "Self-Incrimination and the New Privacy," 1967 *Supreme Court Review* 193, 214–224; Bernard D. Meltzer, "Required Records, the McCarran Act, and the Privilege against Self-Incrimination," 18 *U. Chi. L. Rev.* 687, 712 (1951).

83. See Marchetti v. United States, 390 U.S. 39 (1968); Grosso v. United States, 390 U.S. 62 (1968).

Fourth Amendment is more clearly designed to protect privacy than the Fifth Amendment is. One might have thought, therefore, that a subpoena which invaded privacy would at least be within the scope of the Fourth Amendment.

A good sign that the Court lacks sympathy for a type of claim is its use of inconsistent reasoning to deny it. In *Miller* the fact that the defendant's financial transactions had been exposed to the scrutiny of the bank's employees before enactment of the challenged statute persuaded the Court that he had no reasonable expectation of privacy that the statute might have destroyed. In *Whalen v. Roe*,[84] the Court upheld the constitutionality of a state law that required keeping records of the identity of people for whom certain dangerous but lawful drugs were prescribed by their physicians. The Court rejected the argument that the statute was an invasion of privacy, noting that the statute limited disclosure of the private information collected under it to the employees of the state health agency. This is just the sort of disclosure that was held in *Miller* to destroy a reasonable expectation of privacy. One might have thought that a statute which destroyed a reasonable expectation of privacy would thereby infringe the constitutional right of privacy.

The Court's attitude in the record-keeping cases would be understandable if it believed that the Fourth Amendment protected only seclusion and that the Constitution creates no general right of privacy. The former view would bar challenges to subpoenas in cases such as *Miller* and the latter would bar challenges to record keeping as in *Shultz* and *Whalen*. What makes the Court's attitude difficult to understand is that its members, including some who concurred in the Court's opinions in *Shultz*, *Whalen*, and *Miller*, believe the Fourth Amendment protects privacy in the sense of secrecy as well as in the sense of seclusion (for example, *Katz*), and also that the Constitution creates a general right of privacy unconfined by any specific language in the Constitution (for example, *Griswold*). The former belief implies that Miller should have been able to object to the subpoena

84. 429 U.S. 589 (1977),

directed at the bank's copies of his financial records. The latter belief implies that analysis is not at an end even if the Fourth Amendment does not entitle a person to prevent the search of a bank's records of his financial transactions, since the constitutional right of privacy extends beyond the specific guarantees of that amendment. The voluntary record-keeping practices of banks strike a balance between the privacy and other interests of their customers. That balance carries with it a presumption of optimality.[85] The Bank Secrecy Act shifted that balance against privacy and, it would seem, thereby infringed, at least *prima facie,* the general right of privacy formulated in *Griswold.*

There is no way to reconcile the Court's view of privacy in *Katz* with its view of privacy in *Miller:* the view that wiretapping is subject to the Fourth Amendment with the view that a statute which forces a bank to photograph its customers' checks and then turn them over to a government agency for use in a criminal prosecution is not. The sexual-privacy cases can be reconciled with the denial of a general right of privacy in the record-keeping cases only by narrowing the concept of privacy so that it covers sexual freedom but not confidentiality: to stand the concept on its head. The Court did this in *Paul v. Davis.*[86] In holding that no constitutionally protected interest was invaded by the circulation of a flyer listing people who had been arrested (but not necessarily convicted) for shoplifting, the Court stated that the plaintiff was making no challenge to "the State's ability to restrict his freedom of action in a sphere contended to be 'private'" but only a "claim that the State may not publicize a record of an official act such as an arrest."[87] The periphery of the right of privacy is made the core, and the core is relegated to the periphery.

The Court's insensitivity to the privacy claims in the record-keeping cases is particularly surprising because there lies ready

85. See text supra, at note 1.
86. 424 U.S. 693 (1976).
87. *Id.* at 713. Similarly, in Smith v. Daily Mail Pub. Co., 443 U.S. 97 (1979), the Court, invalidating a statute forbidding newspapers to print the names of juvenile delinquents, remarked that "there is no issue here of privacy." *Id.* at 105.

at hand, in the Court's racial and sexual discrimination decisions discussed in Part IV, a constitutional theory for recognizing such claims. Discrimination is largely a matter of basing decisions on incomplete information: generalizing from a person's
race or sex to his or her character or ability. If discrimination is unconstitutional state action, it is largely because in
certain areas we want to force the government to make individualized assessments. The desire to allow people to conceal certain information about themselves is related to the same
concern with basing decisions on proxies rather than on individualized assessment. The argument for allowing someone to
conceal his arrest record from an employer is that the employer
will use such information as an inappropriate, an "unfair,"
proxy for assessing the applicant's fitness for the job, and this is
the same argument as that for forbidding employers to use race
as an employment criterion. Dislike for using proxies in making
decisions about people could have provided the basis for a constitutional theory of privacy of information that could in turn
have been used to guide analysis in record-keeping cases.

Conclusion

This part of the book ends far from where it began, in the
topsy-turvy world of the Supreme Court's constitutional privacy
adjudication, where "privacy" means, for example, the right of
married and unmarried people, adults and children, to buy
contraceptives and to have an abortion. When there is a clash
between the right of privacy in its traditional senses and the
right of those who invade privacy in the name of sexual freedom or the publicizing of sexual activity, it is generally the latter
who prevail. It is as if the Court had become infected with the
student radicalism of the late 1960s and early 1970s, with its
emphasis on candor at the expense of privacy, its slogans of
"doing your own thing" and "letting it all hang out."[88] *Erznoznik*,
where the right of movie exhibitors to show nude scenes on

---

88. *Cf.* the quotation from Professor Tribe in note 66, supra.

drive-in screens visible from the public highways was held to prevail over the right of the user of the highway to prevent such invasions of his privacy and sensibilities, and *Cox,* where the right to publicize a dead rape victim's name was held to prevail over the right of the victim's parents to the privacy of their grief, when taken together with *Griswold* and the other sexual-privacy cases and with the suggestion in *Paul v. Davis* and *Smith v. Daily Mail* that the right of privacy is a right to act and not a right to keep information private, suggest a tendency on the part of the Supreme Court to confuse privacy with sexual freedom and display. Perhaps the concept of privacy has been so abused in the sexual-privacy cases that some justices now have difficulty recognizing a real privacy claim.

One might have inferred from a few recent decisions (*Pacifica, Hutchinson,* and *Wolston*) a growing sensitivity by the Court to the claims of privacy in an intelligible sense, were it not for the very recent decision in *Bell v. Wolfish.*[89] One of the issues in *Wolfish* was whether it was a violation of the Fourth Amendment for the custodians of a federal prison visually to search what are euphemistically termed the "body cavities" of male and female inmates after visits by a person from outside the prison. These searches were conducted after every visit, whether or not there was any reason to believe that the visitors had conveyed a weapon or contraband to the inmate for concealment in the inmate's body cavities. Among the inmates so searched were pretrial detainees, that is, persons who had not yet been convicted of the crime for which they were being detained; these were in fact the plaintiffs in the case.

The Court, including justices such as Blackmun who believe it an impermissible invasion of privacy to forbid the sale of contraceptives to children,[90] upheld body-cavity searches in an opinion which suggests in passing that prison inmates—even detainees who have not yet been convicted of the crime for

89. 441 U.S. 520 (1979).
90. See Carey v. Population Services Int'l, 431 U.S. 678, 691–699 (1977) (opinion of Justice Brennan, joined by Justices Stewart, Marshall, and Blackmun).

which they are being detained—may have no Fourth Amendment rights whatever.[91] It cut no ice with the Court that the searches were not based upon probable cause, were "because of time pressures . . . frequently conducted in the presence of other inmates" and "caused some inmates to forego personal visits,"[92] and were employed despite elaborate screening of visitors and surveillance of the visits themselves. Given the well-known security problems of American jails, the Court's decision in *Wolfish* may have been correct. But it is not the decision of men who set a high value on privacy, and I have difficulty understanding the set of mind that brushes aside the privacy claims in cases like *Wolfish* and *Erznoznik* and *Cox* and *Miller,* yet regards limiting the sale or use of contraceptives as inconsistent with a due regard for privacy.

91. See 441 U.S. at 558.
92. *Id.* at 577 (Justice Marshall, dissenting).

IV

THE SUPREME COURT AND DISCRIMINATION

12
The Law and Economics
of Discrimination

In moving from privacy to discrimination, this book may once again seem to be changing direction abruptly. In fact the subjects are closely related. The desire to protect privacy in the sense of secrecy and the desire to prohibit racial and related forms of discrimination have a common basis in a reluctance to base judgments of people on partial information about them, whether it is information about their arrest record or about their race. Chapters 13 and 14 discuss the Supreme Court's recent decisions in the area of reverse discrimination or affirmative action, the cutting edge of antidiscrimination policy today. This chapter examines the economics and constitutional law of discrimination. I examine the distributive effects of discrimination and describe the information-costs theory of discrimination. I present an economic approach to justifying and defining the Fourteenth Amendment's "state action" requirement, and question the statutes that forbid purely private discrimination.

Some people prefer not to associate with members of particular racial, religious, or ethnic groups different from their own and will even pay a price to indulge this preference, this "taste for discrimination." Although there are pecuniary gains to trade between blacks and whites—to blacks working for whites or vice versa, whites selling houses to blacks, and so forth (just as there are pecuniary gains to any kind of trade)—such trade imposes nonpecuniary but real costs on those who dislike association with members of the other race. These costs are analogous to transportation costs in international trade, and like transportation costs they reduce the amount of trading and of the association incidental to it.[1]

What is the impact of reduced exchange on the wealth of the groups involved? Assume that whites do not like to associate with blacks, but that blacks are indifferent to the racial identity of those with whom they associate. The incomes of many whites will be lower than they would be if they did not have such a taste. They forgo advantageous exchanges if, for example, they refuse to sell their houses to blacks who are willing to pay higher prices than white purchasers. The racial preference of the whites will also reduce the incomes of the blacks by preventing them from making advantageous exchanges with whites. However, the reduction in the blacks' incomes will be proportionately greater than the reduction in the whites' incomes. Because blacks are only a small part of the economy, the number of advantageous exchanges that blacks can make with whites is greater than the number of advantageous transactions that whites can make with blacks. The white sector is so large as to be virtually self-sufficient; the black sector is much smaller and more dependent on trade with the white.

In an unregulated, competitive market, there are economic forces working to minimize discrimination. In a market of many sellers, the intensity of prejudice against blacks can be expected to vary considerably. Some sellers will have only a mild prejudice and so will not forgo as many advantageous transactions with blacks as their more prejudiced competitors. The costs of these sellers will therefore be lower, which will enable them to increase their share of the market. The least prejudiced sellers will come to dominate the market in much the same way as people who are least afraid of heights come to dominate occupations that require working at heights; they demand a smaller premium for working at such a job.

Under monopoly, the tendency for the market gradually to be taken over by firms with the least prejudice against blacks is not so strong. The single seller in the market will be, on aver-

1. See Gary S. Becker, *The Economics of Discrimination* (2d ed. 1971), on which my analysis in this part of the chapter is based.

age, as prejudiced as the average, not as the least prejudiced, member of the community. Freely transferable monopolies, however, such as patents, will tend to come into the hands of the least prejudiced. The efficient exploitation of a monopoly that requires association with blacks is less valuable to a highly prejudiced owner—who suffers either a reduction in his pecuniary income by forgoing advantageous transactions or a nonpecuniary cost by making such transactions—than it would be to a less prejudiced owner. Therefore, the less prejudiced will tend to purchase monopolies from the more prejudiced.

But not all monopolies are freely transferable. And if the monopoly is regulated, the market forces working against discrimination are apt to be weakened still further. One way to evade a profit ceiling is by substituting nonpecuniary for pecuniary income, since the former is very difficult for a regulatory agency to control; and the satisfactions that prejudiced people derive from not associating with a minority group are a form of nonpecuniary income. Stated otherwise, the cost of discrimination to the discriminators is less where, because of regulation, the pecuniary income forgone as a result of discrimination is smaller than it would be without regulation.[2]

Labor unions that have monopoly power impair the effectiveness of competition in minimizing discrimination. A monopolistic union will increase the incomes of its members above their alternative incomes in other occupations. This disparity in turn will induce workers in other occupations to seek entry into the union. The union cannot take all comers, because if it increases the supply of labor it will be unable to maintain the monopoly price that it is charging employers. Thus the need arises to ration membership in the union. The union could auction off vacancies as they occur or permit members to sell their membership (this is the method used to fill vacancies on the New York Stock Exchange, which was until recently a cartel of stockbrokers) or adopt various nonprice criteria, such as nepotism or

2. See Armen A. Alchian & Reuben Kessel, "Competition, Monopoly, and the Pursuit of Money," in *Aspects of Labor Economics: A Conference of the Universities–National Bureau Committee for Economic Research* 157 (Nat. Bur. Econ. Research 1962).

race. The usual practice has been to use nonprice criteria, and membership in the white race was widely used. In effect, the members of the union took a part of their monopoly profits in the form of freedom from associations that were distasteful to them. In the absence of monopolistic unions, the least prejudiced workers would have an advantage in the job market comparable to that enjoyed by the least prejudiced sellers in the product market. Employers would not have to pay them so high a premium to work with black employees whom the employers might want to hire for reasons of efficiency.

Thus governmental policy, which is responsible for profit controls on monopolists and, in part, for strong labor unions, may increase discrimination above the level that would exist in an unregulated market. The effect is even greater when governments enact and enforce laws that require discrimination, as was long the practice in the southern states. To be sure, such laws will not be enacted unless there is a strong preference in the community for not associating with blacks. But it does not follow that the law adds nothing to private feeling. There may be a minority of whites who have relatively little taste for discrimination and might be unwilling to bear the expense of maintaining separate public rest rooms, schools, and other facilities in their community. In a southern state that had no law against integrated public schools, most school districts might still maintain segregated schools if permitted by federal law, but those districts whose white residents were not prepared to pay a significant price to avoid associating with blacks would not. The total amount of discrimination in the state would be less.

In *Brown v. Board of Education*,[3] the Supreme Court declared unconstitutional under the equal protection clause of the Fourteenth Amendment state laws requiring or permitting racial segregation of public schools. The Court held that segregated education was inherently unequal because it instilled a sense of inferiority in black children. There is an economic as well as a psychological basis for rejecting the notion of "separate but

---

3. 347 U.S. 483 (1954).

equal." Segregation reduces the opportunities for associations between races, associations that would be especially valuable to the blacks because of the dominant economic position of the whites in the society. The Court had recognized the point in an earlier case, *Sweatt v. Painter*.[4] In holding that blacks must be admitted to state law schools, the Court observed that black students in a segregated law school would have no opportunity to develop professional contacts with the students most likely to occupy important positions in the bench and bar after graduation. It rejected the argument that this disadvantage was offset by the disadvantage to white students of being barred from association with black law students, noting that the weak position of the blacks in the profession made such associations less valuable to white students.

The *Brown* decision has been criticized on the ground that it denies freedom of association to whites at the same time that it promotes the freedom of association of blacks and that there is no "neutral principle" by which to choose between the associational preferences of whites and of blacks.[5] But economic analysis suggests a way of distinguishing between the associational preferences of prejudiced whites and of nonprejudiced blacks. Because blacks are an economic minority, the costs to them of the whites' prejudice are proportionately greater than the costs to the whites. This is not to say that discrimination is inefficient but that discrimination has systematic redistributive effects that could be used as the premise of a neutral, though not a wealth-maximizing, antidiscrimination principle.

The Fourteenth Amendment provides that no *state* shall deny the equal protection of its laws, and it is not always clear whether discrimination should be viewed as state or private action. Three levels of state involvement in discrimination may be distinguished: a law or other official action that orders discrimination, the practice of discrimination by a public enterprise, and state involvement in private enterprises that practice discrimi-

4. 339 U.S. 629 (1950).
5. See Herbert Wechsler, "Toward Neutral Principles of Constitutional Law," 73 *Harv. L. Rev.* 1 (1959).

nation but not in the decision to discriminate. Both the first and second levels of state involvement entered into the *Brown* case, but they were not distinguished. One aspect of the Court's decision was the invalidation of laws requiring segregation in all public schools in a state. Such laws presumably enact the prejudices of the more prejudiced half of the population and thus produce greater discrimination than if the decision to segregate were left up to each public school district. The second aspect of the decision was the invalidation of state laws permitting local school districts to segregate at their option. When the decision whether or not to segregate is left to each local school district, it is not so obvious that the amount of discrimination will be different from what there would be if all education were private; but probably there will be more discrimination. A public school system is a nontransferable monopoly (private education is not so good a substitute as to deprive the school district of all monopoly power), and nontransferable monopolies can be expected to discriminate more, on average, than competitive firms or freely transferable monopolies. Since most governmental services are nontransferable monopolies, this point has general application to state agencies.[6]

The analysis is different if the decision to discriminate is made by a private individual or firm, albeit the state is involved to some extent in the private activity. The question, I believe, should be whether the state involvement would make a decision to discriminate more likely than if the state were not involved. State involvement through regulation of public utilities or common carriers increases the likelihood that the firm will follow

6. This assumes that the public agency is staffed by people who have at least the average taste for discrimination in the community. If the agency is controlled by people less prejudiced than the average of the community, it may discriminate even less than a competitive market would do. One might assume that today public agencies, especially at the federal level, are staffed by people who are less prejudiced than the average, but a recent study of male-female and black-white wage differentials among employees of the Department of Health, Education and Welfare suggests that employment practices within government are no freer from prejudice than those in the private sector. See George J. Borjas, "Discrimination in HEW: Is the Doctor Sick or Are the Patients Healthy?" 21 *J. Law & Econ.* 97 (1978).

discriminatory policies. In this case the firm's discrimination could be viewed as state action for purposes of applying the Fourteenth Amendment. However, where state involvement does not increase the likelihood of discrimination, there is no basis for attributing to the state a private decision to discriminate. The state maintains an extensive system of land title recordation and is otherwise deeply involved in the regulation of land use, but these activities do not increase the probability that a white homeowner will refuse to sell his house to a black buyer because of distaste for association with blacks.

The foregoing analysis suggests not a narrower but a different definition of state action from that employed by the courts. It would support a prohibition under the Fourteenth Amendment of racial discrimination by trade unions, for the governmental policies that have fostered the growth of monopolistic unions have thereby increased the likelihood of racial discrimination in employment. But it would not forbid discrimination by the private concessionaire in a public office building[7] unless the public authority had encouraged the concessionaire to discriminate.

Suppose state involvement takes the form of legal enforcement of a private decision to discriminate. May racial covenants be enforced?[8] May the city of Macon, Georgia, as trustee of a park donated by Senator Bacon, comply with the racial condition in the gift?[9] Does the equal protection clause preclude recourse to civil and criminal trespass remedies by shopkeepers who do not want to have black customers? It is hard to show that without legal protection of property rights there would be less discrimination. There might be more, at least in communities in which the taste for discrimination was widespread, because without a system of legally protected property rights more economic activity would have to be directed by political decision rather than by the market. It is true but trivial that if the state

7. As in Burton v. Wilmington Parking Authority, 365 U.S. 715 (1961).
8. See Shelley v. Kraemer, 334 U.S. 1 (1948).
9. See Evans v. Newton, 382 U.S. 296 (1966).

enforced all private decisions except those to discriminate, the cost of discrimination would be higher and the incidence lower. This is equivalent to saying that the state's failure to punish private discrimination is discriminatory state action, a view that would nullify the constitutional requirement of state action.

To be sure, in the restrictive-convenant and charitable-gift cases the effect of enforcing a racial condition would be to create more discrimination than the members of society today want, assuming a secular decline in the taste for discrimination.[10] But it is fortuitous whether the result of a perpetual condition is more or less discrimination than contemporaries want. Were there a secular increase rather than a decline in racial discrimination, enforcing racially motivated deed or gift restrictions (such as a provision in a foundation charter declaring that the purpose of the foundation was to promote racial integration) might produce less discrimination than contemporaries wanted.

If the approach to the state-action requirement that I am advocating were adopted, the constitutional prohibition against racial discrimination could be justified not only by the distributive effects of discrimination (greater costs imposed on the minority than on the majority), but also by the fact that discriminatory state action produces more discrimination than a free market would. This ground is not available to justify laws that forbid purely private discrimination.

The most commonly advanced justifications for the federal laws forbidding private discrimination in the sale and rental of real estate, in employment, and in restaurants, hotels, and other places of public accommodation are first that these laws are necessary to eliminate the effects of centuries of discriminatory legislation and second that they promote interstate commerce. The

10. The discussion in Chapters 6 and 7 of information costs may be relevant in explaining this decline. As those costs fall over time, individualized assessment of people becomes more feasible, so less reliance is placed on race and other attributes that are crude proxies for individual characteristics. It cannot be assumed, however, that the decline in discrimination is permanent and continuous. Costs of information are not the only sources of discrimination, and information costs cannot be assumed to be always and everywhere falling.

second justification strikes many people as contrived, yet it makes economic sense. Discrimination reduces transactions between blacks and whites, and many of the transactions would be in interstate commerce, even narrowly defined. It is the first justification that is dubious, because of its well-nigh infinite reach. Virtually any deprivation from which black people suffer today may be attributable in part to past discrimination fostered by discriminatory laws or other governmental policies. If black children on average do not perform well in northern schools, it may be because the returns to education for black people have traditionally been low as a result of discrimination in employment against educated blacks; this discrimination in turn may have been influenced by the discriminatory governmental policies of the southern states from which many northern blacks originally came.

Laws forbidding discrimination in employment present interesting questions of proof, statutory purpose, remedy, and efficacy. Even if a firm is located in an area having a large black population, it may have no black employees for reasons unrelated to discrimination by either the management or the white workers. There may be no blacks with the requisite training or aptitude, or blacks may not like the type of work or may simply be unaware of job openings at the firm. If any of these reasons are operative, it becomes necessary to decide whether the purpose of the law is simply to prevent discrimination or whether it is designed to improve the condition of blacks regardless of discrimination. There are economic reasons for preferring the narrower interpretation, even if one accepts the appropriateness of redistributing wealth in favor of blacks. If an employer is compelled to hire unqualified blacks or pay them a premium to induce them to do work they do not like or advertise in the black community jobs in which very few blacks are interested, the firm sustains costs in excess of the benefits to the blacks who are hired. The unqualified black employee imposes productivity losses that he does not recoup in higher wages. The premium paid to the black employee who does not like his job is a cost to the firm but not a benefit to the employee: it only offsets the nonpecuniary cost of the job to him. The expense of advertising jobs in the black community may not confer a commensurate benefit on the blacks if the advertising fails to generate a significant flow of qualified applicants. Since the major part of the additional costs are passed on to the firm's consumers, these methods of improving the welfare of black people tend to be regressive as well as costly.

Laws forbidding employment discrimination are costly even when applied to employers who in fact discriminate. The employer may have to pay a higher wage to those white workers who have both a taste for discrimination and attractive alternative opportunities in firms that do not have black employees. If they lack such opportunities, the elimination of discrimination may impose no pecuniary costs—by hypothesis the workers have no choice but to accept association with blacks—but it will impose nonpecuniary costs in the form of distasteful association. And the costs are unlikely to be offset by the gains of black workers for whom jobs in the firm are superior to their alternative opportunities, nor will they be offset by the economic advantages that increased trading with blacks brings to the firm and hence to its customers; if there were such offsetting gains, the blacks would probably have been hired without legal pressure.

What is the appropriate remedy in a job discrimination case in which a violation has been adjudged? If the employer has discriminated against blacks, he should, in my judgment, be required to pay the damages of any black person against whom he has discriminated (perhaps doubled or trebled to facilitate enforcement where damages are small). This type of judgment both compensates and deters and seems preferable to an injunctive remedy requiring the employer to hire a specified number or percentage of blacks. The injunction forces him to lay off white workers or, what amounts to the same thing, to favor black over white job applicants until the quota fixed in the decree is attained. Such an injunction, by imposing costs on white employees (who may be untainted by discrimination) in order to improve the condition of black workers, operates as a capricious and regressive tax on the white working class. Moreover, many of the blacks who benefit from the decree may not have been discriminated against by the firm, and many of those discriminated against may not benefit from the decree.

The analysis is even more complicated if the employees share responsibility with the employer for the discrimination. The employees may have barred blacks from their union, or the employer may have discriminated only because of his workers' taste for discrimination—he himself may not have that taste. In this case, the appropriate remedy is a judgment of damages against the workers or their union. Injunctive relief would again be inappropriate.

Thus far I have assumed that whatever their other effects, laws forbidding discrimination (however defined) will improve the net welfare of the victims of discrimination. But this is not certain. For example, a study of state fair employment laws found that, while the laws indeed increased the demand for black workers, the provisions requiring that blacks be paid as much as whites caused disemployment of blacks, and the two effects canceled each other out.[11]

It is often urged that to rectify historical injustices, blacks should be given preferential treatment—for example, law schools should set lower admission standards for blacks than for whites even if the admission criteria provide unbiased estimates of black academic performance. "Reverse discrimination" of this sort is attacked on the ground that any use of racial criteria to allocate burdens or benefits is unconstitutional, and defended on the ground that reverse discrimination is fundamentally unlike discrimination against blacks. Are the two forms of discrimination fundamentally unlike? Answering this question requires that we go behind the assumption that discrimination is simply a taste, and inquire into its causes.

11. See William M. Landes, "The Economics of Fair Employment Laws," 76 *J. Pol. Econ.* 507 (1968), and for a survey of the literature on the effects of antidiscrimination laws, Richard Butler & James J. Heckman, "The Government's Impact on the Labor Market Status of Black Americans: A Critical Review," in *Equal Rights and Industrial Relations* 235 (Ind. Rel. Res. Assn. Ser. 1977).

Discrimination against racial or other groups has a number of possible causes. Sheer malevolence and irrationality may be factors in some cases. Discrimination is sometimes anticompetitive —this appears to have been a factor in the internment during World War II of California's Japanese residents—and sometimes exploitative, as in the case of Negro slavery; race enters as a convenient factor identifying the members of the competing or exploited group. In recent times, however, the most important factor responsible for discrimination probably has been information costs.[12] To the extent that race or some attribute similarly difficult to conceal (sex, accent) is positively correlated with undesired characteristics or negatively correlated with desired characteristics, it is rational for people to use the attribute as a proxy for the underlying characteristic with which it is correlated. If experience has taught me (perhaps incorrectly) that most Mycenaeans have a strong garlic breath, I can economize on information costs by declining to join a club that accepts Mycenaeans as members. To be sure, I may thereby be forgoing a valuable association with some Mycenaeans who do not have a strong garlic breath, but the costs in valuable associations forgone may be smaller than the information costs of making a more extensive sampling of Mycenaeans. Discrimination so motivated is no different in its fundamental economic character (its distributive effects may of course be different) from a decision to stop buying Brand X toothpaste because of an unhappy experience with a previous purchase of it, albeit the next experience with the brand might have been better. It is no different in its fundamental economic character from the use of information about a person's criminal record to infer his likely fitness as

12. On the information-costs theory of discrimination see Kenneth Arrow, "The Theory of Discrimination," in *Discrimination in Labor Markets* 3, 24–26 (Orley Ashenfelter & Albert Rees eds. 1973); Edmund S. Phelps, "The Statistical Theory of Racism and Sexism," 62 *Am. Econ. Rev. Papers and Proceedings* 287, 292–294 (1973). And for empirical evidence see Richard Sutch & Roger Ransom, "The Ex-Slave in the Post-Bellum South: A Study of the Economic Impact of Racism in a Market Environment," 33 *J. Econ. Hist.* 131 (1973).

an employee, an example of the use of proxies to economize on information costs that was discussed in Chapter 9.

The fact that much racial discrimination may be efficient does not mean that it is or should be lawful. It does suggest, however, that the "balancing" approach sometimes used in constitutional cases might, if honestly followed in racial cases, result in upholding many instances of racial discrimination on efficiency grounds, even if distributive effects were also weighed in the balance. Stated otherwise, people who advocate the balancing approach, confident that discrimination will never be sustained because it is always irrational, may be in for a rude shock. This issue is pursued further in the following two chapers.

13

The *DeFunis* Case
and Reverse Discrimination

This chapter and the next will examine the three major cases in which the Supreme Court has been asked to pass on the validity of schemes of reverse discrimination or affirmative action. The first of these cases, *DeFunis v. Odegaard*,[1] was dismissed by the Court on grounds of mootness, with the result that there was no decision on the merits of the challenged racial scheme. In the next case, *Bakke v. Regents of the University of California*,[2] the Court invalidated a state scheme of reverse discrimination, but none of the opinions of the justices commanded majority support. In the third case, *United Steelworkers of America v. Weber*,[3] the Court upheld the lawfulness of an affirmative-action scheme challenged under one of the federal civil rights statutes but did not decide any constitutional question.

The facts of *DeFunis* are briefly as follows. Marco DeFunis applied for and was denied admission to the first-year class of the University of Washington Law School, a state institution. The law school's admissions process involved first determining from the applicant's college grades and the results of his law school aptitude test (LSAT) his expected grade-point average in the first year of law school. If the expected average was above a certain level, the applicant was automatically admitted. Below this level the applicants were divided into two groups, one consisting of all applicants who were black, Chicano, American Indian, or Filipino, the other of the remaining applicants. About 20 percent of the places in the entering class were reserved for mem-

1. 416 U.S. 312 (1974).
2. 438 U.S. 265 (1978).
3. 443 U.S. 193 (1979).

bers of the first group. An effort was made to identify the most promising members within each group, but qualifications were not compared across groups. Thirty-six of the thirty-seven admittees in the favored-minorities group had expected first-year averages lower than that of DeFunis, who was one of the rejected applicants in the second group. The avowed purpose of according preferential treatment to the four minority groups was to increase their representation in the law school student body and in the legal profession.

DeFunis brought an action for injunctive relief against the university, charging that it had discriminated against him on account of his race (white), in violation of the equal protection clause of the Fourteenth Amendment. The trial court agreed and ordered him admitted to the first-year class. The Washington Supreme Court reversed,[4] but its order was stayed by Justice Douglas pending review by the United States Supreme Court. By the time the case was briefed in the Supreme Court, DeFunis—who had been admitted under a temporary restraining order entered before the trial court's final decision—was in his final year of law school, and counsel for the university advised the Court that DeFunis would be permitted to complete the year regardless of the outcome of the litigation. It was on this basis that the Court held the case moot, Justice Douglas filed a separate opinion in which he declared that preferential racial treatment was unconstitutional, but that the case should be remanded for a trial on the question whether the law school aptitude test discriminates against members of disadvantaged minorities.

The Reasonableness of Reverse Discrimination

What reasons might be offered for the reverse discrimination[5] practiced by the University of Washington Law School?

4. 82 Wash. 2d 11, 507 P.2d 1169 (1973).

5. For a prescient discussion of the problems of reverse discrimination, see John Kaplan, "Equal Justice in an Unequal World: Equality for the Negro—The Problem of Special Treatment," 61 *Nw. U. L. Rev.* 363 (1966). And for thoughtful criticism of the

1. Justice Douglas stated that the conventional predictors of law school success are inaccurate with respect to members of disadvantaged minorities. There is apparently no basis for this conjecture,[6] but if that had been the rationale of the University of Washington Law School's admissions procedure (it was not), the case would not have been one of preferential treatment.

2. A popular basis for preferential treatment in school admissions is the desire to increase the diversity of the student body in order to enhance the quality of the students' educational experience. An *amicus curiae* brief filed on behalf of Harvard University advanced this ground, although it was not the University of Washington Law School's ground for preferential admissions and would not have justified its policy.[7]

For a diversity argument to be convincing, it must identify a differentiating factor that is relevant to the educational experience. No one would argue that in selecting the first-year class, a law school should strive for diversity in the height of the students, or in their weight, pulchritude, posture, depth of voice, or blood pressure, or that it should give a preference to (or disfavor) albinos or people with freckles or double chins. Diversity in these superficial physical respects contributes nothing to the legal education of the students. Race *per se*—that is, race com-

---

argument in this chapter, see Terrance Sandalow, "Racial Preferences in Higher Education: Political Responsibility and the Judicial Role," 42 *U. Chi. L. Rev.* 653 (1975).

6. See John Hart Ely, "The Constitutionality of Reverse Racial Discrimination," 41 *U. Chi. L. Rev.* 723, 725–726 n.22 (1974). A variant of Justice Douglas's argument, also suggested in his opinion, is that even if the conventional criteria predict academic performance as accurately for the minority-group members as for others, they do not predict the value of their contribution to society as lawyers (after graduation) so well. Such an argument may perhaps have been implicit in the University of Washington Law School's expressed basis for its preferential admissions policy—to increase the proportion of minority-group members in the legal profession. I discuss this later as part of a more general consideration of the underrepresentation argument for preferential treatment.

7. The law school set a target of 20 percent minority admissions, which is roughly equal to the proportion of the four favored minorities in the United States population as a whole. There is little connection between seeking *proportional* representation of minorities, on the one hand, and, on the other, enhancing the quality of the educational experience by providing *some* representation for members of minority groups who could not gain admission on the basis of academic promise alone.

pletely divorced from certain characteristics that may be strongly correlated with but do not always accompany it—is also, and in a similar sense, irrelevant to diversity. There are black people (and Chicanos, Filipinos, and so on) who differ only in the most superficial physical characteristics from whites —who have the same tastes, manners, experiences, aptitudes, and aspirations as the whites with whom one might compare them (here, white law school applicants). According such people preferential treatment to increase the diversity of the student body would be equivalent to giving preferential treatment to albinos—except that race is frequently correlated with other attributes that are arguably relevant to meaningful diversity, and albinism is not. The average black applicant for admission is more likely than the average white to have known prejudice at first hand, and his experience, communicated to his fellow students (and teachers) both inside and outside the classroom, might enrich the educational process. The use of a racial proxy in making admissions decisions will produce some inaccuracy—blacks will be admitted who lack the attributes that contribute to genuine diversity[8]—but this cost of using a racial proxy may be less than the cost saved of having to investigate the actual characteristics of each applicant.

The objection to this approach is that it closely resembles, and could be viewed as imparting legitimacy to, the case for regarding discrimination against racial minorities as proper because it is generally efficient. Recalling the analysis of "statistical" discrimination in the last chapter, suppose that a particular racial or ethnic identity is correlated with characteristics that are widely disliked for reasons not patently exploitative, anticompetitive, or irrational. A substantial proportion of the members of the group may be loud, poor,[9] hostile, irresponsible, poorly

8. Thus the Harvard University brief describes "minority status" as "a useful although not invariably reliable indicator of a kind of special social, economic or cultural background." Brief of Harvard University as *Amicus Curiae*, DeFunis v. Odegaard, at 28; see also pp. 14, 16.

9. Poverty is another proxy for undesired characteristics. Some poor people (college students, clergymen, and bankrupts are examples) are distinguishable from the nonpoor mainly by the fact of being poor rather than by social or cultural differences.

educated,[10] dangerously irascible, or ill-mannered, or have different tastes, values, and work habits from our own, or speak an unintelligible patois.[11] To be averse to association (in housing, recreation, schooling, or employment) with an *individual* because he possesses such a characteristic would not ordinarily be regarded as a sign of prejudice. To be "prejudiced" means, rather, to ascribe to all members of a group defined by a racial or similarly arbitrary characteristic attributes typically or frequently possessed by members of the group, without considering whether an individual member has that characteristic—sometimes without being willing even to consider evidence that he does not.[12]

A policy against hostile discrimination could be undermined by a program of benevolent discrimination rooted in the same habit of mind—that of using race or ethnic origin to establish a presumption, and in the case of a racially preferential admissions program a conclusive presumption, that an individual possesses some attribute, that is, some educationally relevant characteristic, such as a background of deprivation or a cultural difference. The danger is increased by the fact that the hostile and the well-disposed discriminators seem to be treating race as a proxy for the same set of characteristics. The characteristics that university admissions officers associate with "black" are the distinctive cultural attributes of many black people who have grown up in an urban slum or in the rural South, and these are

10. On black versus white educational achievement see James S. Coleman et al., *Equality of Educational Opportunity* 20–21, 217–233 (1966).

11. The proportion of the racial or ethnic group who actually possess the disfavored characteristic may, of course, be exaggerated, since obtaining accurate information about the characteristics of the average member may be costly too.

12. An "arbitrary characteristic" in this sense is one whose only significance is as a proxy for some other characteristic. To dislike short people because one finds them repulsive is not prejudice; to dislike short people because one thinks that short people tend to have aggressive personalities is an example of prejudice, since not all short people in fact possess such personalities.

An extreme form of prejudice, not relevant to my discussion here, is to dislike people for a characteristic they do not in fact typically possess. This type of discrimination is effectively counteracted by contact with the group discriminated against. "Rational prejudice," which I believe to be more common, at least today, is reinforced by contact.

the same characteristics that the white bigot ascribes to every black, although he uses a different terminology (for example, "lazy" rather than "unmotivated").

The argument that reverse discrimination resembles and in a certain way legitimizes racial prejudice is reinforced by considering some features of the actual implementation of a racial preference policy. To administer such a policy one needs an operational definition of membership in the favored group because the applicant cannot be relied upon to classify himself correctly. The correct racial classification is not always obvious; and since a benefit attaches to membership in particular racial groups, applicants have an incentive to misrepresent their race. Thus admissions officials confront the problem both of determining what constitutes membership in a racial group and of requiring appropriate evidence that an applicant belongs to it.[13] In the case of blacks, it is necessary to determine what percentage of Negro ancestry should be required of an applicant claiming preferential treatment as a black. Additional problems of definition, and also of proof, arise with respect to Chicanos. If the president of Mexico marries an American woman and they have a child who is brought up in the United States, is the child a Chicano? Or is the term meant to imply some connection with life in a *barrio*? With regard to proof, Chicanos are less distinctive in physical appearance than most blacks; and the possession or lack of a Spanish surname is not decisive evidence. Puerto Ricans, Spaniards, and Latin Americans other than Mexicans also have Spanish surnames; and a Chicano might be the cnilc of a Chicano woman and a non-Chicano man. Similar problems exist with respect to American Indians. Many Americans have some Indian blood without being recognizable as Indian or having a characteristically Indian name. This problem could be avoided by limiting preferential treatment to Indians on reser-

13. For a good discussion of the problems of racial classification created by schemes of benevolent racial discrimination, see Boris I. Bittker, *The Case for Black Reparations*, ch. 10 (1973). According to the record in the *DeFunis* case, the University of Washington used self-classification. But this is probably not a viable policy in the long run, depending as it does wholly on the good faith of the applicant.

vations, but such a limitation would be difficult to justify to Indians who have left the reservation and may have encountered substantial difficulties in adjusting to life on the outside. A solution to all such problems is to delegate the determination of whether an applicant is entitled to preferential treatment to the student association for the group in which he claims membership (such as the Black Students' Union), but the dangers of serious abuse in such a course are evident.[14]

My point is not that the administrative problems,[15] and therefore costs, of implementing a program of racial preferences in admissions should be decisive against adoption of such a program. The problems of definition and proof are relevant to the present discussion because they illustrate the distinction between racial or ethnic identity *per se* and the relevant characteristics for which that identity is a proxy. Suppose a family has so little Negro blood that it has been able to pass as white and has done so, suppressing all cultural traits that might betray its "true" identity. The family has a child who has been brought up

14. Such organizations may define group membership in terms of an individual's commitment to the political goals of the organization rather than in terms of "objective" (genealogical) factors. This suggests an issue DeFunis might have raised but did not. Apparently he could have argued with some force that the University of Washington Law School's admissions committee, especially its student members, gave preferential treatment to political activists of a left or liberal persuasion; that such treatment by a state institution violated the First Amendment; and that DeFunis was harmed by this preference since he was not politically active. The evidence that might support such an argument is reviewed in Chief Justice Hale's dissenting opinion in the Supreme Court of Washington. 82 Wash. 2d 11, 55–56, 507 P.2d 1169, 1194 (1973). DeFunis did argue that the admissions procedure was arbitrary—it was in evaluating that argument that Hale discussed the evidence in question—but he did not make a First Amendment claim, nor did he press his challenge to the arbitrariness of the admissions procedure in the Supreme Court.

15. Some of them are of the universities' own making. For example, some American Indians do not like to be referred to by that term; they prefer "native American." Out of deference to their sensibility (and without regard to the fact that other native-born Americans may consider presumptuous the Indians' attempt to appropriate the term), the admissions form of one university that has a preferential admissions policy toward Indians contains a box in which the applicant can check "native American." Many non-Indian Americans born in this country check the box without knowing that the term is limited to Indians. So whenever an applicant does check the box, the university sends him a follow-up letter asking him whether he meant that he was an American Indian.

as a white but knows that he has some Negro ancestors and who, in applying for admission to law school, claims entitlement to preferential treatment as a black. Should his claim be honored? If it is, the law school's action is like the decision of a country club to deny this individual membership on the sole ground that it does not admit blacks. If the admissions committee takes the position that a single black great-great grandparent "makes a difference," if only as a matter of administrative convenience, on what basis can one criticize the country club (or employer or school board) that reaches the same conclusion on the same ground?

Another point is that using race as a proxy for characteristics thought to be relevant to the educational experience results in discrimination against people who have the characteristics, but not the racial identity. Suppose DeFunis had been an Appalachian white who had encountered and overcome greater economic and cultural handicaps to obtaining an education and preparing himself for a career as a lawyer than some fraction of the applicants accorded preferential treatment on racial grounds.[16] It would still be possible to justify his exclusion from the favored class on the ground of administrative convenience by invoking a presumption that disadvantaged individuals are a greater proportion of the favored groups than of white applicants. But the result of deferring to administrative costs in this instance would be systematically to discriminate against disadvantaged subgroups within the white majority, for no better reason than that the group lacks one of the racial or ethnic characteristics used for administrative convenience to determine entitlement to preferential treatment.

Where, as in the *DeFunis* case itself, racial preference is based

16. Most poor Americans are white. See U.S. Dept. of Commerce, Bureau of the Census, *1970 Census of Population—Subject Reports—Low-Income Population* 53, 61 (1973). And most members of generally disadvantaged minorities are not poor. See U.S. Dept. of Commerce, Bureau of the Census, *U.S. Census of Population: 1970—Detailed Characteristics*, tabs. 250, 347 (1973). One would, in fact, expect the nonpoor members of minority groups to be overrepresented, relative to the poor members of their groups, among law-school and other university applicants.

on simply a desire to increase the number of black lawyers, apparently so that they will be proportionately equal to the number of white lawyers, the diversity ground that I have been discussing falls away. But several other grounds are possible: making amends for past discrimination; putting the minority group where it would have been but for the handicaps imposed by discrimination; improving the level of professional services received by the group; and encouraging the aspirations of its members by providing suitable role models. These grounds have now to be considered.

3. The "reparations" ground is unpersuasive because the members of the minority group who receive preferential treatment will often not be victims of discrimination, and the nonminority people excluded because of the preferences are unlikely to have perpetrated, or in any demonstrable sense benefited from, the discrimination.[17] Indian reparations may be a distinct case, based on treaty (equivalent to contractual) obligations; also distinguishable is the use of racial quotas as part of a decree to remedy unlawful discrimination.

4. Many groups are underrepresented in various occupations for reasons of taste, opportunity, or aptitude unrelated to discrimination. There is no basis for a presumption that were it not for past discrimination the four minorities favored by the University of Washington Law School would supply 20 percent of the nation's lawyers.

5. There is no evidence as to the number or proportion of minority-group law school graduates who seek in their professional careers to serve the special interests of their minority

17. One could spend many profitless hours discussing whether DeFunis is better or worse off as the result of the history of racial discrimination in this country. Perhaps he is better off because, but for a history of discrimination, there would be a larger pool of qualified black applicants for a law school education. Perhaps he is worse off because, but for that history, fewer blacks (and members of other minorities) would be interested in becoming lawyers. Perhaps if there had never been discrimination against blacks, there would never have been slavery in the United States, and without slavery, it is possible, indeed probable, that the black population in the United States would be insignificant, in which event the real income of whites might be higher—or lower—than it is.

group rather than follow the normal patterns of professional advancement.[18]

6. The "role model" argument is similarly *ad hoc* and conjectural. So long as a significant number of members of a minority group enter the legal profession and succeed in it (one of the justices of the Supreme Court is black, after all), others will know that it is not closed to them. There is no compelling need for proportional representation.[19]

The ultimate logic of the underrepresentation argument that underlies grounds 3 to 6 is that the percentage of members of each minority racial and ethnic group in each desirable occupation, and in each level of achievement within the occupation, should be raised to equality with its percentage of the total population (either of the entire nation or, in some versions, of some region or local area). The proponents of racial proportional representation do not as yet urge adoption of the standard of complete proportional equality, but there seems to be no logical stopping point short of it within the structure of their argument. This is true despite their soothing assurance that affirma-

18. Those who argue that they do are careful to state the argument in a form that assures they will not be embarrassed by facts. Thus the *amicus* brief submitted by the Council on Legal Education Opportunity in the *DeFunis* case states (p. 24): "Since the greatest needs for legal services exist in the socioeconomically disadvantaged areas, a preference for students from those areas might be justified by the belief that such students would return to their communities after graduation. (Important values may be served even if they do not return—for example, the diversification of the bar and the creation of 'role models' for younger members of historically underrepresented groups. Thus there need be no proof of a commitment to return to the community of origin to justify such a preference.)"

19. Anyone who was serious about the role model point would want the minorities to be represented in the professions in inverse proportion to their percentage of the population. Suppose Indigos were 10 percent of the population and Ultramarines only 1 percent. If the percentage of Indigo lawyers was raised to 10 to supply adequate role models for young Indigos, the percentage of Ultramarine lawyers should also be raised to 10, for only in that way will the Ultramarine role models be as visible to young Ultramarines. (If only 1 percent of lawyers were Ultramarine, the young Ultramarine would rarely hear of or encounter Ultramarine lawyers on the federal bench or in other positions of prominence.) Conversely, if the role model needs of the Ultramarines are satisfied by proportional representation, the role model needs of the Indigos will be equally well satisfied if 1 percent of the nation's lawyers are Indigo.

tive action is required only in a period of transition to a society in which, all vestiges of discrimination having been eliminated by affirmative action, society can resume a policy of color-blindness. If occupational preferences and abilities are not randomly distributed across all racial and ethnic groups, then governmental intervention in the labor markets (and in the educational process insofar as it affects occupational choice and success) will have to continue forever to secure proportional equality in the desirable occupations. This kind of intervention would distort the allocation of labor and drive a wedge between individual merit and economic and professional success, thereby undermining the incentives on which a free society depends.

A superficially attractive variant of the underrepresentation argument is that at the present time the demand for minority lawyers is greater than that for white lawyers because of the special needs of minority-group members for legal representation and because of their preference for having members of their own group represent them. Therefore they should be given preferential treatment in admissions. But to accept this argument would again be to embrace the intellectual basis for the kinds of racial and ethnic discrimination that we do not like, for it would justify excluding an individual black who had greater academic promise than some white applicant, on the ground that prejudice or other factors would limit the contribution that the black could make to the profession.[20]

20. A similar type of argument would be that women should be treated less favorably than men with respect to admission to law school because the average lifetime earnings of female lawyers are lower than those of male lawyers. See U.S. Dept. of Commerce, Bureau of the Census, *U.S. Census of Population 1970—Occupational Characteristics* 280, 282 (1973). Hence, it could be argued, the demand for male lawyers is greater than the demand for female lawyers. Such an argument would be unconvincing if places in the entering class of law school were simply auctioned to the highest bidders. Then the class would be composed of those who placed the highest value on a law school education, with value being influenced by earnings prospects. But when places are not rationed by price, it is appropriate—in the absence of a private or public policy against discrimination—to award places in accordance with the law school's judgment of the value that each applicant can derive from attending law school, a value that may be affected by racial or sexual discrimination against the applicant.

A version of this kind of argument appears in the *amicus* brief of the Council on Legal

The Constitutional Issue

Did the University of Washington Law School deny white people equal protection when it established a racially preferential admissions program? John Ely answers this question in the negative. He concedes that a policy of discrimination, favorable or unfavorable, might be adopted simply because the costs of individualized treatment were thought to exceed its benefits, but argues that when members of one racial group—such as the white majority of a state legislature—are appraising the costs and benefits of proposed discrimination against another racial group, the comparison is likely to be distorted by conscious or unconscious racial hostility.[21] Hence discrimination *against* a racial minority should be suspect under the Fourteenth Amendment, but discrimination in favor of a minority should not be, because it does not involve the danger of majority exploitation of a minority.

But this argument in fact provides a mode of justifying discrimination *against* racial minorities. Suppose the Post Office were able to demonstrate so convincingly as to rebut any inference of racial hostility that blacks had, on average, inferior aptitudes to whites for supervisory positions, that the costs to the postal system of inadequate supervisors were very great, and that the costs of conducting the inquiries necessary to ascertain whether an individual black had the requisite aptitudes were also great relative to the probability of discovering qualified blacks. It would follow from Ely's analysis that the Post Office

---

Education Opportunity, an organization that gives prelaw training to members of disadvantaged minorities. The brief states (pp. 23–24) that CLEO graduates "begin each year with a guaranteed stipend in addition to whatever scholarship, loan and workstudy funds are provided by the school itself. Many other applicants bring to law school pressing financial needs with less hopeful prospects for their alleviation. An admissions committee might reasonably conclude that a minority student, thus assisted, was a better risk than a nonminority student less well provided for." In other words, it is proper to give a preference to an applicant who has more money, because he is less likely to be distracted from his studies by pressing financial needs than a poorer applicant.

21. Ely, supra note 6, at 729, 732–733.

could adopt a rule barring blacks from supervisory positions. By condemning only inefficient discriminations, Ely drastically curtails the scope of the equal protection clause if I am correct that most discrimination in contemporary society is the result of the costs of information rather than irrationality, exploitation, or the suppression of competition.

Ronald Dworkin makes a different argument for treating discrimination against blacks differently from discrimination against whites, an argument based on his concept of "external preferences."[22] He thinks it would be wrong to outlaw all racial classifications because various arguments, both utilitarian and what he calls "ideal," can be made in their favor; both sorts of argument, he notes, are made by proponents of reverse discrimination. He concedes that utilitarian arguments can also be made on behalf of discrimination against blacks, but these arguments, he says, relate solely to external preferences. He asks what arguments the admissions committee of the University of Texas Law School might have made in *Sweatt v. Painter* (discussed in the last chapter) to justify not admitting blacks, and he answers that the committee, "though composed of men and women who themselves held no prejudices, [might have] decided that the Texas economy demanded more white lawyers than they could educate, but could find no use for black lawyers at all," or that "alumni gifts to the law school would fall off drastically if it admitted a black student."[23] These justifications, unlike those which support reverse discrimination, are rooted in external preferences—the prejudice of Texans against blacks, which reduces the demand for black lawyers and would discourage alumni gifts to a law school which admitted them—and therefore, Dworkin argues, should not be given weight in a constitutional analysis.

Dworkin goes on to argue that a law school which admits applicants on the basis of intelligence is not similarly guilty of using external preferences to justify its admission policies. But

22. See Ronald Dworkin, *Taking Rights Seriously,* ch. 9 (1977); and Chapter 3 of this book.

23. *Id.* at 230.

this argument suggests that he is unaware of the economic or statistical theory of discrimination,[24] which holds that people discriminate on grounds of race or sex or IQ simply because these are convenient proxies for the underlying personal characteristics they are interested in. Thus the University of Texas Law School admissions committee might have been able to use the same kind of argument for not admitting blacks as they might use for not admitting applicants who scored below 600 on the LSAT, and it is not an argument based on external preferences.

How, then, should the constitutional question in *DeFunis* have been resolved? One polar approach to constructing a constitutional rule for discrimination is to be guided completely by the expressed intent of the framers of the Fourteenth Amendment. If the scope of the amendment were determined in this way, DeFunis would have no leg to stand on. Discrimination against whites in admission to institutions of higher learning would have seemed so bizarre to the framers of the Fourteenth Amendment that we can be confident they did not intend to erect a constitutional barrier against such discrimination. But it is also clear that the framers did not contemplate that the amendment would compel equal treatment of blacks in public education.[25] In any event, this approach to interpretation of a constitutional provision is unsound. The costs of amending the Constitution argue for a liberal interpretation of its provisions.[26] A new constitutional amendment should not be needed to prevent states from imposing on blacks forms of discrimination unknown to the framers of the Fourteenth Amendment.

The opposite extreme would be to view the equal protection clause as authorizing the justices of the Supreme Court to enact into constitutional doctrine their personal values with respect to

24. He is not alone in this oversight. See, e.g., Jay Newman, "Prejudice as Prejudgment," 90 *Ethics* 47 (1979).

25. See Alexander M. Bickel, "The Original Understanding and the Segregation Decision," 69 *Harv. L. Rev.* 1 (1955).

26. See Isaac Ehrlich & Richard A. Posner, "An Economic Analysis of Legal Rulemaking," 3 *J. Leg. Stud.* 257, 280 (1974).

social questions, such as poverty, racial discrimination, and equality between the sexes. The arguments against the Court's assuming the role of superlegislature have been made so compellingly by others[27] that I shall not discuss this approach.

The middle course is to derive from the specific purposes of the constitutional framers a rule that, while sufficiently general to avoid constant recourse to the amendment process, is sufficiently precise and objective to limit a judge's exercise of personal whim and preference. Such a rule would be that it is not permissible for the government to distribute benefits and costs on racial or ethnic grounds. Even though it may often be efficient to sort people by race or ethnic origin because racial or ethnic identity may be a good proxy for functional classifications, efficiency is rejected as a basis for governmental action in this context. Permitting discrimination to be justified on efficiency grounds, as Professor Ely would, would not only thwart the purpose of the equal protection clause by allowing much, perhaps most, discrimination to continue, but it would give the judges the power to pick and choose among discriminatory measures on the basis of personal values, for the weighing of the relevant costs and benefits would inevitably be largely subjective.

One may object that the principle I propose is itself subjective and arbitrary, because only race and ethnic origin are subject to it, not all of the immutable or involuntary characteristics which are used as proxies. Height, youth, sex, and low IQ are some of the other immutable characteristics used as criteria for governmental regulation:[28] on what objective basis can they be distinguished from genealogy? First, if the constitutional principle were defined in terms of *all* involuntary characteristics, it would violate the requirement that a constitutional principle bind the judges. Since no one could argue that no involuntary characteristic should ever be used as a criterion of public regulation, the

27. See in particular the neglected contribution of Robert H. Bork, "Neutral Principles and Some First Amendment Problems," 47 *Ind. L. J.* 1 (1971)

28. IQ is not valued in itself, but as a predictor (only partially accurate) of academic or some other sort of intellectual performance.

principle would give the judges interpreting it carte blanche to pick and choose among groups defined by an immutable characteristic. Second, racial and ethnic differences are generally smaller, from a performance or functional standpoint, than sexual and age differences. A rule forbidding blacks to work in mines, one forbidding women to work in mines, and one forbidding children to work in mines may all be discriminatory, but one must strain to regard them as identical. In contrast, it would be very difficult to distinguish a rule forbidding Chicanos, Jews, American Indians, or Italian-Americans to work in mines from a rule forbidding blacks to work in mines.[29]

It remains to consider whether an exception to the rule forbidding discrimination on racial or ethnic grounds should be recognized where the discrimination can be said to favor a racial or ethnic minority and the race discriminated against is the white race. Such an exception would require the court not only to consider whether there was discrimination but to decide whether the discrimination helped or hurt a particular racial group and to weigh the competing claims of different groups. The additional inquiries would rob the principle of its precision and objectivity. In the *Brown* case the Court had no good evidence before it that segregated education in fact harmed blacks. The questions critical to the point where not even asked: Would blacks have fared better under a system of no public education (assuming that whites would prefer such a system to integrated public education)? Under a system where students were sorted by IQ? By family income? In later cases the Court stopped asking whether segregation actually hurt the blacks. (Today some blacks favor segregation.) It has long been argued that some types of restrictions on blacks, such as "benign" housing quotas, actually benefit them.[30] The arguments for these restrictions,

29. The congressional debates preceding the enactment of the Fourteenth Amendment indicate an awareness that its protections could not be denied to other racial-ethnic groups besides the blacks, e.g., the Chinese. See references indexed in Alfred Avins, *The Reconstruction Amendments Debates* 746 (1967).

30. See Bruce L. Ackerman, "Integration for Subsidized Housing and the Question of Racial Occupancy Controls," 26 *Stan. L. Rev.* 245 (1974), advocating this position.

spongy as they are, are no weaker than many arguments that the Court accepts in upholding state action challenged under the equal protection clause in nonracial areas. The arguments about the proper characterization of discrimination that is nominally in favor of racial minorities have a similar sponginess. Is the position of the whites in this country so unassailable that they cannot be harmed by racial quotas? Or is the impact of such quotas likely to be concentrated on particular, and perhaps vulnerable, subgroups within the white majority? Do racial quotas actually help the minorities intended to be benefited, or harm them by impairing their self-esteem or by legitimating stereotypical thinking about race? Are whites entitled to claim minority status when they are a minority within the political subdivision that enacted the measure discriminating against whites? If so, then by similar reasoning would blacks lack standing to complain about an ordinance discriminating against them enacted by Newark, New Jersey, or Washington, D.C., or other cities in which blacks are a majority of the population eligible to vote?

I am prepared to recognize one minor qualification to the principle that racial or ethnic criteria should not be used to determine the distribution of government benefits and burdens. Suppose a prison decided to segregate its inmates by race, not as a method of preference or exclusion but simply to reduce violence stemming from the racial hostilities of both black and white prisoners. If every prisoner is content with the separation, the issue of its constitutionality is moot. But if a black prisoner, say, would prefer integration for whatever reason, then he is the victim of a racially based exclusion and in terms of principle is in no different position from that of the black parent who wants his children to be able to attend an integrated school. To ask whether racial exclusion may not have overriding benefits for both races in particular circumstances is to place the antidiscrimination principle at the mercy of the vagaries of empirical conjecture and thereby free the judge to enact his personal values into constitutional doctrine. Nevertheless, if a race riot breaks out in a prison, the warden must be permitted to segregate the races to minimize bloodshed. But to acknowledge that the antidiscrimination principle requires a safety valve[31] is not the same thing as treating race as merely a "suspect" classification.

The extreme form, which I reject, of the safety-valve argument is that preferential treatment of blacks and other militant minorities is the price the white majority must pay for avoiding unrest and violence, of which the race riots of the 1960s may have been only the portents. Although university administrators publicly justify their preferential admissions policies in terms of increasing diversity, rectifying historical injustices, and the like, in private many of them admit that appeasing student militancy was the dominant factor in adopting the policies.

Is fear of a minority's potential for imposing costs on the majority through violence or other means an appropriate, if unarticulated, justification for discrimination in favor of the minority? The answer depends in part on one's view of the political process. The Court's expressed view, perhaps dictated by its dependence on the good will of the legislative branch, is that the political process is one of honestly attempting to promote efficiency, or justice, or some other equally general conception of the public good. Under this "public interest" theory, extortion is an inadequate justification for legislative or other governmental action.[32] However, as noted in earlier chapters, the public-interest theory of government action is under attack as having no good analytical basis and being inconsistent in actual experience with governmental policies and programs. Many of them are better explained as the outcome of a power struggle—clothed in a rhetoric of public interest that is a mere figleaf—among interest groups.

31. And therefore that the Court had to consider the government's arguments for subjecting the Japanese residents of California to curfews and concentration camps during World War II, albeit it may have given the arguments too much weight. See Hirabayashi v. United States, 320 U.S. 81 (1943); Korematsu v. United States, 323 U.S. 214 (1944).

32. Cf. Cooper v. Aaron, 358 U.S. 1, 21–22 (1958). But cf. NLRB v. Jones & Laughlin Steel Corp., 301 U.S. 1, 41–43 (1937).

If this is a correct description of the political process—not of its every outcome, but of an important and perhaps central tendency—then many, perhaps most, statutes, if evaluated honestly and realistically, would be found to lack any true basis in the public interest. Indeed, the output of the governmental process would be seen to consist largely of discrimination, in the sense of an effort to redistribute wealth in one form or another from one group to another, founded on a group's superior ability to manipulate the political process rather than on any principle of justice or efficiency.[33] Yet it would be odd to condemn as

33. This view of the governmental process is damaging to Professor Ely's attempt to distinguish between suspect and nonsuspect classifications on the basis of whether the majority group is discriminating against itself or against a minority. See Ely, supra note 6, at 733. Much or most legislation, racial and otherwise, is an attempt by one group in the community to advance itself at the expense of another, so that if Ely were consistent in applying his principle he would have to conclude that most legislation was suspect and should be subjected to close scrutiny by the courts—which it could not withstand. Ely does suggest that there is a difference between racial and other sorts of legislative discrimination in that a white legislator is unlikely to be fully conscious of his prejudice against blacks, whereas no such blind spot would prevent him from seeing that a law fixing minimum prices for milk would transfer wealth from milk consumers to producers while at the same time reducing the efficiency of the agricultural market. *Id.* at 733, n.44. But this attempted distinction reveals that Ely does not accept fully the implications of the new realism about the political process. He assumes that a legislator's scruples have an important influence on legislation, so that a person's blindness about his own prejudices might indeed affect the legislative process. If the new realism is correct, scruples are unimportant—the milk producers get minimum prices because they have political muscle, not because they convince the legislators that raising the price of milk serves the public interest. In any event, Ely offers no reason for thinking that the kind of person who dislikes blacks without knowing it is not also likely to think he is voting his conscience when he supports milk price supports in order to improve his reelection chances.

Another questionable element in Ely's implicit theory of the political process is the assumption, implausible and nowhere examined by him, that legislators are principals rather than agents. When he mentions "the group that controls the decision making process," *id.* at 735, he apparently means not the racial majority of the electorate but the racial majority of the legislature. Evidently, a legislature consisting of the black servants of white plantation owners would be free to enact legislation discriminating against blacks. Identifying "the group that controls the decision making process" involves plumbing the murkiest depths of political theory. Who controls the admissions process at the University of Washington Law School? The admissions committee? The law school faculty? The university administration? The university trustees? The state legislature? The governor of Washington? HEW? See also note 40, infra.

unconstitutional the most characteristic product of a democratic (perhaps of any) political system.

The new realism about the political process calls for a reexamination of the role of a constitutional court. If it is true that we have a government of powers and interests rather than of general-welfare maximization, and if this pattern is an inevitable, and perhaps ultimately a desirable, feature of our society (the impartial pursuit of the public interest might incite a revolution by powerful groups who are disadvantaged by that pursuit), then it would be a mistake to require that legislation, to withstand a challenge based on alleged arbitrariness or discrimination, be reasonably related to some general social goal. The real "justification" for most legislation is simply that it is the product of the constitutionally created political process of our society.

This justification would seem to provide a sufficient basis for rejecting any general constitutional challenge to legislation, for example the minimum wage, as inefficient or inequitable (the minimum wage is both).[34] It would seem to provide a decisive objection to Professor Gunther's proposal that the equal-protection clause be interpreted as requiring, in the case of economically discriminatory legislation (such as the statute upheld in *Williamson v. Lee Optical Co.*[35] forbidding opticians to replace eyeglass frames without a prescription), that the means chosen to carry out the avowed legislative purpose be reasonably related to that purpose.[36] If, as seems clear, the true purpose of the statute in *Lee Optical* was to protect optometrists from competition (the avowed purpose was to promote public health), the

34. By increasing the cost of labor, the minimum wage reduces the demand for it. The resulting unemployment effects are concentrated among marginal workers, in particular black teenagers. These effects are well documented. See, e.g., John M. Peterson & Charles T. Stewart, Jr., *Employment Effects of Minimum Wage Rates* (1969); Marvin Kosters & Finis Welch, "The Effects of Minimum Wages on the Distribution of Changes in Aggregate Employment," 62 *Am. Econ. Rev.* 323 (1972).

35. 348 U.S. 483 (1955).

36. See Gerald Gunther, "The Supreme Court 1971 Term—Foreword: In Search of Evolving Doctrine on a Changing Court: A Model for a Newer Equal Protection," 86 *Harv. L. Rev.* 1, 20–21, 23 (1972).

statute would be unconstitutional under Gunther's approach, but the law would be valid if the state declared its true, unseemly purpose.[37] What is to be gained by using the equal protection clause to rub the noses of state legislators in the realities of the interest-group politics out of which legislation arises? If the purpose is to alter the characteristic process and product of a democratic political system, it is a purpose both unlikely to be achieved and unreasonable to attribute to the framers of the Fourteenth Amendment.

While realism about the political process provides a compelling justification for declining to subject legislation in general to a constitutional requirement that it be in the public interest,[38] it provides no justification for upholding legislation that infringes upon a clear and definite constitutional goal, such as the outlawry of governmental racial discrimination. If a constitutional right means anything, it means that infringement is not permissible merely because desired by the political organs. Thus it is not a legitimate ground for refusing to apply a constitutional principle that the group benefiting from the nonapplication (in *DeFunis*, certain minority groups) has enough political or extrapolitical muscle to make life uncomfortable for public officials who do not yield to its demands. The implicit threat of certain minority group members to "make trouble," either in the university or in the larger society, if their demands for discrimination are not met is no more entitled to weight in a constitutional analysis than the threat of the majority to make trouble if their demands for discrimination are not met. Indeed, the very distinction between "minority" and "majority" tends to disappear in a careful analysis of the nature of the political process.[39] The

37. See *id.* at 45–46.

38. There may be extreme cases of discriminatory state action, however, not involving racial or ethnic criteria but so palpably inconsistent with "the equal protection of the laws" as to be unconstitutional, such as forbidding left-handed people to obtain drivers' licenses in order to reduce automobile air pollution.

39. Which is which in the following news story, *Wall Street Journal,* July 29, 1974, p. 10:

Temple University has paid an out-of-court settlement of $5,000 to an historian who claims he was denied a faculty position because he is white.

essence of a realistic analysis of that process is recognition that public policy is procured by and on behalf of minorities—interest groups, such as optometrists and dairy farmers and retail druggists and owners of television stations, that are much smaller than the population—rather than by some undifferentiated majority. The segregation of the armed forces in World War II was not the result of majority preference; it was a concession to a minority composed mainly of white Southerners.[40]

To summarize briefly, while any public policy against efficient discrimination, that is, discrimination based on the costs of individualized assessment, is by definition impossible to justify on

---

The case is believed to be the first in which such a payment was made. It was one of more than 100 reverse-discrimination complaints filed by the National American Jewish Committee with the Department of Health, Education and Welfare over the past 10 years.

The complaint was brought by Martin Goldman, a 34-year-old lecturer in black history at Clark University in Massachusetts, who applied for a position in 1972 at Temple's Institute of Pan-African Studies.

He said that after applying for a job, the institute's director, Odeyo Ayaga, telephoned him and asked him to come to Philadelphia for an interview. He said Mr. Ayaga told him that he was "the most qualified applicant they had."

At the end of the telephone conversation, Mr. Goldman said he told Mr. Ayaga that he was white, and Mr. Ayaga immediately withdrew the job offer.

Mr. Goldman filed his complaint after a second conversation with a representative of the school, a secretary at Temple's black studies program, who he said told him the job was for blacks only.

Mr. Goldman, a native of Philadelphia and an alumnus of Temple, said he singled out that university in his complaint because it was "the only place stupid enough to openly admit the reasons they refused to consider me for a job." . . .

Mr. Goldman said that from 1971 to 1973 he sent out job resumes to more than 100 universities seeking teachers of black history, a field in which he holds a master's degree, and that he was never offered a job.

"I would say that any white kid who wants to study black history is an utter fool. It is a field that has been closed off for political and social reasons to white scholars," Mr. Goldman said.

Since its inception in 1969, Temple's Institute of Pan African Studies has never employed a white faculty member, according to a university spokesman. Except for one Oriental, the staff is all black.

I wonder how Professor Ely would classify this type of discrimination—as a majority exploiting a minority, viewing the Institute of Pan African Studies as the discriminator, or as a majority exploiting itself, viewing Temple University as the discriminator?

40. The "social peace" argument for discrimination in favor of a militant minority was made on behalf of white segregationists, a regional minority, in opposing the desegregation of the public schools in the South. See Cooper v. Aaron, 358 U.S. 1 (1958).

efficiency grounds, in the case of discrimination against an economic minority, such as the blacks in this country, a distributive argument is available. The argument is that discrimination imposes proportionally greater costs on the minority than on the discriminating majority. This distributive ground is not available, however, to justify reverse discrimination based simply on the threat of a minority group to impose costs on the majority if they do not redistribute wealth to it, over and above the redistribution brought about by outlawing discrimination against minorities. Nor have I been able to discover any other persuasive ground for justifying reverse discrimination.

14

Bakke, Weber, and Beyond

Bakke

The medical school of the University of California at Davis, a state university, reserved sixteen of the one hundred places in the entering class for economically or educationally disadvantaged individuals from four racial-ethnic groups: Negro, Asian, American Indian, and Chicano (Mexican-American). A disadvantaged applicant who was not a member of one of these four racial-ethnic groups was not eligible for the special admissions program. Although members of the designated racial-ethnic groups could also compete for the remaining eighty-four places in the regular application process, within the special admissions program they were not evaluated in comparison with regular applicants but only with each other. The average test scores and other measures of academic promise of those admitted under the special program were far below those of other entrants and of many rejected applicants, including Allan Bakke.

Bakke sued the university, alleging that his exclusion from the entering class resulted from racial discrimination in violation of the equal protection clause of the Fourteenth Amendment, Title VI of the Civil Rights Act of 1964,[1] and the California Constitution. The California Supreme Court upheld Bakke's equal protection claim, holding that racial criteria could not be used to determine admission to a state educational insti-

---

1. Title VI forbids racial discrimination by recipients of federal financial assistance. 42 U.S.C. § 2000d (1976).

tution,[2] but declined to consider his other grounds. The U.S. Supreme Court affirmed the judgment of the California Supreme Court insofar as it ordered Bakke admitted to the Davis medical school, but reversed the judgment insofar as it enjoined the university from taking any account of race in its admissions decisions.[3]

The Supreme Court was sharply divided. Justice Stevens, in an opinion concurred in by Chief Justice Burger and Justices Stewart and Rehnquist, voted to affirm the judgment of the California Supreme Court in its entirety on the ground that the use of race as a factor in selecting students for admission to federally aided educational institutions violated Title VI of the Civil Rights Act; he did not reach the question whether it might also violate the Fourteenth Amendment. Justice Powell, who cast the fifth vote to affirm the judgment as to Bakke's admission, wrote that although universities can sometimes take race into account in admissions decisions, the type of program used by Davis was impermissible. He based this conclusion on the Fourteenth Amendment because, unlike Justice Stevens, he considered the standard of Title VI to be the same as the constitutional standard. Justices Brennan, White, Marshall, and Blackmun voted in a joint opinion to reverse the judgment of the California Supreme Court in its entirety. Justice Powell's fifth vote completed a majority for reversing the part of the judgment that enjoined the university from giving any consideration to race in its admissions decisions.

Bakke was a rerun of *DeFunis*, but because there was no majority opinion the case is not a source of much guidance for the future. Justice Powell's pivotal role in the case makes his the most interesting opinion to study for clues to the future course of the Court's adjudication in reverse discrimination and affirmative action cases, although it is hardly a clear opinion, and al-

2. Bakke v. Regents of the University of California, 18 Cal. 3d 34, 553 P.2d 1152, 132 Cal. Rptr. 680 (1976), aff'd in part, rev'd in part, 438 U.S. 265 (1978).

3. Regents of the University of California v. Bakke, 438 U.S. 265 (1978). The Commentary on the *Bakke* case is voluminous. See, e.g., symposia at 67 *Calif. L. Rev.* 1 (1979); and 90 *Ethics* 81 (1979).

though the *Weber* case, discussed later in this chapter, indicates that the effects of *Bakke* may be limited largely to school (including college and university) admissions and to recipients of federal funds.

By way of background to Powell's opinion, it is important to understand that although the equal protection clause of the Fourteenth Amendment was originally intended to protect the newly emancipated black slave from discriminatory state action, it has long been used also as a vehicle for reviewing state action that discriminates on grounds unrelated to such characteristics as race or national origin. Thus legislation taxing railroads more heavily than other business firms is regularly challenged and sometimes invalidated under the equal protection clause. The Supreme Court, unwilling to become enmeshed in detailed review of the fairness of state tax and regulatory laws, has generally upheld legislation in such areas whenever it can be shown that the alleged discrimination bears some rational relation to a constitutionally permissible state policy.

If this approach were applied to racial discrimination, it would blunt the central thrust of the equal protection clause. for, as emphasized in the last chapter, a good deal of racially discriminatory state action could probably be justified under a broad "rationality" standard. For example, since the educational performance of blacks is on average lower than that of whites, it might be "rational"—in the generous sense of the term that the Court uses in economic cases—to assign blacks to separate schools, just as second graders are "segregated" from third graders, or bright children "segregated" from dull children in schools that employ track systems. Powerful arguments can be made that such racially discriminatory measures would be excessive, that the administrative convenience of racial classification would be outweighed by the social costs of stigmatizing certain individuals as deviant or inferior, that racially correlated behavioral differences are themselves products of discrimination, and so forth; but none of these arguments is so compelling that it would carry the day under the relaxed rationality standard of review used in economic cases, where the Court extends every indulgence to the state's justification for the challenged discrimination.

In fact, the Court has long subjected racial and ethnic discrimination to a "strict scrutiny" test which reverses the presumption of legality attached to governmental action reviewed under the rationality standard and indeed places a nearly insurmountable burden of proof on the state to justify discrimination. A critical threshold issue in *Bakke* was whether discrimination against whites was to be tested under the rationality standard or under the strict scrutiny standard. Justice Powell, the "swing" vote on the Court, decided that the latter was correct. He refused to accord constitutional significance to the distinction between "quotas" and "goals," observing that the Davis special admissions program involved "a purposeful, acknowledged use of racial criteria."[4] He stated: "The guarantee of equal protection cannot mean one thing when applied to one individual and something else when applied to a person of another color. If both are not accorded the same protection, then it is not equal."[5] He rejected the argument that since Bakke, as a white male, was not a member of a "discrete and insular minority" requiring special protection from the majoritarian political process, the Davis special admissions program did not call for strict scrutiny: "Racial and ethnic distinctions of any sort are inherently suspect and thus call for the most exacting judicial examination."[6]

Justice Powell pointed out that by the time the equal protection clause was revitalized as a shield for individual liberties in the late 1930s, "it was no longer possible to peg the guarantees of the Fourteenth Amendment to the struggle for equality of one racial minority [blacks]," for the nation "had become a nation of minorities," each of which "had to struggle—and to some extent struggles still—to overcome the prejudices not of a monolithic majority, but of a majority composed of various minority groups."[7]

4. 438 U.S. at 289.
5. *Id*. at 289-290.
6. *Id*. at 291.
7. *Id*. at 292 (footnotes omitted) and n.32, quoting 41 C.F.R. § 60-50.1(b) (1977).

The concepts of "majority" and "minority" necessarily reflect temporary arrangements and political judgments. As observed above, the white "majority" itself is composed of various minority groups, most of which can lay claim to a history of prior discrimination at the hands of the state and private individuals . . . There is no principled basis for deciding which groups would merit "heightened judicial solicitude" and which would not . . . The kind of variable sociological and political analysis necessary to produce such rankings simply does not lie within the judicial competence —even if they otherwise were politically feasible and socially desirable.[8]

The four groups singled out for preferential treatment by the Davis medical school are not the only groups that have been discriminated against in this country. Others include Puerto Ricans, Jews, Catholics, Mormons, Irish, Italians, Poles, Scandinavians, Germans, Hungarians, and women. To be sure, many of these groups have overcome the handicaps imposed by discrimination, but the same is true of the Asians accorded preference by the Davis medical school along with blacks, Mexican Americans, and American Indians. The logic of reverse discrimination would seem to require that courts consider including at least some of these additional groups among those to be accorded preferential treatment. Yet the result might be discrimination by a coalition of minorities, constituting in the aggregate a clear majority, against a minority consisting of white Anglo-Saxon Protestants, or perhaps just of the males in this group.

Justice Powell thus rejected the view that discrimination against members of the white "majority" for a "benign" purpose is not suspect and hence not subject to strict scrutiny:

There are serious problems of justice connected with the idea of preference itself. First, it may not always be clear that a so-called preference is in fact benign. Courts may be

8. 438 U.S. at 295-297 (footnotes omitted).

asked to validate burdens imposed upon individual members of particular groups in order to advance the group's general interest. Nothing in the Constitution supports the notion that individuals may be asked to suffer otherwise impermissible burdens in order to enhance the societal standing of their ethnic groups. Second, preferential programs may only reinforce common stereotypes holding that certain groups are unable to achieve success without special protection based on a factor having no relationship to individual worth. Third, there is a measure of inequity in forcing innocent persons in respondent's position to bear the burdens of redressing grievances not of their making.[9]

Applying the strict scrutiny standard, under which "'a State must show that its purpose or interest is both constitutionally permissible and substantial, and that its use of the classification is "necessary . . . to the accomplishment" of its purpose or the safeguarding of its interest,'"[10] Justice Powell found that two of the medical school's proffered reasons were insubstantial on their face, a third was based on an unproven factual premise, and the fourth, though potentially substantial, had been implemented improperly.

The first reason offered by the medical school was the interest in "'reducing the historic deficit of traditionally disfavored minorities in medical schools and the medical profession.'"[11] Justice Powell rejected out of hand this basis for the program: "Preferring members of any group for no reason other than race or ethnic origin is discrimination for its own sake."[12]

He rejected the second reason, "countering the effects of societal discrimination," for want of any judicial, legislative, or administrative findings of discrimination on which the medical

9. *Id.* at 298 (citations omitted).
10. *Id.* at 305 (quoting *In re* Griffiths, 413 U.S. 717, 722-723 [1973]).
11. *Id.* at 306.
12. *Id.* at 307.

school might have based its preferential admissions policy.[13] This raises the question whether the Davis special admissions program would have withstood challenge if prior to the time it was conceived and implemented the California legislature had found that the medical school had discriminated unlawfully. The answer is shrouded in ambiguity. Although Justice Powell stated that the Davis medical school neither made nor was competent to make findings of past unlawful discrimination, he nowhere indicated which legislative and administrative bodies do have the authority to make such findings.[14]

If Justice Powell intended to recognize the authority of any legislative body or its delegate to identify and remedy unlawful discrimination, he created an enormous loophole in the constitutional principle he announced. Reverse discrimination might be predicated on a legislative finding of past discrimination through a two-stage process. In the first stage the legislature would "find" that some group has been victimized by some institution, and in the second the legislature or a delegate of it, such as the Davis medical school, would adopt a policy of reverse discrimination as a "remedy." Since legislative fact-findings are essentially unreviewable in court, a legislature that wanted to practice or authorize reverse discrimination could subject institutions to ostensibly "remedial" action simply by making conclusory, unsupported findings of culpable discrimination.

Probably he intended no such loophole. Presumably he realized that a constitutional principle which any legislative body is free to disregard by an empty recital of "fact" is not a constitutional principle worthy of the name.[15] In acknowledging that re-

---

13. *Id.*

14. Reverse discrimination is an accepted remedy against an employer or institution that has been found guilty, in an *adjudicatory* proceeding, of unlawful discrimination. As pointed out in Chapter 12, this remedy is dubious in that its brunt is often borne by innocent parties, but its justification is that an equity court must be given discretion in fashioning a decree that will prevent the recurrence of the wrong. The question of reverse discrimination as a remedy recurs in the discussion of *Weber*.

15. Justice Brennan, in a footnote to his opinion, interpreted Justice Powell's opinion as sanctioning a discriminatory policy based on any legislative body's findings of past unlawful discrimination. See 438 U.S. at 366-367 n.42. Because the University of Cali-

medial measures employing racial classifications may be based
on a legislative or administrative finding of unlawful discrimination, Justice Powell was probably referring to the express
powers of Congress under section 5 of the Fourteenth Amendment to implement the substantive prohibitions of those
amendments—powers that state legislatures have not been
given.[16]

---

fornia's Board of Regents is itself a quasi-legislative body with the power to set university policy, under Justice Brennan's reading of Powell's opinion the special admissions
program at Davis would have been invulnerable to attack if predicated on the Regents'
findings of constitutional or statutory violations by the medical school. Justice Brennan
thus criticized as "form over substance" Justice Powell's insistence that a legislative, administrative, or adjudicatory finding of past discrimination precede the adoption of a
remedial measure embodying racial classifications. *Id.*

16. With respect to the scope of Congress's power under section 5 of the Fourteenth
Amendment to remedy unlawful discrimination, see Katzenbach v. Morgan, 384 U.S.
641, 651 n.10 (1966), where the Court stated that section 5 "does not grant Congress
power . . . to enact statutes so as in effect to dilute the equal protection and due process decisions of this Court. We emphasize that Congress' power under § 5 is limited to
adopting measures to enforce the guarantees of the Amendment; § 5 grants Congress
no power to restrict, abrogate, or dilute these guarantees." Thus, even if Congress were
to conclude that public universities had unlawfully discriminated against certain minorities in the past, it might not have the power to enact "remedial" legislation requiring
the offending schools to reserve a fixed number of spaces for members of these groups.
Such a law would abrogate the guarantees of the Fourteenth Amendment as interpreted by Justice Powell's holding that the equal protection clause forbids the use of
racial and ethnic quotas in school admissions.

In the recent case of Fullilove v. Klutznick, 100 S. Ct. 2758 (1980), the Supreme Court
upheld a federal statute requiring that at least 10 percent of federal funds granted for
local public works projects be used to procure services or supplies from businesses
owned by members of specified racial minority groups. As usual in this area, the majority was unable to agree on a single opinion. But the various opinions place great emphasis on the legislative findings that the legislation was necessary to remedy specific
disadvantages caused by prior discrimination. In fact, a procedure was provided "to
prevent unjust participation in the program by those minority firms whose access to
public contracting opportunities is not impaired by the effects of prior discrimination."
Id. at 2776. Since the statute was being challenged on its face rather than as applied,
the adequacy of this procedural mechanism in practice was not in issue. In these circumstances, it was perhaps reasonable for the Court to conclude that the statute was a
specific remedy for actual discrimination against minorities rather than a preference
for minorities that was only notionally related to past discrimination against (other)
members of the minority group. It is clear, however, that the idea of reverse discrimination as "remedy" is sufficiently broad and vague that it may sap *Bakke* of much of its
significance—a point to which I return later in this chapter in discussing the *Weber* decision.

The third reason offered by the Davis medical school for its discriminatory admissions program was the state interest in "increasing the number of physicians who will practice in communities currently underserved."[17] Justice Powell summarily rejected this reason for want of any evidence that Davis's special treatment of preferred groups furthered this state interest.[18]

Powell was more hospitable to Davis's fourth asserted justification—that the special admissions program furthered its interest in "the educational benefits that flow from an ethnically diverse student body."[19] He began with the premise that the school's quest for a diverse student body is a compelling interest, reasoning that "academic freedom, though not a specifically enumerated constitutional right, long has been viewed as a special concern of the First Amendment," and a university's academic freedom "includes the selection of its student body."[20] Because interaction among students of diverse backgrounds may contribute in important ways to the education of both graduate and undergraduate students, and because racial and ethnic diversity is one aspect of diversity of backgrounds, Justice Powell concluded that it is permissible for a medical school to take race and ethnic origin into account in selecting its students.

If this conclusion were not qualified later in the opinion, it would have to be regarded, for the reasons explained in the last chapter, as reflecting, however dimly, racial stereotyping. However, while accepting racial and ethnic diversity as a permissible factor in student selection, Justice Powell rejected, as an unnecessarily and hence impermissibly discriminatory method of promoting such diversity, the Davis medical school's practice of reserving a fixed number of places in the entering class for members of particular groups. This approach, he thought, gave excessive weight to the racial or ethnic factor in the overall quest for diversity. It is constitutionally permissible to use race or ethnic origin as one factor in the admissions decision, but not as the only factor:

17. 438 U.S. at 306.
18. *Id*. at 310.
19. *Id*. at 306.
20. *Id*. at 312.

The file of a particular black applicant may be examined for his potential contribution to diversity without the factor of race being decisive when compared, for example, with that of an applicant identified as an Italian-American if the latter is thought to exhibit qualities more likely to promote beneficial educational pluralism. Such qualities could include exceptional personal talents, unique work or service experience, leadership potential, maturity, demonstrated compassion, a history of overcoming disadvantage, ability to communicate with the poor, or other qualifications deemed important. In short, an admissions program operated in this way is flexible enough to consider all pertinent elements of diversity in light of the particular qualifications of each applicant, and to place them on the same footing for consideration, although not necessarily according them the same weight.[21]

It is possible to read this language in a way that attenuates the racialist character of allowing race *per se* to be considered an aspect of meaningful diversity. Powell was perhaps saying that a university may use race to create a rebuttable presumption that an applicant has a contribution to make to a diverse student body, but that race may not create an irrebuttable presumption. The university may not refuse to weigh a white's claim to contribute greater diversity than the black applicant. This interpretation is bolstered by Powell's use of the term "competitive consideration of race and ethnic origin,"[22] which implies that a diversity claim based purely on race or ethnic origin must always be open to challenge by a white who claims to have more to contribute to the genuine, as distinct from purely racial and ethnic, diversity of the class. Powell approvingly quoted—and included as an appendix to his opinion—the policy of Harvard College, which declares: "A farm boy from Idaho can bring something to Harvard College that a Bostonian cannot offer.

21. *Id.* at 317.
22. *Id.* at 320.

Similarly, a black student can *usually* bring something that a white person cannot offer."[23] Usually, but not always. Were Harvard a public institution, a farm boy who was turned down in favor of an academically inferior Boston Brahmin who happened to be black would have a good claim that his constitutional rights had been violated.

If this interpretation of the Powell opinion is correct, the dispensation it grants for the practice of reverse discrimination is a limited one. It amounts to allowing a university to create a rebuttable presumption that members of particular racial or ethnic groups are, by virtue of their race or ethnicity, likely to contribute an element of meaningful diversity to the student body.

It may be significant that the opinion nowhere endorses the Davis medical school's decision to accord favored status to those minorities which happen to have political influence in the community. According to statistics mentioned in Powell's opinion, of the eighty-four students admitted to the Davis medical school under the regular admissions program in 1973 and 1974, an average of nine were Asian,[24] which is more than 10 percent. Yet Asians make up less than three percent of the population of California.[25] Davis's special admissions program thus singled out for preferential treatment a group that was already "over-represented" in the student body. I conjecture that Asians were included in Davis's special admissions program as the political price for according preferential treatment to minorities under-represented in the general admissions program. But under Powell's analysis of discrimination, a university is not permitted to assemble a list of favored minority groups without regard to

23. *Id.* at 323 (emphasis added). Justice Powell's analysis does not justify the cynical comment that Davis's mistake was to reserve a fixed number of spaces for designated minorities, rather than to attempt to conceal its racial quota under a blanket of reassuring rhetoric in the style of Harvard College. Powell indicated that an excluded white applicant to Harvard would have the same constitutional claim as Bakke if pretrial discovery or other investigation revealed that Harvard, while pretending to treat race and ethnic origin merely as one diversity factor to be weighed against others, was actually implementing a scheme similar to that of Davis. See *id.* at 318.

24. Computed from *id.* at 395 n.6.

25. Brief for the United States as Amicus Curiae at 4 n.3. See also *id.* at 46–47 n.51.

their cultural distinctness and underrepresentation in the school. The City University of New York is not free to make a preferential admissions policy politically attractive by designating Jews as a preferred group along with blacks and Puerto Ricans.

A few observations about the other opinions in the *Bakke* case are in order. The opinion of Justices Brennan, White, Marshall, and Blackmun agrees with Justice Powell that mere rationality is too liberal a standard for testing reverse discrimination, but argues that strict scrutiny is too stringent a standard and proposes an intermediate test: "[to justify] racial classifications established for ostensibly benign purpose . . . an important and articulated purpose for [their] use must be shown . . . [and] any statute must be stricken that stigmatizes any group or that singles out those least well represented in the political process to bear the brunt of a benign purpose."[26] This standard is unworkable because, as pointed out by Justice Powell, the concepts of "stigma" and "least well represented in the political process" cannot be given concrete meaning in the litigation process.[27] Moreover, the intermediate standard is dangerously lax with regard to discrimination of the old-fashioned sort. It will be recalled that such discrimination is tested under the standard of strict scrutiny, a test it invariably flunks. Under the Brennan group's approach, however, if the racial classification is one "established for ostensibly benign purposes," that fact alone takes it out of the strict scrutiny category and subjects it to the more permissive intermediate standard. This implies that to avoid strict scrutiny a racist legislature would only have to recite that it was putting blacks in separate schools for their own good—an "ostensibly benign" purpose.

The Brennan group's suggested standard for reverse discrimination in favor of blacks stands in striking contrast to Justice Brennan's own position, in cases alleging sexual discrimination, on reverse discrimination in favor of women. For example,

26. 438 U.S. at 361.
27. See *id.* at 294 n.34.

in *Craig v. Boren*,[28] Brennan wrote the opinion for the Court invalidating a state statute under which females could buy beer at age eighteen but males could not until age twenty-one. The opinion states that "classifications by gender must serve important governmental objectives and must be substantially related to achievement of those objectives."[29] Cases forbidding discrimination against males and against females are cited indiscriminatorily for this proposition. There is no suggestion in the opinion that discrimination in favor of women might be distinguishable from discrimination against them, except in the comment that "Oklahoma does not suggest that the age-sex differential was enacted to ensure the availability of 3.2% beer for women as compensation for previous deprivations."[30]

In another case Justice Brennan, dissenting from a decision upholding a state statute granting widows (but not widowers) an annual $500 property tax exemption, stated that the correct standard in a case of discrimination against men is whether "the challenged legislation serves overriding or compelling interests that cannot be achieved either by a more carefully tailored legislative classification or by the use of feasible, less drastic means."[31] This is a strict scrutiny standard. If applied to Davis's quota system, with its unexplained preference for a group already overrepresented in the student population, Brennan's standard for reverse sex discrimination cases would surely have required invalidating the quota system. I do not understand why Justice Brennan thinks that males are entitled to a more generous constitutional standard vis-à-vis females than whites vis-à-vis blacks.

The Brennan group's opinion in *Bakke* passes over in silence —as does Justice Marshall's dissenting opinion—the most questionable feature of Davis's quota system, the inclusion of Asians

28. 429 U.S. 190 (1976).
29. *Id.* at 197.
30. *Id.* at 198 n.6.
31. Kahn v. Shavin, 416 U.S. 351, 357-358 (1974). See also Schlesinger v. Ballard, 419 U.S. 498, 511-521 (1975), Brennan, J., dissenting. By a curious coincidence, the *Kahn* decision appears after *DeFunis* in the *United States Reports*.

among the preferred minority groups.[32] All of the discussion in the Brennan group's opinion is of blacks and Chicanos, and all of the discussion in Justice Marshall's opinion is of blacks. One reason the Brennan group thought the Davis program constitutional was that the percentage of places reserved for the favored minorities, 16 percent, was less than the percentage of the favored minorities in the California population, 22 percent. But 22 percent is the sum of only the blacks and Chicanos; no statistics about Asians are presented in any of the opinions. It is one thing to argue for preferential treatment of racial or ethnic groups that have in some sense "underachieved" and quite another to include another minority which has been successful without the benefit of preferential treatment

Had the Brennan group and Justice Marshall addressed the anomaly of including Asians in the special admissions program, they might have been led to reconsider a fundamental though unstated premise of their opinions—that but for discrimination the percentage of black doctors would be approximately equal to the percentage of blacks in the population as a whole. This premise underlay the conclusion that Davis's special admissions program was justifiable by the same sort of logic that allows the use of a racial quota in a decree seeking to remedy past discrimination—that is, as an attempt to undo the consequences of discrimination. But once it is recognized that some minority groups are "overrepresented" in the medical profession, the premise that blacks would not be underrepresented were it not for discrimination is undermined. By the iron logic of arithmetic, not every group can achieve proportionate representation in a profession in which some groups are overrepresented for reasons unrelated to discrimination in their favor; some other group or groups will have to be underrepresented to balance the statistics. Blacks may be one such group. Evidently Asian Americans have some special aptitude for or interest in medi-

---

32. Although American Indians were also included, there is no evidence that any American Indian was ever admitted to the medical school at Davis under the special admissions program.

cine; why else are they overrepresented in the entering class of the Davis medical school? This suggests that medical aptitude or interest is not evenly distributed among racial and ethnic groups. Furthermore, if a group with a history of being discriminated against in this country, such as Asian Americans, has been able nonetheless to achieve disproportionately strong representation in the medical profession, the failure of blacks to achieve proportionate representation cannot automatically be ascribed to the history of discrimination against them.

A second puzzle in the Brennan group and Marshall opinions is the absence of any reference to *McDonald v. Santa Fe Trail Transportation Co.,*[33] decided by the Supreme Court two years before *Bakke.* The Court, in an opinion written by Justice Marshall, held that discrimination against a white person violated both Title VII of the Civil Rights Act of 1964,[34] which forbids discrimination in employment, and section 1981 of Title 43,[35] one of the Reconstruction civil rights statutes. The case involved two white employees and one black employee who were found to have engaged in the same misconduct; only the whites were fired. The Court held that these statutes forbid discrimination against whites in favor of a black, despite the lack of any clear legislative history in support of such a result and despite seemingly contrary language in section 1981 itself. That section provides that all persons shall have the same right to make contracts as is "enjoyed by white citizens," thus making white persons the standard and not the protected class. In *McDonald* Justice Marshall regarded racial discrimination as the same thing whether directed against whites or against blacks. Although that decision was based on statutes other than Title VI, there was, as with Title VI, no evidence of a legislative intent to enact a standard of discrimination different from the constitutional standard. Equating reverse discrimination with old-fashioned discrimination is therefore not the novelty that the Bren-

---

33. 427 U.S. 273 (1976).
34. 42 U.S.C. §§ 2000e to 2000e-17 (1976).
35. 42 U.S.C. § 1981 (1976).

nan and Marshall opinions in *Bakke* imply. But Justice Marshall's method in *Bakke* of treating different civil rights statutes as incorporating unrelated standards of discrimination was a portent of the *Weber* decision.

Before turning to that decision, I want to speculate briefly on the implications of *Bakke* for the future of affirmative action. The term refers to efforts to rectify the continuing effects of past discrimination, as distinct from simply ceasing to discriminate. The Davis medical school's special admissions program was a species of affirmative action. Certain features made it especially vulnerable. First, since people feel a natural anxiety about the qualifications of the doctors who treat them, the idea of an "affirmative action" doctor is particularly troubling. True, the students admitted under the special program had, in theory, to meet the same academic standards for graduation as the regular entrants. But some universities will, if necessary, bend their standards to assure that not too many of their special students flunk out. Second, the Davis program mysteriously included among their preferred minorities Asian-Americans, although this group was patently not in need of preferential treatment vis-à-vis whites. Third, Davis refused to accord any special consideration to disadvantaged whites, thus failing to acknowledge that some whites might be as deserving of a break in the admissions process as a member of one of the preferred minority groups. Fourth, and related, setting aside a fixed number of places for the chosen minorities could not fail to trigger memories of the quotas so long used in American higher education to limit the numbers of Jews and Catholics admitted to elite schools.

Supporters of affirmative action might hope that future decisions will limit the *Bakke* holding to these rather special facts, but precedents are rarely so narrowly construed. The question remains, to what extent will various forms of affirmative action be held subject to the strict scrutiny standard?

It seems unlikely that the *Bakke* decision will be applied to "remedial affirmative action" following a judicial determination of unlawful discrimination. This form of affirmative action constitutes an accepted judicial practice which can be easily (perhaps too easily) justified as an exercise of the traditionally broad discretion of an equity court with regard to remedy. At the other end of the spectrum from the overt quotas often found in remedial decrees is the practice of simply searching harder for black applicants, whether for school admission or for employment, than for white ones. Strictly speaking, this is racial discrimination, but the adverse effects on whites are probably too slight and attenuated to constitute a denial of equal protection of the laws. I reach the same conclusion, for slightly different reasons, with regard to the practice among some universities of giving larger scholarships to blacks than to equally needy whites. This is discrimination, but it is ancillary to lawful discrimination, since in pursuing the lawful goal of achieving student body diversity, universities will sometimes have to compete financially for a limited pool of qualified minority applicants.

The intermediate case is that of preferential treatment in employment, including academic employment. In many universities a slightly less qualified black may be hired in deliberate preference to a slightly more qualified white, and the same practice exists in many business and law firms and other nonacademic institutions. This is racial discrimination, subject under Justice Powell's view to strict scrutiny, and the interests that Powell found sufficient to justify discrimination in favor of blacks in the college admissions process do not apply. A manufacturer of aircraft has no interest in having a racially diversified board of directors—no interest that I would take seriously at least—nor does a university have a valid interest in having a racially diversified faculty in its graduate accounting department. One can of course assert an interest in providing "role models" for blacks, but this involves the kind of facile psychologizing that Justice Powell rejected in responding to Davis's argument that black doctors are more likely than white doctors to practice in medically underserved communities.

The cutting edge of affirmative action is not college or university admissions; it is employment. This is where a strict scrutiny standard, consistently and honestly applied, could profoundly affect existing government policy. Although HEW and other government enforcers tend to abjure the use of terms such as "quota" and instead describe affirmative action in terms of "search," "best efforts," "targets," and "goals," the effect of HEW's practices is to induce many universities and other employers to discriminate in favor of members of the favored groups—blacks, women, or whomever. Members of these groups are hired in preference to better-qualified white males because that is the easiest way for an employer to get the government off its back. This is discrimination, and where the employer is a public institution the victim of the discrimination would seem to have, under the logic of Justice Powell's opinion, a powerful constitutional case for relief. The employee's rights depend in the first instance on whether the prohibition against discrimination in Title VII is interpreted to be coextensive with the constitutional standards announced in Justice Powell's opinion. The *McDonald* decision implies that it will be so construed. But *Weber* unexpectedly, though perhaps justifiably, held otherwise and thereby limited the effect of *Bakke* in employment cases.

Weber

In *United Steelworkers of America v. Weber*,[36] the Kaiser Aluminum & Chemical Corp. had negotiated a collective bargaining agreement with the United Steelworkers union in which half the places in an on-the-job training program were reserved for black employees until the fraction of black craft workers in the covered plants was equal to the fraction of blacks in the work force where the plants were located. Weber, a white employee, applied for admission to the training program but was denied because of the quota; except for the quota, Weber's seniority would have entitled him to admission. Weber brought suit under Title VII, which forbids racial discrimination in employment. He did not challenge his exclusion under the Fourteenth

36. 443 U.S. 193 (1979).

Amendment's equal protection clause as had DeFunis and Bakke in their reverse-discrimination cases, because the employer and the union were both private entities and so the state action requirement of the Fourteenth Amendment (discussed in Chapter 12) was not satisfied.

The Court, with Justice Rehnquist and Chief Justice Burger dissenting, held that the Kaiser-Steelworkers plan did not violate Title VII, notwithstanding the express racial quota. The *McDonald* case was distinguished on the ground that the Kaiser plan did "not require the discharge of white workers and their replacement with new black hires" but was "an affirmative action plan voluntarily adopted by private parties to eliminate traditional patterns of racial segregation."[37] This distinction is at first glance hard to fathom. If Kaiser and the Steelworkers had negotiated a collective bargaining agreement providing for a ceiling in black employment in some job classification where blacks, because of traditional patterns of racial segregation, were overrepresented (perhaps some low-paying unskilled job), the discriminatory character of the agreement would not be excused because it was voluntary and was intended to eliminate traditional patterns of racial segregation.

Having set *McDonald* to one side, the Court examined the legislative history of Title VII, where it found no persuasive indication that Congress had intended to prohibit voluntary affirmative action plans. Justice Rehnquist, in a long dissenting opinion, painstakingly examined the legislative history and found numerous references to the unlawfulness of reverse discrimination under Title VII.[38] For example, Senator Saltonstall had stated that Title VII would provide "no preferential treatment for any group of citizens. In fact, it specifically prohibits such treatment."[39]

Although the legislative history seems to support Justice Rehnquist, there is one consideration that both supports and

37. *Id*. at 209, 201.
38. See *id*. at 219-255
39. 110 Cong. Rec. 12691 (1964).

narrows the scope of the Court's decision. At the Gramercy, Louisiana, plant where Weber worked, fewer that 2 percent of the skilled craft workers were black, although 39 percent of the local labor force was black. While it is perilous to infer discrimination from underrepresentation, the disparity in the above percentages, coupled with the long history of racial discrimination in the South, suggests that Kaiser and the Steelworkers may have been in jeopardy of legal action charging them with discrimination at the Gramercy plant. If they had been sued and had lost, the court's decree might have included just the sort of quota agreed on by Kaiser and the Steelworkers. To forbid them to anticipate and head off a suit by voluntarily adopting the sort of program they could expect the court to impose is to encourage litigation and discourage voluntary compliance with the law. In fact, according to Justice Blackmun's concurring opinion, Kaiser adopted the challenged quota only "after critical reviews from the Office of Federal Contract Compliance . . . and modeled it along the lines of a Title VII consent decree later entered for the steel industry."[40]

If *Weber* was indeed decided on this "anticipatory compliance" ground, the case leaves *Bakke* unimpaired in its factual context (school admissions), since few schools are arguably engaged in discrimination against blacks and other minorities in their admissions procedures. But notice that under *Weber* the lawfulness of affirmative action in employment seems to depend critically on the standards for adjudicating cases involving allegations of discrimination *against* members of minority groups. The looser those standards—the more willing the courts are to base findings of discrimination on statistics of underrepresentation—the wider will be the net of potential liability, and the easier it will be for a firm or a union to argue convincingly that reverse discrimination is merely in anticipation and avoidance of a suit charging discrimination.

The Supreme Court has not spoken its last word on reverse discrimination or affirmative action. Justice Powell's opinion in

40. See 443 U.S. at 210.

the *Bakke* case recognizes the inconsistency between condemning old-fashioned discrimination and applauding reverse discrimination; the inconsistency lies in the fact that both types are
rational adaptations to the same high information costs. The
Weber case raises the question, however, whether reverse discrimination may not be the inevitable concomitant of a policy
against racial and related forms of discrimination, because it is a
potential mode of compliance, anticipatory or post hoc, with
laws prohibiting discrimination against blacks and other minorities.

The dilemma of reverse discrimination ties directly into a
major theme of this book, the importance of information costs
in shaping social institutions. Just as discrimination is itself frequently a response to the costs of information about individual
capabilities and dispositions, so the cost of determining whether
it has occurred invites reverse discrimination as a method of reducing legal risk. The dilemma would be avoided, of course, if
there were no public policy against "statistical" discrimination;
and there would not be if the ethics of wealth maximization discussed in Part I controlled, as it does not, the determination of
public policy.

This point illustrates how the economic perspective enables
one to see that widely different issues of social policy have a
common analytical core. The same tools that can be used to understand the Supreme Court's decisions in the "affirmative action" area can also, I contend, be used to understand the problems of utilitarian and Kantian ethics, the social and legal
arrangements of primitive and ancient societies, and the concept and law of privacy.

Index